NEW LIMITS ON
EUROPEAN AGRICULTURE

Other Research Volumes from
The Atlantic Institute for International Affairs

*BANKS AND THE BALANCE OF PAYMENTS: PRIVATE
LENDING IN THE INTERNATIONAL ADJUSTMENT
PROCESS*
Benjamin J. Cohen, in collaboration with Fabio Basagni

THE INTERNAL FABRIC OF WESTERN SECURITY
Gregory Flynn with Josef Joffe, Yves Laulan, Laurence Martin, and
Stefano Silvestri

THE PUBLIC AND ATLANTIC DEFENSE
edited by Gregory Flynn and Hans Rattinger

THE FUTURE OF BERLIN
edited by Martin J. Hillenbrand

*NATIONAL INDUSTRIAL STRATEGIES AND THE WORLD
ECONOMY*
edited by John Pinder

*TOWARDS INDUSTRIAL DEMOCRACY: EUROPE, JAPAN AND
THE UNITED STATES*
edited by Benjamin C. Roberts

JAPANESE DIRECT FOREIGN INVESTMENT
Sueo Sekiguchi

NEW LIMITS ON EUROPEAN AGRICULTURE

Politics and the Common Agricultural Policy

FRANÇOIS DUCHÊNE

EDWARD SZCZEPANIK

WILFRID LEGG

An
Atlantic Institute for International Affairs
Research Volume

ROWMAN & ALLANHELD

PUBLISHERS

CROOM HELM
London & Sydney

ROWMAN & ALLANHELD

Published in the United States of America in 1985
by Rowman & Allanheld, Publishers
(a division of Littlefield, Adams & Company)
81 Adams Drive, Totowa, New Jersey 07512

Library of Congress Cataloging in Publication Data

Duchêne, François
  New limits on European agriculture.

  (Atlantic Institute for International Affairs
research volume)
  Bibliography: p. 252
  Includes index.
1. Agriculture and state—European Economic
Community countries. I. Szczepanik, Edward F.
II. Legg, Wilfrid. III. Title. IV. Series.
HD1920.5.D78 1985   338.1'84   85-1981
ISBN 0-8476-7375-8

First published 1985 by
Croom Helm Ltd
Provident House, Burrell Row,
Beckenham, Kent BR3 1AT

Croom Helm Australia Pty Ltd, First Floor,
139 King Street, Sydney, NSW 2001, Australia

British Library Cataloging in Publication Data

Duchêne, François
  New limits on European agriculture : politics
  and the common agricultural policy.
  1. Agriculture and state—European Economic
  Community countries
  I. Title   II. Szczepanik, Edward   III. Legg,
  Wilfrid
  338.1'81   HD1920.5.Z8

ISBN 0-7099-0858-X

85 86 87 / 10 9 8 7 6 5 4 3 2 1
Printed in the United States of America

Contents

Tables and Figures

Acknowledgments

In undertaking to research this subject, it was apparent that a small team could not expect to survey, unaided, such a wide ground. The results that were achieved during the research in the Sussex European Research Centre could not have been attained without the substantial help of a number of experts from many nations, from the EC and from other international bodies like the OECD, who gave much time, knowledge, ideas and contacts. The director of the project and the researchers have incurred large debts of gratitude, which it is more than a formal duty to acknowledge.

Thanks for making possible the work must go to the Rockefeller Foundation and Rockefeller Brothers Fund, which made the grants to launch the research and have shown great patience and understanding in funding extra costs due to inflation and providing time for a number of valuable but unforeseen expansions of activity and scope.

The initial involvement and expertise of John Marsh, professor of Agricultural Economics at Aberdeen University, were fundamental in launching the enterprise. Subsequently, his intellectual inspiration as a member of the steering committee was central to its progress. Many aspects of the present work reflect his advice on general and specified matters. He is not, however, responsible for the results, which, for good or ill, must rest with the authors.

A special debt is due to one of the architects of the common agricultural policy, Bernd Heringa, a former director of policy planning of the Directorate-General of Agriculture in the European Commission, and a close collaborator of Sicco Mansholt, the principle creator of the Community's common agricultural policy (CAP). Mr. Heringa, on the steering committee, gave the project the benefit of his unrivalled experience of the politics of the common agricultural policy in its formative years, helped broaden the researchers' vision to the whole European Community, offered invaluable contacts, and himself contributed to one of the studies of which this volume is composed.

The authors have also to thank the many parliamentarians, officials, agricultural economists and other experts, both in and out of universities, and representatives of the food industry, who have helped through discussion at the various meetings which have punctuated the research, or in response to drafts and papers and in some cases by making substantial written contributions of their own.

Professor Tibor Barna, of Sussex University, a member of the steering committee, directed a study, carried out at the Sussex European Research Centre, on "Production and Trade in High Income Countries," which was funded by a contract from the FAO in the framework of its major project, "Agriculture towards the year 2000" and published, under the former title, as Number 6 in the Sussex European Research Centre's series of Sussex European Papers (1980). This study laid the ground for setting the CAP in an international context. The researchers responsible for the present volume collaborated with Professor Barna. So did Dr. Robert Bideleux, on Soviet and East European agriculture, and Ms. Magdalena Reid, whose statistical contributions are much appreciated.

Just as the chapter in the present work on international aspects owes much to a distinct but related study, so Chapter 3, "National Agricultures and Policies," would have been inconceivable without a number of reports, two of them over a hundred pages long, contributed by well-known national experts. These studies, though collectively much too long to be incorporated in the present work, have nevertheless provided greater depth, variety and confidence than the book could otherwise have enjoyed. It is often difficult, in assessing the CAP, to gauge the collective importance of the individual national policies in the grand design. One of the problems is the diversity this implies. Together, however, the essays make abundantly clear just how crucial the national policies are as a shadow CAP. They provide a sense of its workings not to be gathered from exclusive concentration on policy-making in Brussels.

The study is particularly indebted to the authors of individual essays on national policies, which are summarized in the text:

Professor Denis Bergmann, of the Institut National de la Recherche Agronomique, Paris: *Food Policy Options of France for the 1990s,* May 1979; expanded into *L'Agriculture Française—Perspectives, Stratégies et Politiques à Long Terme,* produced at INRA in December 1979.

Professor Stefan Tangermann, of Goettingen University, whose text has been independently published, by the Goettingen Institut füer Agraroekonomie, 1982, as *Agricultural and Food Policy in Germany.*

Professor Adam Pepelasis, then governor of the Agricultural Bank of Greece, with the assistance of *Marika Frangaki: Greek Agriculture in the EEC,* incorporated in *The Tenth Member—Economic Aspects,* published by the Sussex European Research Centre as No. 7 in the series of Sussex European Papers, 1980.

In addition, detailed criticisms and suggestions on various other member states have been contributed by Professor G. Fabriani, of the University of Naples, who made available an advance copy of his book, *L'agricoltura in Italia tra sviluppo e crisi (1945–77),* and commented on the Italian draft; Professor G. R. Boddez, of the Catholic University of Leuven, and R. de Craene-Dossche, Agricultural Counsellor of the Belgian Embassy in London, for contributions on Belgium; and *Mr. Bernd Heringa,* on the Netherlands; *Professor J. S. Marsh,* on the United Kingdom; The Irish Department of Agriculture, especially Ms. C. A. Cahill, and the Irish Institute of Agricultural Research, notably Deputy Director Mr. Michael O'Sullivan, and Messrs. Patrick G. Cox and Brendan Kearney, on Ireland; and Professor C. Thomsen, of the Royal Veterinary and Agricultural University, Copenhagen, for contributions on Denmark.

This does not exhaust the list of contributions. A number of international experts from agriculture and the food industry have taken part in seminars during the course of the work. Senior officials at the European Commission in Brussels and the Agricultural Division of the OECD in Paris provided invaluable encouragement and cooperation. The common agricultural policy being under widespread attack, the European Commission tends to receive its due share of brickbats. Nevertheless, its super-abundant publications on agriculture are a unique store-house of comparative information. They also have the advantage, in most cases, of continuity from year to year. There is a relative openness on the part of international bureaucracies, which perform a major service in raising the general level of awareness. They are, in this way, an unacknowledged stimulus to much-needed public debate. Special mention should be made of Dr. Günther Thiede, now retired from the anonymity of the European Commission's Statistical Office, whose researchers on supply balances in grain equivalents have made possible many comparisons that would otherwise be frustratingly out of reach.

The present study has thus benefited from numerous *inputs* of time, thought and information from many sources. Yet the responsibility for the *output*, that is, for the uses to which the contributions have been directed, must inevitably lie, and lie alone, with the authors of this volume.

Last but, as anyone who has sought to publish a study of this kind will appreciate, not least, thanks are due to the Atlantic Institute. The Institute has a distinguished record of publications on the common agricultural policy. Two of its previous reports—*A Future for European Agriculture* (1970), edited by Pierre Uri, and *European Agriculture in an Uncertain World* (1975), edited by John Marsh—have in their time led the way in expert and creative analysis of the issues. It is a privilege to follow in their footsteps.

François Duchêne
Edward Szczepanik
Wilfrid Legg

Note to Readers

Readers who have time only for a summary of the argument can obtain an outline from reading, in the usual sequence, Chapter 1, Chapter 3—the last section only, and Chapter 5. Greater depth of information and argument will be obtained, naturally, from perusing the whole text. The above chapters nevertheless offer the basic evidence and conclusions.

The text was completed in January 1984. Given the nature of the analysis, no general attempt has been made to modify it in the light of the decisions of the Community in mid-1984. The last section of Chapter 1, however, has been revised to incorporate them. The broad argument is not changed by those decisions.

Introduction

Studies of the common agricultural policy (CAP) of the European Community (EC) abound in all its languages. There is intense interest in a subject that covers an important and traditionally special section of society and that is also the extreme, indeed virtually unique, example of a more or less federal European policy. The CAP is an isolated relic of the ambitions of the founding fathers of the European Community. It also remains the boldest experiment in political economy in Europe for decades, and is thus doubly political. It is the repository of the peculiar romanticism that still surrounds agriculture, despite the ever-increasing industrialization of farms and food production. And, for once, as a proxy for European integration, agriculture is not in the rural margin of urban society, but a part of what might almost pass for "high politics."

Why another book when there are already so many? In this case, reasons concerning perspective and timing apply. The perspective of the present analysis is less economic and more political and historical than most, and this fact affects conclusions more than might appear at first sight. An examination of its history shows that the CAP was not merely set up to complete the common market, promote an economic union and so pave the way for a politically united Europe, although all of these were certainly motives of the founding fathers of the Community. It was also designed to finesse a number of problems arising out of national agricultural policies at the time of its inception in the late 1950s. A particular aim was to postpone—if possible avoid altogether—placing limits on farm production, even though national surpluses were already beginning to emerge. This and other evasions were built into the CAP and have hobbled it ever since. In many ways, the problems it has constantly faced are merely the logical consequence of the ambiguities wished on it at birth. Some academic experts on the CAP have argued that "European agriculture is not in serious difficulties at the moment; the CAP, however, is fighting for its survival" (Josling and Pearson, 1982). But if some at least of the troubles of the CAP come from an older failure to balance agricultural policies in the member states, the two aspects of the question may not be so easily disconnected. West European agriculture as well as the CAP will now have to face long postponed decisions.

One clear implication of this is a feature of the CAP which, again, is not normally stressed: the extent to which it is a juxtaposition of national policies that continue on their own sweet way—all the more because the CAP, by monopolizing attention, draws a veil over what they are and signify. The CAP is in some senses a fusion of the policies of the member states in a single European system; but it is also in other senses, a very unfused accumulation of persisting national ambitions and political pressures. To some extent, of course, this is normal in any political system. One should expect national motives and interests, like the motives and interests of the farming profession, to play an enormous role in any European agricultural policy. This would be true of a centralized national system, or a mature federal one like the United States, as it must be of an embryonic federal (if it's indeed federal) one like the European Community. The existence of special interests is not what marks off the CAP from other regimes. What is special about it is that forces inside the system can destroy the CAP itself and work against as well as within it. No picture of the evolving situation is complete without an understanding of these centrifugal forces, turning on the alternative centers of authority of the European institutions and the national capitals. The specially European problem the crisis of agriculture poses within the CAP is whether the tension put upon the system will weaken or strengthen, dilute or reinforce, the common policy-making framework and thereby the European as against the national context. It is characteristic of the Community's collective and far from unitary nature that crises at the level of specific policies necessarily pose critical questions about the system as a whole. The framework cannot be taken for granted. This is part of the political drama that always lies behind the technicalities of the CAP.

A second justification for presenting another study of the CAP relates to timing. The CAP is clearly in crisis, in the real sense of the word. In a certain sense, it has nearly always been in crisis. Crisis, in a Community of Six, Nine or Ten countries, seems to be indispensible to the smallest decisions. But the present crisis is of a different order, comparable to the throes of its original creation. At one level, this crisis has occurred because the original funds—or rather the legal tax base—provided for the CAP by agreements in 1970 have run out and given the opportunity in effect for a renegotiation of the bases of the system. At another and deeper level, it is due to the fact that agricultural output in the Community, after three decades of virtually unchecked growth has at last come up against limits in world demand that it cannot deal with by buying-in surpluses or providing subsidies to sales at home or abroad. These newly experienced limits are themselves related to another new development.

Traditionally, the European Community—more precisely Western Europe and above all Britain and Germany—have been regarded as the world's quintessential food importing market. This has been true for a century, since the opening of grainlands in the distant continents and the development of efficient forms of transport to sell cheaply to the cities of Europe. Western Europe is still far and away the world's greatest import market if one takes account of tropical foodstuffs and the enormous quantities of feed imported to build up livestock production in the Community (Appendix Table 4). But this general picture conceals the fact that, if one excludes the raw materials of agricultural production, the Community in 1979, for the first time and after a steady 30-year rise in output (which is continuing into the 1980s and will go on continuing unless major changes occur), crossed a watershed and became a net exporter of the temperate-region foods it produces (Appendix Table 2). It is by far the biggest food exporter in the world after the United States, the only one in any way comparable (Appendix Table 4). This development is closely tied up with the expansionary forces that have marked west European agriculture since the war, and it has important international implications for the future.

The most obvious immediate symptoms of crises are the quarrels, which became overt in 1982, with the United States and other traditional or would-be exporters over the Community's food export subsidies. Since all countries more or less protect their farmers, so that their sales abroad can all be taken to be in some way artificially priced, these quarrels over market shares offer a rich field for quibbles, debating points, embattled bureaucratic negotiations and, possibly, serious conflicts between countries that could affect international politics as a whole. It is no accident, at any rate, that the issue has become pressing at the precise moment when the world food market, which was unprecedentedly buoyant throughout the 1970s, suddenly went flat after the Iranian revolution of 1979–80, the second energy crisis, and renewed reces-sion. Since production in the exporting countries has continued to rise, the competition for markets and the problems of farmers suddenly became very intense.

However, the short-term issue should not obscure longer-run implications. The 1970s have accentuated the picture of, broadly, a Western farm economy, buoyed up by high price policies, producing more and more food for the world market. They have also sharpened the complementary picture of the Socialist and developing economies—often pursuing low price policies—running into cumulative food deficits as rising incomes produce a rapid increase in demand for food. Both the high price tendencies in the West and the low price tendencies elsewhere have roots that are political at least as much as economic. High output in the West is a reflection of high productivity, but not only of high productivity. Very often, and certainly in the European Community, it reflects the power of mass lobbies to push the governments of representative democracies to provide high supports and prices. In the Third World, low output is often a reflection of the government's fear of unrest in the slums of the ever-growing cities. *Panis* is subsidized, if not *circenses*, so that prices to farmers tend to be set too low to incite them to sufficient production. The same is true in most, though not all, of the Socialist countries, for reasons going back to the early Soviet record of squeezing agriculture to provide the capital for rapid industrialization. Choices made then have hardened into the belief that the security of the political establishment is bound up with these policies, which have failed, in the USSR, to deliver the goods to the towns in the quantity and quality required.

The shift of Western Europe from the camp of the importers to that of the exporters has to be seen in that perspective. Whereas Europeans have been used to settling their agricultural problems largely in isolation, by reference to national or Community criteria, they will now, as exporters, influence and be influenced by the international situation. Agriculture will necessarily take on more mercantile and international connotations for Western Europe. This situation is new, and beyond headlines about quarrels with the United States in GATT, little attention has been paid to the implications of such a profound change. So far, the dialogue has been largely between the farmers and CAP critics within each country or between member states of the Community. The circle of decision-making will inevitably widen, and "agro-power," as the accidents of the language ambiguously term it, will become a necessary dimension of the policy debate.

Because of the fundamental nature of the changes affecting Community agriculture and the CAP, and because of the persistence of surpluses as a symptom of the impact of a new context on traditional policies, this book both analyzes the lessons of the CAP in the 1970s and looks at policy options relevant in the next phase of agricultural policy within the European Community. It is divided into two parts. The first, "Contexts," consists of two chapters. Chapter 1 is an historical analysis of the antecedents of the CAP dating from World War II and its development since the treaties of Rome, establishing the European Economic and Atomic Energy Communities, signed on 25 March 1957. Chapter 2 examines the rapid emergence of the European Community as a major force in world food markets in the 1970s and looks at some implications for the next phase of its development. These two chapters set the scene for the policy issues discussed in the second part, "Structures and Policies," consisting of three chapters. Chapter 3 offers a survey of the agricultural policies of each of the member states of the European Community of Ten. The purpose is to relate the CAP to national goals and show the forces likely to affect the evolution of farm policy in the CAP or in any successor policy or policies. This balances the usual focus on the CAP with a clearer idea of the national and sectoral forces with which any agricultural policy-making on the territories of the member states will have to reckon. Chapter 4 also analyzes forces likely to determine attitudes toward policy, but takes a different cut through the problems. It concentrates on convergences and divergences in the situations of the countries and their agricultural sectors that can influence alignments and divisions of outlook and interest when new choices have to be confronted. Chapter 5 considers policy options for the Community and for agriculture in the Community zone.

Notes appear at the end of each chapter. References and the Glossary are at the end of the book. Tables relating most specifically to the various chapters are included in the text. The collection of tables providing data for the study as a whole appear in the "Statistical Appendix" at the end of the volume.

Part I
CONTEXTS

1   The Common Agricultural Policy

Two Faces

Open debate is, or is reputed to be, one of the foundations of the democratic political process. The ways in which it is referred to normally assume a domestic context. The traditional guarantees, such as the responsibility of governments to representative parliaments, secret and universal suffrage, the right to establish political parties potentially opposed to those in power, an independent judiciary, free speech, and so on, all tend to assume domestic politics as a self-sufficient system. This is natural, since the problems of open politics largely concern modes and instruments of operation and these are bound to focus where the main authority resides, in national governments. Yet, in practice, it is often rather difficult to generate domestic debate on the basics of policy. Choices tend to be circumscribed by inner circles of well-entrenched lobbies, by corporate power structures and by numerous past compromises. In such settings, only specialists are likely to have a clear idea of the choices implicit in policy. Clarity may not be that easy even for specialists. In the relatively closed arena in which much domestic policy-making is carried on, the inner meaning of choices tends with time to be buried under rituals of collective agreement which few are anxious or strong enough to question, still less challenge. The potentials of the courses followed, and the feasible alternatives are often not fully explored. Corporatist policies, in short, inhibit free debate on fundamentals. This is especially true of sectors where vested interests are high and on which the general ideological debate is not particularly focused. In many ways, agriculture is a prime specimen of such a sector. Because of the weight of the farm and rural electorates, because of the traditional image of farming, because of its separate appearance in a predominantly urban world, agriculture tends to be the domain of the profession itself and of specialist politicians, officials, or academics. The specialists develop a consensus, which is little understood by the public at large, and few feel qualified to question the half-truths of the day and fewer still to deny the emperor's clothes. Open debate in such a sector is apt to be a relative concept, certainly not free of discreet political bullying, and superficial or narrow patterns of thought and behavior can become virtually unassailable once they have been sanctified as a national style.

For these reasons, a more open debate can sometimes come from comparing and confronting different national policies in the collective setting of an international organization. When the different national structures and political choices are contrasted, the underlying alternatives and the particular avenues selected by each of the participants become much clearer. Even so, governments are jealous guardians of their prerogatives. Normally, there is a compact of politeness and restraint between them. It is the homage all pay to their common assumption of individual sovereignty. The secretariats of international organizations suppress many a thought in the name of this wary courtesy. Thus, the real confrontation of policies emerges only when the governments are forced, or have maneuvered themselves, into a common policy they have to assume together. At this point, the differences between national preferences and the forces behind them surface far more distinctly. The interests and choices of the partner nations are starkly juxtaposed as each fights for its way against those of the others in the system. The issues and commitments that tend to be muffled in the narrower national consensus stick out as different or even opposed systems in the confrontations between nations over common policies. This is especially the case when joint policy-making is far-reaching, though it is difficult to generalize because the cases of far-reaching joint policy-making are so rare. In fact, the European Community's (EC) common agricultural policy, the CAP, is virtually unique in the scope and depth of the commitments undertaken by the member states. Debate on agricultural issues has thus acquired a new dimension in the controversies over policy in the CAP. For this reason, it is one of the most revealing areas for the study of the political process in the second half of the twentieth century.

However, another consequence of this unwonted political prominence is that concern with the CAP is dual and inherently ambiguous. To the agricultural practitioner or specialist, it is primarily of interest because of its implications for the sector and profession. For anyone chiefly preoccupied with European integration, it is apt to be valued for very different reasons. To those at one end of the range, it is the outstanding federal achievement of a political new deal betrayed by the revival of nationalism since de Gaulle. It is all the more precious and sacrosanct for being under threat, and any change that might sap its uniqueness is to be viewed with extreme suspicion. To critics of the European Community at the other end of the range, the CAP's weaknesses are unforgivable; it is the repository of all the follies of protectionism (a curious charge, incidentally, when one considers the general stance of some of the critics). Thus, the CAP is far from being only an agricultural policy. It is the more or less muted political battleground of all the forces for and against European federation, and attitudes towards it often have little to do with agriculture. The loyalties generated by such broad political debates can also be exploited by particular interests in agriculture for their own ends. The potential permutations are numerous. Indeed, without these overtones, the CAP would not have existed in the first place and would not now attract such passionate attention. The circle of discourse would be more specialized and narrower. Much of the political controversy would be missing.

The fact that the most federalist policy inside the Community was born to the accompaniment of threats of crisis and disruption by General de Gaulle, the prime ideological opponent of "supranationality" and champion of *l'Europe des patries*, is symbolic of all these ambiguities in the CAP. Any political economy of the problems it currently poses must be alive to the sometimes distinct needs that arise from the agricultural content of the CAP on the one hand and the political framework on the other. The two are married today, but they need not always be so; and a failure to meet the sectoral problems of the CAP out of exaggerated concern with the political ones, or a willingness to pursue with excessive single-mindedness agricultural interests under cover of the general European ideal, could each have the effect of producing a divorce between the two and of harming one or the other or more likely both.

The fact is that the CAP, like all important political phenomena, serves several ends at once. The CAP, as has already been noted, was set up partly to solve a number of problems posed in the agricultures of the founding states at the end of the 1950s. The working out of these problems is one aspect of the theme. It was also set up to lay the foundations of an economic union seen as the intermediate step between the customs union of the European Economic Community (EEC) and an ultimate political union of the member states. This is a second aspect. The CAP was established on the assumption that a strong centralized decision-making system in the EC would lead to the overriding of national vetoes and so in some sense mobilize the economies of the member states behind effective common purposes. When, however, General de Gaulle successfully reintroduced the national veto into Community decision-making, the assumptions of the system were largely reversed. Now, the collective of the member states, or rather the convoy, is forced to move at the speed of the slowest ship; and if the slowest ship proposes not to move at all, the whole fleet is usually stalled.[1] In these new circumstances, it could be, and has been, argued that there would be more progress, in toto, if each nation were to move at its own speed. A partial or complete reversion to national policies would produce more real flexibility and adjustment to the needs of change. The debate over this set of issues is one of the main strands in controversy over the CAP and any reform.

Another consequence of the CAP, inherent in the concept, and which remains despite modifications of the original intent, is that it does band together the member states in a Community distinct from all other countries. It potentially mobilizes the whole region as an entity in its relations with the rest of the world. This is not, in practice, denied by the insufficiencies of policy-making within the CAP. Whether the system moves forward under its existing momentum, combining political inertia with quite rapid technical progress, or changes the underlying thrust of its policies, Western Europe as a whole, or the core of it represented by the EC, makes a major impact on the international scene.

All these different aspects are crucial to appreciating the CAP. It is not possible to deal with any one of them without taking all the others into account.

Surpluses and Prices

There is almost universal agreement on two propositions concerning the CAP. One is that it suffers from a chronic condition of oversupply. The other is that this is due to high farm prices, politically determined under the CAP's managed system. Yet anyone who takes these propositions literally is liable to miss important nuances. For instance, on 31 December 1981, the stocks of commodities in surplus in EC intervention stores amounted to no more than 27 days' consumption for wheat, 68 days for skimmed milk powder, 11 days for beef and 3 days for butter. If that was a butter mountain, it had given birth to a mouse (*ASC 1982*, pp. 267, 330, 391–92, and 401). To take a more substantial case, the European Commission has produced evidence that, between 1973 and 1981, farm prices, at constant rates, fell between 2 percent and 5 percent in all but one of the six founder states of the Community, the lone exception being Germany, where they rose 1 percent. (Com-EC, 1982a, pp. 9–64). The idea of continuous price increases in the common agricultural policy is clearly far from always correct. The question remains how such figures can be reconciled with the known problems of the CAP.

The paradox concerning stocks is superficial. The reasons for their being so low in 1981 was that large quantities had been sold at highly subsidised prices to domestic consumers or for export. At the extreme, normal sales of skimmed milk powder, that is, without subsidy, represented less than 9 percent of total disposal (*ASC 1981*, p. 369). Overproduction is clear in large expenditures by the Community's agricultural fund (EAGGF) either for stocking commodities unsellable at prevailing prices or for subsidizing their disposal as exports and sometimes as concessional sales to selected groups of consumers in the member states (Appendix Table 11). Stocks and export subsidies tend, naturally enough, to fall when world prices rise, as from 1980 to 1981, and to rise when world prices fall, or are low, as between 1976 and 1979 and after 1982. In 1983, butter stocks soared to a level twice as high as ever before. By early October, they reached 862,000 tons, equivalent to more than seven months' consumption (Com-EC, 1983g).

However, whether the Community is a relatively dear producer or not is a complex question. For almost all times and products, the "entry" prices imposed by the Community on food imports have been substantially higher than the "normally lowest available Third Country offer price," as the European Commission's annual report on *The Agricultural Situation in the Community* (ASC) puts it. On the basis of this definition, for most times and products, CAP prices have been between 1½ and 4 times the "entry" prices of imports delivered to its ports, with dairy products conspicuous at the top end of the range. But the definition itself is subject to question. Community producer prices are not as high as the "entry" price, which has a protective purpose. In 1981, CAP wheat and barley "entry" prices were about 40 percent above the lowest Third Country offers, but support prices in Community member states were themselves 25 percent below the "entry" price (Koester, 1982, p. 15 and Table 3).[2] Further, how would world export prices change if the EC, as the world's largest import market, were to allow freer entry? For a number of products they would certainly rise (Koester, Table 10, p. 28).[3] The cheapest producers can be marginal in total world supply. New Zealand and Australia, for example, produce less than 7 percent as much milk as North America and Western Europe (FAO, 1980b). Comparisons have to be mainly with the United States, which is, in basic crops, the world's residual supplier. American grain and meat prices are substantially lower than European ones, but whether the prices of the grass-based foods, milk and dairy products in the Community or U.S. are higher or lower depends on the dollar exchange rates (Table 1.1).[4]

Even if one skirts the controversies about the representative character of world prices, high domestic prices do not necessarily generate surpluses. A country can well have prices way above those of commodities internationally traded and still move increasingly into deficit. There has been just such a case inside the Community itself: Italy during the 1960s. Shortly after the Community was set up, in 1959, Italy had a level of self-supply of food which has been calculated at 91 percent (Appendix Table 2).[5] From then until 1973, during which time CAP prices were introduced, there was a drastic change. Italy's level of self-supply fell as low as 78 percent in 1973. The reason was that though Italian producer prices rose by the Community average of a quarter and production by a third, consumption grew still faster—by a half. The Italian pattern was quite different from that of the other states of the Community, where supply was outrunning home demand. Italy was not only growing faster than they. Because she was initially much poorer, Italian consumers spent relatively more of their rapidly increasing incomes in the 1960s on food. In particular, they switched to eating meat. Very roughly, and varying between countries, systems and years, meat is equivalent to between five and eight times its weight in grain (with pigs and poultry below five and beef eight) (Thiede, 1980, p. 4; Eurostat, 1983b, pp. 133–35). Italy could not supply this surge of demand quickly enough, though at the time she had the highest rate of growth of beef production in the Community (Table 1.7). From 1963 to 1973, beef consumption rose by 71 percent, but indigenous production only by 39 percent (OECD), 1975, p. 82). She had to import not only meat but feed to raise her indigenous herd. This was not an isolated phenomenon. Spain, also a high-cost producer of meat, equally went into deficit on farm trade during the booming 1960s and early 1970s and for the same reasons.[6] Whether high prices produce surpluses depends on how rapidly consumption as well as output is rising. It is such a simple point it is surprising how often it is, by implication, neglected.

Where demand is static or declining, a small increase, or even a fall, in production (in the case of potatoes, for example) may produce surpluses. Food production in the Community countries, certainly the largest ones, has not grown particularly fast. It has grown more slowly than in the Soviet Union, whose farm production is widely considered to have been a failure.[7] Only in some poorer EC-12 countries like Greece, Ireland and Spain, or exceptionally the Netherlands, has the growth of farm output been more rapid. EC

Table 1.1   Unit Values of Some Major Farm Products in the USA and EC in 1980 (dollars per ton)

Commodity	United States			European Community			US-EC Comparisons		
	Output (million tons)	Value (billion $)	Value per Ton ($1 ton)	Output (million tons)	Value (billion $)[a]	Value per Ton ($1 ton)	EC Values per Ton as Percent US Values[a]	US Output at EC Values (billion $)	EC Output at US Values (billion $)
Wheat	64.5	10.4	161	51.1	11.1	219	136	14.0	8.2
Feedgrains	198.9	18.3	92	68.3	8.5	124	135	24.7	6.3
Oilcrops	58.9	15.5	263	2.9	2.6	912	347	52.8	0.8
Beef and veal	10.0	31.5	3150	5.8	23.7	4080	130	40.9	18.3
Pork	7.5	8.9	1187	9.4	18.5	1970	166	14.8	11.2
Poultry	8.4	5.9	702	4.0	6.7	1670	238	14.1	2.8
Milk	58.3	16.6	285	110.9	30.9	278	98	16.3	31.6
Total above		107.1			102.0			177.6	79.2
Total farm output		139.5			156.9				

[a]See Note 4 for the importance of the exchange rate—the rapidly changing dollar rate to the ECU —in all US-EC comparisons of value. The EC figures are established in ECUs. The ECU was worth $1.392 in 1980. By 1981 the ECU was worth $1.116 on the exchanges, and by 1982 had fallen under par to $0.980. Variations in the exchange rate that are not related to domestic purchasing power can powerfully affect comparisons.

Source: US Statistical Abstract 1981; Com-EC, ASC 1981.

Table 1.2   **Percentage Increases in Prices, and in Production and Consumption (in grain equivalents), of All Agricultural Products in the EC and Its Six Member States between 1957-1960 (= 100) and 1968-1969**

Country	Prices	Production Consumption (1968/69 in grain equivalent)	
Belgium/Luxembourg	130	130	116
France	137	146	131
Germany	104	137	125
Italy	123	134	150
Netherlands	123	141	120
EC-6	123	140	132

Source: Hermann Priebe, "The Changing Role of Agriculture," in Carlo M. Cipolla, ed., *The Fontana Economic History of Europe*, The Twentieth Century, Vol. 5 (2), p. 430, from Eurostat sources.

surpluses are not due to high rates of growth of output. The balancing item is demand, the growth of which has been increasingly sluggish.

Since the end of the 1950s, there has been no more than a moderate growth of demand at any time in the Community, except in Italy, and a slowing down in the 1970s to near stagnation. Western Europe's population is growing more slowly than that of any other region. It is aging. It is already on the average well fed, some might say too well. Expenditure on food has risen much more slowly since the war than consumption in general. Not only are income elasticities of demand for food low in the Community, they have been declining as real per capita incomes increase. Recession has accentuated the trend. In short, in the basic sense that the growth in the domestic European demand for food has become very low, agriculture is, quite simply, a "declining" industry.

The gradual but cumulative overhauling of demand by supply implies that, to balance the two, prices to producers should have fallen. The general impression seems to be that CAP producer prices have risen. This is not borne out by a comparison of national producer prices with the general price index (GDP deflator) or with the costs of inputs on the farm. Between 1950 and 1980, prices paid to farmers in the Community's member states fell compared with general prices, in all cases markedly and in most very substantially indeed (Table 1.3). Irish prices seem to have fallen the least in real terms, but even their average rate of decline seems to have been nearly 1 percent a year.

There have been variations from period to period within this general decline, of course. Between 1960 and 1965, when the CAP was being negotiated, producer prices in the founder states fell much less than in the actual transition to the CAP which followed. From 1970 to 1975, real producer prices rose in Italy and two of three states of the first enlargement,

Table 1.3 Trends of Real Prices Received by Agricultural Producers of the EC-9, 1950–1980 (percentage rise [+] or fall [−] in real prices between start and end of each 5-year period)

Period	Character of Period	Founder States					States of First Enlargement—1973		
		Belgium	France	Germany	Italy	Netherlands	Denmark	Ireland	U.K.
A: 1950–55		−9	−10	+12	−16	−10		+1	
1955–60	Rome Treaty 1957	−6	+4	−6	−11	−17	−15	−15	−19
B: 1960–65	Negotiation CAP	+4	−4	+1	0	+2[a]	−10	−7	
1965–70	CAP enters into effect 1965–1968	−14	−4	−28	−29	−14	−13	−12	−7[b]
C: 1970–75	End boom and first enlargement 1973	−14	−4	−2	+8	−8	0	+18	+21
1975–80	Recession	−14	−11	−11	−10	−15	−7	−8	−19

[a] OECD, *Agricultural and Food Statistics*, 1969.
[b] 1965–1969.

Note: Data are incomplete in some countries and not always comparable from period to period.

Source: A: FAO, *Production Yearbook 1962*; Price Deflators Consumer Price Index, Com-EC, Eurostat, *Basic Statistics of the Community 1978*, Table 112, p. 139.

B: FAO, *Production Yearbooks, 1970 and 1971*; GDP deflators 1960–1980, *European Economy*, November 1983, Table 17.

C: FAO, *Production Yearbooks, 1976*; Com-EC, *ASC 1981*, pp. 200–201; GDP deflators 1960–1980, *European Economy*, November 1983, Table 17.

Britain and Ireland. Nevertheless, the dominant trend over three decades has been a substantial fall in real farm prices across the board.

The relative shifts in prices to farmers as against their costs of production (Table 1.4), which are most relevant to farm incomes, give fairly similar results. They also bring out the extent to which national farm prices rose between 1960 and 1965, in Ireland as well as the founder states negotiating the CAP. The dominant tendency for them since 1965 has been to fall, as they did in the 1950s, especially in Benelux, and overall during the recession years since 1973. Relative producer prices rose in both Denmark and Ireland before entry into the EC in 1973 and fell once they were inside (in a way somewhat similar to the founder states in the 1960s). Unfortunately comparable figures for Britain only exist after 1973.

In general one gets the impression that in the 1950s farm prices fell steeply everywhere except in Germany and France. From 1960 to 1965, farm prices in the founder states marked time or slightly rose, though compared to general prices they continued to fall in Denmark and Ireland. Prices fell everywhere from 1965 to 1970, and even from 1970 to 1975 except in Italy and especially in Britain and Ireland. In the later 1970s, they once again fell in all the Community states. For the three decades as a whole prices have fallen most in Italy, Belgium, Denmark and the Netherlands, three of them the countries with the highest farm incomes in 1980. This seems more than a coincidence. For the rest the figures suggest that contrary to conventional wisdom, the CAP's record is fairly average for the European course.

General indices fail to show trends on particular commodities, where one can deal with comparable volumes and some of the worst practical problems have been posed. However, the comparison of trends in constant prices for wheat, sugarbeet, milk, and beef, with the record of production, confirms the picture already presented (Tables 1.5 to 1.8). In all these major items, except beef, real producer prices have fallen in nearly every country, often steeply, while output has risen nearly everywhere, also in most cases steeply, though the effects are more marked for crops than for livestock products. There are, of course, variations. Though the UK for wheat, Ireland for beef, and France for sugar had particularly striking records of growth of output, in general the most responsive countries were, outstandingly, the Netherlands and Ireland and, to a lesser extent, Britain, France, and Germany. The weakest supply responses to price tended to be those of Denmark and Italy. In only two cases—milk in Denmark and beef in Britain—has production risen less than real prices between 1963 and 1979.

The picture is clear: prices have fallen substantially over three decades, yet output has risen. This argues for powerful expansionary forces in supply. In the EC, yields per hectare have increased steadily since 1950: for wheat (2.5 times), barley (1.7 times), and milk (1.5 times) (UN ECE-FAO, 1954, Table 4; and FAO 1980). The evidence is reinforced by the sharp reduction in the traditional resources devoted to agriculture since the war in contrast to the interwar years. Before the years immediately preceding each of the two world wars, the workforce on the land fell by only 10 percent, while the cultivated

Table 1.4 Gain or Loss in Farm Producer Prices as Against Prices Paid for Inputs into Production (Intermediate Consumption) in Successive 5-Year Periods, 1950–1980 (percentage rise [+] or fall [–])

| Period | Character of Period | Founder States | | | | | States of First Enlargement—1973 | | |
		Belgium	France	Germany	Italy	Netherlands	Denmark	Ireland	U.K.
1950–55		–15		+5	–2	–15		–5	
1955–60	Rome Treaty 1957	–9		–8	+4	–22		+7	
1960–65	Negotiation CAP	+1	+7	+5	+5	+9[a]	–1	+12	
1965–70	CAP enters into effect 1965–1968	–10	+3	–16	–17		+10	0	
1970–75	First Enlargement 1973	+2	–8	–5	–9	–4	–3	–11	
1975–80	Recession	–11	–8	–8	+8	–11	0	–3	–13

[a] OECD, *Agricultural and Food Statistics, 1969.*

Note: Data are incomplete in some countries and not always comparable from period to period.

Source: See Table I—for 1950–70; 1970–1980, Com-EC, *ASC 1981* p. 182.

Table 1.5 Trends in Prices and Output 1962-63 to 1978-79: WHEAT (percentage variation: base year for each column = 100)

Country	Output[a]					Prices (constant currencies of 1962)[b]				
	1963-68	1968-73	1973-76	1976-79	1963-79	1963-68	1968-73	1973-76	1976-79	1963-79
Belgium-Luxembourg[c]	1.4	17.7	-21.0	18.6	11.7	-14.7	-17.1	-8.3	-7.9	-40.3
Denmark	-18.1	31.3	-0.3	9.2	17.0	-24.1	-10.4	-1.3	-9.4	-39.2
France	16.7	25.6	-11.8	32.2	70.8	-9.4	-11.3	-5.6	-7.6	-29.9
Germany	30.4	15.8	-2.6	19.8	76.1	-20.3	-21.7	0.2	-6.9	-41.8
Ireland	4.4	-30.7	-13.3	14.9	-28.0	3.1	-31.4	33.5	-6.8	-12.0
Italy	8.5	-4.1	-10.3	11.9	4.5	-22.8	-14.8	10.9	-5.9	-31.3
Netherlands	15.2	2.4	-11.5	32.2	38.1	-13.3	-24.2	-15.1	-12.5	-51.2
United Kingdom	53.0	42.7	-8.8	53.1	204.8	-20.7	-1.0	2.0	5.9	-15.2
EC-9	18.0	16.7	-9.7	27.5	58.6	-16.1[d]	-13.2[d]	0.03[d]	-5.4[d]	-31.1[d]

[a] 1963 = average 1961-65; 1968 etc. = average 1967-69, etc.
[b] GDP deflator 1979 = 1978 etc.
[c] Prices, Belgium only.
[d] Average weighted by output of each member state.

Sources: Output: FAO, *Production Yearbooks* (annual); OECD, *Food Consumption Statistics 1964-1978*, Paris, 1981.
Prices: Com-EC, *Agricultural Markets*, June 1980; and *European Economy*, November 1983, Table 17 (GDP Deflators).

Table 1.6   Trends in Prices and Output 1962-63 to 1978-79: SUGAR (percentage variation: base year for each column = 100)

Country	Output[a]					Prices (constant currencies of 1962)[b]				
	1963-68	1968-73	1973-76	1976-79	1963-79	1963-68	1968-73	1973-76	1976-79	1963-79
Belgium[c]	41.5	2.4	8.7	19.8	88.8	-5.3	-18.4	-8.3	-7.9	-29.9
Denmark	12.1	6.5	24.9	8.1	61.2	-21.7	0.1	-11.4	-6.2	-34.8
France	11.2	23.4	15.2	31.0	106.9	-2.6	11.9	1.0	-17.0	-8.6
Germany	16.5	8.1	17.4	17.0	73.1	-6.6	-27.3	2.2	-14.7	-40.8
Ireland	11.9	4.0	12.8	10.2	44.8	-0.9	-39.6	47.6	-5.8	-16.7
Italy	38.1	-27.8	33.4	24.2	65.2	5.4	-14.0	39.5	-14.7	7.8
Netherlands	37.3	-2.6	17.0	14.0	78.4	-9.7	-18.4	2.4	-24.8	-43.2
United Kingdom	9.5	-16.0	-5.5	56.6	36.2	-11.1	-13.5	10.8	14.4	-2.5
EC-9	20.2	1.9	16.1	24.9	77.4	-4.8[d]	-10.2[d]	6.9[d]	-12.9[d]	-18.5[d]

[a,b]See Table 1.5 above.
[c]Luxembourg produces no sugar.
[d]See Table 1.5 above.

Note: 16 percent sugar content in sugarbeet.

Source: See Table 1.5 above.

Table 1.7 Trends in Prices and Output 1962-63 to 1978-79: MILK (percentage variation: base year for each column = 100)

Country	Output[a]					Prices (constant currencies of 1962)[b]				
	1963-68	1968-73	1973-76	1976-79	1963-79	1963-68	1968-73	1973-76	1976-79	1963-79
Belgium-Luxembourg[c]	2.4	-6.7	-0.2	5.0	0.0	5.3	-15.1	-6.7	-3.8	-19.8
Denmark	0.7	-7.7	6.7	3.6	2.7		5.5[d]	2.4	-0.3	(7.7)
France	27.2	4.2	-1.0	7.9	41.6	-9.4	12.6	-5.1	-11.1	-13.9
Germany	6.8	-3.9	4.2	7.9	15.4		-11.5[e]	-4.0	-3.8	(-11.5)
Ireland	26.9	-5.7	11.4	24.3	65.8	3.2	-10.8	29.0	9.3	29.9
Italy	20.9	-1.1	-2.3	11.2	29.8	4.1	6.1	6.6	6.1	25.0
Netherlands	10.0	21.3	12.1	10.5	65.3	-8.4	-15.2	-10.4	-6.5	-34.9
United Kingdom	5.3	14.2	0.5	10.5	33.5	-1.7	-9.2	9.2	-10.2	-12.4
EC-9	13.3	2.9	2.6	9.2	30.6			1.6[f]	-5.2[f]	

a,b,c See Table 1.5 above.
 d 1968 = 100.
 e 1969 = 100.
 f See footnote d, Table 1.5.

Note: 3.7 percent fat content.

Source: Output: Com-EC, Eurostat, *Cronos* series.
 Prices: see Table 1.5 above.

Table 1.8   Trends in Prices and Output 1962-63 to 1978-79: BEEF (percentage variation: base year for each column = 100)

Country	Output[a]					Prices (constant currencies of 1962)[b]				
	1963-68	1968-73	1973-76	1976-79	1963-79	1963-68	1968-73	1973-76	1976-79	1963-79
Belgium-Luxembourg[c]	2.1	9.5	9.0	-0.3	21.4	15.7	10.2	-22.9	-3.7	-5.3
Denmark	13.9	-10.2	30.4	5.0	40.0	-8.4	44.0	-13.9	-3.9	9.1
France	11.7	-10.1	23.2	1.4	25.4	-1.7	31.2	-20.4	3.3	6.1
Germany	2.0	-0.6	13.6	8.1	24.5	5.4	7.5	-10.7	-11.0	-9.9
Ireland	48.5	7.3	58.5	18.3	198.5	-3.5	21.0	0.5	21.0	42.1
Italy	43.2	10.4	-5.1	8.5	62.7	1.8	6.7	7.6	-9.0	6.4
Netherlands	-5.2	0.3	27.6	2.5	24.4	10.3	0.5	-20.0	-11.7	-21.7
United Kingdom	-4.2	-5.3	24.3	-1.3	11.2	1.2	29.0	-18.1	12.0	19.7
EC-9	10.1	-1.8	16.9	4.5	32.1	2.1[d]	18.7[d]	-12.0[d]	-0.9[d]	4.2[d]

a,b,c,dSee Table 1.5 above.

Source: Output: OECD, Meat Balances in OECD Member Countries 1963-1976, Paris 1978, p. 8; Com-EC, ASC 1980, p. 367.
Prices: see Table 1.5 above.

area remained much the same and output rose marginally. Since 1950, in the six founding states of the Community, manpower on the farms has shrunk by two-thirds and the land area some 10 percent, yet output has risen about three-quarters.[8] This has not been the result simply of Europe borrowing new methods from America after the war. In the United States too, technology and yields accelerated. "Following a period of slow growth during the first four decades of this century, American agriculture underwent a second revolution during the next four decades. Farm output doubled during this period, with all of the growth attributable to productivity per unit of input."[9] It is clear that to avoid excess supply, real prices would have had to fall further even than they did in Europe.

What seems to have happened is that agriculture entered a new era of technological exploitation of biological possibilities. The general economic boom that raised living standards and job opportunities off the farms to new levels also made farming as a society open to the new methods in a way it had not previously been. In the single generation since the war, Western Europe has made a qualitative leap from the traditional peasant agriculture to industrial farming. One mode of production, dependent on horsepower and manpower, has virtually disappeared. It has been replaced by one based on tractors, chemicals, and, ultimately, cheap oil. The tractor has not only brought greater power to the producer. It has opened the door on a whole panoply of new techniques and systems. Mechanization has helped consolidate holdings, and larger farms benefit greatly from economies of scale. But they also have proportionally higher overheads: intermediate consumption in farming has steadily grown (Table 1.9). This in turn has made more intensive management and marketing techniques essential as well as profitable. There has been an increased demand for knowledge and for improved inputs from industry and from research. Bio-engineering even shows signs of taking over as the engine of technical progress now that energy costs have risen and become more uncertain, and the flight from the land has eaten into (but not yet exhausted) the old potential for cutting labor. Over wide areas of the Community, agriculture has ceased to be the large but diminished remnant of the civilization of our ancestors, uneasy in the margin of our own. It has become a science-based industry not all that different from the others. The social context has also been transformed. "The peasant village, familiar throughout European history, does not exist any more . . . the villages accommodate people of all vocations that have been drawn into the wake of increasing urbanisation" (Priebe, 1976, p. 421).

Two other factors have underlain these changes. The first is that the biological potential of plant life is far greater than revealed by traditional levels of productivity on the land. The possibilities for the systematic reduction of the gap between actual and maximum theoretical yields are enormous (Thiede, 1975; OECD, 1983a). The second is that there is, and has always been, a substantial difference between best practice and average, let alone laggard, performance on the farms.[10] Though some regions have much higher natural potential than others, for example for milk, both these facts mean

Table 1.9   Intermediate Consumption in Agriculture (value production inputs ÷ value final agricultural production × 100)

	1956–58	1980	1981
Belgium	32.7	58.6	57.5
Denmark	36.9	56.7	54.5
France	24.7	45.3	47.3
Germany	33.3	55.1	56.0
Greece	9.7	22.5	23.4
Ireland	—	46.3	48.4
Italy	15.6	29.0	31.9
Luxembourg	—	39.3	39.6
Netherlands	40.5	55.9	52.5
Spain	10.7	35.9	—
UK	53.7	55.2	54.6

[a] 1978.

Source: 1956–58: "Output, Expenses and Income of Agriculture in European Countries," Sixth Report, UN: FAO & ECE; quoted in Gale Johnson, *World Agriculture in Disarray*, Fontana (1973), p. 70. 1980: Com-EC, *Agricultural Situation in the Community (ASC) 1981*, pp. 178–79; *Anuario de Estadistica Agraria 1980* (Madrid), p. 610; *ASC 1982*, pp. 192–93.

there are great reserves of productivity in Western Europe, which can be exploited when economic conditions are favorable. In fact, it would need exceptionally depressed economic conditions, or highly deflationary management, or a notably flexible group of producers, to rein in the underlying buoyancy of output. None of these has prevailed in the past 30 years on the farms. Agriculture and the CAP have lived essentially under pressure from supply. Thus, if, from the point of view of demand in Europe, agriculture has been essentially a "declining" industry, on the contrary, from the point of view of supply, it has been fundamentally a dynamic one. This is the dilemma of the Community and its common agricultural policy.

Policy and Prices

All this is obvious enough now. It was not at all obvious at the end of the war. Wartime and immediate postwar food shortages made higher production seem a strategic necessity. This was reinforced by the European countries' critical shortage of foreign exchange, at first relieved only by Marshall Aid. Such experiences made high levels of autonomy in food, traditional in most countries, appear a self-evident public duty. Even in a country such as Britain, till 1931 a land of laissez-faire farming, the Agriculture Act of 1947 set the target of raising net output 50 percent above pre-war levels by 1951–52 (that is, 20 percent above the levels reached by 1947) (Tracy, 1964, p. 255). Production responded well. As early as 1951, agricultural output in the OEEC area, including West Germany, exceeded prewar levels (OEEC, 1959, p. 21).

The inner logic of the welfare state and the rising tide of an incipient boom which was rapidly increasing incomes in European societies added another preoccupation. Improving the relatively low average incomes on the farms in most European countries became a major concern for governments. Electoral interests and notions of social order both played a role. The family farm was seen in many countries as an anchor of social stability in a continent which had first been shaken to the foundations and then subjected to rapid change. Between 1945 and 1953, the governments of the larger European countries increased price supports to raise farm output and income. In retrospect, these decisions seem to have been crucial, because, in effect, they fixed the point of departure of postwar policies and prices.

Before the CAP was established, two aspects of these policies began to be evident to observers. The first was that price supports did not greatly increase average farm earnings relative to those in other occupations. Significantly, in the 1950s, most of the countries where average farm returns were fairly comparable with those in the national economy at large—such as Britain, Belgium, and the Netherlands—already had a relatively low proportion of manpower on the land (though Denmark has proportionately more). Elsewhere, labor on the land was abundant and average farm earnings usually ranged from 40 percent to 60 percent of the average national intersectoral income. Price support policies did not greatly change this situation before the CAP was instituted; nor has the CAP greatly changed them since (Appendix Table 18) except, in some countries, for the worse.

However, earnings from agriculture do not tell the full story of farmers' incomes. For one thing, farmers, as businessmen, own or work capital—land, buildings, equipment—and when its value rises, as it did in the 1960s and 1970s, they make capital gains. (In the 1930s some of them had sustained such severe capital losses that they were ruined.) Moreover, the business carries some of their cost of living (transportation and food being obvious cases). The farm provides the holder with more wealth than earnings measure. A second complication is that many farmers, or their families, have earnings off the land. In 1977, 27 percent of all holders of farms in the Community had a second job. A study in Britain in 1979 also showed that on average British fulltime holders earned on the farm only 54 percent of the family couple's total income. West Germany has a particularly high proportion of part-time farmers, and the federal government's annual Agricultural Report to the Bonn parliament regularly demonstrates that the shorter the time a holder works on the farm, the *higher* (on average) the income. Paradoxical as such results may seem, they accord with results in North America. In the U.S. in 1977, farmers on the average earned 61 percent of their incomes away from the farm![11] This at least makes it more plausible that the purely agricultural statistics should make farmers out to be poor, while in northern countries at least they tend, on the whole, to be seen as well-off. Such complexities can lead to confusion in assessing standards of living and to difficulties in administering policies across the board. They do not, however, dispose of the problems posed by the discouraging returns for income from the land. At least one-third of all farmers have neither full time work on the land nor a second job. This large minority do suffer from the low incomes which CAP price supports have failed to correct; and many full-time holders of small-sized farms are not necessarily much better off.

A second feature characteristic of debates about the CAP also appeared long before the latter's emergence on the scene. The UN, ECE-FAO report, *European Agriculture: A Statement of Problems*, drafted in 1953 was already preoccupied with surpluses:

> Some of the measures used to dispose of agricultural surpluses, such as giving milk to school-children, are highly valuable from a nutritional and social point of view; but this can scarcely be argued for others, such as the transformation of wine and sugarbeet into industrial alcohol. Even when such measures serve desirable social needs, however, they are frequently developed as by-products of a rigid production structure rather than strictly on their own merits (pp. 37–38).

Far from receding, these pressures increased in the course of the 1950s. The European Commission's first report, published in 1959, well before there was any such thing as a CAP, spoke of wheat surpluses in Italy and Belgium, growing sugar stocks in Germany, Italy and Belgium, and difficulties with dairy products, especially butter, in all six founder states of the Community. The Dutch government was even moved in 1958 to apprise the barely installed EEC Commission of the "difficult situation" in dairy products (de Bruin, 1978, p. 481).

In retrospect, these consequences seem self-evident. To raise the prices of commodities increases the returns to all factors of production—land and capital as well as labor. The rewards are the higher the more efficient (and often in practice the larger) the farm (Com-EC, 1969, p. 72). The incentives to increase production are high, particularly if the guarantees, as often in the CAP, are open-ended. Supply is likely to be buoyant, particularly in a period of technological innovation. But where society has reached a stage in the consumption cycle, as Western Europe has, where the extra income of consumers is spent less and less on food and more and more on other goods, there are too few outlets for this expanding supply. To clear the markets, real prices have to fall unless government, as in the CAP, provides "political" outlets by some kind of subsidy, such as public purchase. The more high prices increase the imbalance between supply and demand in favor of supply, the more prices, left to themselves, would fall. The public purse, though deep, is not infinite. Sooner or later, the logic of expanding production in the face of stagnant demand must lead to falling real prices.

Thus, for agriculture as a whole (as distinct from the most efficient farmers), higher production is no solution, but aggravates the underlying imbalances. In these circumstances, the only remedy is to cut costs. If labor on the farms resists declining incomes, it constitutes a relatively rising cost and reduces profit margins. Numbers on the land therefore have to fall to increase incomes per head.

It follows that the only long-term way to raise average farm incomes is to cut the labor force to the point where the market gives farmworkers returns equal, on average, to those of workers in other sectors. The steep reductions in the Community labor force on the land have not sufficed in most countries. Average incomes on the farm only come within crying distance of average national incomes where numbers on the land are low.

Why, then, were price support policies so widely adopted and stuck to after the war? In 1950, the active population on the land accounted for some 30 percent of the workforce of the six founder states of the Community. The electoral power of such a mass was enormous, especially as these voters were in general mainstays of the right-of-center governments in office. Farmers' organizations are well aware that it is easier to obtain subsidies from consumers through high prices than from budgets, where the costs may become disconcertingly visible, as they did in Britain in the late 1960s or have now become in the Community.[12] Indeed, with such a huge contingent of poor producers, it was doubtful that individual incomes could significantly be raised through the budget. A further factor was the historical experience forming the background to decisions at the time. It was difficult, in the early 1950s, to have confidence that the boom would last or to foresee the potential of the technological changes already under way. Price supports had, in all but a handful of countries such as Denmark, been the traditional staple of farm policy before the war. Politically, all forces converged on the solution of price support. The only differences were over means. Britain, with a relatively small farm sector, was able to fund the difference between low prices to consumers and higher ones to producers by budget subsidies to the farmers—so-called "deficiency payments." These subsidies were, significantly, very large (see Table 1.10). This would have been too big a load for the budget in countries with a large farm sector, who thus concentrated on making the unorganized consumer pay the bulk of support.

This collective choice was merely confirmed when the CAP was established. In 1960, the national systems of the founder states all followed the same broad pattern. All managed their domestic agricultural support primarily through prices paid by the consumer above those prevailing on world markets. To buttress this high-priced production against competition from imports, all imposed duties or controls. All had some form of state finance to buy in and stock surpluses or subsidize otherwise unsellable exports. Most, though not all, offered open-ended guarantees of purchase on important commodities, especially grains. In essence, the CAP simply transferred these arrangements from their separate national planes onto a single Community one. There would be common Community prices; common trade controls to insulate those commodities against cheaper imports from outside the Community; and a common European fund to buy in and stock agricultural surpluses and, if

Table 1.10   Price Subsidies (Price Supports) to Agriculture in 1956 in Various Countries Later to Become Members of the EC

Country	Price Support as Percent Output Value at National Prices 1956	Price Support per Head of Active Agricultural Workforce in £s, 1956
Britain	24	251
Germany	18	53
France	15	69
Italy	14	31
Belgium	5	41
Netherlands	5	28
Ireland	4	17
Denmark	3	19

Source: Gavin McCrone, *The Economics of Subsidising Agriculture*, London 1962, p. 51.

need be, to subsidize sales to special groups of consumers at home or, more generally, to markets abroad.

Here again, the CAP has largely continued practices with immediate antecedents in national postwar policies and roots deep in history. It is very much tied to the expectations of peasant agriculture as such. It is not, for instance, a food policy. It is very specifically about agriculture, although since the war, food industry and distribution have been competing more and more sharply with the farmers for the consumers' expenditure. Such choices have meant that policies born of low productivity in a slow-moving environment have become increasingly ill-fitted to deal with high productivity in a fast-moving one. The past quarter-century has for the first time broken with the old continuities, while the CAP has not. The difficulties of the CAP come mainly from its conservative elements, not the radical ones, which are political and European rather than grounded in agriculture itself.

The irony is that the CAP was initially viewed as a remedy for the imbalances already surfacing in the national context. However, as so often happens in such situations, the idea of what constituted a remedy differed sharply with each of the parties to the negotiation. For the main formal architect of the CAP, the former Dutch agricultural minister and first European commissioner for agriculture, Sicco Mansholt, the initial aim was to eliminate surpluses. He declared in 1958 a determination not to repeat "the errors" of the past: "Since it has recently become apparent that excessive support for prices and markets easily leads to overproduction, it is easy to see the limitations of price as a means of underpinning incomes."[13] This was not at all the top priority as the exporting countries saw it. What they wanted was free and preferential access to the large and rapidly growing German import market. For the Netherlands, France and Italy alike, agricultural exports were a vital element of the balance of payments. A quarter of all Dutch and Italian exports came from the farms and as did about a seventh of those of France.[14] The opportunity to cash in on this by replacing non-European exporters on the German market was too good to be missed. Moreover, there were, for the French, balance-of-power reasons for forcing the issue. With half the agricultural area of the Community of Six, France perceived a need to balance the disproportionate advantages she feared Germany, as the dominant manufactuirng power, might gain from the industrial Common Market. France was to be compensated for the industrial risks she took by free access to Germany's food markets.

French pressure settled the issue of whether the CAP would exist or not. Only France could push the Germans to give way in the name of European unification. But the Netherlands and Italy were at least as interested as France in securing German outlets. The Dutch in particular were far and away the most advanced agricultural producers, transformers, and traders in the Community, particularly in dairy products where, at the time, they accounted for two-thirds of all Community exports. If the French forced through the CAP, the form it took was largely due to the Dutch. It was they who first struggled for the kind of CAP that finally emerged. It was their dairy producers, along with the big French cereal and sugarbeet growers, who, per head, profited most from it. The French, before 1961, were inclined to think in the limited terms of bilateral long-term contracts with Germany for wheat and sugar, the two export products which interested the farmers of the Paris basin who dominated the French lobbies.[15]

The high price countries (the net importers Belgium, Germany, and Luxembourg, as well as Italy for "northern" products) had yet a third view of the CAP. If they were (reluctantly) to open their import markets to their partners, they could not allow the real incomes of their numerous and politically influential farmers to be undercut. They therefore resisted all price cuts. Low prices might have suited the lower price exporters (the Dutch in dairy products, the French for cereals and sugarbeet, and the Italians for fruit and vegetables) by undercutting farm output in Belgium and Germany. But farmers in these latter countries had no intention of becoming sacrificial lambs. They stubbornly opposed the Mansholt idea of competitive, low price specialization. The reduction of 9 percent in German cereals prices, painfully negotiated when common European price levels were at last decided at the end of 1964, was more than made up by the high prices subsequently fixed for milk (a decision in which Belgium and Italy played a notable part). French and Dutch milk prices were raised a quarter to accommodate the Belgians, Germans, and Italians (UN, ECE-FAO, 1967: UN, ECE, 1968). Ironically, the only exporting country which succeeded in avoiding high price supports was Italy for fruit and vegetables. She was not to know that, as a result of commercial shortcomings, she would fail to oust Dutch horticulture and Spanish citrus exporters (who are not even in the Common Market) from their dominant positions in the richer northern markets.

The compromise between the founder states on which the CAP was established reflected these divergent preoccupations. On the one hand, there would be free access by Community producers to all the member states' markets. This was an important concession to the exporters. On the other hand, real prices to producers would not be cut more than marginally in any commodity. This was the condition of unhampered trade. It meant that prices were aligned virtually on the highest cost producers in the highest cost member states and that there must be commensurately high levels of protection against imports from non-Community countries. It was a straight defeat for Mansholt's reforming hopes concerning prices.

In short, the decision taken when the CAP was set up established a single framework for agriculture, but failed to resolve the underlying contradictions, or competition, between national policies. To that extent, the CAP confirmed the pre-existing national traditions and tended to heighten, while postponing, the potential conflicts. The CAP cannot be blamed for the present agricultural crisis in the sense that all its main features were politially fixed before it was even conceived. The Community has compounded the problem in that deals among the six or ten, let alone twelve, countries have increased the temptation to reach the immediately least embarrassing compromise rather than face the longer-term economic trade-offs and sociopolitical choices which would be hard enough to tackle in a single centralized national system. Accordingly, the Community has ultimately aggravated the pre-existing problem by taking the easiest, that is, the most expansive, route out of the initial political difficulties. But in doing so, the CAP has been a reflection, not a cause, of the pressures behind expansion.

Mansholt, realizing that he had failed to correct the national "errors of the past," then turned to his very Dutch favorite of a structural policy. He proposed in 1968 the plan that bears his name, aiming at profound changes in the pattern of Community farming. He wanted a common policy of Community subsidies to encourage smallholders to leave the land and re-train in other occupations (if young enough to do so), while the minimum size of farm should rise to 80–120 hectares for wheat, 40–60 cows for milk, 150–200 head of cattle for beef production, and so on, by 1980—all of them stratospherically above average levels at the time. The agricultural area would have to fall from 71 to 65 million hectares, and the labour force from 20 percent of the total working population of the Community of Six in 1960 to 6 percent by 1980 (Com-EC, 1969, p.51). The idea was to modernize agriculture in order, first, to make it more competitive and, second, to reduce the differences between incomes on and off the farm and, at least as important, between varying types of farmer. This would ultimately create the conditions in which real prices could be reduced by basing them on costs nearer those of the more efficient producers.

The governments refused to endorse this far-reaching policy and still less to allow the Commission to carry it out. It is notable that the two major initiatives of the later 1970s in Community structural policy, involving special aid for hill-farmers (1975) and the Mediterranean zones (1978), were pushed through in response to specific national preoccupations. In 1975, the British were looking for compensation for the costs to them of the CAP. In 1978, the Italians were looking for long-term ways to ensure they would not have a net deficit in their Community budget payments.

The weakness of the Community's hold on structural policy can be gauged from its budgetary scope. Mansholt had envisaged that the agricultural fund would account for half the Community's farm budget. The rump reform he managed to obtain, and its successors during the 1970s, have resulted in structural expenditure representing only 5 percent of the Community's farm budget. The national agricultural budgets, on the other hand, were together (depending on the definition) as large, or twice as large, as the Community's fund (Appendix Table 10). In 1977, for which data (though incomplete) are available, national tax reliefs or subsidies to production, marketing, and capital represented 40 to 45 percent of farm investment in the Community (except for the UK).[16] Often investment would not have taken place without this component, which was crucial and could be strategic. The last lines of the Mansholt plan, writing of the national structural plans sprouting at the time, were clear about the implications:

> In practice, the efforts which are deployed often aim less at integrating agriculture in the economy of the Community as a whole than at affecting the competitive advantage of national sales on the common market. An opening up of frontiers in the Community that leads to competition on a national basis could prove dangerous for the balance of markets [Com-EC, 1969, p.499].

The course of the CAP in the years since could hardly be more succinctly summarized.

Three factors are probably responsible for the conditions in which the CAP was established. The first was the refusal of the member states to tackle the difficult internal issues posed by the development of agriculture since the war. This was partly because they dared not flout their powerful farm interests, and partly because their constant preoccupation with balances of payment encouraged them to expand their farm sector whenever it seemed to offer the prospect of promoting exports or reducing imports.

The second was that the federalists, including Mansholt himself, cared even more for a step that led to economic and ultimately, they hoped, political union, than they did for the agricultural reforms they perceived were necessary. They were in any case in no position to prevail on prices.

The third factor was that the CAP, by opening up the import markets of Germany and, as it later proved, Italy and Britain, gave the exporters maneuvering room. There was slack in the European import markets for exporters with preferential access. This gave time that would not otherwise have been available to continue on the trajectory of the 1950s. It became possible to postpone inside the wider Community the resolution of the issues posed in the narrower national settings before the Treaty of Rome was signed.

"Fuite en Avant"★

The two factors which, for twenty years, gave room for farm expansion within the CAP were both nonrenewable. One was the change of diet associated with the postwar economic "miracles". For the first time, this produced a middle-class way of life for the majority of the population. Demand for food was less affected by high growth than most other forms of consumption. Nevertheless, total food imports into the Community countries, in value and from all sources, after allowing for inflation, rose by half between 1960 and 1980 (see Table 1.11). This is not enormous—equivalent to about 2 percent a year—but it did provide some leeway for all suppliers. It was also more substantial in tonnage than value because of falling farm prices in real terms. It had a particularly striking consequence, already noted, as a result of the explosion of the Italian food import market. Here, a large new outlet was opened up; net food imports rose as much in Italy from 1960 to 1980 as they did in the far larger German economy.[17] The second factor was the massive exploitation of the preferential Community market created by the CAP. Whereas at constant prices, imports from countries outside the Community, which in 1960 outvalued EC intra-trade 3 to 1, fell 5 percent between 1960 and 1980, trade between member states more than tripled to outstrip them. All the increase in farm trade went to the member states who, in 1960, accounted for a mere quarter of it. Because of the fall in real farm prices, the story in terms of volumes is still more dramatic. Imports, by weight, into the European Community–9 doubled, but imports between Community countries grew nine times.[18] Since, in the formation of the CAP, Community countries shifted their sources of supply to their partners at the expense of outsiders, the problems of domestic expansion in the area became manageable.

There has, on the surface, been a cyclical pattern in what has in fact been a steadily mounting pressure of expansion of supply. In 1958, three of the six founder states had increasing export potential for which they sought new outlets: the Netherlands particularly for dairy products, France for cereals and sugar, and Italy for fruit. One country, West Germany, was a major market, which on its own accounted for not far short of half of the food imports from all sources, external and internal, of the original Community. As expected, the establishment of the CAP did provide a preferential market and afford relief. At constant prices, the value of exports of the six founder members rose by a third to third countries between 1960 and 1970, and between the six themselves nearly doubled. Italy's hopes of flourishing as an exporter were dashed and her farm deficit grew fast. Between 1960 and the last year before enlargement in 1972, Italy and Germany accounted together for nearly 60 percent of the increase in imports among the member states. On the side of the exporters, France supplied 40 percent and the Netherlands 24

★ This useful and common French phrase (literally "forward flight") is untranslatable but means, roughly, "an attempt to accelerate out of trouble." There is no connotation in it of expectations of either success or failure.

Table 1.11   Evolution of Food Trade of the EC-9, 1960–1980, in Value, at Constant Prices (in billions of ECUs of 1960) (SITC 0 + 1 + 22 + 29 + 4)

Year	Trade within EC-9 (imports = exports)	Trade with World		Trade All Sources	
		Imports	Exports	Imports	Exports
1960	2.8	9.1	2.1	12.0	5.0
1980	9.3	8.6	5.0	17.9	14.3
1980 (1960 = 1)	3.3	0.95	2.3	1.5	2.9

Source: Appendix Table 6.

percent of the growth in the same period.[19] As they had hoped, France's cereal growers benefitted greatly from the new dispensation, though proportionately Holland was at least as successful. What was not so expected was that the one country for which optimists in the exporting countries had assigned a passive importer's role, West Germany, should turn about and vigorously increase the proportion of her farm exports too (Appendix Table 7). As German food exports started from a very low level, this was not so visible as it was to become in the 1970s. Nevertheless, German exports to the Six grew over five times at constant prices between 1962 and 1972 and by that last year had overtaken those of Italy. By 1972, the Community of Six had risen virtually to self-sufficiency, and in breadgrains, sugar, and dairy products, the very commodities which had posed the greatest initial problems, surpluses were rearing their head again as an active issue.

From this point of view, the first enlargement of the Community, which brought in the archetypal importer of farm produce, Britain, was a potential godsend. As with the initial creation of the CAP, the expansion of the Community and its preference in agricultural trade afforded relief. But, once again, only a little time was really gained. The upward march of production as against consumption continued, all the more rapidly because the rate of growth of consumption fell markedly after the onset of recession in 1973 (Appendix Table 1). Once again, the importing country itself contributed to the trend with more than average abandon. Considerable stress was laid on the fact that in the 1970s Germany's coverage of farm imports by exports rose with the Community partners (Appendix Table 7) from 29 percent in 1970 to 52 percent in 1980 (Hu, 1979, pp. 453ff). Less attention was paid to the figures showing that Britain's coverage actually rose substantially faster in the same period. By 1980, Britain's ratio of exports to imports from the Community, which stood at 23 percent in 1970, had shot up to 54 percent (Appendix Table 7). On the threshold of the 1980s, the Community faced much the same surplus problems as ten or twenty years before, or rather a situation somewhat worse.

Now the second enlargement, towards the Mediterranean, is, or may be, in process. Greece joined the Community in 1981 and Spain and Portugal appear to have improved prospects of being allowed to do so. Here again, their markets may afford relief. On this occasion, however, the margins for growth are only a fraction of what they were in their time with Germany and Britain, even if outside exporters are supplanted. As the figures in Table 1.12 indicate, any relief would not be likely to last long. Moreover, the three new aspirants to entry, or rather Spain, unlike Germany and Britain, are major traditional exporters of some important commodities, the so-called Mediterranean products, such as citrus fruit, early vegetables, olive oil, wine, and so on. Higher CAP prices are likely to lead them to produce and export still more (Com-EC, 1978c, pp. 191–198; 1982c; and Bourrinet and Stioui, 1982, pp. 21–27). Surpluses threaten to break out in commodities which have not hitherto created major difficulties. This poses risks of competition mainly between the relatively poor producers of the southern regions of the Community. Moreover, behind the Three, there is no further large import market waiting to be exploited by an expanding Community. In short, the preferential European *Lebensraum* for soaking up surpluses is being progressively filled up, as the tide of self-sufficiency rises in one after another of the potential outlets. This is one reason why the second enlargement of the Community poses problems that are just as intractable for agriculture as the entry of Britain, despite structures which, on the face of it, seem more complementary.

Table 1.12 Preferential Markets for EC Food Exporters Opened Up by Various Stages of the Development of the EC (in billions of current ECUs and as percentages of exporting member countries sales)

		The importer's(s') Food Imports (excl. from prospective EC partners)	The EC Partners' Food Exports (excl. to prospective EC partners)	Importers' Markets as Percentage Exporters' Sales
1960	Germany (imports) and other five founding states of the EC (exports)	1.9	1.6	121
1972	Britain (imports) and EC-6 (exports)	3.9	3.5	111
1980	Greece, Portugal and Spain (imports) and EC-9 (exports)	3.7	17.7	21

Note: All figures are in billion ECUs at current prices and exchange rates and cover SITC 0 + 1 + 22 + 29 + 4. Excl. = excluding.

Source: Com-EC, Eurostat, *Monthly External Trade Bulletins, European Economy*, Nov. 1983, Table 41, OECD, *Trade by Commodities*.

Table 1.13   Food Trade Between EC States: Coverage of Imports by Exports in Percent (SITC 0 + 1 + 22 + 29 + 4)

Country	1960	1981[a]
Belgium-Luxembourg	66	92
Denmark	1213	331
France	182	136
Germany	13	55
Greece	–	74
Ireland	611	150
Italy	160	50
Netherlands	892	295
United Kingdom	11	54

[a] EC-10

Source: See Appendix Table 7.

This development is illustrated by the coverage of imports of agricultural products by exports in trade between the member states since 1960 (Table 1.13). The pattern, revealed in Table 1.13, is absolutely regular. The net exporters (more than 100 per cent) in intra-Community trade of 1960 all see their export coverage decline. The net importers in intra-Community trade of 1960 (less than 100 per cent) all see their export coverage rise.

This could, in principle, be consonant with an increased specialization of trade, and provide a yardstick of the integration of markets. Indeed, on the evidence of the 1970s, there may have been some: Italy in tinned fruit and vegetables, France in flour, Germany in dairy products, and the Netherlands in tobacco, which were already the leading exporters in the Community in 1974, further increased their lead by 1980. This could reflect a degree of real division of labor. There has also been some specialization in output. "Cereal production, already located at the start of the Community period in large farm areas, is concentrated today in three growth poles: the Paris region, the east of England (east Anglia) and north Germany, which account for more than 50 percent of the Community harvest " (Henry et al., 1981, p. 22). To a lesser extent, milk production as well as pigs, poultry, and eggs close to Dutch and other north European ports importing cheap animal feed, or fruit and vegetables (around large conurbations), have increasingly focused on areas with clear locational advantages.

Yet this is specialization with a difference. It is a strange division of labor which extends milk production into the Italian *Mezzogiorno*.[20] Britain's coverage of imports by exports within the Community rose between 1972 and 1980 from 6 percent to 100 percent for cereals, 8 percent to 76 percent for dairy products and from 16 percent to 34 percent for sugar (Thiede, 1980; Eurostat, 1983b). All of these are products in surplus in the Community. Trade in sugar and cereals within the Community actually fell between 1978 and 1981 because, the Commission noted in 1980, "of production increases in deficit countries such as Italy and the UK" (ASC 1980, pp. 68, 76). The general conclusion must be that in standard products at least, the channels of trade within the EC, hitherto buoyant, are beginning to silt up because ever-increasing output in each country is filling the erstwhile market gaps. That, of course, is the reverse of specialization and confirms Mansholt's strictures.

Such an evolution is not simply due to the CAP. The export-import ratios of Britain and Germany rose in close parallel from the late 1950s onwards, although Britain joined the Community fifteen years after Germany (Appendix Table 7). In the Mediterranean, the growth of imports noted in Italy was more or less common to all the southern European countries. As with prices, trade parallels inside and outside the EC suggest that in Western Europe wider economic forces and wider similarities of policy than the CAP have been at work. However, whatever the causes, the results are plain and cumulative.

The implications are most easily appreciated by looking at the growth of supply and demand during the past three decades. The growth of output (Appendix Table 1) has been remarkably steady for those thirty years. The rate has oscillated for the six founder states around 3 percent per annum in the 1950s (value) and 1960s (volume) and fell only to 2.6 percent (volume) during the recession since 1973. This steadiness is all the more remarkable if one recalls the considerable ups and downs in the evolution of real farm prices (that is, of farmers' prices compared to others in the economy). It is therefore reasonable to assume that there may have to be a considerable change in policy or the environment for the rate of growth to fall substantially. Demand has apparently been more variable. The growth of demand for food averaged 4.1 percent annually (in value) for the Six in the 1950s. At this period, the shift in European habits from starchy foods (potatoes, cereals) to meat, fruit, and vegetables was in full swing. But by the 1960s affluence was moving increasingly into other sectors of demand. Food consumption growth was less, about 2.6 percent per annum in volume in the decade. Then, in 1973, recession came on top of changes in spending habits and growth of consumption fell to 1.5 percent per annum in volume. (Appendix Table 1). Even here, however, there is more continuity than meets the eye. The proportionate fall in the growth of food consumption between the 1950s and 1960s is almost identical with that between the 1960s and 1970s: about 40 percent in either case.[21] Thus, in the 1950s, production in the six founder states rose less rapidly than consumption (though this was not true of all products). In the 1960s, production began to outpace consumption across the board, but the Community of Six was still not self-sufficient and there was some leeway. In the 1970s, production continued to grow almost as fast as in the boom years, but the growth of consumption fell further. The tendency to oversupply has accelerated and been felt with increasing sharpness.

The result has been for the Community member states to be more and more prone to export abroad. All of the Community of Nine, with the exception of Italy and the Netherlands, have greatly increased their food exports to the rest of the world since 1958 in comparison with their imports from it (Appendix Table 7). For the EC-9 as a whole, the ratio of exports to imports in food trade with the rest of the world rose from 24 percent in 1960 to 33 percent in 1970 and then, accelerating, to 58 percent in 1980, and 71 percent in 1981 (Appendix Table 5), though it fell again to 65 percent in deep recession in 1982 and 1983. Some of the details by commodity, shown in Table 1.14, are particularly instructive as one can read from them the developments not merely in abstract currencies but in actual weight of goods. In many sectors, as Table 1-E shows, imports from third countries actually fell between 1974 and 1980. The exceptions, of which fruit and vegetables and feed for livestock are of major importance, nevertheless are few.[22]

Accordingly, in 1979, the Community of Nine crossed an important commercial and political watershed. For the first time, it became a net exporter of temperate foodstuffs. Its percentage of self-supply that year reached 103 percent, on a curve rising (Appendix Table 2) to 108 in 1981. Six years before, in 1973, the percentage had been only 94. This statement needs qualifying for more than one reason, the most important of which is that it excludes the animal feed—the raw materials—which the Community imports in large quantities to raise livestock. Taking these imports into account, the Community's level of self-sufficiency was only 89 percent in 1979, up from 83 percent in 1973. But though this reservation is important, by 1981 the level reached 97 percent on the most restrictive yardstick, and the fact that in final farm products the Community is already a net exporter is an enormously significant development. For a century, after all, Western Europe, meaning essentially from this point of view the member states of the Community, had been *the* food importer of the world. The region's role is rapidly changing.

Potentially, this development transforms the environment for Community policy-making in agriculture. On the one hand, new opportunities on the world market could help—and in the 1970s have helped—to relieve the

---

Table 1.14   The Balance of EC Exports To, and Imports From, the Rest of the World for Some Major Agricultural Commodities, 1974 and 1981

Value of EC-9 Agricultural Output in 1981	Commodity	Exports to Non-EC Markets Expressed as a Percentage of Imports from Them, by Weight 1974	1981
12.2	Cereals	27	107
2.9	Sugar	43	145
10.7	Fruit and vegetables	17	15
19.6	Dairy products	530	746
33.8	Fresh meat (all)	37	134

Source: Com-EC, *Analytical Tables of Foreign Trade, Nimexe 1974 and 1981*, Vol. Z: *Countries – Products.*

Community's internal problems. On the other, once a country or region becomes a significant exporter, it loses much of the control over the context it enjoys at home. As Denis Bergmann pointed out (1979, p. 5) "An exporting agriculture cannot control prices; it has to live with them."[23]

It is one thing to persuade Community consumers to pay prices to which they have long been accustomed (and which depend as much on the food industry and distribution as on farmers). It is another, even for a dominant exporter, as OPEC has found, to manipulate export prices when world demand simply is not there. Similarly, it is one thing to conduct policy within the Community on the basis of home producers replacing outsiders in the markets of the member states; it is quite another to undercut established exporters in other parts of the world. Such developments shift the ground on which established compromises in the CAP have been built. As a result they impinge even on politics inside the Community. The tensions do not halt on the doorstep. They break into the house.

How are markets to be profitably won for production that cannot be sold at home? Who is to pay for new markets when sales are subsidized? These are exactly the questions the CAP was designed to answer twenty years ago. As old agreements on Community revenues run out of steam, as they have done in the early 1980s, the familiar bargains they underpinned are also put in question.

So, in one guise or another, all the problems the founding states of the Community hoped in 1960 to finesse through the CAP are reappearing a quarter of a century later after the exploitation of the major import markets that once existed, or as in Italy have since appeared, in the region itself. The calculation that the CAP would allow the member states to avoid policy choices has, at the most, bought time. It has seen millions of farmers and their children leave the land without too much social upheaval. Yet it has provided no release from the basic dilemmas. They have simply grown with the years and the wider market. Hopes of release from choice then extend to the world market. They are apparently confirmed when world markets boom. When world markets fall again, as in an unstable situation they always do, the costs reappear magnified. Conflicts involve third countries and so are less malleable. Domestically, the calls on resources make it possible to question the consensus established when the CAP was set up. But there is now no cushion such as the CAP itself provided in the last phase. Either a new one has to be created—but how? where? and on what consensus?—or the problems postponed a generation ago have at last to be faced.

Policy Responses

The imbalances in the CAP have led to abundant official and unofficial policy suggestions and responses. Three in particular can be distinguished, based on the different sources from which they have come: lay and academic comment, especially but not only in countries with a tradition of criticism of CAP, intellectual or otherwise, such as Britain or Germany;[24] policy proposals put forward by the Commission; and the responses of national governments.

LAY CRITIQUES: INCOME SUPPORTS

The dominant strain in nonofficial comment, often very critical of surpluses, has been to distinguish between the productive and welfare functions of the CAP. At least as early as 1970, experts proposed that CAP guarantees of producer prices should be reduced across the board to make markets balance, and the poorer farmers compensated for losses by direct aids to income. The basic insight behind such ideas, which have been repeatedly advanced, is the enormous gap between the productive potential, and income, of the marginal farms, with three-quarters of the holdings, and the largest or most efficient ones, with three-quarters of the output (Table 1.15).[25]

The "Stocktaking of the CAP" carried out by the European Commission in 1975 enunciated the basic principle that "to support incomes, it is necessary to fix prices at a high enough level to provide a living for the marginal farmers."[26] This is the reverse of what Mansholt argued for, and necessarily provides large

Table 1.15   Distribution of Productive Capacity in the EC-9, 1975–1979

	Size of Sector		Smallholdings		Largeholdings	
Sector	Holdings (percent)	Value of Final Production 1980 (percent)	Holdings (percent)	Area[a] or Headage[b] (percent)	Holdings (percent)	Area[a] or Headage[b] (percent)
Cereals	61	12.6	52	8	8	53
Cattle[c]	50	15.8[d]	48	10	19	59
Laying hens	50	3.4	97	15	0.2	56
Pigs	37	11.5	51	2	8	75
Dairy cows	35	19.2	55	15	12	44
Potatoes	33	1.9	59	11	9	54
Vines	31	4.8	48	8	6	49
Broilers	26	4.2	97	7	0.5	73
Fruit	10	4.0	43	6	7	47
Sheep	10	1.8	39	2	5	48
Sugarbeet	6	2.7	41	7	14	56
Crops under glass	1.5	—	52	9	8	41
All above	—	81.9[e]	57[f]	9[g]	8[f]	56[g]

[a] For crops.
[b] For livestock.
[c] Including dairy cows.
[d] Beef and veal, but not milk.

[e] Excluding crops under glass.
[f] Arithmetical average.
[g] Arithmetical average weighted by proportion of value of final production.

Source: Com-EC, *ASC 1982*, pp. 194–95 and 312. Community farm structure surveys 1975 and 1977; bovine and pig surveys 1979.

profits to the much more productive farms at the other end of the scale. In the late 1960s, the Mansholt Plan noted that unit costs of production fell by a third for cereals produced on farms of 70 hectares as against 30 hectares (already twice the average Community size); and labor and capital costs per cow by more than 40 percent when the herd grew from 10 to 40 head. (Com-EC, 1969, p. 72). The structural survey of 1975 showed that 60 percent of Community farms were then under 10 hectares and covered only 13.5 percent of the agricultural area (*ASC 1980*, p. 250).

Two major consequences follow from such a policy applied to widely differing conditions—the one economic, the other social. From the economic point of view, prices attuned to the weakest farms are bound to encourage expansion among those that are much more efficient. Support prices would have to fall steeply for incentives to the more productive farms to be cut to the point where output is under control. Nobody knows how big such reductions would have to be. For what it is worth, some close observers of the CAP guessed in 1979 that it would be necessary to reduce agricultural incomes by 20 to 30 percent from their then levels to begin to inhibit surpluses in the dairy sector. The Commission itself suggested in October 1981 that the gap in US and European domestic prices for cereals, then of 20 percent, should be gradually reduced between then and 1988.[27] Such estimates at least give some idea of the political determination that would be necessary to establish control through prices alone.

The second implication, of great social importance, is the wide spread of incomes between the poorest and wealthiest holdings. Average farm incomes in the richest regions of the Community are about ten times those in the poorest. The Community's Farm Accounts Data Network (FADN) for "1975" (that is, 1974–76), provided an extreme range of 21:1 between a group of 77 Dutch farms producing cereals, sugarbeet and potatoes and averaging 78 hectares each, and 21 Umbrian holdings, mainly of vineyards, on an average of $2^{1/4}$ hectares each. The German official Agricultural Report of 1980 provided a range of 44:1 in group average family incomes on different individual farms in the single Land (State) of Hessen![28]

Since smallholders are very unevenly distributed across the European Community, these enormous disparities have regional implications. Of the holdings between 1 and 5 hectares in the Community in 1977, 56 percent were situated in Italy, 19 percent in Greece, 11 percent in Germany, and 9 percent in France, leaving only 5 percent among all the remaining six members of a Community of Ten. As we have already seen, smallholdings and part-time work are not necessarily synonymous with low incomes. Nevertheless, concentrations of the two often are associated. Italy and Greece have much the lowest incomes on the land, and German incomes are lowest where numbers are highest. The correspondance is less close in France, but even there applies in the case of Rhône-Alpes (Eurostat, 1974, p.155; Com-EC, 1978b; ASC, various). It is in character with the policy of price supports, geared to high production, that Community budget payments for surpluses favor the productive holdings and richer regions. A whole series of reports, official and unofficial, have shown that most of the regions receiving the largest sums (at least until 1978) were rich and that most of those receiving the least were poor. There are partial exceptions, which can usually be identified as beneficiaries of a particular regime, such as Apulia through olive oil subsidies.[29]

While Community agriculture has largely changed from a peasant to an industrial one, it has travelled only part of the way—especially in the Mediterranean, the south and west of France, and in Ireland. It still retains a highly dualistic structure, with marked regional differences. The European Commission carried out a survey of the structure of holdings in 1975 which showed that after a generation of smallholders leaving the land, the average size of holdings in the Nine was still under 15 hectares. There were still 12.7 million people putting in some regular work on the farms, nearly 90 percent of them family members; and 72 percent of the total were part-time (ASC 1982, p.119). Moreover, 44 percent of farmers themselves devoted less than half their time to farming; and of these, half had no gainful activity other than farming (ASC 1980, p.22). Outside Britain, Denmark and Benelux, the peasant inheritance of Western Europe was still very much in evidence.

Community agriculture has a powerful head and body, provided by relatively few but highly productive farms. These constitute the "economic" sector. There is also a long tail at the extremity of which almost 60 percent of farms seem to control less than 10 percent of farm resources (Table 1.15). This is the "welfare" sector. It is difficult for a single undifferentiated policy to deal with such divergent conditions. If prices are fixed to maintain the incomes of the poor, inflation in land and other values keeps out the young newcomers and the richer farmers are stimulated to produce too much. If prices are reduced to balance supply and demand, the poorer farmers could face catastropic inadequacies of income. By treating two societies according to single criteria, the CAP has impaled itself upon a dilemma. The European Commission began trying to unhook itself in the later 1970s, but not along the lines recommended by lay critics.

THE COMMISSION: FROM ACCOUNTANCY TO LIMITS

Commission policies have moved through a number of fairly distinct periods. Mansholt stamped his imprint on the first. Despite his initial failure to stop the establishment of official CAP support prices at virtually the highest national levels, he worked hard to rein in prices thereafter. He hoped that over the long-term, price constraints would finally inhibit production. As it was, in the short term, surpluses posed problems. Their pressure, and dissensions between the six member states, as they then were, prevented price support decisions being taken from 1968 to 1970, a time when inflation was already accelerating (Table 1.16). This amounted to a fall in real support prices which partly corrected the high price decisions at the creation of the CAP. There may even have been some effect on output. At any rate, the three years from 1968 to 1971 were unique in that milk production for once marked time (Eurostat, Cronos).

Table 1.16   Trends in Official CAP Support Prices from 1968–69 to 1984–85 (percent per annum)

Year		1 Increase in National Currencies (weighted average, percent for EC)	2 Inflation in National Currencies (weighted average, percent for EC; calendar years, i.e., 1968–69 = 1968, etc.)	3 Net Increase in National Currencies (weighted average, percent for EC at constant price)
EC-6	1968–69	0.0	2.8	−2.7
	1969–70	0.0	5.1	−4.9
	1970–71	0.0	6.6	−6.2
	1971–72	(3.5)[a]	6.9	na
	1972–73	(8.0)[a]	6.1	+na
EC-9	1973–74	21.0	8.1	+11.9
	1974–75	14.0	12.4	+1.4
	1975–76	10.1	14.8	−4.1
	1976–77	8.1	10.4	−2.1
	1977–78	5.9	9.6	−3.3
	1978–79	7.6	8.4	−0.7
	1979–80	6.4	9.3	−2.7
	1980–81	5.7	10.7	−4.5
EC-10	1981–82	10.9	9.1	+1.6
	1982–83	12.2	9.0	+2.9
	1983–84	6.9	6.3	+0.6
	1984–85	3.3	5.1	−1.7

[a] EC prices only, without conversion to national currencies. Prices in national currencies would certainly be higher than in European units of account.

na = not available.

Sources:
  Col. 1: Edmund Neville-Rolfe, *The Politics of Agriculture in the European Community*, European Centre for Political Studies, PSI, London 1984; Table 8.1, pp. 248–49, column 7.
  Col. 2: Derived from Com-EC, 1983i, *European Economy*, November 1983, Tables 6 and 17, with corrections for changing EC membership.
  Col. 3: Col. 1 divided by Col. 2.

But in Mansholt's last year, 1972, price supports increased again. His departure and replacement by another former Dutch minister of agriculture, Petrus Lardinois, coincided with new conditions. In 1973–74, the first energy crisis added to the inflation that cut into farmers' earnings. In 1974–75, the boom in international food prices reduced the Community's need to subsidize exports and lightened the burden on the budget (Appendix Table 11). Both strengthened the temptation to raise support prices. As a result, this was a period of laxity in price policy which added gratuitously to later embarrassments (Table 1.16).

These reappeared very soon. By 1976, world food prices had already fallen. Community farm budgets duly began to climb again, to a new peak in 1979 (Appendix Table 11). This coincided with the tenure of the Commission's farm post by Finn Gundelach, a Dane who had worked at GATT. From 1975 (in Lardinois' last period) to Gundelach's sudden death in January 1981, the Commission reverted to Mansholt's "prudent" pricing and even tightened the rhetoric to "rigorous" (Com-EC, Price proposals, 1979, 18).[30] The problems and priorities were clearly stated:

> First, the imbalance between supply and demand in several major agricultural markets is worsening. Secondly, income disparities within the agricultural sector remain substantial. Thirdly, monetary upheavals have disrupted the common agricultural market. By itself, the CAP cannot solve the agri-monetary problem. It can only partially help to eliminate income disparities. But it must accept the overall responsibility for restoring market equilibrium [Com-EC 1978d].

From 1975 to 1980 increases in price support were held below the rate of inflation in the member states. Cumulatively, this amounted to a substantial squeeze in real support by the Community.

Nevertheless, the restraints of 1975 to 1981 only modestly outweighed the increases of 1972 to 1974, just as the restraints of 1968 to 1971 probably did not annul the increases in supports conceded during the setting up of the CAP. Support prices are not, of course, identical with the actual market prices in the member states already discussed. But in either case, it was clear that price falls in real terms were far from compensating for the steady rise in productivity on the farms. Production and the levels of self-sufficiency in Community farming continued to rise. So did the basic levels of Community spending on agriculture which rose gradually, with ups and downs, toward the ceiling on Community tax resources (Appendix Table 11). In short, the Commission's attempts, insofar as they were coherently pursued, to control output through long-term price cuts ultimately failed in the 1970s.

For this reason, Commission policies seemed in many ways designed to contain the budgetary consequences of surpluses—about which it was possible to act in the short-term—rather than to persuade the member states of the need to control output, a weary task which would obviously require a prolonged struggle. There are many examples of this bias toward what was called an "accountant's policy."

For instance, in 1977, the Commission persuaded the Council to accept one of its longstanding ideas, that producers themselves pay part of the costs of funding the CAP. A "co-responsibility levy" of 1.5 percent (later raised to 2.5 percent) was instituted for milk (Com-EC, Price Proposals, 1977, 58). This levy was soon built in to negotiators' calculations and raised the milk price higher than it would otherwise have been. But if this did little for consumers, it certainly helped the budget. In the peak year, 1982, the levy covered nearly

14 percent of the Community's spending on milk (Com-EC, 1983a, p.26). In the same year, the sugar levy actually covered 56 percent of spending on sugar (ibid. pp.26, 34). Neither halted the rise of output. Another device was the export cartel, agreed in GATT in 1979 with New Zealand (and with the de facto support of the US) to hold up world dairy prices (Neville-Rolfe, p.386). These arrangements worked to the associates' advantage when world markets were strong in 1980–81, but as is the way with cartels, not so well when they weakened from the third quarter of 1982 (International Dairy Arrangement, 1982, p.11).

The accountant's policy was inherently flawed. It addressed only financial symptoms and could not indefinitely mask the underlying problem of over-supply. Accordingly, from 1980 onwards, the Commission shifted policy toward the surpluses as such. In December 1980 and October 1981, it produced "reflections," and then "guidelines," for agriculture which marked a watershed (Com-EC, 1980c and 1981a).

The accent this time was not on "prudent" pricing in the old form, though the term remained. The second energy crisis squeezed farm incomes after 1979 even more than the first had done. World food markets revived, again as after the first energy crisis, so that the pressures on the Community budget were relieved. Under the new farm commissioner, Poul Dalsager, hitherto Denmark's minister of agriculture, there was a slight but distinct rise from 1981 to 1983 in CAP real price supports (Table 1.16). But this was not really a reversion to the Lardinois years. Output was still rising. The Community's financial crisis would visibly return as soon as world markets weakened. This was only a matter of time, and it clearly concentrated minds in Brussels.

The Commission was now compelled, and perhaps realistically able for the first time, to put forward more radical ideas. Three were central to the reflections and guidelines. The first was to place limits (now called "guarantee thresholds") on the hitherto open-ended price supports offered under the CAP. Beyond given tonnages, CAP support prices would be reduced or withdrawn, or (still more stringently for milk) replaced by taxes on excess output: if sufficiently swingeing and strictly applied, the latter in effect amount to production quotas (Com-EC, 1980c, p.18).

Second, guaranteed prices should be reduced across the board for the basic commodity cereals, whose price is not only important in itself but a key ingredient in the costs and mixtures of feed for livestock—the northern parts of the Community's principal agricultural activity. The Commission proposed that the gap between Community internal grain prices and those in the US (Table 1.1) be "progressively reduced" in the years up to 1988. This was the first time since the creation of the CAP the Commission had publicly committed itself to large cuts in price supports. It marked a major conceptual break with the past (Com-EC, 1981a, pp.26–31).

Third, national investment policies must be made compatible with Commu-nity limits on output. The guidelines gave an illustrative (and "not exhaus-tive") list of major sectors in which there was "no control": fruit and vegetables, cereals, beef, skimmed-milk, olive oil and wine. Since these exceptions were no accident, the demand amounted to a reassertion of Mansholt's attempts to institute a Community structural policy (Com-EC, 1981a, pp.22–24).

On balance, and despite the proposals for cereals, the Commission's thoughts leaned towards limits on support and towards production quotas more than towards price cuts across the board. Since this approach was likely, at least initially, to maintain price guarantees on basic quantities, it also reduced the pressure for income aids to small producers that would be necessary if support prices were cut for all deliveries. The Commission envisaged only peripheral income aids for small milk farmers, of a kind that had existed since 1977,[31] and a minor extension to beef and veal producers (Com-EC, 1981a, pp.21–22). The longterm policy of lower prices offset by income aids favored by lay commentators was not exactly written off, but the main thrust of policy at least for milk, was plainly towards production quotas. Whatever the pros and cons of this approach, it was at least a new departure.

NATIONAL STATES AND POLITICAL WILL

In the Community, however, it is not the Commission, acting as pilot, but the convoy of the governments which decides on the course to be taken. The main force behind the policies of expansion of the initial CAP has been the member states and the main obstacle to reform has been the reluctance of the Council of Ministers to rein in either CAP price supports or farm output.

It has sometimes been argued that the CAP is too rigid. Technically, this is hard to understand. Far from being a one-track system, the CAP is virtually a total network of the various management techniques available to farm administrators. According to commodities and times the instruments have varied from free trade, through simple tariff protection and quality controls, via minimum prices and "voluntary" restrictions on imports, to subsidies for producers, exporters and consumers, income aids for smallholders, intervention buying at low or high prices, guarantee thresholds, "superlevies" (as taxes on excess output are called), production quotas and so on. It is hard to see what weapons are missing from this immense and varied arsenal. The problem is not the insufficient elasticity of the CAP as a technial device or series of devices, but the political consensus about the ends to which the wealth of instruments should be directed.

Expanding output is the easiest way to placate farmers and, at least in appearance, to improve net national exports. National governments are as sensitive to pleas that real incomes are being eroded in the farm sector as in any other branch of the economy they administer. It is the expression, in the CAP, of the familiar maxim of the difficulty of compressing real incomes. It is not surprising that the governments, already struggling with urban unemployment, have been reluctant to face the rural music too. This is obviously a political, not a technical, phenomenon.

National placation of the countryside has been a recurrent counterpoint to Community efforts to compress farm earnings. When Community bounties fail, governments frequently step in, often with little pretence of reference to Community norms. This has been practiced more or less continuously through national "structural" policies which have many effects parallel to price increases. There have also been numerous examples of national income payments.[32] All these tend to strip the CAP of its institutional mask of European policy.

Expansion itself has been a screen for powerful national forces in agriculture. Little by little, it has eroded all three pillars sustaining the original concept of the CAP: common prices, common markets and common budgets. Common prices applied fully for only two years (July 1967 to August 1969), before inflation and instabilities in exchange rates more or less insulated national price levels from each other (Chapter 4 below). Free access to each other's markets is reduced in practice if not principle by the increase in self-sufficiency of each member state. The common budget is potentially called in question by quotas for contributions of the kind Britain has sought since 1979 and by national attempts to sidestep Community restraints on farm prices.

The political stakes for the Community in this at once artificial and anarchic expansion have been obvious enough. Tensions between different groups inside the Community could theoretically appear at many levels: between rich and poor farmers; between taxpayers or consumers and producers; between urban and rural interests; between regions the CAP favors more or less; and so on. Because many of the problems are in essence social, they would normally, in an integrated state, be channeled through parties and lead to the ritualized claims and conflicts between groups which are the stuff of politics in a unified democratic society. Because, within the Community, the tensions across society are superimposed on the semi-international balance of power between member states and Community institutions, this is not so. In practice, pressures surface primarily as conflicts between member states and about the political nature of the Community. International groupings, or confederations, are apt to be cemented by pressures from outside, but pulled apart by centrifugal forces from within, in this case between the member states. Disputes about transfers of income bring tensions to bear directly on these fissures. They are not merely about strains within the system. They raise questions potentially about its very future.

What may be less obvious are the stakes for national policies on the land. Even if renationalization were to take place on a significant scale, it would not eliminate the costs of applying remedies. It would merely redistribute them among different states, regions and groups of farmers. Exporting countries would have to pay higher costs of adjustment or export them onto world markets. At times, the world market might expand enough to let them do so. Alternatively, exporters might be able to persuade their Community partners to fund the export subsidies required. But somewhere, sometime, the limits would have to appear, as they did in 1984. The irony is that the CAP was established precisely to avoid, or at least postpone, such unwelcome choices at the national level. If national remedies were sought, the wheel would have turned full circle.

All these implications, hidden by expansion, came into the open when it became evident free growth could no longer continue. There was several reasons why this became unavoidable in the early 1980s and neither before nor later. The first reason was that expenditure, from 1979 onwards, was in sight of reaching, and indeed breaching, the ceiling of funds freely available to the Community. When world markets expanded, as in 1980–1981, the pressure receded, when they went slack, as from 1976 to 1979 and again from 1982 to 1984, it returned with redoubled force. (Appendix, Table 11)

The institutional basis of the CAP was the "common market organizations" painfully agreed upon by the founding states in the mid-1960s; but they could not have operated long without the "decision of Luxembourg" of 21 April 1970 (Strasser, 1975) which provided ample potential funds on which to run them and so constituted a virtual second foundation of the CAP.

1970 was the year of the *relance européenne* engineered by the newly installed triumvirate of Pompidou in France, Brandt in Germany and Heath in Britain. An essential part of it was the lifting by Pompidou of de Gaulle's veto on Britain's entry into the Community. However, from the French point of view, it was necessary to guard against Britain undermining the model of the CAP so recently put together, as it was predictable she would be tempted to do. So the French made it a condition that the necessary funds to run the CAP for an indefinite period should be made available. The Community already had access to the revenues from customs duties and their equivalent in agriculture, the variable levies on food imports, but these alone were not enough. It was therefore decided to give the Community the formally independent tax base ("own resources") envisaged in the Treaty of Rome but denied by de Gaulle in the crisis of 1965, up to 1 percent tax on value added in each of the member states (VAT). It was these funds which made possible the Community's agricultural expansion during the 1970s. By 1983, however, after a first warning in 1979, these resources no longer sufficed. The financial room for growth provided by the Luxembourg decision of 1970 had run out. So, with it, did the lease on life of the initial model of the CAP.

Of course, the ceiling of the Community's "own resources" could simply have been raised. This introduces the second reason for the crisis coming when it did. The exceptional costs for Britain of the CAP became evident at the end of the transition period to her full membership of the Community which came in 1979 (Appendix table 14). Britain's determination to place a limit on her contribution first surfaced in the last year of the Callaghan government, 1979, and then, from 1980 onwards, was relentlessly pressed by Mrs. Thatcher. Given the intergovernmental norms of the Community system of decision-making and the constitutional need for national Parliaments to ratify any raising of the Luxembourg tax ceiling, this alone would have been enough to force the issue. The ability to reach a compromise, however, was dependent on a partially concordant financial approach by the other member states, especially the most powerful, Germany and France.

That this concordant attitude in fact existed was the third reason for the reform of the CAP coming in 1983–84. Hitherto, the investment of each country in the CAP tended to follow whether it had a positive account or not with the Community, measured by the commercial as well as financial balance. More deeply still, it was rooted in the national desire to maintain expansion on the farms. In one way or another, this meant that all Britain's partners (indeed Britain herself) were committed to expansion throughout the 1970s. The factor which changed all that was the policies adopted nationally after the second energy crisis in order to choke off inflation and especially to cut down the ever-growing portion public budgets had previously been taking of national wealth.

In July 1982, the French socialist government gave up the attempt it had made, on assuming office 15 months earlier, to expand its way out of recession. After that *volte-face*, there was an unprecedented consensus between the Community governments on policies of tight credit and budget retrenchment. The trends of expenditure in the Community cut across the cost-cutting mood in the national capitals. The bases of limits on the CAP were laid at the level of macroeconomic policy, where there would probably never have been a consensus for them in agriculture alone.

The budget of the Community is not large compared with national public spending. In 1981, for instance, it came to 0.8 percent of Community GDP, which is pretty modest against a range in the member states for public expenditure from 39 percent (UK) to 53 percent (Belgium) in the same year (Eurostat, 1984a, p. 76). At a time of cutbacks, however, trends mattered more than absolute amounts. Balancing troughs and peaks, the CAP's budget rose about 5 percent a year at constant prices between 1973 and 1983 (Appendix Table 11), whereas EC GDP rose in the same period by less than 2 percent a year. The recurring tendency for CAP budget costs to explode—as they did, by 65 percent at constant prices, between 1975 and 1979, or over 20 percent in the single year from 1982 to 1983–politicised the contrast even more sharply. The anomaly of a booming Community budget in the midst of national recessions was bound to become untenable.

This was the basis for the 1984 compromise in the Community by which the CAP was in effect transformed. Basically, this involved an agreement, on the one hand to rein in production by increasing Community payments to agriculture at a slower pace than the revenues of the Community and, most stringently, by imposing quotas on milk production as the urgent problem; and on the other hand, to envisage a future extension of Community funding, in January, 1986, by raising the tax base of "own resources" to 1.4 percent of value added in the member states.

The compromise was of major importance for two reasons. One was that a brake was at last applied to agricultural output. The relief in Brussels could be heard even through the Commission's bureaucratic prose: "for the first time ever, the average prices in ECU adopted by the Council (− 0.5 percent) actually fall short of the prices proposed by the Commission (+ 0.8 percent)" (Com-EC, 1984b, p. 5). Though the controls are not systematic and almost certainly, for the future, still not sufficiently broad or deep for products other than milk, they nevertheless constitute a vital precedent for policy-makers.

The other reason, implicit in the first, is political. The 1984 compromise demonstrated that there was no effective will on the part of the collective of the member states to break up the CAP. Again, the relief in Brussels was audible: "the rationalisation advocated by the Commission rather than the renationalisation of the CAP has at last prevailed" (Com-EC, 1984b, p. 8).

At the same time, the lacunae in the 1984 compromise underline the difficulties ahead. Though cereal prices have been held or cut 1 percent in ECU (except hard wheat, mainly a Mediterranean crop), there is no mention of the Commission's target of a long-term reduction in the gap with U.S. prices. Though quotas on milk and the extension of guarantee thresholds to new products—they now include cereals, sugar, oilseeds, cotton, dried grapes and processed tomatoes—all suggest nascent commitment to output controls, longterm price policies are missing.

There are also significant loose ends. An increase of 0.4 percent in VAT receipts is unlikely to last the EC and CAP for more than a very few years unless supply controls are further tightened in future. That means more pain in prospect and the familiar pressures from farmers to relax the noose. Governments may have to face turbulence in future in several countries. Even without that, the difficulties of achieving agreement on finance, despite the compromise, have been demonstrated once more in continuing dissensions on the supplementary payments to close the large gap in the Community budget for 1984, before the new VAT regime enters into force.

The constrictions placed by the 1984 decisions on Community quotas and prices have also produced the predictable rash of national aids to farmers facing losses.[33] These may or may not prove compatible in the longer term with Community policies and control; only time will tell. But the remainder they provide of the social and political strains in the member states indicates that tensions between "rationalization" and "renationalization" of the CAP have not been waved away by the wand of a single compromise, however strategic. Agriculture and the Community will no doubt continue to live with at least latent crisis for years to come.

Notes

1. One can, however, overplay the force of the national veto in the Council of Ministers. The decision-making system was described with more nuance by David Owen, then U.K. Foreign Minister, in evidence on 8 February 1978 to the House of Lords Select Committee on the European Communities. He stressed the constraints created by the interweaving of member states' interests across a broad front. This made it difficult for any country to exert a systematic veto irrespective of the priorities of a heavy majority of its partners. See House of Lords, 1978, pp. 290–304; Owen, 1978; and Curry, 1982 b., p. 92. On 18 May 1982, a majority of the member states exceptionally forced through farm prices for 1982–1983 over a British veto. *Financial Times*, "EEC Farm Vote: how Britain was outflanked", 20 May 1982.

2. One way to compare world and Community prices is to look at the trade returns per unit of Community exports in the Community and to the outside world (Table 1.A). This depends, however, very much on the $-ECU exchange rate, since most trade is denominated in U.S. dollars. See note 4 below.

Table 1.A

SITC Category		Average Prices of Exports in EC9 as Percent of Prices of Exports to Rest of World		
		1979	1980	1981
041	Wheat	156	138	129
046	Wheat flour	173	142	128
061	Sugar (refined)	131	109	76
023	Butter	206	175	139
011.11	Beef on the bone	220	212	204
011.40	Poultry	158	148	133
112.12	Wine	60	73	61

Source: Com-EC, *Analytical Tables of Foreign Trade—SITC Rev. 2.*

3. The calculations conclude that total abrogration of EC import restrictions for grains would raise world prices for: Barley, 14.3 percent; wheat, 9.6 percent; maize, 2.2 percent. The Community is essentially an exporter of wheat, wheat flour, and barley. See Table 5.4 of this study.

4. Comparisons of American and Community support prices are hard to establish. One method is used in Table 1.1. Another approach can be based on the U.S. Mission to the European Communities, Brussels, comparative figures for 1980–81 in *US-EC Agriculture in Brief*, April 1981 and for 1983–84 in the equivalent text for this later period. These figures concern EC intervention prices and U.S. target prices, which are the support prices in the respective systems (EC and U.S. "target" prices do not correspond) (see Table 1.B). All EC prices fall heavily against U.S. prices; however, from April 1981 to November 1982, the U.S. dollar appreciated over one-third against the Community's ECU. This accounted for most of the changes.

Table 1.B

	Support Price of EC as Percentage of US Target Price	
	1980–81	1983–84
Wheat	186	125
Maize	238	151
Milk	111	87
Skimmed milk powder	83	66
Butter	123	100
Cheese	127	104

Further, the U.S. and EC systems do not match. EC intervention prices mean more or less what they seem to mean. U.S. target prices tend to overstate the guarantees offered to American farmers on grains. American farmers have a choice between accepting market prices and escaping all government controls, or opting for deficiency payments (technically, loans) calculated on the target price, but only on certain conditions. The two most important are: (1) the "allocation" factor fixed by the Federal Government every year, depending on market needs and desired production goals, and which can and often does reduce the real support price several percentage points below the theoretical target price; and (2) the "set-aside," which is an obligation not to produce (or produce only approved alternative crops) on a portion of one's land. The "set-aside" has gone as high as 20 percent of the area sown to wheat. Farmers usually make up for a third or so of this loss by higher productivity but it still represents a substantial reduction of the guaranteed price. Set-asides have applied consistently since 1968 except for a few years in the late 1970s. The system is extremely complex, as is made clear in Gardner, 1982.

5. Thiede, 1980; Eurostat, 1983b, pp. 129–53. These cover the years 1973–78 (in identical detail), 1979 (aggregates only), and 1980–81 (in refined detail and for the Ten instead of the Nine). The years 1957–61 to 1969 are analyzed by the same methods but in more aggregate presentation in Thiede, 1970, pp. 228–75, dealing with the Six founder members. These sources make it possible to establish largely comparable supply balances from 1957–61 to 1968–69 and again from 1973 to 1981 with a major gap 1970–72 and a partial one in 1979. The 1979–80 and 1980–81 figures are also more complete than earlier ones for fruit, sugar, and oilseeds, without the new series being made retroactive. All products are reduced to "grain equivalents"—i.e., given values in tons of grain as the basic unit. Such equivalents, though carefully established and agreed, are necessarily conventional and open to criticism. (Koester [1982, pp. 32–33], for instance, argues that EC estimates of the grain equivalent of pork are too high and so afford concealed protection when import levies are based on them.)

The method also leaves out of account changing values of farm products, which tend to fall over time in relation to the prices of other goods and services in the economy. So totals in grain equivalents can diverge quite substantially from calculations of output by value added or of productivity in prices: they are, e.g., inappropriate for discussions of farmers' incomes. On the other hand, they give a stable basis for comparing volumes of output, consumption and trade of different products over periods of time—all that goes into "supply balances"—and are invaluable, e.g., for establishing self-sufficiency ratios.

6. The trade coverage (i.e. exports expressed as percentage of imports) of southern members of a would-be EC-12 evolved as follows between 1964 and 1980:

	1964	1970–72	1980
Greece[a]	157	127	143
Italy	49	40	43
Portugal	99	72	44
Spain	123	103	88

[a]1982 = 99

All the southern countries except Greece saw their balances move sharply into deficit in the boom years. Greece kept her end up until she joined the EC.

7. FAO, *Production Yearbooks 1978* and *1980* show production rising between 1967–69 and 1977–79 as follows (1967–69 = 100):

Spain	146	France	116
Netherlands	143	Belgium	114
Greece	135	Italy	114
Ireland	135	Germany	113
USSR	123	Denmark	105
U.K.	121	Portugal	84

Portugal was hit by the revolution after 1974.

8. Mitchell, 1976, for the period before each war; for 1950–54, Com-EC 1958b, pp. 62 and 70.

9. Sanderson, 1982, p. 400. OECD, 1983a, gives instances for the U.K.: "it has been estimated that plant breeding accounted for 65 percent of the increase in wheat yields in the 20 years since the end of the 1940s. . . . During the 1970s, all of the yield improvement is attributed to the introduction of superior varieties."

10. In 1975, regional yields of barley ranged from 4.1 tons per hectare on average in Scotland to 1.2 tons per hectare in Calabria; and of milk from 5.6 tons per year per cow in Liguria (sic) and 4.8 in the Netherlands to 0.5 in Calabria (*ASC 1979*, pp. 330–31.) The range between farms at the extremes is still greater.

11. *ASC 1981*, p 287; Hill, 1983, pp. 35–48: "the proportion of farming couples with another gainful occupation is probably nearer one-third. . . . In Britain about three-quarters of part-time farmers gain their non-farm income as proprietors of second businesses. . . . most do not rely on their farms for their main source of income. . . . the Inland Revenue's Survey of Personal Incomes (SPI) data suggest that farmers' incomes are disproportionately represented among the high income groups." For the United States, see Paarlberg, 1980, p. 195. For Germany, the *Agrarbericht, 1982*, pp. 70 and 229, shows average incomes for 1981–82 for different farmers compared in Table 1.C.

Table 1.C

	Full time (DM)		Part time (half +) (DM)		Spare time (half −) (DM)	
Income on farm	28	587	16	615	6	310
Income off farm	1	689	17	905	35	311
Total Income	30	276	34	520	42	621
Full-timer's income = 100		100		114		137

12. Ries, 1978, p. 111: "the lobbies understood perfectly well that the scope of the structural problem was such that any official socio-structural policies would mobilise quite inadequate funds. . . . For this reason, they always focussed their demands essentially on market policies and in particular on price guarantees and import protection" (translation).

13. de Bruin, 1978, p. 388. Mansholt gave the speech in Stuttgart on 17 October 1958. See also Com-EC, 1958a, p. 70, para. 94: "Production of the major products is increasing more vigorously than consumption, surpluses are appearing on the various markets and their disposal is causing serious difficulties and worries. The first rule for a market policy within the framework of a common agricultural policy must, therefore, be to try to create an organic equilibrium between production and a market for the products."

14. Com-EC, 1958b, pp. 117–18: agricultural exports (SITC categories 0, Food, and 1, Beverages and Tobacco; see fn. 19) accounted in 1957 for 28 percent of all Dutch exports, 24 percent of Italian and 15 percent of French.

15. de Bruin, 1978, p. 154, quoting W. van Oosten, speech at the Agricultural University of Wageningen, "De Nederlandse Landbouw in de Gemeenschappelijke Markt," 11 September 1965. In 1960, the Dutch accounted for 64 percent of the cheese traded between the Six, 70 percent of the pork, 79 percent of the butter and 88 percent of the eggs. By 1979, these proportions, in the EC-9, had shrunk, for instance to 24 percent for butter and 31 percent for cheese. In absolute terms, the trade had risen substantially. For French policy, ibid., pp. 426, 486.

16. Investments in farming in the Community (except the U.K.) in 1977 came to 11.7 billion ECUs and national aids to 4.5 billion ECUs (*ASC 1978*, pp. 168–69; *ASC 1980* pp. 244–45 and 255). German (p. 141) and French semi-official investigations (House of Lords, 1982, p. 141) estimate that tax exemptions for farmers were worth DM 2 billion and FFrs. 3 billion in 1978 = 1.3 billion ECUs against the Commission's published figure of only 0.6 billion ECUs (*ASC 1979*, p. 168).

17. Eurostat 1982 b. Between 1960 and 1980, Germany's imports from all sources, Community and other, increased by 1610 million ECUs at constant 1960 prices (i.e., 69 percent), while Italy's rose by 1,564 million ECUs (i.e., 210 percent, proportionally three times as much). Constant prices are calculated from Eurostat, 1976 and 1980, as well as *ASC*

1980, p. 224, and Com-EC, 1984a, relating to the Council's common agricultural price decisions for 1982–84, Annex 3. All calculations refer to implicit GDP deflators.

18. The figures in the text are in values. Weight is a more constant measure of trends in each product though not (because of changing prices) overall. In weight, imports into the six founding EC states developed between 1958 and 1978 (when trade between EC states reached its peak relative to trade with the rest of the world) as shown in Table 1.D. The table brings out the concentration of the growth of imports from outside the EC on animal feed, and to a lesser extent meat, fruit and vegetables. Sugar imports into the EC-6 from outside the EC have virtually disappeared since 1978 (except from the French sugar islands to France). 03 (Fish), 07 (Coffee, cocoa, tea, etc.) and 09 (Patent foods, such as soups, mustards, etcetera) have been left out.

Table 1.D

SITC Code		Growth Imports 1958–78 (1958 = 1)		Imports 1978 (thous. tons)	
		Intra	Extra	Intra	Extra
00	Live animals	18.4	0.9	866	363
01	Meat	19.2	2.5	2188	873
02	Dairy products	40.6	1.8	4063	176
04	Cereals	11.6	1.3	14000	15146
05	Fruit and veg.	3.7	2.2	8122	14172
06	Sugar and confec.	18.8	2.1	1202	2117
08	Animal feed	6.1	7.4	5518	13976
11	Drink	22.8	0.3	8668	710
12	Tobacco	15.5	1.9	186	333
22	Oilseeds (animal feed)	42.3	3.7	1565	11786
42	Oilcake (animal feed)	21.7	3.1	1890	2249

19. There are two internationally accepted ways of establishing trade statistics. One code, elaborated by the United Nations for economic analysis, is the Standard International Trade Classification (SITC). It is organized in ten major categories, from 0 to 9. Detail can be refined from two- to five-digit subdivisions up to a maximum of 1,924 headings. The SITC Code has been twice revised, in 1961 and in 1975. The differences between Rev. 1 and 2 are significant for dried milk products. The agricultural categories generally used are: 0 (Food), 1 (Beverages and Tobacco), 22 (Oilseeds), 29 (Vegetable and Animal Raw Materials), and 4 (Fats and Oils). Sometimes, only 0 + 1 are used. Some lesser categories are occasionally included, such as 592.11 (starches), but not here.

The second code, derived from the Brussels Customs Code formally known as the Customs Cooperation Council Nomenclature (CCCN), in EC publications "Nimexe," consists of 100 basic categories from 00 to 99. These break down as far as six-digit subgroups, and a maximum of 7,500 headings, which are therefore more detailed than the SITC. Correspondence between the two codes is complicated. The agricultural chapters of the Nimexe code, from 00 to 24, cover overwhelmingly the same ground as SITC 0 + 1 + 4 + 22 + 29.

While EC uses both SITC and Nimexe codes in its statistics, the OECD sticks to SITC. For details see Eurostat, 1982a.

20. European Parliament, 1982, p. 72; and Henry and RICAP, 1981, p. 23. The combination of cheap animal feed, coming in principally through Rotterdam, and high prices for pigs, poultry, eggs, and milk, based not only on high Community cereal prices but also, according to Koester, on excessive ratios for converting grain into meat, provides powerful incentives for production to develop along the Rhine river-canal complex. Since export subsidies are also calculated according to these ratios, they may stimulate EC poultry exports: Koester, 1982, p. 32.

21. Because the figures in appendix Table 1 for the 1950s are in values and for the 1960s and 1970s in volume (grain equivalents), they are not comparable. Since real farm prices fell in the 1950s—faster in most EC countries than in the 1960s—values tend to underrate the volumes involved. This implies that the fall in consumption was steeper, proportionately, from the 1950s to 1960s (during the boom years) than it was from the 1960s to 1970s (even though the latter decade was infected by recession from 1974 onwards). This could suggest a structural development rather than a cyclical one.

22. The annual average changes in the volume of trade for a number of commodities between 1973-74 and 1979-80 are shown in Table 1.E.

Table 1.E

	EC with Third Countries		Intra-EC
	Imports	Exports (percent per annum)	(Imports)
Cereals	−3.5	2.8	−0.2
Sugar	−0.7	22.0	−2.2
Wine	−3.1	14.7	7.3
Vegetables	2.6	2.7	5.0
Olive oil	−10.9	62.9	37.2
Butter	−4.6	2.5	−0.8
Beef and veal	−3.4	21.5	5.8
Poultry	2.8	15.6	2.3
Eggs	−7.0	2.9	8.7

Source: ASC 1981, pp. 224–27.

23. "Une agriculture exportatrice ne peut guère avoir la maîtrise de ses prix: elle doit les subir."

24. Some of the earliest critics have been French: See Adrien Ziegler, with a preface by Edgard Pisani; the official French *Rapport Vedel*, Paris, 1969, whose conclusions were similar to, but more radical than, those of the Mansholt Plan; Pierre Uri (the author of the Spaak Report, which provided the intellectual underpinnings of the Treaty of Rome) and Denis Bergmann, as co-authors of the Atlantic Institute's *A Future for European Agriculture*, Paris, 1970.

25. These proportions, common in Commission discussions, have not been published in such a form. The order of magnitude can be inferred, e.g. from *ASC 1981*, Table 91, p. 303.

26. Com-EC 1975, p. 15. This directly contradicts the "First Report" (Com-EC, 1958a, p. 70), and the Mansholt Plan (Com-EC, 1969, pp. 34–35), both of which warned specifically against fixing prices "at a level which enabled even those enterprises to cover their expenses which, owing to their inferior structures, were producing at high costs."

27. Agra-Europe, 1978 p. 82. Cereals: Com-EC, 1981a, pp. 27–29. Sugar: House of Lords, 1980a, reports that Commission sources said that to replace the quota regime by a pure price regime of equivalent production effect would require a price cut of about 15 percent. "However it is not possible to make a reliable estimate" of price cuts necessary to balance supply and demand with some allowance for stocks "since the change both of price and quantity . . . goes well beyond the known range of economic experience" (Ministry of Agriculture memorandum, p. 80).

28. *Agrarbericht, 1980*, p. 213. The Centre National pour l'Aménagement des Structures des Exploitations Agricoles (CNASEA) in France, *Contribution à une nouvelle politique de l'exploitation agricole*, has figures, p. 112, which suggest that in 1976 the income per annual labor unit in France ranged from 5,000 francs a year for the bottom 20 percent of farms of 10 to 20 hectares (not the smallest) rearing beef, to 85,000 francs for the top 20 percent of arable farms of 70 to 100 hectares—a range of 17:1.

29. Henry, 1981. According to Table 13, pp. 66–68, income per worker in agriculture (average EC-9 = 100) ranged from 270.6 in Schleswig-Holstein to 28.6 in Molise in 1976–77. According to Table 15, the only Italian region to obtain more than an average share of Community farm funds was Apulia. Regions "where the farm income is low and stagnant" account for 47 percent of the land area and 56 percent of the agricultural workforce of the EC-9. The main concentrations are in the Mezzogiorno, the whole of Ireland, the Scottish Highlands and the French Massif Central: *ASC 1980*, p. 52.

30. The phrase "prudent price policies" is at least as old as the Mansholt Plan (Com-EC 1969, p. 16).

31. Com-EC, *Official Journal*, L 131, 26 May 1977, p. 6; C32, 7 February 1983, p. 50; L 132, 21 May 1983, p. 8. In 1983, the decision was taken to provide 120 million ECUs of Community funds for the member states to distribute to smallholders. The sum is marginal. For Finn Gundelach's reluctance to envisage direct income aids, see Com-EC, 1979a, reproducing his speech to the Agricultural Committee of the European Parliament of 2 October 1979.

32. When the German DM (Deutschmark) was repeatedly revalued upwards between 1969 and 1973, the Federal Government accorded German farmers tax reliefs on national VAT payments to the tune of DM 1.7 billion a year from 1970 to 1973 (equivalent to $464 millions in 1970, rising to $639 millions in 1973). This was to compensate for losses incurred through the reduced DM values of CAP prices denominated in now devalued European units of account. (Com-EC 1978–79. "Chronological table of events concerning MCAs") German final producton in 1971 was worth DM 37.7 billions (*ASC 1972*. Table I/3.3).

When the squeeze on farm incomes due to the first energy crisis coincided with a cyclical downturn in the beef market, this led to unrest on the land. The French government provided subsidies for each cow and pig; and the Belgian announced regional subsidies for livestock (Neville-Rolfe. 1984. 268).

The second energy crisis again squeezed farm incomes, and Presidents Giscard and Mitterrand, in two separate moves in 1980 and 1981, gave some FFrs. 10 billions in all (about $1.7 billions) to French farmers (OECD 1983b, p. 65; Ministère de l'Agriculture. 1982). In 1980, French agricultural gross value added amounted to FFrs. 100.4 billions (*ASC 1981*. p. 179) and in 1981 to FFrs. 106.5 billions (*ASC 1982*, p. 192).

Prior agreement of the Commission was sought for none of the initial moves launching these national aids.

33. *Financial Times*, "Milk scheme delays aggravate discontent," 18 July 1984, reports British, Dutch, French and German national aid schemes to encourage farmers to stop producing milk. These have Community endorsement.

The Community compromise in the Council of Ministers of 31 March 1984 included an agreement to let the German government compensate German farmers for DM losses as a result of the gradual elimination of MCAs till the end of 1988 (see Chapter 4). As in 1970 to 1973, it was proposed that, between July 1984 and the end of 1988, they be relieved of tax payments up to 3 percent of German VAT (Com-EC 1984b, p. 19).

At the European Council (i.e., the "summit" of heads of Community governments) of 25–26 June 1984, Chancellor Kohl of Germany wrested reluctant assent from the other leaders for the ceiling of German VAT reliefs for farmers to be raised to 5 percent between 1984 and 1988 (Agence Europe, 28 June 1984).

2 The Community in the World

The Second Largest Food Exporter

Since the world market is, or has come to seem, the new frontier for an expanding Community agriculture, it can no longer be ignored. Yet, until very recently indeed, public discussion of farm policies in the Community and in most member states has been curiously insulated from world trade. The potential demand for Community exports is invoked as a slogan by some and thought of by many as a necessary consequence of the population explosion in the developing world. But in general, public awareness of the profound changes underway is at best embryonic. Occasional headlines, for instance on tough talk in GATT, may reflect a new situation, but that is not the same thing as digesting their implications. In politically relevant and public terms, this has hardly begun.

One can divine at least two reasons—apart from the usual visceral reluctance to change mental horizons—for this innocence of context. The first and most obvious has been the natural concentration on markets in the Community, which provided far and away the richest initial opportunities. This is easy to gauge from the fact that in 1960 the food exports of the nine member states of the European Community of 1980 to each other were only 1.3 times as valuable as those to the rest of the world, whereas by the later 1970s the proportion in favor of intra-Community trade had risen to 2.3 to one. It then fell back, by 1980 to 1.9 to one (Appendix Table 6) and was still at that level in 1982. As long as internal trade remained buoyant, until 1978 in fact, changes in the Community foreground distracted attention from those also taking place in the background of food trade with the rest of the world. Yet the Community states' coverage of world food imports by their own exports outside EC frontiers was steadily growing throughout two decades, with the pace accelerating in the later 1970s. The ratio of exports in food trade with the rest of the world, which was 44 percent in 1976, rose to 49 percent in 1978, to 66 percent in 1980, and reached 74 percent in 1982.[1] Such a progression in only six years is dramatic. It reflects a pressure of exports which can no longer be left out of account.

The second distraction from a gathering reality has been more subtle. The Community has been, and still remains, the world's greatest importer of agricultural products. It is still heavily in deficit in the total account of all these commodities. The Community's own publications show that imports in 1980 amounted to $58.8 billion against exports of only $27.2 billion (*ASC 1981*, p.

229). Such a disproportion seems to leave little room for a special preoccupation with exports, large though the sums are on both sides of the balance sheet. The point, however, is that such figures, valid enough as far as they go, are very misleading. For one thing, they include a virtually irrelevant series of agricultural raw materials for industry, such as cotton, wool, and rubber, which the Community imports in large quantities and does not export at all. For another, there are three different types of food, and while the Community is very much a net importer in two of them, the significant fact is that it has become a big net exporter in the third. Lumping them all together conceals the important development. The first type of trade is in those foods of which the Community is a nonproducer or minor producer and where there is virtually no competition. This applies to all the tropical fruit and spices and, partially, to the Mediterranean fruit and vegetables. The second type of product is the oilseeds and feed other than cereals for stock-raising, which, again, are only partially in competition with domestic Community output. Finally, there are the finished goods of temperate agriculture that are the main domain of the Community's own farms and (to a lesser degree) food industries. These are three very distinct categories. Just how different they are can be gauged from the trade figures once they are broken down (even in a general way) to take account of these factors (Table 2.1).

In aggregate, the Community remains a net importer, though by nothing like the margin the figures including industrial raw materials would suggest. It also remains a deficit area in a deeper sense, in as much as its dominant animal production (56 percent of all farm output in 1980) would need to adjust, and for a while at least might be severely curtailed, if imports of feed were abruptly cut off. The imports seem to cover about one-sixth of the total nutrition and food supply for the Community's livestock.[2] To this extent, apparent self-sufficiency is not a measure of Community food "security." In all these ways, the traditional picture remains accurate, but it is nevertheless highly misleading because so partial. The strong export surplus on temperate foods that it conceals is of major practical and political importance and does not at all fit the traditional image of Europe as an importer. The Community's deficit reflects, in part, the extent to which its agriculture has in effect become a transforming rather than a primary industry (emphasizing livestock, dairy products, wine, and spirits rather than crops). Its imports are overwhelmingly in agricultural raw materials of agriculture and industry, as well, of course, as the fruit of climates very different from its own. In the temperate products of its farms and food industry, it is a massive exporter both in absolute terms and relative to other suppliers.

The scale of the phenomenon needs to be emphasized. It is a major development, not a minor one, on the international scale. The EC has become a force in world trade. It is a much larger food exporter than ones long familiar such as Argentina, Australia, and Canada, or the other major newcomer, Brazil. Only the United States had much larger food exports (Appendix Table 4). The EC is now the largest of all exporters of meat, dairy products, beverages, barley, wheat flour, and potatoes; it is the world's runner-up in

Table 2.1 EC Trade in Food and Feed with the Rest of the World, 1981 (in billions of ECUs) (SITC 0 + 1 + 22 + 29 + 4)

	Imports	Exports	Exports (as percent of imports)
Tropical–Mediterranean products[a]	13.6	3.1	23
Animal feed[b]	9.6	2.0	21
Temperate foods[c]	9.4	19.1	204
Total	32.6	24.2	74

[a] SITC 05 (fruits and vegetables), 07 (coffee, tea, spices), 12 (tobacco).
[b] SITC 08 (feedstuffs), 22 (oilseeds), 4 (fats and oils).
[c] SITC 00 (live animals), 01 (meat), 02 (dairy), 04 (cereals), 06 (sugar), 09 (patent foods), 11 (beverages), 29 (plants and flowers). 03 (fish) is excluded.

Note: Coverage of temperate foods in 1960 was 60 percent compared to 204 percent in 1981. For the two internationally accepted ways of establishing trade statistics, see Chapter 1, note 19.

Source: Table 5 from Com-EC, Eurostat, *Analytical Tables of Foreign Trade SITC Rev. 2, 1981.*

sugar and eggs and in every individual meat; and it is a significant fourth in wheat and even in oilcakes, although it has a massive deficit in oilseeds (Table 2.2). These are not minor commodities. They cover nearly three-quarters of gross agricultural output in the European Community (Appendix Table 12).

Whereas the dominance of the United States in world food markets tends to be exercised massively in a few basic crops, which underpin the world's food system, especially grains and oilseeds for livestock, the European Community ranges widely over a spectrum of commodities. Outside the basic crops and cotton, tobacco, poultry, fruit and vegetables, the United States is not a prominent exporter (cereals, fats, and feedstuffs accounted for 77 percent of her food exports in 1980) (U.S. Dept. of Commerce, Bureau of the Census, 1982). The Community's strength is focussed mainly on the transforming sectors, where the United States is not particularly prominent. Moreover, EC capacity is increasing steadily, not least in commodities such as sugar, cereals, beef, dairy products, and wine, where supply is rising against near-stagnant or even falling demand at home.

The impact of the European Community on food export markets is largely a product of the past twenty years and especially of the 1970s. This is not immediately apparent from aggregate figures because the present member states, taken together, were already the world's second exporting group before 1960 (had anyone thought of them as such). It is only when one looks at individual key commodities that the changes stand out. As Table 2.3 indicates,

Table 2.2 EC-9 Agricultural Exports to World, 1980

Commodity	Sector Output as Percent Value Added in EC9 Agriculture	EC-9 Agricultural Exports Percent World Exports By Volume	Rank in World Exports	Tonnage to World (millions)	Tonnage to World (thousands)	Tonnage by Other Major Exporters (millions or thousands; as EC-9)
Wheat	7.2	8.0	4	7.5		US 36.9, Can 17.4, Austrl 15.0, Arg 4.6
Wheat flour		52.9	1	3.6		US 1.5, Can 0.7, USSR 0.6
Barley	3.2	33.8	1	4.3		Austrl 3.0, Can 2.7, US 1.5
Potatoes	1.9	37.4	1		981	Can 254, Pol 176, Cyp 174, Egy 144, Leb 125
Sugar	2.7	16.1	2	4.3		Cuba 6.2, Braz 2.6, Austrl 2.2, Philipp 1.6
Wine	4.8	29.4	1		929	Spain 578, Bulg 267, Hung 233, Alg 170
Beef	15.8	22.6	2		527	Austrl 580, E. Europe 253, NZ 216, Arg 204, Yugo 58
Pork	11.5	14.6	2		83	Can 114
Poultry	4.2	28.2	1		337	US 332, Arg 170, Hung 135
Fresh meat		17.4	1		983	Austrl 779, NZ 634, US 466, Arg 385
Eggs (in shell)	3.4	16.6	2		67	PRC 76, US 54
Milk powder		59.4	1	1.1		NZ 284, US 138, Austrl 108, Can 80
Butter	19.2	61.5	1		548	NZ 231, Austrl 23, USSR 18
Cheese		45.4	1		330	NZ 69, Switz 63, Austrl 61, Find 46, Austria 41
Feed	—	4.9	4	2.7		US 7.7, Braz 7.0, Arg 1.8, India 1.2
Margarine	—	[62.7]			103	
Beer	—	39.5	1		556	CSR 197, Can 188, US 133, DDR 40, Pol 40, Singapore 30

73.9

Source: Com-EC, Eurostat, *Analytical Tables of Foreign Trade SITC Rev. 2, 1980.* FAO *Trade Yearbook 1980.*

Table 2.3 Percentage of World Exports Contributed by EC-9 (excluding trade between themselves)

Commodity	1960 (percent)	1970 (percent)	1980 (percent)
Grains	3.8	7.9	8.5
Sugar	7.8	4.9	16.1
Milk powder	0.9	35.3	59.4
Butter	5.8	26.6	61.5
Meat	5.9	7.6	17.4

Source: See Table 2.4

the weight of the Community's member states in world exports of certain major products was modest in 1960 and even, with the exception of dairy products, in 1970, but major for all except some grains (essentially maize) by 1980. The rise of the Community as an exporter is even more apparent when one looks at the proportion of the *increase* in world exports for each decade for which it has been responsible (Table 2.4). In the 1970s, it has accounted for a third of the increase in meat as a whole, over half that of sugar, nine-tenths of milk powder and 140 percent of butter (sic)—in effect, in this commodity, displacing other exporters.

The significance of the emergence of the Community as an exporter needs to be placed in the international context of the growth of food trade by regions (Table 2.5). Four points stand out from this table. First, the West, broadly defined to include Australia and New Zealand, has been virtually alone in increasing exports of food notably faster than imports during the 1970s.

Second, within the West, the United States has been far and away the most rapidly growing exporter during the decade. This reflects its position as the residual breadbasket of the world. In 1980 it supplied two-thirds of the world's wheat, coarse grain, and soya-bean exports. This is greater than the dominance of the oil trade by Saudi Arabia.

Third, the European Community has been relatively the next fastest growing exporter, ahead of Oceania. The UNCTAD *Trade and Development Report, 1981* brings out starkly how much the greatest relative increase in share of food exports since 1961–65 can be attributed to the industrial economies *other* than the traditional "low-cost agricultural exporters." This group, in which the EC plays the largest part, has, between 1961–65 and 1976–80, according to UNCTAD, increased its share of world food exports from 18 percent to 28 percent. The traditional low-cost exporters themselves, in the latter period, accounted for only 33 percent of food exports (but 62 percent of those of cereals) (UNCTAD, 1981).

Fourth and last, all the other regions in the world, with the important exception of the developing market economies in the West Pacific area, have

Table 2.4 Distribution by Regions of Increase in Volume of World Exports of Key Agricultural Commodities, 1960–1980

| SITC Group | Commodity | Volume of World Exports in tons[a] | | | Volume Growth of World Exports[a] | | Percentage of Increase of World Export 1960–1970 (col. 1) and 1970–1980 (col. 2)[a] Contributed by | | | | | |
| | | | | | | | European Community[a] | | N. America and Oceania | | Rest of World | |
		1960	1970	1980	1960–1970	1970–1980	(1)	(2)	(1)	(2)	(1)	(2)
041–046	Grains (million tons)[b]	67.5	105.5	206.7	38.0	101.2	15	9	60	89	25	2
061[c]	Sugar (million tons)	17.1	21.0	26.6	3.9	5.6	–8	58	20	28	88	14
022[d]	Milk powder (thousand tons)	410	1033	1883	623	850	58	88	39	2	3	10
023	Butter (thousand tons)	430	623	892	193	269	72	142	29	–16	–1	–26
011	Meat (million tons)	1.9	3.4	5.6	1.5	2.2	10	33	37	44	54	23

[a] Excluding EC-9 Intra-Trade
[b] SITC Rev. 1 and Rev. 2 046 wheat flour in wheat equivalent (i.e. product weight × 1.389).
[c] SITC Rev. 1 and Rev. 2 0611 and 0612 (0611 refined sugar 1 ton = 0611; raw sugar 1.087 tons.)
[d] For 1960, SITC 022 milk and cream, evaporated, condensed, dried;
For 1970, SITC Rev. 1 022.2, milk and cream, solid or powdered (i.e. excluding evaporated and condensed);
For 1980, SITC Rev. 2 022.42/43, milk and cream, dried or granulated, with less than 1.5 percent fat (022.42) or more than 1.5 percent fat (022.43);
The 1960 figures are not, therefore, strictly comparable with those of 1970 and 1980, the effect being to underrate growth in exports 1960–1970.

Source: FAO Trade Yearbooks for 1966, 1975 and 1980; OEEC and OECD, Statistical Bulletins of Foreign Trade, Series C, Trade by Commodities, for 1960, 1970, and 1980.

Table 2.5   Exports of Agricultural Products by Volume Relative to Imports by Major
World Regions, 1970–1980

Region	Growth of Food Exports by Volume (1970^x = 100)	Ratio of Growth of Food Exports to Imports by Volume (percent)	Agricultural Exports Relative to Imports 1980 by Value (imports = 100)
North America	239	219	213
Western Europe	191	145	73
Far East LDCs	169	102	116
Oceania	162	126	966
"Other Developed"[a]	148	95	22
Latin American LDCs	134	50	224
Near East LDCs	132	36	26
Asian CPEs[b]	113	49	44
European CPEs + USSR[b]	91	36	35
African LDCs	78	32	110

[a] Israel, Japan, South Africa.
[b] CPE = Centrally Planned Economies.
[x] 1970 = average 1969–71.

Source: FAO, *Trade Yearbook 1980*, Tables 2 and 4, pp. 24 and 36; Table 6, p. 44.

become relatively more dependent on imports. This may not be serious for the agriculturally poor Middle East, which has other assets, or Latin America, but it is striking for the Socialist countries and Latin America and potentially catastrophic for the arid parts of Africa. On balance, the trend towards a Western producer of food supplying the rest of the world (except Latin America and East Asia), which was potential not dramatic in the 1960s, became much more marked, indeed one of the basics of the international economic structure, during the 1970s.[3]

More than that, during the 1970s, signs began to indicate that the food balances of the world might indeed be shifting toward a new environment of greater pressures on production. The first suspicions were prompted by the wild boom of 1974–75, when world commodity prices tripled and a World Food Conference gathered in Rome in 1974 to be addressed by Dr. Kissinger on the risks of world famine. The theme seemed all too apposite in the wake of the "oil shock" of the winter of 1973–74, particularly as developments in the world food market were for a brief period almost as dramatic. But within two years, world food prices, having attained their highest levels in real terms since an international food market came into existence in the 1880s, fell again to their lowest levels in real terms since the war. Three years later still, by 1980, sugar prices, followed by those of grains, again rose substantially. But then, once again, by 1982, after three abundant harvests, and in the midst of world recession, the incomes of US farmers fell 30 percent, and threats of a "trade war" with the EC dominated the GATT ministerial conference of November.[4] Such instability had not been experienced since the Korean boom of 1951–52, and now there was no war scare to explain it. Were these new instabilities rooted in more durable changes?

Figures put together by the U.S. Department of Agriculture suggest that, between 1950 and 1980, world food production outside the United States increased by 2.8 percent per annum, whereas consumption rose fractionally faster, by 2.85 percent per annum (Table 2.6) (O'Brien, 1981, pp. 2–26). This minute discrepancy, initially negligible, had cumulative effects. In particular, it resulted in a more than proportionate increase in world food trade, which grew at a rate of 5.3 percent per annum, or almost twice as fast as output in the same period. Moreover, the trend, far from slowing down during the post-1973 depression, actually accelerated. Thus, whereas non-American production rose by 2.95 percent per annum between 1950 and 1972 and consumption rose by 3 percent per annum, both sides of the equation fell in the 1970s—but production notably more than consumption, so that the gap between them grew. Production between 1972 and 1980 rose outside the U.S. by 2.3 percent per annum and consumption by 2.55 percent per annum. Thus, the gap between non-U.S. output and consumption, which in the 22 years from 1950

Table 2.6 World Agricultural Production, Consumption, and Trade Growth Rates

| | Compound Annual Growth Rates (percent) | |
	1950-72	1972-80
World		
Production	2.85	2.35
Consumption	2.85	2.35
Trade	4.95	6.25
World excluding U.S.		
Production	2.95	2.30
Consumption	3.00	2.55
Trade	4.70	5.65
U.S.		
Production	2.05	2.80
Consumption	1.90	1.20
Trade	5.50	8.90

Source: Patrick M. O'Brien, "Global Prospects for Agriculture," in *Agricultural-Food Policy Review: Perspectives for the 1980s*, pp. 2–26, U.S. Department of Agriculture, April 1981.

to 1972 averaged 0.05 percent per annum, rose between 1972 and 1980 to an average of 0.25 percent per annum—relatively speaking a fivefold increase.

These differences were necessarily reflected in the acceleration of the growth of world trade. Whereas between 1950 and 1972 world trade grew by an annual average of 4.95 percent, between 1972 and 1980 the rate rose to 6.25 percent, which seems to be without precedent over such a period. The main shift was registered in American exports, which grew from 5.5 percent per annum in 1950–72 to the exceptionally high 8.9 percent per annum in 1972–80. Non-American rates of growth in exports also rose, from 4.7 percent per annum in 1950-72 to 5.65 percent per annum in 1972–80 (Table 2.6).

The increasing role of trade in the system has been no mere statistical freak, as can be seen from the crucial grain trade. In 1960, world grain exports were equivalent to only 7 percent of world production. In the 1960s, 18 percent of the extra output in the decade was being traded, and in the 1970s the proportion rose even faster, to 30 percent (Table 2.7). Food demand (or more properly perhaps demand for animal feed) was becoming increasingly dependent for its satisfaction on traded supplies, overwhelmingly provided by the U.S. (Table 2.4). The buoyancy of trade has not been confined to grains. It has been almost as strong for milk powder and substantial also for meat and even butter (Table 2.4). The fact that, contrary to expectations of what demand would concentrate on, meat and dairy products have expanded rapidly is of particular significance for the Community, as the world's leading exporter of these products.

In short, changes in world food trade not only in the boom of the twenty years from 1953 to 1973 but even more, perhaps surprisingly, during the recession of the 1970s, have prompted the question whether a new phase has opened in agriculture as in other areas of the international system. On the face of it, for two decades at least there has been an accelerating demand for food

Table 2.7   Growth of World Grain Imports in Relation to Production, 1960–1970 and 1970–1980

	Millions of Tons		Percent Growth	Millions of Tons	Percent Growth
	1960	1970	1960–70	1980	1970–80
World grain imports[a]	64.6	103.0	59	207.2	101
World grain production	997.6	1215.4	22	1570.7	29
Imports[a] as percent of production	6.5	8.5	17.6	13.2	29.3

[a] Excludes intra-EC9 trade.

Source: FAO, *Trade and Production Yearbooks* (various); OEEC and OECD *Statistical Bulletins of Foreign Trade, Series C, Trade by Commodities.*

exports from the West to the rest of the world. This is a clear break from the previous century when Western Europe was the great magnet for imports from the new continents and at one time Russia. Will these changes prove deep and durable? And, if so, what are the implications for Western European agriculture? In particular, is there any sense in which European exports may in future not merely represent the inexorable pressure of surpluses brimming over from an overprotected environment, but a partial answer to the long-term needs of the international food system and beyond that a hungry mankind?

Will Real Food Prices Continue to Fall?

Unlike the previous decade, the early 1980s are an unsatisfactory time to ask whether there may be a growing need for food exports from Europe. Between the second energy crisis of 1979–80 and the signs of recovery from deep recession in 1983–84, food trade was almost static.[5] This created a crisis in the United States, the dominant grain exporter, where the growth of output not only continued but, encouraged by exceptionally favorable weather in three years out of four, actually accelerated. Previous strains on supply soon turned into overproduction; and the reversal could not have come at a worse time. Domestic inflation in the U.S. and remedial public policies overwhelmingly reliant on high interest rates, simultaneously raised production costs. A cost-price squeeze followed and cut heavily into farmers' incomes.[6] Diplomatic symptoms of changed times appeared rapidly, both in the cancellation of the U.S. grain embargo against the USSR for the invasion of Afghanistan, and in conflicts between the U.S. and the European Community over the latter's food exports. Noisy disputation filled the ministerial conference of the GATT in November 1982 and was followed by the warning shot of American subsidized sales of wheat flour to the largest importer, Egypt, in January 1983 and then, again, of butter and cheese in July. This was openly designed to displace the Europeans, guilty, in American eyes, of unfair sales practices.[7] The threat of a trade war between the two great powers of world commerce was temporarily averted but continued to lurk in the background of tense negotiations. At such an extreme of the pendular swing, it was easy to think of the opposite experience of the 1970s as a closed chapter. Food prices on international markets would, on balance, continue to fall; normality would be restored.

Indeed, this may be so. Nevertheless, to assume continuity and pass over the phenomenal surge of the 1970s without another look at its potential, would be to fall into the recurrent trap of extrapolating from short-term cycles. No doubt, some of the developments of the 1970s are quite specific. The sudden wealth of the OPEC exporters or the equally sudden failure of the Soviet Union to keep up with its own rising demand for food, cannot be repeated in precisely these ways, if only because they have already taken place. Yet the growth of food trade in 1970s was too broad and went too deep to be seen only in terms of these major surprises of the system. Not merely the 1970s, but the 1960s as well, were remarkable for the way in which (1) a number of fast-growing medium-income market economies, mostly oil exporters and "newly industrializing countries," or NICs in the OECD parlance, (2) Japan, and (3) Socialist states virtually monopolized the increase in world farm imports (Table 2.8).[8] From 1970–1980, this minority of 36 states accounted for almost three-quarters of the increase in world imports of dried milk, for 90 percent of those of meat, for 101 percent (sic) of those of grains, 129 percent of those of sugar, and 132 per cent of those of butter, to take only the major temperate commodities of most concern to the European Community.

This fantastic concentration of the growth of food trade on a minority of countries has a number of implications. One is that the increase of world food trade in 1960 to 1980 has been due primarily to rising incomes in a middle tier of fast-growing countries and not to the general increase of population in the world and more particularly in the developing areas. Thirty-five percent of the world's people, including all the poorest, together accounted for less than 7 percent of world agricultural inputs in 1980. In many of the poorest countries, especially in Africa, food consumption per head has unfortunately fallen in the 1970s, and they lacked the foreign exchange to make up for the shortages by major increases in imports (FAO, 1980 b, Tables 6 and 7; FAO, 1980 c, Tables 3 and 4). In other words, on the evidence of the past two decades, the motor of the food trade is overwhelmingly rising incomes, not population as such.

Second, the force behind the new importers' hunger for imports was the shift from starchy foods to livestock consumption as personal incomes rose. This, in effect, meant moving away from consuming basic crops, the poor man's diet, to meat-eating, the characteristic of urban populations as living standards rise. Meats are luxury foods and call for heavy recourse to grains and other feed. Hence, the acceleration in word demand and trade.

Table 2.8 World Imports of Key Agricultural Commodities, 1960–80: Distribution of Growth of World Imports by Country Groups in Volume (World = 100)

Commodity	1960–70			1970–80		
	EC-9	27 FGME[a]	9 CPE[b]	EC-9	27 FGME	9 CPE
Grains	7	54	25	−8	53	48
Sugar	−14	30	51	−32	90	39
Milk powder	0	51	16	0	64	9
Butter	−19	58	−1	−53	67	65
Meat	8	31	15	−14	62	25

[a] Fast-growing market economies.
[b] Centrally planned economies.

Note: Table excludes trade within EC-9.

Source: See Table 2.4.

Third, though the growth in world trade tends to be associated with the Soviet Union, in fact the 27 market economies in the group collectively played a larger role than the nine centrally planned economies for every commodity except sugar in the nineteen-sixties (Table 2.8).

Fourth, viewed in broad terms, the essence of what occurred was the extension to a whole new stratum of countries in Eastern and Southern Europe, the Middle East, East Asia and substantial parts of Latin America, of the shift to a richer diet which came in Western Europe between the 1880s and 1950s and in Japan in the decades after the second world war. This spread of more prosperous eating habits has already affected something like a quarter of humanity (a half if one includes China) and is not likely to burn itself out in a hurry (FAO, 1980 b, Table 3). Consumption levels in most of the new countries are still well behind those of the West. That is the case even to some extent for Eastern Europe.[9] In these conditions, the resumption of general economic growth could revive the rapid increase in demand for foods which are inherently expensive. There is a basic buoyancy in the long-term demand for food which became obvious in the 1970s and of which future account has to be taken. Behind particular surprises, like the sudden burst of import demand from the USSR, lies a more widespread phenomenon.

The experience of the 1970s also revealed limits in the supply of food. This is more a matter of relative speeds of growth of supply and demand than of absolute constraints on production. If, for instance, years of low demand follow those of high demand, supply capacities can catch up even without significant changes in technology. The balance of supply and demand is full of variables, most of them representing time, and cannot be projected with certainty. Nevertheless, some limits did, in the 1970s, become evident in the capacity of U.S. output to keep up with demand. This was crucial because the United States provided over two-thirds of the enormous increase in world exports of grains and soya beans, the two basic crops that made possible the worldwide expansion of animal-rearing.[10]

Although American production rose faster between 1972 and 1980 than from 1950 to 1972, this was achieved by using up the best reserves of productive land which farmers were previously paid, in the "set-aside" program, not to cultivate. The rate of growth of yields of basic crops fell by about a third, from about 2.1 percent per annum in the 1950s and 1960s to about 1.5 percent per annum in the 1970s (O'Brien, 1981, p. 11). In the future, the growth of acreage of crops could hardly exceed 0.5 percent per annum of less good land. The implication was that if world demand began to grow again on anything like the scale of the 1970s, American rates of improvement in yields would have to increase once more. Declining trends since the 1950s would have to be reversed. To achieve that, American supply might have to become more expensive than in the recent past (O'Brien, p. 20). Given the American domination of world markets for basic crops, the historic fall of agricultural prices relative to others might be halted and even reversed (Figure 2.1).

Finally, there is a political reason for taking the evidence of the 1970s

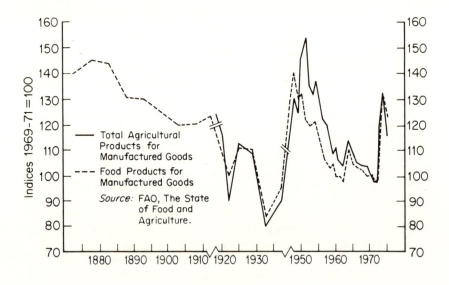

Figure 2.1.

Long-Term Trends in Indices of World (Market economies only)
Terms of Trade of Food and Agricultural Products for Manufactured
Goods (World export unit value indices, 1969-71 = 100).

seriously and asking whether food might not become dearer to supply. In the
European Community, assumptions of cheap food reinforce conventional
wisdom. The CAP has always been criticized on the implicit assumption of
falling real prices for food on world markets. In these conditions, it is clear
that there can be little room for exports from the EC. Yet, in fact, during the
1970s, the Community did find extra outlets for exports, and not only because
of subsidies. Community sales of dairy products in 1981, for instance, were
underpinned by strong world markets. If one could establish plausible
hypotheses of the growth of food demand to the end of the century, one would
have a set of tests for the practical limits of growth in the CAP. The tests
would be particularly interesting if they were not designed for the purpose of
investigating, still less justifying, the expansionary ambitions of the European
farm lobbies.

It so happens that, in the expansive conditions of the end of the 1970s, two
such studies of future food trade were made by non-European organizations.
The first was a series of econometric projections by the United States
Department of Agriculture (USDA) (O'Brien, 1981—hereafter USDA I; and
USDA, 1981—hereafter USDA II). The other was *Agriculture towards 2000* by
the FAO.[11] Both studies appeared in two versions, the later one in each case
betraying more caution than the first. The USDA projections go to 1985 in the
first case and to 1990 in the second, concentrating on the likely world demand

for U.S. basic crops (grains, oilseeds and cotton). They rest on a detailed data base, with regional and national supply balances for grains and cotton around the world, and are explicit about general growth and commodity price assumptions. The FAO projections, extending to the year 2000, are concerned primarily with the export outlook for 90 developing market economies in a wide variety of commodities; they include China only for grains (Table 2.9). The projections are based on extrapolations of trends between the early 1960s and 1975 corrected for what seem plausible rates of growth and balances of supply and demand.

Two major preoccupations emerge from the USDA studies, particularly the first. This is that the century-old trend for food prices to fall in real terms (that

Table 2.9   Net Import Balances of Developing Countries, 1963–2000, and Trend Projections (millions of tons: − = exports)

	FAO I	FAO II	FAO II All LDCs Incl. China	FAO II 90 Countries Scenario B [a]
	90 Countries			
Grains				
1963	10.3			
1975	32.5			
1979		36.4	52.5	
2000	153.0	132.0	165.0	105.2
Milk (whole milk equivalent)				
1963	4.9			
1975	8.3			
1979		13.0	15.0	
2000	67.0	22.0	25.0	
Meat (carcass wt.)				
1963	−0.8			
1975	−0.4			
1979	0		0.3	
2000	15.0	2.5	3.0	0.2

[a]   90 LDCs Growth Rates
(percent per annum)

1980–2000	Trend Projections	Scenario B
Total agricultural production	2.8	3.1
Total agricultural demand	2.9	3.2
Total agricultural imports		3.4
Total agricultural exports		2.8

Source: FAO, *Agriculture: Toward 2000 (1979)*, "FAO I," pp. 26, 181–82. FAO, *Agriculture: Toward 2000 (1981)*, "FAO II," ch. 2, and milk and meat balances communicated to the author.

is, compared to prices of other goods) might be reversed in the 1980s. The earlier USDA study of April 1981 assumed that U.S. farm production would have to grow 3 percent per annum to meet world demand, and real prices rise "1 to 3 percent per year, compared with declines averaging 1 to 2 percent per year for the postwar period" (USDA I, p. 20). Behind its drab statistical facade, this conclusion was radical. It reflected the immediate shock of the second energy crisis of 1979–80 and assumed among other things that ethanol production from corn to reduce energy imports would raise American domestic demand for agriculture in the early 1980s from 1.1 percent a year to 1.5 percent a year. The later report, reflecting the subsequent recession, implicitly played down ethanol production. The general findings were also suitably toned down. "Strong growth in demand for farm products, combined with the impact of high production costs," were now "projected to push nominal costs up sharply, possibly at or even marginally above the inflation rate" (USDA II, p. 7). However, even in this watered-down version, in which U.S. production was to grow by 2.6 percent (± 0.1 percent) per annum, the argument was maintained that the age of falling food prices was probably coming to an end. There was a further implication: since the U.S. is the breadbasket of the world, international grain prices, and those of meat and dairy products which partly depend on them, would also be likely to stop falling in real terms and might even rise.

The second preoccupation emerging from the USDA reports was the fear of heightened short-term instability of markets, a growing variability in demand and supply balances from year to year. The exploitation of reserve land in the U.S. in the 1970s; the potential increase in dependence on marginal lands in the 1980s; limits on water supply for irrigation; and the rising dependence of world trade on the US (on USDA computations 40 percent of the volume of world farm trade in 1980, against 25 percent in 1970)—all pointed towards greater variations from year to year in the balance of world demand and supply for basic commodities. Taking running fifteen-year periods, the annual variability in foreign demand for American grains and oilseeds trebled from 1950–64 to 1966–80 while the demand for them only doubled. Supply, too, was seen to be very variable, especially in the case of maize. The variations from year to year in maize production in the exporting countries were equivalent to 63 percent of world trade in 1975 and over 100 percent in 1971 (USDA II, pp. 5, 79, and 82; OECD 1980b, p. 81).

The USDA projections offered enlightenment for Europe only on grains. This left in the shadow two other sectors of prime importance to the Community—meat and dairy products. Here, FAO's *Agriculture Towards 2000* was more explicit. As with USDA, there were two studies, the first more dramatic than the second. The innovative contribution of the first study, in 1979, was in pointing out that if existing trends for production and consumption continued, the import demand of 90 developing countries, including all the main ones but China, would rise spectacularly between 1975 and 2000, not only for grains, which was no great surprise, but for milk and meat, which was the first time such a possibility had been expressed (Table 2.9). The second study, issued in 1981, played down this startling conclusion, mainly, it seems, on two grounds. The first was that the rather mechanical projections in the earlier version produced a number of incompatibilities between future farm imports for developing countries and farm exports for developed ones. The second was that any attempt by the developing countries to meet the bulk of the extra demand from home production (FAO's hope), implied general sustained growth rates of 7 to 8 percent a year, which had never been attained at the height of the boom and were all the more unlikely during a recession. The changes in the second version made for moderate reductions in the projected trade in grains, and much larger ones for milk and above all meat, where the prospects became far more modest.

Even in their more cautious second versions, the USDA and FAO studies raise issues of considerable significance for the European Community. If prices were really to stop falling, this should help the Community, on the past record, to reduce the gap between European and world market prices and so take some of the political and financial sting out of it. Since Community prices have tended to fall in real terms, but not fast enough, stable or rising world prices might reduce the financial and political costs of reaching some balances in the EC's own farm policies. Increasing instability in world markets could also make it easier for the Community to unload stocks at remunerative prices in years when suppliers elsewhere are tight (as it did in 1974–75), or to substitute higher-cost domestic grains, in the place of imports, to feed livestock.

It seems, in fact, that the effect of this would not necessarily be major. Josling and Pearson have found that the difference in expenditure for the Community of assuming at the extreme a rise of 2 percent per annum in real prices on world markets and at the other a fall of 2 percent per annum of world prices, might well not come to more than 13 to 16 percent either way (Josling and Pearson, 1982, pp. 16–17). This is far from negligible, but more limited than the authors themselves expected. Favorable trends in world prices would not, then, necessarily or even probably be a substitute for a long-term policy to control supplies. Yet they could gain time and so make a policy of controls easier to adjust to and accept. The implications of FAO's findings are also of importance, if confirmed. They suggest that unless there are considerable changes away from past trends, meat and dairy products, the staple EC food exports, might play a more prominent role than is widely assumed (particularly in depression, as in 1983–84) in the growth of world trade in food. For all these reasons, it is necessary to look more closely at the assumptions worked out most explicitly in the USDA report and to address the central question: how plausible a pointer to the future can one take the experience of the 1970s to be?

FUTURE FOOD BALANCES

A simulation carried out by the International Energy Agency (IEA) in 1982, assumed that, from 1985 to 2000, the OECD countries could sustain an average growth of 3.2 percent a year without creating the conditions for more oil crises and renewed depressions. At these rates of development, unemployment in the rich countries would fall "gradually" after 1985 (OECD, IEA, 1982, pp. 23-25). Since average unemployment in OECD Europe was over 10 percent at the end of 1982, this implies significant unemployment until well into the 1990s (OECD, main Economic Indicators, monthly). The IEA scenario of growth coincides with the "low" FAO estimate to the end of the century (Table 2.10). Both also coincide—if that is a coincidence—with the actual average rate of growth recorded by the advanced industrial economies during the 1970s. USDA is slightly more pessimistic, with a projection of 3 percent a year for the 1980s. Both USDA and FAO virtually reproduce, once again, the growth rates of the 1970s for their estimates of the likely performance of the developing countries. But whereas this procedure may seem plausible enough for the rich, conditions have changed enough for it to seem decidedly optimistic for the poor.

Whereas in the 1960s, the developing countries grew about 1.2 times as fast as the developed, in the 1970s their relative performance improved sharply, to 1.75. This striking shift to greater apparent self-reliance offers one significant explanation why the difficult 1970s did not in the end match the depression of the dismal 1930s. But the conditions of the 1970s were very special. There was a huge and sudden transfer of funds from the rich to the comparatively *nouveaux riches* of OPEC. This was passed on, through OPEC's massive dollar balances and the Western banks where they were deposited, to the middle income and Socialist countries, whose investment prospects were deemed at the time more attractive than those of the recession-ridden West. Some newly industrializing countries grew faster in the 1970s, despite ambient recession, than they had before.[12] Moreover, unemployment in the West was still low by the standards of the early 1980s. Under 3 percent of workers in OECD Europe were unemployed in 1973, and 5 percent on the eve of the second energy crisis in 1979, against over 10 percent at the end of 1983. (OECD, *Main Economic Indicators*). Consequently, protectionism had not become the force it was a decade later. Even if recession is outgrown, the 1980s seem likely to be markedly less favorable to potentially fast-growing developing countries than conditions ten years earlier. Although the developing countries may on balance have become more self-reliant than in the 1960s, they should be more affected by trade and market restriction in the rich countries than they were in the idiosyncratic 1970s. Yet both the USDA and FAO projections implicitly ignore these uncomfortable considerations. They imply that developing countries could, in the 1980s, actually grow slightly faster, relative to the rich, than they did in the 1970s (Table 2.10). In contrast to this, USDA drastically cuts growth expectations for the Socialist countries. In general, these are halved in comparison with the 1970s.

Naturally, such assumptions are reflected in USDA's projections for food trade in the 1980s. The continued growth of demand in the faster-growing developing, or newly industrializing, countries, remains the centerpiece of expectations:

> the transition towards stronger livestock demand in the more affluent developing countries was assumed to continue and, in selected cases, to

Table 2.10 World Growth Rates and Projections (annual, percent)

| | Actual | | UNCTAD | USDA | World Bank | | OECD Interfutures Scenario B2 | FAO Scenarios | |
| | 1960–70 | 1970–80 | 1980–90 | 1980–90 | Low 1980–90 | High | 1975–2000 | Low (B) 1980–2000 | High (A) 1980–2000 |
	(1)	(2)	(3)	(4)	(5)	(6)	(7)	(8)	(9)
Market economies									
Developed	4.9	3.2	2.4	(3.0)	2.8	3.7	3.5	3.2	3.8
Developing	5.9	5.6	4.2	(5.6)	4.6	5.7	6.0	5.7	7.0
Socialist economies									
Developed	6.6	5.3	3.5	(2.4)	3.9	3.9			
Developing	6.8	5.5	5.0	(4.6)a	5.3	5.3			
World	(5.4)	(4.0)	(3.0)	(3.4)	(3.4)	(4.1)	(4.4)		
Growth elasticity LDCs b	1.20	1.75	1.75	1.87	1.64	1.54	1.71	1.78	1.84

aChina only.
bGrowth elasticity: ratio of growth rate for developing market countries to that of the developed market economies.

Source: UNCTAD, Trade and Development Report 1981, Table 29, p. 85 for cols. 1, 2, 3, 5, and 6.
USDA, Problems and Prospects for U.S. Agriculture in the 1980s, November 1981, pp. 15–16, for col. 4.
OECD, Interfutures.
FAO, Agriculture: Toward 2000 (1981), p. 31 for cols. 8 and 9.
World Bank, World Development Report 1980, Table 1, "Basic Indicators," 1978, has provided the weighting for aggregating the USDA figures in col. 4 and for computing world growth rates in cols. 1–6. All figures obtained in this way are set in parentheses. The weighting corresponds to the distribution of GDP in 1978 expressed in dollars at current exchange rates.

accelerate. As a result of these forces, foreign demand was projected to grow 2.5–2.7 percent per year, compared with 2.7 to 2.8 percent per year over the postwar period to date [USDA II, p. 5].

In short, even if growth slows down somewhat, the shift to meat-eating will still virtually maintain a growth in demand like that from 1972 to 1980. This could well make too little of the effects of slower OECD growth on the previously fast-growing middle income economies. The rate of growth of food demand outside the US would only have to fall by a tenth, while output growth was maintained, for the gap between demand and supply in the importing developing countries largely to disappear. Unlike other developing countries, fast-growers have often registered good, and some of them outstanding, rates of increase of domestic food output.[13] If these countries can keep up such performances, their import needs could dwindle in the light of the slower general growth in their domestic incomes (though this could affect their agricultural output too). USDA probably overestimates demand from the intermediate market economies in the next decade, if not necessarily in the 1990s.

On the other hand, the bias in USDA computations for the Socialist states seems to lean strongly the other way. The projections provide for a *fall* of 22 million tons, or 32 percent in Socialist net imports of grain between 1980 and 1989 against an *increase* of 41 million tons in the 1970s. This would cancel two-fifths of the expected increase of 52 million tons in the demand for grains from the developing countries.[14] If the assumption were incorrect, and even if actual imports into the Socialist countries were to be static, this would still represent an increase of 22 million tons in demand compared to the cuts USDA expects. This is a notable counterweight to any exaggerated expectations of the developing market economies. A large cut in Socialist imports is therefore a key assumption. It implies one of three possibilities: the Socialist countries have no foreign exchange; they can ignore the pressure of consumer demand; or productivity can be greatly improved on the land.

Lack of foreign exchange is clear in Eastern Europe and some believe the Soviet Union itself will run short, as indigenous oil and gold fall in quantity or price or both (Brown, 1982). But the Soviet Union is building up natural gas sales (OECD, IEA, 1982, p. 182), and some observers argue that selling energy for food is economic in Soviet conditions.[15] Even China, despite rising grain output, has rapidly built up, and because of insufficient inland transport maintained, wheat imports into the eastern coastal cities of over 10 million tons a year (*Financial Times*, 1984b).[16]

Given the stages of development of the Socialist economies, where food remains an important item in budgets and consumption of livestock products is still on average behind Western levels, any growth is likely to turn into a substantial demand for food. This can no doubt be suppressed in the USSR if the authorities so determine. But threatened increases in food prices were the starting point of the three Polish crises of 1970, 1976, and 1980. Even in the USSR, compliance may not be eternally assumed; and agriculture, once at the bottom of Stalin's scale of priorities, had, by the early 1980s, in the words of Leonid Brezhnev shortly before his death, become "the most serious political and economic problem facing the country" (*Financial Times*, 1982c; *The Times*, 1982).

The USSR now invests relatively far more in agriculture than the sector's contribution to national wealth.[17] Yet, Soviet food production seems to have fallen in virtually every major commodity from peaks situated variously between 1973 and 1979.[18] Soviet grain output for 1980–82 was over 20 percent below the average of the three previous harvests and nearly 30 percent below the target average for the Eleventh Plan years of 1981–85. Moreover, the Plan revisions of 1982 expressed some pessimism about the future in carrying forward only slightly increased targets to 1990. If this Plan were successful it would be possible to accommodate in the 1980s an increase in consumption similar to the 1970s and at the same time eliminate imports. But there is no special reason to assume this must be so; and if the performance of the 1970s is repeated, Soviet net imports of grain could rise to over 80 million tons by 1990.[19]

The weather tends to be blamed in the USSR for the meager returns to the enormous investment on the land. Outsiders stress inadequate prices, inherited from the policy of subsidizing urban food supplies. Yet, there are reasons for suspecting the problem in the USSR goes deeper, into the heart of a system of bureaucratic as opposed to entrepreneurial management. Other Socialist countries have applied a wide variety of systems on the land, with an equally wide range of success.[20] But collective farming, rooted in the Stalinist revolution, evokes deep commitments and fears of change in the Soviet political establishment. Reform could well continue to be inadequate, as most observers have judged the efforts of 1982.[21] In these conditions, any political sense of a need to keep the population well fed could push the leadership in some Socialist countries, especially the two giants, the USSR and China, to continue to import food even against other priorities. Socialist demand is, therefore, a particularly uncertain quantity. All observers assume the USSR could cut imports rapidly if it really tried. But if they overrate the prospects of the USSR really trying, its impact on demand could continue to be enormous. On balance, any misperceptions by USDA are likely to err on the side of underestimating demand from the Socialist countries.

The effects of these various assumptions can perhaps best be gauged through the USDA projections for grains in the 1980s (Table 2.11). Grains and oilseeds between them account for 70 percent of US farm exports and 30 percent of US farm output and dominate the USDA assessments of the impact of world trade on domestic US costs on the land. A number of points emerge from Table 2.11. The first is that a slowdown in demand is assumed for the 1980s, but it is limited if one takes account of the fact that for the 1980s a nine-year period is taken against one of ten years for the previous decade. Second, demand falls more than supply, which suggests over-optimism in the projections. Third, if allowance is made for the number of years, the projections provide for a slightly accelerated demand by developing countries. This

Table 2.11   Growth of World Trade in Grains 1970-1980 and Projections 1980-1989
(changes in millions of metric tons net)

	Actual 1970–80	Forecasts 1980–89
United States	+72.7	+43.9
Argentina, Australia, Canada ("Trio")	+19.5	+20.9
Europe, Japan (traditional importers)	+17.3	–13.5
Centrally planned economies (CPEs)	–41.4	+22.1
LDCs (excluding CPEs)	–55.5	–51.5
Increase in net supply	+109.5	+86.9
Increase in net demand	–96.9	–65.0
Increase in net supply 1980s % 1970s		79.4
Increase in net demand 1980s % 1970		67.1
U.S. as percent total increase in supply	66.4	50.5
Trio as percent total increase in supply	17.8	24.1
U.S.: Trio increase in supply	3.7	2.1

+ = increase in net supply, either by a rise in net exports *or* reduction in net imports;
− = increase in net demand, either by a fall in net exports or a rise in net imports.

Source: For 1970 and 1980: FAO, *Trade Yearbooks*, 1972 and 1980; for 1989: USDA,
Economic Research Service, *Fall 1981 Baseline*, pp. 54-75. All figures are net,
i.e., balances of exports and imports.

possible exaggeration of opportunity is, however, substantially damped down by the enormous reversal assumed for the Socialist states. As a result, the growth of demand is assumed to decline by a third compared with the previous decade (or a quarter, if adjustment is made for a full ten years). Fourth, the United States is presented as taking a significantly smaller share of the presumed increase in trade than in the 1970s, compared with the minor traditional exporters, Argentina, Australia, and Canada. The United States took nearly four times as much of the new trade as they did in the 1970s but would, in the coming period, take little over twice. To this extent, the USDA projections seem fairly cautious; and much the same can be said of those for oilseeds, where the historic American share of the world market is even greater than for cereals.

However, the plausibility of the argument hinges on two further variables. One of them is whether the limits on supply already discussed are really as tight as USDA argues. Behind the stress on areas of cropland and yields lie technological assumptions. The USDA experts expect no major break-throughs in production such as nitrogen fixation (to reduce the fertilizer needs of grains) until the 1990s. Caution about technological prospects lies behind the conclusion that an acceleration in the growth of yields may call for higher real farm prices. USDA expectations of higher prices were also influenced by the revival of the energy crisis after 1979. USDA I assumed this would constrain supply by raising costs; and also increase demand, notably for fuel production from the bio-mass. USDA's first estimates of real farm price increases of 1–3 percent a year to 1985 hinged to a considerable extent on the "gasohol" program to replace imported oil by fuel from 14 to 22 million extra tons of maize a year by 1985 (O'Brien, USDA I, p. 18). What happened instead was that the second energy crisis, though it did indeed raise costs, cut dead the growth of international demand for grains. Recession, declining fuel demand and prices also put an end to any large "gasohol" program. Depression took over from the anticipated strains on supply. Yet the first crisis produced quite different outcomes. By transferring income to new countries, not only the oil exporters, it actually helped in the medium-term to increase farm trade. In a shifting context, like causes do not necessarily have like effects.

The uncertainties are compounded by the fact that the second energy crisis, prompted by revolution in Iran, demonstrated that social chaos might have an even bigger impact on the energy market than deliberate policies. It could lead to sudden major breakdowns in supply. Studies suggest that such interruptions of supply would have much sharper effects on production costs, including on the farm, than even very big price increases for energy (Dvoskin and Heady, 1976, p. 5). The energy situation is, therefore, another and potentially major source of uncertainties. Energy variations tend above all, perhaps, to magnify the conceivable swings from supply shortage to failure of demand according to circumstances. They amplify the potential instability of the market, which is, in some ways, the main worry of those responsible for agricultural policy. This instability will be greater to the extent that the IEA proves right in fearing a renewal of the underlying tensions on energy markets after 1985.[22]

The short-term fact remains that, in the United States from 1980 to 1982, the areas harvested for grains and oilseeds and yields all expanded faster than USDA predicted. The period is, however, too short to offer a basis for conclusions. 1980 was the one relatively poor harvest in a quartet of otherwise abundant ones from 1979. If one takes 1980 as the base, supply growth seems buoyant. But if one takes 1979, a peak year, as the base, the changes seem very modest.[23] Since the weather, favorable in the three bumper years, can produce variations of 10 to 15 percent either way from what later proves to be the trend, the latter is effectively hidden by the vagaries of what, on the past climatic record, is an exceptional period. There remains at least the possibility that supply in the United States may be more elastic than the USDA experts have judged.

The same could be said of the minor exporters who have expanded their sales very substantially in the same years.[24] They were, of course, favored by the American embargo on sales to the USSR, though this did less to restrict exports of grains than to redistribute trade channels, the US concentrating on customers other than the USSR, and the rival exporters taking its place to some extent on the forbidden market.[25] On the other hand, the trio of traditional minor exporters—Argentina, Australia and Canada—have between them only half the land under cereals and half the yields per acre of the United States, so that they are, even collectively, a much smaller feature in the picture (FAO 1980b, pp. 93–94). Supply responses may be stronger than USDA has argued, especially if technology advances rather faster than its very cautious estimates for the 1980s; but nothing yet provides a base for a committed judgment.

On the second variable, however, it is possible to be more categorical. Next to the reversal, compared with the 1970s, of the supposed trends for imports by the Socialist countries, the most striking assumption, reflected in Table 2.11, is the assertion that the major traditional importers, Western Europe and Japan, will substantially increase their net grain imports. During the 1970s, exactly the opposite happened: their net imports fell by a substantial amount (and, therefore, appear as an increase in net supplies in the table). This was due essentially to the fact that the European Community is now a net exporter of cereals, its large exports of wheat outbalancing its dwindling imports of feedgrains (as against oilseeds and cereal substitutes). There is nothing so far to indicate a change of direction. If the Community's exports of grains were to increase in the 1980s with anything like the strength of the expansion of the last decade, USDA's projections would, worldwide, envisage virtually the same increase in supply as in the 1970s but only half the demand, with the LDCs as the only expanding market. This is, of course, impossible. To achieve any kind of balance, the Socialist countries' imports would, contrary to USDA's expectations, have to increase at the unprecedented rate of the 1970s. The implication is simple. It is quite probable that, far from being a marginal region which can go its own way, ignoring the world market and largely ignored by it, the European Community would, in some circumstances, as a newcomer, become a swing producer making the difference between a sellers' and a buyers' market for grains (and other foods). Supply tendencies in the Community must, therefore, be addressed in a much broader setting than has so far been the custom.

New Frontiers and Constraints

European Commission reports in the early 1980s have underlined the implications for the future of trends in supply and demand inside the Community. The clearest cases were probably four major commodities—cereals, sugar, milk and beef—which between them account for just over half of EC gross agricultural output (Com-EC, 1981a; Com-EC 1983a;).

USDA's projections for *cereals*, which assume that the European Community will marginally reduce net exports of grains in the 1980s, obtain no warrant from the record of steady and substantial growth of European production in the face of high but falling real prices. A crude extrapolation of Community trends in the last seven, recession-ridden years of the 1970s, after the EC's first enlargement and the oil shock of 1973–74, implies, in the Commission's rough published estimates, an increase in output of grains of

1.7 percent per annum against near stagnation—a growth of 0.35 percent per annum—in domestic demand. Such a rate, continued unchecked to 1990. would imply a surplus of over 12 million tons in Community output and by the year 2000, of nearly 30 million tons, against the marginal deficit of 2 million tons in 1980. Since the Community remains an importer of feedgrains, this most plausibly means that the rapid growth of tonnages of wheat available for export would continue. This emerges more clearly still from the Commission's detailed statistical breakdown for 1973–81. These figures, extrapolated, would imply net wheat exports of 27 million tons in 1990 and 47 million tons by 2000 against 9 million tons in 1981. For feedgrains, net imports of 4 million tons in 1981 would turn into 3 million tons of exports by 1991 and 13 million tons by 2000. The more detailed figures, in short, point to surpluses both in 1990 and 2000 about twice as high as those put forward by the European Commission (Table 2.12). These figures are consonant with the econometric projections of Koester and Josling and Pearson who project net grain surpluses of about 28–30 million tons by 1990 on current trends, (Josling and Pearson, 1982, Table 12; and Koester, 1982, Table 7). They are quite incompatible with USDA projections, especially for wheat. USDA wheat estimates envisage that the U.S. and the three traditional minor exporters, Argentina, Australia and Canada, would increase their exports by somewhat more than the 10 million tons by which the wheat trade is supposed to expand between 1981 and 1989; and that the Community's net exports would marginally decline (the difference going to stock). The EC projections, on the other hand, would eat up the margin of growth on the Commission's parameters and bite deeply into the export markets of the U.S. and the traditional trio on those of Thiede. In fact, the Thiede projections applied to those of USDA would result in supply in the 1980s growing 2¼ times as fast as demand. Either way, the contrast with USDA projections recalls the title of a French book on the East-West conflict: "One Bed for Two Dreams " (Fontaine, 1982). The one way they could possibly be reconciled would be if the increase in total grain exports and stocks during the next decade were to be of the same order of magnitude as the unprecedented performance of the last one. Even in this case, the EC would corner the extra market. Otherwise, on the projections proposed by USDA, there would, as in 1982, be a glut. Prices would be under heavy pressure to fall. Far from operating on a market overwhelmingly defined by others, the Community would itself be a major factor determining international conditions and world prices.

This is already the case for *dairy products*. In this sector, unlike cereals, there is no question of the cheapest producers also becoming the dominant suppliers. The productive potential of New Zealand is too small (FAO 1980b). The United States, which is a much bigger producer and, like the Community, has accumulated substantial stocks by 1983, is also, like the Community, a high cost producer. On the other hand, the U.S. has already demonstrated that it could, if it so wished, subsidize large exports of dairy products.[26]

For the future, the only substantial estimates are those advanced by the FAO. In the earlier version of *Agriculture: Toward 2000* (FAO I), the demand

Table 2.12 Extrapolations to 1990 and 2000 of EC Supply and Demand Trends for Cereals, Sugar, Milk, and Beef from 1973 to 1980 and 1981 (millions of metric tons; + = net exports; − = net imports)

Commodity	Based on estimates in EC Commission Report on Agricultural Aspects of "Mandate" of 30 May 1980[a]			Based on balances by Gunther Thiede of EC Food Production and Consumption in Grain equivalents 1973–81[b]			Based on "Basic Policy" Scenario in Josling and Pearson Study of Future EC Budget Costs to 1990[c]
	1980	1990	2000	1981	1990	2000	1990
Cereals	−2	12	30	9	24	47	29.6
Wheat				−4	3	13	
Feedgrains				2	12	24	
Sugar			33				6.4
Milk:				11	20	35	13.6
1.6 percent growth output per annum	18	29	45				
2.4 percent growth output per annum[d]	9	28	55				
Beef and veal	0.2		1.6–2.6	0.04	2.3	5.2	1.7

[a] Com-EC, *Guidelines for European Agriculture: Memorandum to Complement the Commission's Report on the Mandate of 30 May 1980,* Com (81) 608 final of 23 October 1981; Com-EC, Bulletin, Supplement 4/83, *Adjustment of the Common Agriculture Policy;* Eurostat, *Cronos* production series.

[b] Gunther Thiede, Com-EC, *Agricultural Statistical Studies, No. 22: Overall Accounts on the Community Supply Situation based on Grain Equivalents,* 1980; "Mengenmaessigen Gesamtrechnungen zur EG-Versorgungslage" *Agrarwirtschaft,* March 1981; Com-EC, Eurostat, *Crop Production 1-1983* (March 1983), pp. 129–53, Table 4.6.

[c] Timothy E. Josling and Scott R. Pearson, *Developments in the Common Agricultural Policy of the European Community,* USDA, ERS, Foreign Agricultural Economic Report 172, Washington, D.C., June 1982.

[d] This is based initially on deliveries to dairies only (98.8 million tons for EC-10 in 1982, against total output of 106.3 million tons). This explains why the 1980 and 1990 figures are less than those of 1.6 percent per annum growth based on total output. However, after 1990 a 2.4 percent growth becomes synonymous with an equivalent growth in total output.

for dairy products of 90 major developing countries (excluding China) by the year 2000 was estimated at the equivalent of 67 million tons of milk, a huge amount compared with FAO's estimate of 8 million tons (in milk equivalent) of dairy products bought by the 90 in 1975 (and even with the total output of the Community itself, as the world's biggest producer, of somewhat over 100 million tons in 1981). This was heavily scaled down in the later version of the report (FAO II), which contains projections of 22 to 25 million tons, an increase of 10 million tons (with the inclusion of China) on what was actually being traded in 1979 (Table 2.9).

How these widely varying estimates of plausible demand square with the supply prospects for the Community depends on the base one takes for Community supply projections. One could, for instance, take the increase in output of total milk produced on the farms from 1973 to 1982, which averaged 1.6 percent per annum; or, again, the rate of increase of milk deliveries to the dairies from 1973 to 1983, which averaged 2.4 percent annum. The differences between such rates and Community demand growth, from 1973 to 1983, of about 0.5 percent per annum, extrapolated to the year 2000, lead to enormous supply–demand gaps, especially if one takes account of the fact that EC supply already outran consumption of dairy products by 13 million tons in 1981. By the year 2000, the excess of extra supply over increased demand in the Community would add a further 27 million tons over 1982 on the basis of a 1.6 percent per annum growth in milk production, and a further 10 million tons in the case of a 2.4 percent increase per annum.

Whichever assumption one takes, the postulated rise in Community milk production would seem to be about three to four times as large as the increment of demand in the developing 90 countries over the next two decades assumed in FAO II (Table 2.9). They would only become feasible if earlier and much higher FAO estimates of demand trends for dairy products—given up in part for balance of payments reasons—were to materialize; or massive new markets were to open up once again in the Socialist states (left out of the FAO calculations). Even then, other exporters would have to take up modest shares of the new markets. This is not impossible. But it is only likely in the "best-case scenario" (from a purely EC point of view) of a general growth in world food trade far more favorable than in the wake of the second energy shock of 1979. That in turn depends at least in part on what plausible sustainable rates of general economic growth can be managed without further energy crises breaking their impetus.

The case of *sugar* goes beyond the bounds of even best-case optimism. FAO projections treat sugar as a major net export of the developing countries—"on trend," 20 million tons by the year 2000. The developing countries exporting cane sugar are on the whole low cost producers. USDA expects the demand for sugar in the United States to fall during the 1980s, because of the competition of cheaper "high fructose corn syrups" derived from maize.[28] These have been denied entry into the Community, but even so European consumption of sugar is expected to stagnate at less than 10 million tons. In these circumstances, the growth of sugar production in the Community of

4.6 percent per annum for 1973–80—or even of 5.7 percent per annum for eight years if one extrapolates from the huge jump in output of 1981–82—leads into realms of statistical fancy (*ASC*, relevant years). At 5.7 percent per annum, the Community's sugar output would grow to 42 million tons a year by the year 2000, four times the Community's own consumption (at least) and a quarter of total world production—even if one assumes that high demand in the developing countries leads to 3 percent growth per annum not merely to 1985, as the World Bank estimated in the late 1970s, but to the end of the century.[29] In these conditions, the Community would be exporting huge quantities of sugar to the main would-be exporters, with lower costs of production than its own! If the Americans chose to export their own corn syrups, matters would become still more surreal. Anything worse for Third World development would be hard to imagine.

Beef and veal are another matter. The Commission assumed, in its Guidelines of 1981 that production in the 1980s would grow by 1.5 to 2 percent per annum at home against consumption rising at a mere 0.5 percent per annum. This could generate exportable supplies of between 1.6 million and 2.6 million tons by 2000 against 1980 Community exports of 0.2 million tons. (Com-EC, 1981a) Thiede's detailed supply balances of 1973–81 imply larger export quantities, rising to 5.2 million tons by the year 2000 (Table 2.12). These are very large quantities set against the 3 million ton deficit for all developing countries for all forms of meat forecast for 2000 in the latest, FAO II "trend" projections, and still more against the 0.2 to 1.1 million ton deficit for all meat under FAO II's "normative" scenarios. Only against the original FAO I "trend" projection of a 15 million ton deficit would the diverging rates of Community production and demand, as extrapolated to 2000, have scope to find a market (Table 2.9). On the other hand, EC output stagnated between 1980 and 1983, more or less balancing demand. Meat projections are more sensitive, it seems, to variations in assumptions than those of cereals, sugar, or milk. The essential shift in FAO thinking has been to reduce the gap between food demand and production in developing countries, on the basis of the record so far, from a deficit of 0.5 percent per annum to one of 0.1 percent per annum. This seems mostly due to a downgrading of the rate of growth in food demand as a result of lower estimates of general growth. The outlook, therefore, is most uncertain.

Crude linear extrapolation of the trends during the 1970s clearly offers no base for forecasting, particularly over a period of twenty years. But as a quantitative illustration of the kinds of problem implicit in Community supply growth rates, it has claims to relevance which transcend the method. The rate of growth of the volume of agricultural output in the EC during three decades (Appendix Table 1) has been so steady as to constitute for the near future virtually a standard of "normality." That is to say, there is no sign it will change unless incentives do.

The rate of growth of demand in the Community may seem less predictable. It is hard to be sure how far the decline in the growth rate since 1973 (Appendix Table 1) is due to recession and how far to the continuing fall in the propensity of consumers to spend extra income on food. On the other hand, there are reasons for being sceptical that the growth of demand for food could increase very much. Between 1950 and 1975, the population of the EC–12 grew by 52.5 millions (0.7 percent per annum). Between 1975 and 2000, it is expected to grow by only 25 millions (0.3 percent per annum).[30] It cannot be assumed that when the economy revives there will be a consistent return to the historically exceptional rates of growth of the 1960s. And it is clear that European food markets are largely saturated. Incomes did rise in the 1970s in the Community. The only major food sectors that grew substantially were pork, poultry and cheese. Most crops fell. In the mid-1970s, for western Europe as a region, the income elasticity of demand was estimated at 0.07 for total food calories, 0.29 for calories of animal origin, and 0.37 for animal proteins (OECD, 1976). The FAO has concluded that food consumption in Western Europe may rise about 0.6 percent per annum between 1975 and 2000 (FAO I).

Food demand in southern Europe is likely to be more buoyant than in the north. But even there, one FAO study of EC enlargement estimates that between 1975–77, the base period, and 1990, production will tend to outstrip consumption in Greece, Portugal and Spain. (FAO 1980a, p142). Thus, while demand may continue to grow faster in the Mediterranean than in the north, the growing import gap, characteristic of the region in the boom years, is likely to close up again. Supply will begin to catch up on demand in southern as in northern Europe.

On balance, it is unlikely that even if general conditions improve, there will be a major revision of demand trends. A revival of demand can moderate the tendency of the Community to generate surpluses, but demand grew faster than today in the 1960s without matching supply. Thus, there is virtually no chance, barring a serious-to-catastrophic energy crisis, of a spontaneous closing of the domestic gap between European rates of growth of supply and demand. Unless some major assumptions change, there seems to be a built-in stability in the trends of demand and supply in the Community.

In these conditions, the main room for maneuver depends on world markets. The 1970s have shown that an entirely new stratum of demand is appearing in the faster-growing middle income countries and that collectively these represent a major section of the world's population. In this, as in other ways, the simple postwar distinction between first, second, and third worlds is being outgrown. When general conditions of growth are favorable, the demand from these countries is exceedingly strong, as it was in the 1970s. Given their state in the cycle of consumption, it is likely that, were growth to resume, they would again become vigorous markets.

An expansion of world markets of 1970s proportions for one and a half decades could, at least in raw figures, absorb many (not all) of the excess supplies of the Community in most commodities. Even then, though, little or no room would be left for other exporters. The Community, selling by subsidy, would take the lion's share. It is doubtful that this could be politically sustained. In the case of sugar, "trends" would expand output beyond any possible power of absorption of the world market. In short, there are possibilities of markets for Community produce that must not be neglected, but, equally clear, the prospects are highly conditional. Policies have to be tailored to a real environment of considerable uncertainty.

The sources of uncertainty are numerous. An important one is that the growth in outlets has not been due to increasing population, as such, but to rising incomes in relatively successful economies. Countries near the subsistence line lack the foreign exchange to buy food. They need help, which should primarily take the form of assistance to build up their own output for a whole host of development reasons (including creating local markets) and may also include some food aid. But food aid is a tax on the givers and it has been made abundantly clear over the years that the will to underwrite such transfers is limited; and that even if it were not, free food might actually depress prices in the receiving countries and undermine incentives to grow their own food. The major markets are the commercial ones. Once that is accepted, it also follows that demand is subject to the vagaries of the economic cycle. The early 1980s, coming after the buoyant food markets of the 1970s, have shown with some force just how uncertain those prospects always are.

Food markets have an inherent instability of their own, due to the short-term ups and downs of the weather, which have been heightened of recent years by other factors. One of the most important is the tendency of the world market to be used as the cushion for the imbalances of domestic policies—surpluses for the Community, deficits for the USSR, and so on—imbalances which might cancel each other out if they appeared in neatly compensating symmetries but most of the time do not, and on occasions supplement one another. The short- and medium-term uncertainties of this kind are compounded by longer-term ones, both in the fast-growing market economies and the Socialist ones, though for different reasons. Most of the fast-growing market economies have rather successful agricultural sectors. This means that if the growth of domestic demand slows down, they may have less need of imports. They may use the respite to catch up on demand. As for the Socialist states, and particularly the Soviet Union, which no one doubts could rapidly solve its agricultural problems if it adopted the right incentives, the questions are primarily political. There is no basis for being reasonably sure that conditions may not change both rapidly and unpredictably.

Even the fears of catastrophe produce uncertainties in that their consequences are not only incalculable within the mental framework people frequently adopt, but that this framework itself proves as often as not to be quite inappropriate to what actually happens. The second energy crisis is an excellent instance of this. Because of the experience of the first energy crisis, the second one was feared—in agriculture—mainly for its effects in increasing the costs of supply. In fact, its effect on demand was so much greater that markets collapsed. Another example could be the crucial one of climatic change, or the lack of it. In the mid-1970s, there was a flurry of speculation that the planet was about to enter a "mini" or even a fullblown ice-age and that this might happen very rapidly. By the early 1980s, publicity was given to

American official reports of a significant heating up of the earth after 1990 as a result of the "glasshouse" effect on the upper atmosphere produced by carbon dioxyde emissions from fossil fuels.[31] Any policy which presumes on a particular future, risks preparing for the wrong crisis and even aggravating vulnerability to others that could occur instead. Thus, reliance on the security of surpluses produced by heavy inputs of animal feeds and energy (though including fertilizers, chemicals, and machinery), all of which are imported, involves a highly dubious "self-sufficiency" and could, if there is another energy crisis, hasten the fate it seeks to avert.

There is nothing surprising in uncertainty. It has a venerable record going back to the creation. But it does break with the special environment of the CAP, which did for a period create for itself an area of predictability which was, historically, exceptional. To break out of the egg of security is uncomfortable. One way to seek to maintain it is to stress the value of abundant output as a cushion against the unexpected.

Such a policy, however, has substantial costs. For one thing, excess supplies depress markets and, other things being equal, the greater the excess, the greater the depressive effect. Unless general demand revived, European surpluses, growing at "trend," would be bound to weigh more and more heavily on world markets. Even then, exports might find no takers, as in the case of milk products: "Exports of skimmed-milk powder and butter decreased dramatically during the last two years and in 1983 will reach only 81 percent of butter exports and 59 percent of skimmed milk exports of 1981" (Com-EC, 1983a, para. 4, p. 35). Someone has to pay for the losses, including the member states and their taxpayers. Hence the budgetary crises of the Community, which are the domestic face of the political problems that arise.

There is also, as a result of the increase in the presence of the Community on world food markets, an increasingly important foreign policy dimension to the political picture. This is likely to be of greater significance than it has been in the past, when European expansion ignored international strategy. As the international effects of the changes that have been taking place build up, this too can become an area of costs that impinge on fields of foreign policy at first sight a long way from agriculture and food.

The quarrels between the Reagan administration and the Community at the GATT ministerial meeting in November 1982, as well as before and since, have given currency to the idea that the Community's external conflicts are essentially with the United States. This oversimplifies the picture. The foreign trade sector is a political irritant at a number of levels and on the import as well as export side of the equation. In practice, the range of countries affected tends to be much the same for imports and exports, but since there are some differences and it is almost quicker to enumerate the regions not affected than those that are, the least confusing approach may be to list the various categories at length, even at the risk of a certain amount of repetition.

One can distinguish up to five or six cases. There are four groups of countries who would lose substantially from the further closing to them of Community markets. One group contains the temperate region exporters—

especially New Zealand for butter, cheese, and lamb, and the United States for oilseeds—who have formally or informally guaranteed outlets in the EC— but also others such as Brazil, Argentina, and South Africa. The second group consists of the Mediterranean exporters who could be cut out of the markets of the Community—largely but not solely—by its extension to Portugal and Spain. These countries export olive oil, citrus and other fruit, and early vegetables. For some of them—Cyprus, Israel, Morocco, and Tunisia in particular—the Community market is very important. Ten percent of the total employment of Tunisia depends on olive groves built up on the prospect of exports to the Community; the groves also have an environmental purpose— to hold back the desert (IAMM, 1980). A third group are the—mostly Asian—developing countries who export cereal substitutes to the Community and have already agreed to limit their sales (ASC 1982, para. 127, p. 76). Curiously enough, they stand to lose by open policies in the Community, since their exports of cereal substitutes are mainly due to the fact that high CAP grain prices also inhibit American sales of maize. A fourth group would be added if, against all expectations, the sugar islands of the West Indies and Indian Ocean, the impoverished "jewels" of the old eighteenth-century British and French empires, were to lose their Community guarantees.

The second general situation concerns countries who stand to lose from Community competition on third markets. Here again, the temperate exporters are prominent. The most notorious incident occurred in 1980 when Australia threatened not to buy the Airbus in retaliation for the Community's lamb regime, agreed upon that year, which threatened Australian outlets in Asia, or so the Australians believed (Com-EC, 1980). In 1982, the United States filed a series of complaints in GATT about EC policies and practices for exports especially of sugar, tinned fruit and raisins, poultry, pasta, wheat flour, and citrus fruit.[32] The US then threatened to start a war of export credits with the Community. The second group are the developing countries. The most obviously affected are the developing sugar exporters other than the Community's own protected partners in the Lome Convention. The refusal of the Community to accept formal restraints has become the major single factor preventing the implementation of the International Sugar Agreement (*Financial Times*, 1982e; *ASC 1982*, para, 122, p. 74). But close associates of the Community, such as Morocco and Tunisia, are also beginning to complain that their potential food exports (such as wine to black Africa) are being pre-empted by subsidized competition from EC member states. In short, the expansion of Community food exports is affecting a widening range of countries throughout the world and the consequences could become increasingly costly to the Community itself.

Up to a point, external opposition drives the member states of the Community together. They were united in their opposition to the United States at the GATT ministerial conference of November 1982. But it is clear from the caution of the United States and the Community after the conference that both sides have a great deal to lose in carrying their quarrel too far. The same applies to the Community's interests in the Mediterranean, which is a region of importance to the member states not just for economic but security reasons. Germany, for one, has been pursuing a strategy of as close an association as possible of the Mediterranean countries with Western Europe. Italy and France sent peace forces to the Lebanon. As for the Third World, the Community, or some of its member states, have set store by claims to a special relationship. This is traditional for the French and British. It also has diplomatic uses at times in marking off Europeans from the United States. If Spain joins the Community, it will be eager to maintain as good relations as possible with Latin America. Since the countries most likely to be affected by the expansion of West European supplies tend to be precisely those with the closest general relations with the Community's member states, what are ostensibly agricultural questions can become caught up with a host of other economic, political, and security issues.

For all these reasons, the verdict has to be that as a new frontier for Community agriculture, the world market does indeed offer prospects, but ones that are highly conditional. World demand could alleviate the problems of the CAP, as in 1974–75 and 1980–82. It is, however, quite impossible to count on it doing so in any steady way. In fact, the forces for expansion in a few branches of Community agriculture are such as to preclude any plausible future satisfying them. It follows, even if it sounds a paradox, that the benefits of a potentially favorable world market can only be fully reaped if Community control over production is vigorously asserted. This would become still more critical were markets, cyclically or for a longer period, to fail. Control does not mean renouncing opportunities for growth. It does mean that agriculture must be considered in the total picture and not as an independent variable responding only to the internal laws of the sector. Given the scale Community food exports have now assumed, the need for flexible control will in future be greater, not less. The rapidly increasing presence of the Community on world markets internationalizes what was hitherto seen as a regional policy and takes it out of the sole discretion of the family.

Notes

1. Eurostat 1982b and Eurostat 1982a. These figures refer to SITC 0 + 1 and leave out SITC 22 + 29 + 4 (see Ch. 1, note 20, supra) so they are not fully comparable with Appendix Table 7.

2. Thiede, 1980, Table 15, puts imports at 17 percent of all animal feed in the late 1970s.

3. These conclusions are not substantially changed by taking statistics from the FAO *Trade Yearbooks* by value instead of volume. The major changes concern Latin America and Africa, whose performances are relatively 20 percent better in value than volume, and socialist Europe and the Near East, whose performances are relatively about 15 percent worse in value than volume.

4. OECD 1980b, Table 6.3, p. 73; *ASC 1981*, pp. 124–27, 323; *Financial Times*, "Compromise statement from Gatt attacked for 'papering over' issues," 30 November 1982, as well as earlier numbers; Com-EC 1984c, Claude Villain, Director-General for Agriculture, Com-EC, addressing Outlook 84 Conference, London 8 February 1984, "The Outlook for Europe's Agriculture."

5. Between 1976–77 and 1980–81, world exports of grains rose over a third from 156 million tons a year to 212 million tons a year; but from 1980–81 to 1982–83 (harvests of 1980 to 1982), world grain exports stagnated: 212 million tons in 1980–81 and 213 million tons in 1982–83. USDA 1982, *Agricultural Outlook*, p. 44.

6. On the basis of 1977 = 100: Prices received by U.S. farmers, 1982—134; prices paid by U.S. farmers, 1982—150 (Ibid., p. 23).

7. *Financial Times*, "Flour sale to Egypt adds force to farm war threats to EEC," 9 January 1983; "Wheat flour sale to Egypt threatens EEC-US ceasefire," 20 January 1983. Com-EC, 1983f, "Sale of Products," specifies that the U.S. State Department on 18 July 1983 notified the EC of the export of 18,000 tons of butter and 10,000 tons of cheese to Egypt as "food aid." Marcel Scotto, *Le Monde*, 2 August 1983, reported the EC had agreed to limit export refunds to cereal sales of 12.3 million tons in 1982–83. But on 26 October 1983, the Commission authorized the sale of 400,000 tons of (French) wheat flour to Egypt with sufficient subsidies to win the contract.

8. The statistics in Table 2.8, as well as the discussions in the text, are based on 36 countries selected, in the case of the market economies, mainly because most of them exceeded GDP growth rates of 5 percent per annum between 1970 and 1978. (World Bank, 1981, Table 2). However, no country with an income level below $7.5 billion in 1978 was included even if its growth rate exceeded 5 percent per annum, on the grounds that the market opportunities were too small to be of general importance. On the other hand, a few countries with growth rates slightly below 5 percent per annum were included on the grounds of their significance as import markets: Czechoslovakia, German Democratic Republic, Israel, Portugal, and Spain. None of these averaged less than 4.4 percent average growth per annum 1970–78. Iraq's annual growth rates in 1970–78 are not available in the World Bank's *World Development Report 1980*, but it has been included on similar grounds.

The 36 countries are: *Market Economies:* (1) Mediterranean: Morocco, Algeria, Tunisia, Egypt, Israel, Syria, Turkey, Greece, Yugoslavia, Spain, Portugal; (2) Africa: Nigeria; (3) West Asia: Iran, Iraq, Saudi Arabia; (4) East Asia: Indonesia, Singapore, Malaysia, Thailand, Philippines, Hong Kong, Japan, Republic of Korea (Taiwan is missing from FAO statistics for political reasons); (5) South America: Mexico, Colombia, Venezuela, Brazil; *Centrally Planned Economies:* (1) East Europe: Bulgaria, Czechoslovakia, German Democratic Republic, Hungary, Poland, Romania, USSR; (2) Asia: PR China, North Korea.

9. U.S. Congress, Joint Economic Committee (1981), using data for 1976, Table 10, p. 22, presents comparisons of meat consumption per annum in the West and the Socialist states (kilos/person per year) (Table 2.A). In the case, however, of the USSR, fish (excluded from the table) is more important than in the other countries considered. USSR consumption of fish in 1976 reached 18 kilos per person per year against 6 in the United States (p. 7).

Table 2.A

West		East	
United States	118	Czechoslovakia	81
France	102	Poland	70
West Germany	92	Hungary	68
UK	70	USSR	46
Italy	67		

10. In 1970, the U.S. accounted for 94 percent of the world soyabean exports, and in 1980, 81 percent (Webb, 1981, pp. 2–98). The U.S. percentage of the increase in world soyabean exports from 1970–1980 was 70 percent (Argentina 19 percent, Brazil 9 percent) (FAO, 1975, and 1980b).

11. FAO in two versions under the same title, *Agriculture: Toward 2000*: 1979 (hereafter FAO I); revised, 1981 (hereafter FAO II).

12. World Bank, *World Development Report 1980*, Table 2.8, p. 11: see Table 2.B below.

Table 2.B

Region or Groups	Average Annual Growth of GNP per person, % p.a.	
	1960–1970	1970–1980
Latin America, Caribbean	2.7	3.5
East Asia and Pacific	4.9	5.6
Oil exporters	2.8	3.5
Low-income oil importers	1.6	0.9
African oil importers	1.6	0.2

13. FAO, *Production Yearbook 1980*, pp. 75–80. For instance, food output *per head* rose, from 1969–71 to 1980, in Syria by 67 percent; in Tunisia, 32; in S. Korea, 21; and in Thailand, 25.

14. In fact, USDA, ERS, *Fall 1981 Baseline Projections*, pp. 54–75, envisages a still larger fall between 1981 and 1989, the outer dates used for detailed cereal supply balances: of 33 million tons or 46 percent. But it seems best to relate the projections for 1988 to the real trade of 1980, not only to provide a factual rather than speculative comparison but also to provide a link with the developments of the previous decade.

15. Jan Vanous, Wharton Economic Forecasting Associates, letter to *New York Times*, 19 November 1982, "Why Russia would rather not feed itself," argues that importing 46 million tons of grain in 1981 cost the equivalent of 29.2 million tons of crude oil equivalent in Soviet conditions, but that producing this amount in the USSR itself would have cost labor and capital capable of producing 159 million tons of oil.

16. According to FAO, *Trade Yearbooks*, the "Asian Centrally Planned Economies" (nearly all PR China) imported 6.3 million tons of cereals on average between 1961 and 1965, 9.1 million tons in 1970, and 20.2 million tons (of which 17.8 million tons went to China) in 1980. The biggest item throughout was wheat.

17. Lester R. Brown, 1982, p. 18: "Since 1966, Soviet investment in agriculture has dwarfed that of the United States. . . . The 24 percent share of national investment devoted to agriculture (27 percent if some sectors servicing agriculture are taken into account) is already high but is to be increased during the next five-year plan 1986–90 to 27-28 percent, or 33-35 percent if the wider sector is included." OECD, 1983b, p. 90. The World Bank, *World Development Report 1980*, Table 3, "Structure of Production", p. 155, estimates that agriculture represented 17 percent of Soviet national income in 1978.

18. Brown, 1982, p. 16, Table 2. Up till 1982 inclusive, the peak production years were 1973 for potatoes; 1974 for sugar; 1977 for milk; 1978 for grains, meat and vegetables; and 1979 for fruit.

19. USDA, ERS, 1982d, Table 2, "Total supply and estimated utilisation of grain, USSR, 1971–72 to 1981–82", p. 21; USDA, ERS, 1981a. The production goals have been as shown in Table 2.C. However, G.R. Allen (1981) argues that, until 1978, Soviet productive performance was reasonably on target.

Table 2.C

	Grains	Milk	Meat
	(millions of tons p.a.)		
Tenth Plan (1976–80)	217	95	15.3
Eleventh Plan (1981–85)	238–243	97–99	17–17.5
Twelfth Plan (1986–90)	250–255	105	20
Output 1980–82 (FAO estimates, *Production Yearbook* 1982)	169.9	89.4	15.2

20. Robert Bideleux (1979) stresses the very wide range of land organisation in Socialist countries between collective and state farms, agro-industrial complexes, commercially

autonomous collectives (mainly in Yugoslavia and Hungary), purchasing and marketing cooperatives, people's communes and even private ownership as the norm (Poland). Success and failure are not clearly related to these regimes (though the correlation with price policies is closer). The USSR and Poland have both done rather poorly, Hungary and the DDR rather well.

21. OECD, 1983b, referring to the USSR's agricultural plans: "Although the programme appears impressive in terms of its proposed capital outlays for agriculture and additional incentives to farmers, it does not indicate a profound re-organisation of the agricultural sector," p. 90.

22. OECD, IEA, Table 1.1, p. 26, shows a growing potential gap between supply and demand in the later 1980s, increasing towards the year 2000. This view is contested in the United States.

23. USDA, ERS, 1982a, p. 24. The series for crop production in the U.S. is as follows (from slump to peak only), 1973 = 100: 1974, 89; 1979, 114; 1980, 100; and 1982, 117. Overall, this would correspond, from 1973 to 1982, to a rate of annual growth of 1.8 percent per annum, but from 1973 to 1980 to zero.

24. See Table 2.D.

Table 2.D

Grain Exports	1969–71	1980	1981	1982
	(av. p.a. million metric tons)			
Canada (wheat, barley, corn)	12.7	20.1	20.5	23.3
Argentina (wheat, corn, sorghum)	9.0	9.5	17.8	15.5

Source: USDA, ERS, 1982c.

25. Brown, 1982, pp. 32 and 37: "The U.S. embargo distorted normal grain trade patterns as the Soviet Union turned to other suppliers, all quite small compared to the United States. Tying up the lion's share of exportable supplies from countries such as Argentina, the Soviet Union forced Japan and other major importers to rely even more heavily than usual on the United States . . . Whether or not the Soviets import their grain directly from the United States is not the relevant issue. The vast U.S. grain exports . . . are what enable the Soviets to import record quantities of grain."

26. By the third quarter of 1982, American butter stocks totalled 245,000 metric tons, and dried milk stocks 514,000 tons (USDA, 1982, p. 32 and conversion factors lbs-to-metric tons, p. 43). EC stocks at the end of 1982 were 147,000 tons of butter and 371,000 tons of dried milk (*ASC 1982*, pp. 391–92).

27. Eurostat, *Cronos* time series for milk production and deliveries to dairies 1960–80; *ASC 1982*, p. 384; Com-EC, 1981a; Com-EC, 1983b; OECD calculations (excluding milk for suckling calves).

28. USDA II, p. 53. Tibor Barna (1980), *Agriculture Towards the Year 2000: Production and Trade in High Income Countries*, p. xiii, singles out sugar as a commodity where less stress on self-sufficiency in the EC (cf. cotton in the USSR) could most help the agricultural exports of developing countries.

29. House of Lords, 1980a, *EEC Sugar Policy*, especially the evidence of Earl Jellicoe, p. 48. Of the exporting countries in the International Sugar Organisation (which the Community has not joined), and which between them had quotas of about 13 million tons in 1978–79, Australia and South Africa accounted for 2.7 million tons (about 21 percent); all the rest were developing countries. *Ibid.*, p. 69.

30. U.N. medium variant population projections, revised 1978, as used for FAO, 1979 and 1981, *Agriculture: Toward 2000*.

31. *Guardian*, "A hot time ahead for Planet Earth," 19 October 1983, quoting a U.S. Environmental Protection Agency report released in Washington on 18 October 1983 and based on earlier projections by the U.S. National Academy of Sciences. The warming of the

earth would begin in the early 1990s melting the polar icecaps, raising coastal waters and disrupting food production. It would be due to the effects of the past burning of fossil fuels and could be mitigated but not prevented.

32. Com-EC, IBI, 1982; Wayne W. Sharpe, Counsellor for Agricultural Affairs of U.S. Mission to the European Communities, *The Role of Agriculture in Transatlantic Relations*, speech to the International Federation of Margarine Associations, 8 June 1982.

Part II

STRUCTURES AND POLICIES

3 National Agricultures and Policies

Introduction

The history of the common agricultural policy shows the inadequacy of any assessment that fails to take into account national policies. The very bases of the CAP have been shaped by the clash of ambitions and domestic problems of the member states. The last decade has repeatedly made it clear that divergent aspirations in the nations are a crucial obstacle to coherent common goals for the CAP. National divergencies also tend to hold up reforms sought by the Commission and this itself incites individual governments to take matters into their own hands. Such patterns of behavior are part of a wider phenomenon, the increasingly intergovernmental character of the Community. It is the very situation the founding fathers were trying to circumvent, and particularly uncomfortable for the CAP because of the latter's isolation as the one area where policy-making has been significantly Europeanized.

Accordingly, any analysis of agriculture in the European context must give the same attention to the individual policies of the member states as it does to that of the EC as a whole. Policy goals pursued inside the Community can be made and unmade by unilateral actions of the member states carried out with relatively little publicity. Even if one assumes compatibility between these policies separately pursued and those jointly promoted, decisions taken at the national level illuminate the purposes working through the CAP. If, as our quotation from the Mansholt Plan has already suggested, one assumes potential incompatibilities between national and common policies, understanding of those differences can be crucial. The purpose of this chapter is to provide assessments of the national agricultural policies. These assessments, though necessarily brief, have in all cases been developed with the aid of recognized national experts.[1]

Of course, giving prior attention to the policies of the member states assumes a good deal. There are levels other than the state at which divergences of interest can appear. Different sectors of farming, or different income groups among farmers, or different regions, may at times seem more appropriate units for policy-making. Yet the fact is that pressures which, in a more centralized regime, might have united and divided social or political families right across the territory irrespective of national frontiers have, in the less integrated Community, surfaced overwhelmingly as conflicts among member states. Whatever other forces may work within member countries, political demands are channelled into the EC system largely (although not entirely) through governments. The attempts of local authorities to bypass them with the Commission have been no more than embryonic and wherever possible squashed. In practice, then, it is vital to look at national policies as such. Anything else would misinterpret the nature of the CAP.

This chapter accordingly consists of surveys of the agricultural situations of each of the ten member countries of the European Community of 1983 (except Luxembourg). Each survey assesses (1) the major issues, (2) the policy approaches, and (3) the critical factors likely to affect the national outlook in future. The conclusion draws some common threads from the national policies.

France

MAJOR ISSUES

France has always seen herself as a great and rich agricultural country with enormous potential. This was even a consolation in the near-century of weakness from 1870 to 1950. Yet for much of that period, her agriculture was virtually stagnant, growing at well below 1 percent per annum. Productivity was low. The agricultural labor force in 1946 still amounted to about 36 percent of the total working population; France was still partly a peasant country (Mitchell, 1976 p. 659). Revival came only after 1945, with the sharp postwar increase in the demand for food, the emergence of favorable non-agricultural employment opportunities for farmers' children and the resulting creation of incentives for structural change and mechanization. The postwar decades (1948–80) were marked by an average rate of growth of agricultural production close to 3 percent per annum. But spending on food, which rose by 3.7 percent per annum from 1959–64 fell to 2.6 percent per annum in 1970–73 and only 1.4 percent per annum in 1974–77. It is unlikely to exceed 0.6 percent per annum in the next twenty years (Bergmann, 1979, p.5). Accordingly, between 1959 and 1981, the country's self-sufficiency ratio in food climbed from 98 percent to 135 percent (Appendix Tables 2 and 7). France has become the second largest food exporting nation in the world, if EC trade is counted and the fifth largest even if it is not (Appendix Table 4). Farm and food industry exports came to 30 percent of the value of agricultural production (Bergmann, 1983b, pp. 17, 19; and Bergmann, 1983a, pp. 270–86).

Yet it is widely felt in the country that the huge potential for production of France's only major natural resource has still not been fully exploited. Shortages of land, labour or capital are no problem. In the view of Denis Bergmann, French farm output could fairly easily expand, as in 1959–80, at about 3 percent per annum, even with lower real prices and reduced energy consumption. The weakness is mainly in human capital: the process of farmers' selection, their education, the advisory services for them, and the competitive spirit in the sector, are all inadequate. Less than 5 percent of farmers had any professional training in 1975 (Delorme and André, 1983). It will take many years to correct these largely social shortcomings.

A second, connected issue has been the relative weakness of the food processing, manufacturing and distributing industries (Appendix Table 20). This has been overcome to a considerable extent in the past two decades. France's hyper- and super-markets account for 40 percent of all food and sundries sales—a world record (*Financial Times*, 18 June 1979; and Bergmann, 1983a, p. 273). Thus, the food industry in France, as in other EC countries, has been caught between high prices paid to farmers and low prices paid by the modern and highly concentrated distribution system. The resulting profit squeeze has powered the French food industry's search for export markets and for new international ventures.

The future of French agricultural exports is the third and central policy issue, as indeed it has been since the 1950s. France's supply was already outrunning domestic demand in major commodities like cereals in the late 1950s, and she had nearly half the farm land of the Community of Six (even in the Community of Ten she has a third) (*ASC 1981*, pp. 266–67). Cereal-growers, long the dominant group in the farm lobbies, more than tripled their output between 1950 and 1980 (FAO, 1970, p. 86). The Community preference has been highly profitable to them, and their sector still represents three-fifths of exports (Appendix Table 9). However, during the 1970s, the progress of French exports in the EC first slowed down and then, in some key areas, such as sales of sugar and cereals to other EC markets after 1978, actually fell.[2] Exports to non-EC countries have become critically important, and in 1981 (though not 1982) provided one of the most buoyant sectors of foreign trade. This was dramatized by President Giscard in a speech delivered on 16 December 1977 in Vassy when he called agriculture the *"pétrole vert de la France."*

POLICY APPROACHES

French agricultural policy assumes that expansion would contribute to a whole range of desirable goals: improve the balance of payments, alleviate unemployment, combat inflation, prevent the economic and social decline of disadvantaged regions, close the gap between farm productivity in France and in agriculturally more advanced countries of the Community, and, quite simply, develop the country's only major natural resource. It is realized that surpluses, especially of dairy products, should be avoided, but intensive farming, in the Netherlands and elsewhere outside France, is claimed to be the main culprit (Auberger, 1980, pp. 516–26). French increases in cereal output are justified-by-long-term deficits in developing countries and by the need to build up adequate stocks to deal with highly unstable world market conditions.[3]

Given the relative decline in the surplus in trade with the rest of the European Community (Appendix Table 7), policy aims at adding value to these exports by further processing, thus increasing earnings from them. The food processing and manufacturing industry was a beneficiary of prime minister Raymond Barre's measures to decontrol prices in 1978. The sector was to be taken into account in subsidies for agriculture, new funds for research and development, and the special service for the agro-food industry in the Ministry of Agriculture. For basic crops, there is a hankering for long-term public contracts, on the pattern of the Soviet–American agreement on cereals, or the Soviet–New Zealand one on butter. Algeria and Egypt are often mentioned.

As for imports, the French tend to interpret the European preference built in to the Treaty of Rome as meaning straight self-sufficiency. They have long been critical of Britain's special concessions for New Zealand. They would like to find ways to slow up the flow of imported animal feed, maize, cereal substitutes and even oilseeds, to "factory" farms (Bergmann, 1983b, *Financial Times*, 1982d).

Similar preoccupations influence the French approach to the enlargement of the Community to Spain. French cereal and dairy farmers, not least in the southwest, could gain new markets in Iberia. But the large wine and horticulture sectors of the Midi fear Spanish competition. The influence of southern and western smallholders on government policies has grown because they now represent two-thirds of French farmers; and the socialists and communists are traditional rivals for southern votes. The numerous and politically combative wine growers of the Languedoc are a special headache. A family can live quite well off a few hectares of vines. It is virtually impossible to find a substitute offering the same combination of income and employment (Institut d' Economie Régionale du Sud-Ouest, 1979). In July 1982, a law passed Parliament setting up marketing organizations which, in the Commission's eyes, so threatened open frontiers in the Community, especially for wine, that it took the French Government to the European Court (*Financial Times*, 1983d; OECD, 1983b).

The national cast of agricultural policy has been reinforced by the vigorous pursuit of "structural" policies since the *lois d' orientation* of 1960 and 1962. These marked a turning point. Previously, officialdom protected agriculture, by tariffs or price supports, in response to pressure from the farm lobbies. It amounted to rather passive protectionism with overtones of patronage. With the advent of the Fifth Republic and the shrinkage of farming as a society within society, government has promoted food as a whole, including manufacturing, in a positive, expansionist way, as one sector among the many others to which similar treatment is accorded. Before the war, government spending represented under 1 percent of agricultural output. In the 1950s, this climbed to 10 percent; in the 1960s to 12 percent; and since 1973 to 16 percent. About half of this, however, represents social security payments which were totally lacking in the past.[4]

Policy, since 1962, has focused on three broad priorities. The first has been to promote a solid stratum of viable, two-person, medium-sized family farms for social, regional, and environmental reasons. Young farmers must be allowed to acquire or operate farms and settle the countryside prosperously in as large numbers as possible to prevent rural "desertification" (CNASEA, 1980; OECD, 1983b; pp. 27–28, 81; *Financial Times*, 1983c). Second, farmers are encouraged to act collectively, mainly through producer or marketing cooperatives (OECD, 1983b, pp. 73, 83, 85). This makes it possible to reap economies of scale without mergers, increases the bargaining power of farmers against manufacturers and retailers, and helps them improve management and marketing, not least to build up exports. Third, value added along the whole length of the food chain from the farmer to the food manufacturer is to be increased by upgrading products and encouraging effective cooperation among the various stages in the sector.

The instruments for structural reform tend to cluster round the *Crédit Agricole* (the world's biggest deposit bank), producer cooperatives, and the so-called *organisations interprofessionnelles,* which link different sectors of the food chain. All of these have developed principally since the war but have roots in the agricultural depression at the end of the last century. The big change is really that under the Fifth Republic a modernizing state has used old institutions to correct what it regards as the under-exploitation of a major national asset.

The *Crédit Agricole* is a combination of a state bank, a cooperative agricultural bank, which benefits from tax relief, and a bank which lends money to house purchasers on mortgage, that is, what in Britain is called a Building Society. Government funds it to subsidize interest rates to preferential borrowers, such as new farmers or cooperatives, purchasers of land, approved modernizers, and so on. As a result, farm borrowing and indebtedness are high. This makes it hard to cut back incomes for fear of ruining farmers, especially young farmers who are encouraged to join the profession.

The *organisations interprofessionnelles,* mainly developed in the 1960s, bring together farmers, food processors, manufacturers and retailers in virtually every sector—beef, cereals, milk, wine, etc. The organizations may be public or unofficial, but even when unofficial, they have, since 1975, powers to collect levies and, hence, potentially of subsidy.[5] They tend, as a French author has put it, to exercise "monopoly constraints with public backing" and in some of their activities "not to conform to Community law."[6] The system also includes an official agency to promote the exports of agriculture and the food industry, the *Société pour l'expanson des ventes de produits agricoles et alimentaires,* or SOPEXA. This long-established system tends to vertical integration; is largely opaque; makes national investment in, and direction of, farming at least partly autonomous; and, in its planning, has little relation to any abstract model of a "common" market.[7]

Land prices nearly doubled in real terms between 1962 and 1976 (Delorme and André, 1983, p. 331). Official SAFERs (*Sociétés d'Aménagement Foncier et d'Etablissement Rural,* or Land Control and Rural Settlement Boards) have been set up, over most of the country, to buy land, sometimes using their right of pre-emption, and resell it at cost. In areas where they have been most active, SAFERs have controlled up to one-third of the land changing hands. In order to satisfy demand as much as possible, they tend to help create or enlarge medium-sized farms averaging 30 to 40 hectares each, well below the levels where most economies of scale can be reaped (80 hectares for grains, 50 dairy cows). Yet farm concentration in France is in reality already far advanced. Of 1.2 million farms in 1980, 0.2 million produced 60 percent of final output; while at the other end of the scale 0.4 million produced only 8 percent.[8]

Part of the determination French governments bring to the promotion of agricultural interests reflects the fact that those interested in farm property far exceed the proportion of the population working on the land. The Napoleonic code specifies that property should be divided equally among the children on the parent's death. About half the land in France is now rented from family members or other owners of often tiny holdings. As a result, probably over 20 percent of the total population, much of it urban, has an interest in the prosperity of French farming, which adds to the government's care for the sector (*Financial Times*, 16 June 1980).

CRITICAL FACTORS

For political reasons, the Midi's problems now form one of the main planks of the French government's attitude towards the CAP. Their solution will probably remain a critical factor in the 1980s. In particular, France wants to bring more products under the umbrella of full CAP support regimes and the CAP to provide more aid for processed foods before further enlargement. France also wants to place strict limits on Spanish and Portuguese imports, impose a long transition period and introduce safeguard clauses to bar imports if they cause market disruption. The pressures could lead the French government to demand, or resort to, changes such as national support for farm incomes, which would amount to a modification of the CAP.

According to Professor Bergmann, successful long-term expansion will require France, like the rest of the EC, to adjust to lower prices (Bergmann, 1983b, pp. 17, 19; and 1983 a, pp. 270–86). This is inevitable to compete with cheap grain exporters on world markets. The key to the success of such a policy is to be found in innovations and their diffusion to farmers. Many of these innovations will require fundamental advances in knowledge, in plant physiology, bioengineering, and perhaps new methods of fermentation crucial to energy saving. A policy of low-cost expansion must include a big component of research, extension services to farmers, and education. However, France will face major obstacles in improving her relative position. Farmers' organizations want to retain control over extension services and are more concerned with using them to maintain their clientele than with productivity drives; and education is a long-term investment and therefore is not easily taken up by politicians geared to constant electioneering.

As regards structures, many of the necessary policy instruments and institutions already exist in France. Many efficient farms already exist. Yet the chances of major improvement are not good. Effective structural policies would have to be selective. This would eliminate most of the smaller farmers and is resisted, especially in recession. Improved policies would involve more intervention on the land market and such unpopular measures as taxation of capital gains on land, changes in inheritance laws, or strict zoning. No French politician with an instinct for survival would campaign for such reforms. Structural change will continue, but probably at a moderate rate.

Any agricultural expansion in France must be export-oriented, since the domestic market is virtually saturated. This implies the acceptance of a whole new set of disciplines. In particular, increased grain exports can be sustained only if prices are cut. With continued genetic improvements, wheat yields, which are more than double those of the great plains of North America, can continue to rise faster than there. This leaves a big margin to absorb higher fertilizer, machinery, and land costs (Bergmann, 1983b, pp. 17, 19; and 1983a, pp. 270–86). Sugarbeet, wheat and barley prices could well be cut since the incomes of big French crop farmers are high.

Exports of some dairy products to the U.S. which is high-price and highly protectionist in this sector, would make economic sense. The west of France, like other parts of the EC (for example, Ireland) is probably a cheaper producer than the U.S. But American protection is unlikely to be dismantled and other markets seem to have been saturated in the 1970s. France could export more beef, for which there are markets, but this would require improvement in pastures and grazing lands. As for wines, spirits and luxury foods, competition is keen and expansion will require greater dynamism in the food and beverage industries.

Price reductions would have substantial effects on farm incomes, especially in view of the increasing significance of purchased inputs. Average income per farm in France stagnated or fell in real terms in the decade after 1973, although this has not been true of all types of farms. The most reasonable solution would be direct income supplements to the most vulnerable farmers in order to offset, at least partly, the effect of price decreases. This was not so far from the initial attitude of the socialist government in 1981. However, the big farmers are adamant against special policies for smallholders, which would leave them exposed. Both the Giscard and Mitterrand subsidies to French farmers for 1981 and 1982 seem to have been based on no careful economic analysis; to have failed to make a strict distinction between large and small farmers; and to have been decided with little or no reference to Community institutions.

One particular factor that has to be taken into account in France is the tradition of peasant violence occasionally throughout the century and of government placation of it. This could become particularly important in the political shift in Europe from an expansionary agriculture to one which is forced to observe limits. France might yet prove a more radical element in the CAP than declared policies and rhetoric would have one believe.

Germany

MAJOR ISSUES

The expectation at the time of the establishment of the CAP was that West Germany would become the major market for the food exporting member states, especially France. In fact, thanks to high farm prices and a generally successful economic and commercial performance, Germany's own food exports in the Community rose, as a proportion of food imports, from 13 percent in 1960 to 57 percent in 1983 (Appendix Table 7). Already, by the mid-1970s, exports of some important commodities, such as dairy products, were larger than those of imports. The increases in Germany's share of intra-EC food trade were particularly striking for milk (45 to 68 percent of EC internal trade between 1971 and 1977), butter (9 to 26 percent), sugar (5 to 26 percent) and wheat (1 to 11 percent) (Com-EC, 1979c, Tables 31–68). These are all products in surplus in the Community.

The long-run tendency for agricultural production to exceed demand is cumulatively becoming the main problem facing Germany's agricultural policy. A declining population and sluggish income growth imply negligible increases in domestic food demand. One officially commissioned study of 1978 estimated that aggregate demand for agricultural products in Germany would grow by only 0.1 percent per annum until 1985. Output, however, would increase at 1.8 percent per annum even if real prices fell by 1 percent per annum. With a 2 percent annual decline in prices, production would still expand at 1.3 percent per annum (Willer and Haase, 1978). It is not surprising that surpluses are beginning to accumulate. Germany is ceasing for all practical purposes to be a net importer.

Accordingly, the main policy issues in Germany turn around remedies for overproduction. Some German academics think there is a need gradually to withdraw 25 to 30 percent of agricultural land from production by the year 2000 in order to restore and maintain market equilibrium (Weinschenk, 1979, pp. 97–106). Slowing down the rate of growth of production could be achieved by progressively lowering real support prices and compensating the farmers through direct income payments independent of the volume of production (Koester and Tangermann, 1977, pp. 7–31). However, the government argues that it would be difficult to finance such payments and that they would involve too much bureaucracy. The reduction of the arable land area, by physical or economic controls, has not been seriously considered.

It has been suggested that changes in farm structure could increase the flexibility of agricultural output in West Germany. Some projections based on past trends suggest further increases in the average size of farm (which was still only 15.3 hectares in 1980), the disappearance of many small farms, and a reduction in the number of full-time farmers by 38 percent, combined with a decline of total agricultural manpower by 43 percent between 1976 and 1990 (Rehrl, 1979, pp. 81–91). But why this should slow down the growth of output is not clear. Manpower on the land fell at almost 5 percent per annum in the 1970s, but output steadily rose. The strong movement, especially in north Germany, against factory farming in poultry and pig production might somewhat slow up expansion. Environmental protection also militates against the increase in farm size, the more intensive use of chemicals, and pollution through livestock production.

One effect of the success of German agriculture has been the growing export of processed foods. These have recently made considerable inroads in all EC countries, including France. They comprise cheese, meat and fish preparations, bread, biscuits, etc. High quality is the main reason for this penetration of new markets, backed up by outstanding cooperation between farmers, the food industries, the trade and the Central Marketing Organization for German Agricultural Industry (known as CMA), which was set up by the government in 1969 (*Financial Times*, 16 November 1978). No other EC country has anything as comprehensive as the CMA. It has a network of offices around the world, including Austria, Belgium, France, Italy, Japan, the Middle East, the U.K. and the U.S. The most important feature of the CMA's activities is the in-store sales promotion and training for supermarket staff at retailers' own training centers. The success of the German food sector in Community markets is likely to become another important food policy issue because it may present a serious threat to less efficient industries in other Community countries.

German agriculture is remarkable for having more part-timers than any other in the Community. According to 1973 — 74 OECD data, 21 percent of agricultural output, 27 percent of agricultural area, and as much as 55 percent of the total number of farms were accounted for by part-time farmers. Certainly in 1977, only 28 percent of Germans on the land worked full-time (*ASC 1981*, p. 286).

One view of part-time farming is that it is an important stage in the process of gradual reduction of agricultural manpower. Another view holds that part-time farming is the most promising branch of agriculture and that its more widespread adoption would solve many policy problems, including market equilibrium and income parity. The German government takes a third view. It regards part-time farmers as an important component in a "healthy mixture" of all types of activity and encourages industry to move to the countryside, so that part-time industrial work can occupy the spare time of those whose farms are too small for present-day needs. Part-time farming is thus considered as essential to the social fabric and regional balance of the country.

POLICY APPROACHES

It seems there will be no willing shifts in agricultural and food objectives in Germany in the near future. The high-price method of allegedly securing acceptable incomes for farmers has been dogma virtually since the war. Yet average net earnings from farming after 35 years of the policy, nationally and in the CAP, are still much lower than in non-farm occupations—indeed, relatively lower in Germany than in any other Community country (Appendix Table 18). True, the higher incomes of part-time farmers make such comparisons potentially misleading. Because of such considerations, the farm income-parity problem is at last beginning to be seen in a more complex light. Increasing attention is given to income distribution within agriculture and to the impact of price support measures on farms of different kinds and sizes. West German agricultural policy is still far from being an incomes policy geared to assisting poor individual farmers instead of the whole farming sector, but it seems to be moving slowly in this direction.

The main pillar of farm income support continues to be the CAP price policy. Germany, therefore, will go on pressing for relatively high prices under the CAP. It is realized, however, that surpluses will limit the scope for future price increases and can be aggravated by low growth. With its small farms, and often high costs, at least in the south, Germany seems an obvious place for attempts to regulate production by quotas, which preserve incomes but are designed to inhibit the future growth of output. The German Ministry of Agriculture came out in favour of such quotas in the course of the negotiations of 1983–84.

Of recent years, the noneconomic services rendered by agriculture to society have received increasing attention in Germany. A sceptical view is that this is because the economic performance of agriculture has become increasingly controversial. Yet it also needs to be seen in the context of the general movement towards a better recognition of noneconomic services which, in the case of agriculture, concerns the environment and regional balances. The recognition is by no means unanimous. Agriculture's positive contribution to conserving the landscape is contrasted with the negative effects of the use of chemicals and other forms of pollution. Both aspects have already become objects of policy. Legislation on admissible kinds and quantities of chemicals used in agriculture and levels of pollution in livestock production can be expected to become increasingly restrictive. Much thought is given in Germany to the harmonization of such legislation in the Community in order to prevent Germany losing any competitive edge.

Although regional policy in Germany has received much emphasis since the 1960s, it has not been incontrovertibly successful. This has become obvious in the recent years of low growth and recession. It is suggested that farming in disadvantaged regions should be subsidized to ensure an acceptable minimum level of agricultural activity in all regions. The need to sustain agriculture to conserve the landscape in these regions is also stressed. This is already achieved in the hill farmers' program of the EC, but some believe these efforts need to be intensified.

In regard to food processing and manufacturing, the concentration of enterprises will probably continue, although at a slower pace. Many companies feel that conditions in Germany are not particularly favorable for food processing because of relatively high labor costs. Gross value added declined in real terms in the mid-1970s (Appendix Table 20). Future investments in this sector may be made less in Germany than elsewhere in the community or outside it.

CRITICAL FACTORS

The main critical factor in West German agricultural policy will be the level of producer prices. The long-term reduction in real prices would have to be very substantial to bring about a better balance between supply and demand. Yet Germany will probably continue to press for high CAP support prices. Monetary developments may even increase this pressure. The government has given, and will continue to give, high priority to price stability, so that

German inflation will probably remain well below the Community average. As in the past, this could well lead to sporadic revaluations of the Deutschmark against other EC currencies. Germany has always sought compensation for this in export subsidies for her farm sales to other Community states (see Chapter 4, Section "Inflation and Market Shares"); while other Community states, especially France, have pressed for the reduction of the prices and the subsidies. She will be tempted to seek a way out of this dilemma by higher common support prices in European currency units. Paradoxically, therefore, in the short run, the lower the relative rate of inflation in Germany, the stronger could be the pressure to increase CAP prices!

An acute conflict could arise between Germany and the EC countries heavily dependent on agricultural exports, notably France, Denmark, Ireland, and the Netherlands. These countries think that, as Germany has the most prosperous industrial society in the Community, she should be prepared to accept the penetration of her food markets by producers whose costs are probably a great deal lower. But it is inconceivable that the Germans, who do not have any free trade tradition in agriculture, would allow the fabric of their rural society to be undermined by competition. The alternative to MCAs could be income aids. These may be more acceptable to the French and if carefully tailored to that end need not be incompatible with a more complete common market in food. The clear fact is that high prices and high output are increasingly destructive of the common agricultural market, in which Germany has a direct and growing stake as a significant exporter.

Financial considerations are likely to have a crucial influence on the future of German agriculture, but they will clash with political ones. Public outlays on the large German farming population have increased at very high rates and will reach unacceptable levels unless there are fundamental reforms. Farmers strongly resist any restriction of these subsidies. It was estimated in 1978 that income tax concessions to farmers approached DM 2 billion ($1 billion) per annum; concrete proposals for reform were suggested by a group of academics. The minister of finance agreed that most of the concessions to farmers should be abolished, but the minister of agriculture, together with the *Bauernverband* (Farmers' Union), put up a stubborn and largely successful defence. In the end, tax concessions to farmers were only modestly reduced. The law of 1980 reorganizing the income taxation of farmers should, when fully implemented, raise effective taxation by about DM 300 million (*Gutachten* (Opinion) 1978; OECD, 1983b, p. 76).

This demonstrates an important factor in German agricultural and food policy—the strength of the farmers' lobby. This is out of all proportion to their numbers, even with a leftwing government, ostensibly not heavily dependent on the farm vote, as the SPD-FDP coalition was from 1969 to 1982. The farmers' leverage was rooted in the delicate balances of coalition-building and sustenance. The long-standing minister of agriculture, the Bavarian Josef Ertl, in office from 1969 to 1983, had his power base in the farmers' vote. His Free Democratic Party, with only 5 to 7 percent of the popular vote, held (and still holds) the balance between the two main political parties. Had the Social Democrats governed alone, farm policy might possibly have changed, but even this is far from certain. The *Bauernverband* is a large and extremely well organized body, with 900,000 members. As with similar groups in other countries, it has tended to be dominated by the larger farmers, so that in 1972 a breakaway union for part-time farmers was formed: the DBLN (Deutscher Bundesverband der Landwirte in Nebenruf). The Christian Democrats are traditionally the farmers' party, and a Bavarian (this time a CSU-Christian Social Unionist) farmer again became minister of agriculture in 1983.

Structural policies in German agriculture will be another critical factor. Germany will be unwilling to accept any major changes in the present balance between national and Community responsibilities, none at least which changes the balance in the Community's favor. The Federal Republic believes that predominantly national control over structural policy is necessary to enable member governments to adjust to differing national circumstances. The same considerations apply to social policy for agriculture and the government would probably resist any attempt to establish Community control over any major element of this policy. As Germany becomes more and more self-sufficient in agricultural products, it could well press for the increased, and not reduced, independence of national agricultural policies.

This is linked with Germany's increasingly reluctant role as traditional paymaster of the CAP (from which her farmers and, indirectly, her industrialists have greatly gained). In the recession years since 1973, financial rigor in Bonn has built up the resistance to further Community spending. This became politically effective in 1983 in the Anglo-German alliance to limit the CAP budget. The Social Democrats, back in opposition, also made political capital out of Germany's funding of the CAP in 1983, in parallel with their revived questioning of Nato orthodoxy. Just as funding the CAP has ultimately been a price of the special relationship with France, so changes in attitude towards the farm funds will involve political calculations that extend far beyond the CAP.

Belgium

MAJOR ISSUES

Like West Germany, Belgium has traditionally been thought of as a food importing country; and, like Germany, has so far very successfully exploited the CAP to her own advantage. She is one of the countries whose agricultural exports have increased as a proportion of total EC trade between 1960 and 1980 (Appendix Table 8). She is a marginal net importer but prospects for exports will be decisive in the next phase. As with all the smaller EC countries, a very large proportion of the gross combined output of agriculture and food manufacturing is traded. Belgium's food exports are more concentrated on the EC than those of any other member state, even the Netherlands and Ireland (Appendix Table 9).

Proportionately to total output, Belgian farming is second only to that of Denmark in reliance on pork (23.3 percent of agricultural production and 12 percent of agricultural exports in 1980) (*ASC 1981*, pp. 174–75). Belgium's main problem in this major sector will probably be to maintain the present level of output. The dramatic expansion in pig production in the 1960s and early 1970s occurred only in Flanders, and environmental brakes are already operating in this densely populated region. Export prospects are not favorable.

Similarly, only slight increases of output of beef and veal (18.3 percent of agricultural production in 1980), mutton and lamb (0.2 percent), poultry (2.9 percent) and cereals (5.6 percent) are to be expected, especially in view of French and Dutch competition. Domestic food consumption as a whole has already reached a very high level, and may even begin to decline, while prospects for basic food exports to other EC countries do not justify expansion in Belgium. Milk (17.5 percent of total agricultural value added in 1980), only produces occasional surpluses, and Belgium would probably not find them too difficult to eliminate as part of Community-wide efforts.

Belgium's special concern with sugar (4.8 percent of agricultural output and 3.2 percent of agricultural exports in 1980) is likely to continue, since soil and climate are both favorable and the processing industry is highly developed. Any expansion, however, would present serious problems of disposal. Belgium would probably strongly resist any attempts to curtail capacity because of the economic and agronomic importance of sugarbeet, the most reliable crop for rotation with cereals. Belgium is a hard bargainer in international sugar negotiations. She may also oppose larger sugar imports into the Community from the developing countries, but the Lomé Agreement will be observed. If need arises, Belgium would probably vote for maintaining EC sugar intervention stocks or even increasing quotas, though sugar production is located on larger farms, with income well above average. Their political weight is also disproportionate.

POLICY APPROACHES

In spite of poor export prospects for the next two decades, the pressure for an expansion of agricultural production may be heavy because of Belgium's generally depressed economic condition. Unemployment rose to some 15 percent of the labor force by 1984 and may well continue to rise. Though agricultural employment is already exceptionally low—Belgium with less than 3 percent of the workforce on the land is comparable with Britain in this respect—encouraging it to fall faster than is happening naturally would aggravate an already serious labor situation. Moreover, the ability of the farmers to resist cuts is very strong because the chronically strained relations between the Flemish and Walloons make the central government sensitive to pressures coming from any well-organized lobby.

CRITICAL FACTORS

About 80 percent of Belgian farmers are organized in the Farmers' Union, the *Boerenbond* (with a large variety of economic interests and about 100,000 mostly Flemish-speaking members) and its subsidiary Walloon section. This lobby exercises great influence through the Flemish Christian Social Party, without which it is virtually impossible to form a government. All Belgian governments, therefore, are likely to give strong support to the CAP and high producer prices.

To promote their interests, the farmers' lobby draws on several arguments. First, farmers' incomes, though, along with those of the Dutch and Danes, among the top group in the Community (Table 4.3), lag behind those in other sectors and have even tended to fall in relative terms (Appendix Table 18). Since the Agricultural Act of 1963, however, the government has been legally committed to income parity. Second, except during the 1972–74 turmoil and following the 1975–76 drought, food prices in the 1970s rose at lower rates than consumer prices in general. Third, producer prices in Belgium do not greatly affect food prices to the consumer. What the housewife pays is more dependent on distribution margins. Fourth, the share of food products in total exports has been rising. Finally, under the CAP, Belgium has, in relation to gross value added in agriculture, been a net beneficiary from the Community's budget to an extent exceeded only by Ireland and the Netherlands (Appendix Table 13). In 1981, however, this ceased to be the case.

Belgium will continue to be a strong supporter of the CAP so long as it provides high producer prices, although increasing competition in the traditional and new lines of agricultural exports may present a continuous and ultimately insurmountable challenge to such a policy. Any new production and export drive is likely to be mainly in the area of high quality dairy and horticultural products, as well as delicatessen and other processed and manufactured foods. The high dependence of Belgian horticulture (13 percent of agricultural production in 1980) on energy supply could become a critical factor for the greenhouse industry, if world energy prices were ever to leap forward again. The inclusion of Greece and eventually Spain and Portugal in the EC could also mean unwelcome competition for the Belgian horticultural sector. Yet this competition should not be overemphasised: non-edible horticulture products, such as flowers, could expand to replace increasing imports.

The Netherlands

MAJOR ISSUES

Few would challenge the claim of the Dutch to be the economic and technical leaders in Community agriculture. For their country's size, they might even claim to be the most successful food producers in the world. Yields are among the highest anywhere (FAO, 1980b, pp. 229-31). Incomes are much the highest per farmer in the Community, even though they still do not reach the average of incomes in other walks of life in the Netherlands themselves (Appendix Table 18). Even in the depressed 1970s, the growth of output, as measured by gross value added, was outstanding, and again the highest in the Community.[9] All this is perhaps summed up in the astonishing fact that, if one includes their exports to their EC partners, the Netherlands are, despite their size, one of the world's largest agricultural exporters, a short neck behind France.[10] In many ways, the Dutch set the standard by which other Community farmers are compelled, however unwillingly, to judge their own performance.

The Dutch have achieved these results by developing a resolutely mercantile and industrial agriculture. Exports represent the highest proportion of GDP of any country of the Community except Ireland and have traditionally been concentrated on Western Europe itself (Appendix Table 9). Three-quarters of Dutch food exports are to outlets within the Community, a proportion exceeded only by Belgium. The Dutch have also concentrated on high value output. The industry is heavily concentrated on three sectors where this can be achieved: horticulture (30 percent of national agricultural value added in 1980), dairy products (28 percent) and the cereal-based livestock products, pigs, poultry, and eggs (26 percent). Costs are cut by importing, with little or no duty, vast amounts of cereal substitutes and oilseeds to provide the bulk feed and proteins for livestock at costs EC grains cannot match. In 1981, the Netherlands imported the equivalent in animal feed of 113 percent of their own total agricultural area. The Netherlands is the country of factory farming par excellence. Whereas the average land area of farms is low, the size, in value of output is, with those of the British, the highest in the Community (*ASC 1981*, p. 293).

Hot-house agriculture could become very expensive in the Netherlands if energy costs were to rise again relative to other prices. Dutch fuel subsidies to the greenhouses have been a source of contention in the Community especially since the second energy crisis of 1979. An agreement with the European Commission of July 1982 provided for their phasing out after 31 March 1983 (*ASC 1982*, p. 154; OECD, 1983b, p. 68). Dutch horticulture is heavily specialized in a few mainline commodities, flowers, lettuce, tomatoes, and cucumbers. Mediterranean producers have the advantages of better climate and possibly of lower wages, but they are less close to the main markets and commercially and technically less well organized. The Italians have failed to oust Dutch tomatoes from the northern European markets although average Dutch selling prices are between one and a half and two times as high.[11]

Water transport has added to Dutch success. The route from Rotterdam, up the Rhine and along the canal systems branching out from it, is the cheapest for bulk transport; and there has been an increasing concentration of Community pig breeding along these routes.[12] Pork and poultry, often combined, provide far and away the highest farm incomes. It is no accident that the Netherlands and Belgium both have a high concentration of these lines and high average farm incomes. There has also been a rapid concentration of both dairy and pig herds, especially during the 1970s (*ASC 1982*, pp. 295-301). The Dutch are very alert to any developments inside the Community to restrain the import of cereal substitutes.

POLICY APPROACHES

The Dutch are the first to recognize that the CAP, which they have profoundly influenced, has been of decisive importance for the expansion of their food exports. The CAP removed the obstacles that might have hampered Dutch access to the German market, in particular. Moreover, because of the high productivity of the sector, the Netherlands have benefitted from Community farm supports almost as much per head as Ireland, Denmark, and Belgium, all of which have much smaller populations (Appendix Table 13). The loss of free access to EC markets would be a disaster.

A very important part in the capacity of the Dutch to exploit their opportunities has been played (as in Denmark) by the sophisticated organization of the sector. The foundation has been the excellent system of farm education, which starts in the school and culminates in the agricultural university of Wageningen. In the early 1970s, the Netherlands had approximately seven extension workers per thousand farmers, as against two in Britain, which also had a relatively advanced agriculture. Many of the advisers are highly specialized (Szczepanik, 1976, p. 122).

The strong structure of institutions has been mainly regulated in recent times by the Industrial Organization Act of 1950 (Sociaal-Economische Raad, 1976, p. 14.; 1966, pp. 33–34; OECD, 1973). It set up, interalia, Commodity Boards (*Produkt Schappen*), which, through a vertical structure, cover all stages in the producton, processing, manufacturing, and distribution of a given chain of food products. Thus, the Meat and Livestock Commodity Board covers livestock production; the trade in live animals; the wholesale trade in meat; livestock products; butchering, and the retail trade in meat products and preserved meats. This type of arrangement creates close institutional links between agriculture and the downstream sectors, including the food industry. There are fourteen such boards, which together provide comprehensive policies covering virtually all agricultural and food products. In addition, there are Industry Boards. Unlike a Commodity Board, an Industry Board is horizontal in character, covering only one branch of industry. At present, there is one Industry Board for Agriculture (*Landbouwschap*) and several for various branches of food processing, manufacturing, and distribution.

Inside this highly corporatist structure, Dutch farmers exercise a powerful influence on policy. This was particularly in evidence when the CAP was established (de Bruin, 1978, especially Chs. XI and XIII). Their influence has been enhanced by the fact that, until recently, the prime minister's powers have been weak compared to those of the individual ministries. Coalition government—the norm in the Netherlands—has reinforced this tendency (de Bruin, pp. 353–57 and especially 358–60). Even when the mainly urban socialists led coalitions, the basis of the deal with the parties to their right was often to give these a relatively free hand in agriculture. This somewhat resembles the situation in Germany.

Within this highly structured framework, Dutch agriculture can carry collective controls to significant lengths. For instance, since 1973, farm enlargement has been inhibited by informal limits operated through the producer cooperatives and the food processors with whom many farmers have production contracts. The aim has been to keep small farmers going. The same preoccupation is visible in "state action." A Guaranteed Special Farm Credit Scheme was introduced from April 1981 to May 1982 to bail out younger farmers who had recently acquired a farm and were caught out by rising interest rates on their debts. The Agricultural Land Transaction Act of 1981 has given the existing Land Offices the duty to vet all transfers of land and the right to pre-empt land in the public interest. The State may also acquire land to lease it out at a rent of 2.5 percent of the purchase price to farmers' children, tenants and young farmers unable to raise funds from other sources (OECD, 1983b, pp. 73,81).

Sales of farm products are coming increasingly under the control of the food processing industries. Integration has become particularly marked in broilers, pork, and veal. Nearly all the production of poultry, veal, and potatoes and half of the pork was sold in 1981 under contract, not on the open market. However, a substantial part of farm produce is traded through cooperatives usually created by the producers themselves. In 1981, they accounted for about 90 percent of the market for milk and about 60 percent for cereals and sugarbeet. In the early 1970s, more than half the supply of feed, 70 percent of fertilizers and 30 percent of agricultural machinery, were sold through cooperatives (OECD, 1973; *ASC 1982* p. 303)

CRITICAL FACTORS

The major problem facing the Netherlands is the danger posed for their traditional reliance on West European outlets by the growing self-sufficiency of all the member states of the EC. EC demand for the Netherlands' standard, low-priced products will clearly decline. The prevailing view in the Netherlands is that long-term adjustment will have to be towards more expensive products such as frozen and dried vegetables, cheese, and meat (especially veal), confectionery, etc. Shifts in quality will not suffice, however; new outlets will have to be sought. This will be a challenge proportionate to the traditional degree of Dutch concentration on European markets. There will have to be a substantial redeployment to new customers and this must take time. The best prospects are those countries which have begun to improve their diets in the past fifteen years: the Soviet bloc, the newly industrializing countries, or the oil exporting ones. In the short run, however, these markets are likely to be much less buoyant than they were in the 1970s.

An export strategy cannot succeed in a vacuum as regards the Community itself. Three issues are especially important: the possible extension of the Community to embrace Iberia, which affects horticulture; the future of imports of animal feed, crucial to livestock production; and the control of surpluses, especially but not only in the dairy sector.

The Dutch seem less concerned with the risks of direct competition from Greece, Portugal, and Spain than with the indirect dangers arising from French and Italian responses to the challenge of the new Mediterranean members. Their attention has focussed on the fear that pressure from France and Italy for special protection against Spain in particular could set off a chain reaction of barriers to trade within the common market in food. The danger was equally visible in French restrictons on the trade in pork early in 1984. As the Dutch are the biggest intra-EC food exporters, this would be highly detrimental to their interests.

The expansion in the past decade of the pork and poultry sector has been based to a considerable extent on feed imported at prices far below those of Community cereals. The signs that France and—from 1983—even the Commission itself may contest this system of industry, in the name of the Community preference for Community products, are certain to lead to the strongest possible Dutch resistance.

Finally, there is widespread recognition in the Netherlands of the need to control dairy surpluses, but how to do so is another matter. The Dutch seem set against reductions in real farm prices in this as in other sectors. They also oppose quotas based on standard yields per cow or hectare, on the grounds that this would prevent the smaller, less efficient and poorer farmers from improving their performance and incomes. They would agree to a reduction in the numbers of dairy herds, provided there were suitable subsidies, income supplements or financial incentives to shift to alternative lines of activity. But what lines offer sufficient prospects? Generally, it is a safe assumption that any change in policy will come about as a result of external rather than domestic pressures.

Italy

MAJOR ISSUES

Italy is the only EC founder country in which, under the CAP, growth of food imports for a time exceeded that of food exports (Appendix Table 7).[13] Accordingly, the main agricultural policy issue in Italy in the 1970s became the reconstruction and modernization of the sector. All political parties agreed it should, as in 1959, satisfy 90 percent and not, as in the early 1970s, less than 80 percent of Italy's total demand for agricultural products (Appendix Table 2). The aim was to reduce the heavy strain on the balance of payments. In 1980, agriculture accounted for about one-third of Italy's trade deficit.

Italy also has to cope with the perennial problem of the underdevelopment of the South—the *Mezzogiorno*—and the hilly "disadvantaged" areas scattered all over the country. In 1977, 70 percent of the small holdings of the EC-9 (between 1 and 5 hectares) were located in Italy, as well as 44 percent of the people working on the farms, even though Italy had less than 19 percent of the Community's agricultural land. In 1980, 24 percent of the labor force still worked on the farms in the Mezzogiorno against 9 percent in northern Italy and an average for the rest of the EC-9 of under 6 percent. (Wade, 1982; Com-EC, *ASC 1982*, p. 282-83,290-91).

This agricultural duality is also reflected in the two different types of commodities produced: "northern" ones (cereals, sugarbeet, meat, dairy, etc.) and "southern" (fruit, vegetables, olive oil, wine, etc.). Until 1978, the CAP subsidised southern products on balance substantially less than northern ones. This hurt Italy on both the budget and trade. She felt, as the poorest of the founder states, that she should be a major beneficiary of the Community's farm funds. In 1978, she was actually a net contributor. On trade, the heavily supported northern commodities constitute Italy's main food imports, while the more lightly protected and subsidized southern ones represent 70 percent of her farm exports. As a result, in 1978 in particular, Italy was substantially in deficit in the Community on both farm fund and food trade accounts (Appendix Table 14). In the later 1970s, for the first time she expressed disgruntlement with the Community, hitherto accepted as an article of faith.

To improve the trade balance, a fall in CAP prices for northern foods might seem to be of interest to Italy. In practice, this has not been the case. Even in Italy, northern products account for half of total output (Table 4.1), more than half of consumption, and virtually the whole food deficit. Increasing self-sufficiency in these products has therefore been the priority and high prices one of the instruments. In the Community, Italy has concentrated on obtaining more subsidies for southern products and aid for "structural" investment, above all in the *Mezzogiorno*. She has been so successful since 1978 that, by 1983, southern products attracted proportionately about the same support from the farm funds as their relative weight in total EC output.[14]

Italy has failed to exploit external markets for processed foods, although some multinational enterprises (especially Unilever) have made considerable progress. Expansion of this part of Italy's food system should, therefore, become another important policy issue.

POLICY APPROACHES

In order to lay down a long-term program for the reconstruction and modernization of the entire agricultural and food system, Italy's political parties, in an unusual display of unanimity, agreed on a series of financial measures under the so-called *Legge Quadrifoglio* ("Shamrock Law") passed by Parliament in December 1977. The *Quadrifoglio* envisaged that over a period of ten years (1978 to 1987) the total sum of Lire 6,970 billion (6.2 percent of GAP in 1976) would be made available for agricultural development, divided as follows: irrigation 43 percent, animal husbandry 15 percent, hill and mountain agriculture 13 percent, horticulture 12 percent, forestry 12 percent, Mediterranean tree cultivation 3 percent, viticulture 3 percent. (Agricoltura, 1977). Of the largest item, irrigation, 60 percent was reserved for the

Mezzogiorno, which was also due to benefit more than the northern regions under other headings.

The *Quadrifoglio* was conceived as the long-term financial basis of a comprehensive five-year plan for agriculture and food. The draft plan envisaged a 2.5 percent annual increase in agricultural output (3.4 percent in cereals and livestock, and 1.5 percent in other products) in order to achieve 90 percent self-sufficiency in ten years' time. It also emphasized the importance of irrigation, recovery of about 400,000 hectares of abandoned agricultural land by 1981, structural improvements (larger and more mechanized units), lowering of production costs through technology (especially seed control and better veterinary services), expansion of agricultural credit, promotion of cooperation societies, and marketing improvements.

Various political events prevented the government from completing the proposed plan and obtaining its approval by Parliament. Towards the end of 1978, a truncated version (*stralcio*) of the *Quadrifolgio* was adopted. The succession of weak coalition governments since then has made it difficult to see any firm prospects for a food and agricultural policy in Italy. The Italian government has also been reducing the functions of the Ministry of Agriculture in Rome and handing some of them over to the regional administrations, which do not have close contact with each other and are not all of equal caliber. The devolution law, which handed these powers to the regions, passed in 1975 has still not taken effect in many of them. Nevertheless, the regions seem already to play some part in subsidizing agriculture, including food exports.[15] In the long run, regional devolution may considerably weaken Italian influence in reshaping the CAP.

CRITICAL FACTORS

In any case, the influence of Italy on the CAP has been more limited than might have been expected of a country for which agriculture is so important. The weakness of Italian governments has been reflected in an absence of effective strategy in agriculture (as in other fields). Italy has pursued high price policies de facto to encourage the output of northern products for which, for obvious reasons, she is less well placed than the regions on the other side of the Alps. Nonetheless, Italy has not escaped deficits, in meat and probably more ineradicably in dairy products. As for southern products, such as fruits and vegetables, the Italian negotiators had thought, when the CAP was established, that their farmers would be able to exploit their climatic advantages. In the event, mainly because of marketing failures, they failed to seize their opportunities. Most spectacularly, the Spaniards, from outside the EC, have maintained a major presence on the North German, Benelux, and British markets for citrus fruits.

Despite these policy weaknesses, Italian self-sufficiency in food rose substantially during the 1970s and by 1981 the level of 1959 had been once more attained (Appendix Table 2). This seems to be mainly because the rate of growth of consumption has fallen off sharply (Appendix Table 1). If recent trends, quite opposed to those of the boom decades, were to persist, Italy would close the import gap in most products and eventually become, like the other Community states, a net exporter.

In fact, one of the problems now beginning to loom, as the Community switches funds to the Mediterranean, is oversupply in new sectors. A prime example is the attempt to help fruit and vegetable growers by aiding the canning industry (especially tomatoes). In 1978, farm fund expenditure on this item was negligible. By 1983 it had multiplied twentyfold to 700 million ECUs, over 4 percent of the farm budget (Com-EC, 1983a, p. 26). Oversupply could even result from the structural reforms envisaged in the various Mediterranean farm development programs. The Pizzutti report of the European Commission estimated in 1976 that, if fully implemented, the plans to increase the area of irrigated land in the *Mezzogiorno* would increase the region's productive capacity by at least 20 percent—no small prospect for an area comprising two-fifths of Italy. Plans to renew the Sicilian vineyards would increase the output of wine by 10 percent, compounding a surplus which the Community could well do without (Com-EC, 1977). It can be, and frequently is, argued with a shrug and a smile, that Italian plans on paper and on the ground do not necessarily resemble each other. But if so, why spend the money?

Despite gains, Italy does have major structural problems. In the mid–1970s she had nearly 70 percent of the EC-9's smallholdings under 5 hectares, of the farms requiring less than half of one worker's time, and of units returning the lowest category of incomes. Yields in the *Mezzogiorno* tend to be around half those of the most productive northern provinces, which themselves tend to be lower than on the other side of the Alps (*ASC 1979*, pp. 330–31). In wide stretches of the mountains and the south, there is little or no alternative employment. The unique if marginal increase in the number of Italian smallholdings between 1975 and 1977 (the latest year for which figures are available for the country) could be a sign of this (*ASC 1982*, p. 290-91). These vulnerabilities are underlined by the prospect of enlarging the Community to Iberia. One report has come to the tentative conclusion that 65,000 jobs may be at stake in agriculture (Com-EC, 1981c, p. 98). This is modest in a workforce on the land of over 3 million, but comes on top of general unemployment and underemployment which is already high and which in any case, may be underestimated. Although, on political grounds, Italy favors the enlargement, she is rightly worried by the threat Spain could pose to her exports of Mediterranean products. Spain has shown herself to be commercially much better organized, especially in citrus fruits. The Italians have argued that they should have price supports high enough to protect their farmers from Spanish competition. The northern member states and the Commission see no reason why new surpluses of unmanageable proportions should be generated.

This dilemma is pushing the Community to new concepts for dealing with the Mediterranean. Any attempt to support agriculture across-the-board in order to maintain employment or incomes in the poorer regions tends to perpetuate the causes of poverty and underemployment by encouraging activities that cannot hope to offer good returns and are bound in the long run to continue to decline. This explains the gradual shift, in the regional and agricultural policies of the Commission, and to some extent the Community, towards "integrated" development programs for poorer areas. In these policies, agriculture figures as one element in a palette of measures designed to reduce regional disparities and not as an isolated focus of attention. This is not easy in many areas, given the lack of industry and services. But new industries or services may offer new prospects; and the strategy in itself offers a better-balanced analysis of many of the broad-based difficulties which the Community has approached too narrowly through the CAP.[16]

United Kingdom

MAJOR ISSUES

Britain is, on the whole, at the furthest extreme from Italy, with its mass of small farms. The main issues facing British agricultural policy derive from the fact that it was dominated for a long time not by landed, but by consumer interests. The early start in industrialization and the consequent profit for Great Britain in fostering exports of manufactures against imports of cheap food for the urban majority allowed no particular preference for domestic food producers. The British food system thus developed within a more competitive framework than that of most other EC countries. Moreover, when cheap grains began to flood in from the Americas, Australia, and Russia in the 1880s, British farms were already relatively large. There was not the interest of the Dutch or Danes in giving smallholders a livelihood by building up a livestock industry for export. Britain remained until the 1930s, when protection began to be reintroduced, and even later, the food importer par excellence.

The result has been a contraction of the agricultural sector (to about 2.5 percent of GDP and total employment in 1982) consisting of capital intensive and, by European standards, large units (by far the biggest in area and roughly equal with the Dutch in turnover).[17] Imports led to a low degree of self-sufficiency in agricultural products (61 percent in 1973, as shown in Appendix Table 2 though that was well up from the 33 percent level of the early 1930s): They also engendered a relative lack of integration between domestic agricultural production and most food manufacturing activities; as well as a much smaller place for agricultural cooperatives than in the EC countries with larger numbers of smallholders, and the development of a competitive food industry with a commercial orientation. The socio-economic problems of marginal producers, except hill farmers, are a minor consideration in Britain. The interests represented are those essentially of large farmers.

The postwar expansion of agriculture was organized under a policy which was an ingenious juxtaposition of past free trade and incipient protection. The aim was to increase domestic self-sufficiency in food while keeping down costs of feed for livestock producers, maintaining low consumer prices, along traditional lines, and helping to keep down industrial costs (since food prices played a large part in wage negotiations). This was done by freely importing "cheap" food at low international market prices, and raising the prices paid to British farmers by government subsidies on output—"deficiency payments"—which supplemented the returns they could get by selling on the competitive domestic markets. In 1956 British subsidies per farmer—UK farmers being relatively few, and Britain relying on subsidies more than price supports—were the highest in Western Europe (Table 1.10). When Britain joined the Community, the deficiency payments had to be abandoned in favor of CAP prices paid by consumers—on average some 20 percent higher than U.K. subsidized farm prices. The memory of the national system lingered on and was used recurrently as a stick with which to beat the CAP by the opposition to the Community. This was specially strong in the Labour left, which saw the Community, at least until 1983, as a major obstacle to a thoroughgoing Socialist Britain. Under both the national and CAP systems, domestic production has increased vigorously.

When the U.K. joined the EC in 1973, she was faced with the possibility of a sharp increase in food prices due to adaptation to higher CAP levels at a time when her own inflation rate was one of the highest, and her economic growth rate one of the lowest, in the Community. The U.K. government sought to keep consumer food prices low. In the event, food prices to the consumer (including manufacturing and distribution) rose less than the general consumer index even during the 1970s, when British producer prices were raised to CAP support levels on top of other increases.

However, even in the inflationary mid-1970s, the determination to stimulate home production was also evident. The Labour government's White Paper of 1975 was, significantly, entitled *Food from Our Own Resources* (U.K., 1975). Then, and since, the retention of the monopoly Milk Marketing Board, the resistance to imports of liquid milk, national subsidies to dairy and sugarbeet farmers, and frontier protection for poultry (condemned by the European Court) have all encouraged home production.

After Germany, the UK is the largest EC food importer from third countries (Appendix Table 4), Thus, from 1978, the U.K. began to contribute, primarily through import levies and customs duties, more to EC revenue than any other member state except Germany. But, because her agriculture is relatively small, she obtained proportionately less than any other from the Community's farm budgets. As a result, the budget began to take the front of the stage in British attitudes to the CAP as soon as the country became a full-fledged member (at the end of the transition period) in 1979. In May 1980, the other member states reluctantly agreed to a three-year formula to refund a large part of the British net contribution to the EC budget. In 1983, the reappearance of this problem coincided with that of the running out of the Community's tax funding system as set up in 1970. Britain linked agreement on the future funding of agriculture to a long term solution of its financial problem, as well as to various CAP reforms, and thus largely precipitated the 1983-84 crisis of the Community.

POLICY APPROACHES

Once the Conservative government came into office in May 1979, the producer orientation of U.K. food policy became increasingly explicit. Between 1974 and 1980, the volume of British food exports increased by 95 percent while food imports diminished by 6 percent. Britain still had the lowest total self-sufficiency ratio in the Community, but between 1973 and 1981 it climbed more than that of any other member state, from 61 percent to 77 percent (Appendix Table 2). In these conditions, the long-term U.K. strategy has appeared to be to limit liabilities to the Community budget while pressing for common prices high enough to stimulate British agricultural production and raise national self-sufficiency.

A study undertaken by the U.K. Ministry of Agriculture in 1979 suggested for 1975–83 possible increases in GAP of 18 percent at constant real prices and of 14 percent at an annual 1 percent fall in real prices (U.K., 1979). These increases represented respectively, annual compound growth rates of 2.1 percent and 1.6 percent (and closely resemble German estimates). Assuming continuing low growth in U.K. demand (Appendix Table 1)—say 0.3 percent per annum, an annual increase of GAP of 1.6 percent from the level of self-sufficiency reached in 1981 would result in virtually complete self-sufficiency by the year 2000 (Appendix Table 2). The implication is a large shift either in foreign trade (reduction in U.K. imports and expansion of exports) or in resource utilization and input composition in British agriculture, or a combination of both. The establishment in 1983, as in France and Germany, of a central marketing organization, "Food from Britain," to develop marketing at home and sales abroad, has underlined a preoccupation with food exports that contrasts, symbolically, and in practice, with 140 years of history since the repeal of the (protectionist) Corn Laws in 1846.[18]

Two other aspects of this production policy should be mentioned. First, even before the U.K. accession to the EC, the fiscal and political limitations on government expenditure led to a restraint in deficiency payments and a shift towards market support for British agriculture (via import control measures). After the full alignment of U.K. and EC prices in 1979, the problem of sensitivity to future rises in food prices diminished because their relative rate of increase slowed down. Restrained annual negotiated price changes are thus quite consistent with a British expansionary policy. Second, the economic and political role of the U.K. in the world will probably continue to diminish and there will be some shift in preference towards domestic (U.K.) supplies in uncertain international markets. These two factors are likely to reduce the pressure in the U.K. for access to its market by third-country exporters. Moreover, since the U.K. resistance to the CAP partly springs from the changes it entailed, that element should also diminish in time. The accommodation of British agricultural and food policy objectives within a revised CAP might be easier in the future.

Because of the marked structural differences between agriculture in the U.K. and in the rest of the EC, the proposals for CAP reform suggested elsewhere in the Community are frequently alien to British producers. For example, preferential treatment of marginal farmers, by quotas or income aids, are opposed by U.K. producers, few of whom are marginal by EC standards, and who accordingly fear discriminatory constraints on their production. Similarly, EC pressure to encourage the use of more indigenous products in food manufacturing has also been resisted by U.K. enterprises, which are used to input mixes and technologies substantially based on imports from outside the EC.

CRITICAL FACTORS

While British public discussion on the CAP has expressed widespread resistance to a system seen as alien and expensive, British policy has in fact used the opportunity to complete the transition from the free food imports appropriate for a dominant exporter of manufactures (1846–1933) to a high degree of self-sufficiency, not unconnected with the country's industrial decline. In retrospect, the CAP has been made to serve what seems a long-term strategy that has not been reflected in the controversies surrounding the CAP and "deficiency payment" systems of agricultural support which filled discussions during the 1960s and 1970s. Britain has also had more influence than any other member state in bringing the CAP crisis to a head because of her refusal to underwrite the financing of the system.

How far can Britain push her farm interests nationally without undermining the CAP and, with it, the balance of interests in the Community and her own non-farm investment in the European policy? How far can Britain's national expansion go without revealing the limits of her room for maneuver on the farms themselves? So far, as a net importer in an expansionary CAP she has not had to face these dilemmas. They will not be so easy to avoid in the future. If Britain continues to expand irrespective of the effects on the CAP, she will be, for example, exporting cereals in a free-for-all against rival EC as well as traditional exporters. If she cannot do so, her farmers will have to accept restraints on output. If these come in response to CAP, not British national, priorities, she will have to apply restraints sooner rather than later. Can the short-term advantages of the net importer be exploited much longer? The Milk Marketing Board has carried out a number of research studies in dairy farming which questioned whether low input systems might not provide better returns in a world of limits than high intensity-high yield production (Hughes, 1978). These issues are not, of course, confined to Britain, which may be better placed than some other countries to solve them. They nevertheless imply a second sharp change of context and focus in a relatively short time, and choices with political as well as social and economic overtones.

Another factor determining the future course of British food policy is likely to be the long-term shift in the proportion of value added and employment from the agricultural to the post-farm sector. At present, of the total labor force engaged in the agro-food system (from the farm input industries to the consumer), probably only about one-fifth is employed directly in agriculture. The whole food system is becoming more controlled through computer technology which, inter alia, tends to a more sensitive translation of consumer demands upstream and a better adjustment of inputs at various stages of the system. Moreover, the sluggishness of demand has increased and will continue to increase competition, both horizontally (among retail food distributors and among food manufacturers) and vertically (between retail food distributors and manufacturers). By the same token, any increases in demand tend to be directed towards the nonagricultural components of food consumption, that is, the post-farm elements which already account for over 52 percent of U.K. household expenditure. All this is likely to lead to further competition and concentration in production and distribution, upstream contracts with agriculture, and changing bargaining relationships between the component sectors of the system. As a result, the focus of food policy may shift from the farm to the food manufacturing enterprise. Curiously enough, however—and in this the food system reflects the special British situation in other industrial sectors—there has been far less integration of the various parts of the food chain in the U.K. than in, say, the Netherlands, Denmark, and Germany and a far less explicit emphasis on food policy than in the past twenty years in France.

Ireland

MAJOR ISSUES

Ireland more nearly resembles the southern EC countries than her northern neighbors in her heavy dependence on agriculture. In 1980, agriculture still accounted for over one-tenth of GDP and nearly one-fifth of the national labor-force.[19] If one adds food manufacturing and the industries supplying agriculture, the food system generated nearly 30 percent of the national wealth in 1970 and employed a commensurate proportion of the labor force, which was 2½ to 3 times the EC averages at the time.[20] The agricultural self-sufficiency ratio, which rose from 184 percent in 1973 to 202 percent in 1981 (Appendix Table 2) was much higher than that of any other EC country except Denmark. Sixty percent of the country's gross agricultural output is exported; and agricultural sales accounted for nearly two-fifths of all exports in 1980. The low import content of agricultural products exported means that agriculture's contribution to the balance of trade is greater than even this suggests: "Agricultural land is the country's major natural resource" (Inter-Departmental Committee on Land Structure Reform, p. 21).

Unlike the southern member states, Ireland is more strongly focussed on cattle than any other member of the Community (except Luxembourg). She has "an equable climate with adequate rainfall and soils which enable grass to grow lusher and for more days in the year than anywhere else in Europe" (Hicks, 1977). Ireland with a low population, also has comparatively plentiful

) percent more than the whole of Benelux, which has over
ation. Pasture covers 80 percent of the agricultural area
–75 and 286–87; Ryan, 1983); and beef and milk account
t of production and about the same proportion of exports.
both advantages and disadvantages. On the one hand,
ably have a comparative advantage over any other EC
e in a competitive market for milk and beef. A comparison
uction in specialized dairy farms in Britain and Ireland in
low-cost, low-yield Irish methods were over twice as
are at the time as high-cost, high-yield British ones. The
herd size in Ireland reduced but did not cancel the Irish
s, 1978). On the other hand, climate has tended to specialize
or where demand is sluggish, surpluses restrict the prospects
es have recently been among the lowest (*ASC 1982*, pp. 116–
18).

The environment for Irish agriculture was dramatically changed by Ireland's accession to the EC in 1973. The sector had struggled through the 1960s in adverse circumstances, familiar to all food exporters in that period of oversupply. Between 40 and 50 percent of gross agricultural production (GAP) was exported—four-fifths of it to the United Kingdom. Preferential access was available there, yet returns were unattractive and other openings severely limited. Farmers' incomes were under continuous pressure. Between 1960 and 1970, government expenditure on farm price-supports grew from 3.6 percent to 19.5 percent of aggregate farm incomes (2.6 percent of GDP). Even so, average per capita incomes fell by 7.3 percent over the decade in comparison with average industrial wages at a time of good general growth. (Sheehy, 1980, pp. 297–310; investment figures, *ASC 1982*, p. 183).

After accession to the EC, the shares of the U.K. in Ireland's exports diminished from 61 percent in 1972 to 39 percent in 1980, while that of other EC countries increased from 16 percent to 30 percent. Real prices received by farmers rose 45 percent between 1971 and 1978 (Sheehy, 1980). Payments from the Community farm funds, per head of population, were higher than for any other country.[21] Per capita real incomes of farmers grew by 63 percent. It has been argued that gains made under the CAP up to 1978 increased total Irish GNP by as much as 15 percent above what it would otherwise have been (Attwood, 1979; and Ryan, 1983).

It is curious that the pace of agricultural expansion (about 3 percent per annum in 1960–80) was not noticeably affected by EC membership, except in milk and to a small extent in barley for animal feed. The Dairy Export Board met the challenge of new markets and greatly increased production—only a minimal use of intervention occurred. However, the fragmentation of the beef industry prevented any significant progress being made either in the production or the marketing of the country's principal product (Sheehy, 1980).

Since 1978, the Irish farmer's love affair with the CAP has suffered rude shocks. Output, which had risen 20 percent in volume between entry into the EC and 1978, suddenly lost impetus and fell 3.5 percent by 1981. This was felt

Table 3.1   Distribution of Irish Farms According to Given Levels of Income Compared
to the Average Gross Wage for a Non-agricultural Worker in the Region
(in percentages)

	Below 80 percent	Between 80 and 120 percent	Above 120 percent
1978-79	46	21	33
1979-80	86	8	6

Source: Com-EC, *Agricultural Situation in the Community, 1982 Report*, p. 119.

the more keenly because the old low-input system of peasant husbandry changed at great speed in the boom of the mid-1970s. In 1976, purchased inputs represented only 33.7 percent of the value of production; by 1981 they had risen to 48.4 percent, above France and within shouting distance of the economic leaders in Benelux, Britain, Denmark, and Germany (Table 1.9). Land prices (a sure sign of a boom in the sector) tripled in real terms between 1969–71 and 1978 (Sheehy, 1980). Irish farmers were now much more vulnerable to the second energy crisis, which broke in 1979. The results were immediately visible in farm incomes (Table 3.1).

This abrupt return to earth was followed in 1983 by the Commission's proposals to bring Community production under control. These raised a storm of protest in Ireland. First, any program of restraint would put an end to the short-lived hopes of prosperity through expansion generated after 1973. Ireland had been less well-off than most Community countries previous to that period. To see the hopes of better times end after such a short release was a deep disappointment. Second, Ireland is more dependent on dairy production than any other member state except Luxembourg (a third of all farm output). Three to 4 percent of the total GDP is involved in milk against, say for Britain, 0.4 percent and even for France 0.7 percent (*ASC 1981*, pp. 172, 174). Given its weight in Community spending, milk is bound to be first in line for measures of restraint.

Yet it was hard to see how Ireland could manage without the CAP. Without it, Irish food exports would fetch lower prices. Ireland would also lose major budgetary advantages. In the bad year of 1981, the farm funds received from the Community came to 40 percent of income derived from Irish agriculture (Ryan, 1983). Even in those lean years, income in agriculture was 10 percent above that of the late 1960s for a farm population which had shrunk by 30 percent (*ASC 1981*, pp. 174, 174). Accordingly, the Irish pressed for favored treatment within the CAP, on grounds of need, not for action outside it.

POLICY APPROACHES

The two main motives of Irish agricultural policy seem to be to raise farmers' incomes as near as possible to the average levels of the rest of the population good substitute for one.

As regards the second preoccupation, farm incomes, prospects for the future are tied up with structural reform. The inter-departmental Committee on Land Structure Reform set up by the government in July 1976 identified, in its final report of May 1978, about one-third of the land as occupied by aging, unmarried smallholders who failed to increase yields or production during the EC boom years. Twenty-three percent of the Irish workforce on the land was over 65 years of age. These seem to be small peasant proprietors, especially in the west, who in effect withhold land from the younger and more efficient farmers better qualified to develop it (Inter-Departmental Committee on Land Structure Reform, 1978, pp. 22, 31, 96-97).

The problem of the small peasantry, somewhat analogous to that of Italy, remains, all the more because of recession and very high unemployment. The Committee on Land Structure Reform concluded that the central problem was to give active younger farmers better access to holdings of reasonable size. The government, through a new Land Agency, should establish a register of qualified applicants for land; impose limits on the value of individual land acquisitions to prevent excessive concentrations; and promote long-term tenancies (Inter-Departmental Committee, 1978, pp. 22, 31, 96-97). In some ways, this resembles French structural policy developed since the early 1960s.

CRITICAL FACTORS

In the long run, the key issue for Ireland's agriculture, which in 1978 exported nearly three-fifths of its output, exceeding all but Denmark in export dependence, is markets (Thiede, 1980, p. 17). As food exports (including the value added by manufacturing) are worth about 80 percent of total farm output, foreign markets will be decisive (Eurostat, 1980, pp. 220, 244). Because of saturation of EC demand, that will have to mean mainly extra-Community markets.

Uncertainty about the future is reflected in a study published by the Economic and Social Research Institute, for the period 1975–90 (Murphy, O'Connell and Sheehy, 1979). According to this study, agricultural production cannot grow more than 2.2 to 2.5 percent between 1975 and 1990. The main limitations appear to arise from deficiencies in agricultural structures and national resources (soil and climate) as well as from the lack of economic incentives to adopt high-yielding technology in a period when demand is sluggish. The expansion of Irish food exports in the EC will be difficult if the CAP persists in high price policies that keep too many less efficient producers in business. Accordingly, cuts in the real price of food would benefit Irish agriculture. Part-time or marginal producers would have to shift to non-agricultural activities, but the more efficient farmers in Ireland, with a comparative advantage for beef and milk, would be able to expand production, tap economies of scale, increase their share of EC markets, lower costs, and so be better equipped to exploit market opportunities in third countries. The food processing sector would also benefit from an expansion in supplies of raw materials at lower prices and would, in turn, be able to expand markets for its finished products.

The Irish food processing sector itself, however, faces built-in constraints on expansion. Much of the domestic market is served by small indigenous firms or by subsidiaries of foreign multi-nationals which export on a limited scale. In industries most geared to exports, beef and dairy products, the amount of value added, and thereby the employment effect, is quite low. Increasing value added would involve the development of higher value products and a marketing battle with strongly entrenched multinational food companies. If present trends continue, by 1990 the Irish food processing industry could be predominantly in their hands and produce about twice its 1973 output with less than 18 percent of the labor force employed at that time (Murphy, O'Connell, and Sheehy, 1979). These trends can only be altered by a large, coordinated effort of the beef and dairy industry; by the Irish government encouraging the creation of Irish-based big firms which could compete with existing multinationals; or by using tax or other incentives to press multinationals to expand production and exports from Irish plants.

The Irish consider the maintenance of price and financial solidarity in the CAP to be crucial. National pricing arrangements or income aids would never be willingly accepted by Ireland. Wealthier member states would be able to support their producers on a scale no poorer member state could afford. Irish policy favors higher EC expenditures on structural measures in the poorer member states and a greater EC harmonization of national aids than now exists.

Denmark

MAJOR ISSUES

A century ago, when cheap grains began to reach Europe from the Americas and Australia, Denmark, like the Netherlands, took advantage of them as feed to shift into efficient livestock production for export. This switch was possible because Denmark had been encouraging the growth of a well-educated class of independent smallholders since before the French Revolution (Tracy, 1964, Chs. 5, 10, 15). From the 1880s onwards, this peasantry, organized in sales cooperatives, developed exports of meat and dairy products to Britain and Germany.[22] Two-thirds of farm production was exported, the highest rate in the world; and animal products formed nearly 90 percent of these exports (OECD, 1974 and 1977). It was a successful formula and Danish farm incomes are still among the highest in the Community (Table 4.3).

However, for the last two decades, Danish agriculture has experienced serious setbacks. In the 1960s, exports were depressed by falling prices for primary products; by rapidly rising production costs under the pull of the belated "industrial revolution" at home; by export concentration on a stagnant British market; and by exclusion from traditional EC markets while the great rival, the Netherlands, exploited the CAP preference in a booming Germany (Appendix Table 8).

Denmark's market share of EC-9 trade shrank from 23 percent to 7 percent between 1960 and 1972. Once the near-equal of the Netherlands in European farm exports, Denmark was a minor actor by the end of the 1960s. Her primary goal, therefore, was to acquire free access to CAP price supports and to German as well as British food markets. The ambition was at last achieved in 1973 by joint membership with Britain of the Community.

Membership of the EC was expected to give Danish farming an enormous boost. In fact, some of these hopes were dashed. Producer prices in Denmark did indeed rise 18 percent (at constant prices) in the single year from 1972 to 1973; and Community farm funds paid out the equivalent of 15 percent of Danish gross agricultural product in the latter year. But the effects were partly blunted by the cancellation at one stroke of all direct national support to agriculture (worth about 11 percent of GAP in 1971–72) (OECD, 1974, 1977). Then, shortly after entry into the EC, came the first energy crisis, recession, accelerating inflation and, in 1975 and 1976, two successive bad harvests. It was only in 1977 and 1978 that Danish farmers began to reap the benefits of the CAP. Investment for a brief period boomed (*ASC 1981*, p. 183).

Unfortunately, this too was short-lived, because the second energy crisis of 1979–80 brought renewed inflation, high interest rates and recession. In 1980, farmers' interest payments were more than three times as high as in 1975, and Denmark came through this period incurring the highest farm debt per hectare in Europe. The collapse of farm incomes in Denmark was as severe as in Ireland that year. The number of forced sales of farms in 1981 rose to 1,500, as against 400 in 1980 and 120 in 1979—a large number in a country with only 116,000 farms in 1977 (*Finansierengsproblemer*, 1981; OECD, 1983b, pp. 24-26 and 134).

The result of two decades of pressure has been a rapid contraction of Danish agriculture. There has also been, for the farmers who remained, a significant fall in relative farm labor incomes measured against the national average wage: from 90 percent in 1960 to 68 percent in 1980 (Appendix Table 18). Yet the cooperatives remain active, farmers have shown considerable powers of adjustment, and the response to the crisis has been increasing concentration in agriculture and in food manufacturing, which remains the first industry of the country. The search for new markets is active: partly through sales of food, Denmark has the best trade balance with Japan of any EC country, and there has been a renewed shift to non-EC markets, which, in 1980, took 35 percent of agricultural exports. However, food manufacturing is still relatively under-developed (Jørgensen, 1978).

POLICY APPROACHES

A food exporter, Denmark is one of the few countries with a tradition of relative free trade in agriculture. The industry has, to a large extent, been self-managing: as early as 1900, 1,541 agricultural cooperatives were processing and exporting meat and dairy products. Then in the 1930s, Imperial Preference in Britain forced the government to intervene. Government export boards regulated prices and licensed exports. When trade recovered in 1950, these boards were turned over to the cooperatives and exporting firms. They negotiated with their own and other governments, fixed minimum prices, imposed export levies and operated funds to iron out the fluctuations in producers' returns.

In the 1960s, when foreign markets were adverse once more, the government intervened again, through the Agricultural Products Marketing Act of 1961 to assure farmers of sufficient returns at least on the home market. Import restrictions and controls over domestic prices were designed to alleviate the effects of falling export prices. Subsidies reduced production costs and sustained incomes (Tracy, 1964, Chs. 5, 10, 15).

It was recognized that a permanent improvement depended on structural reforms. The Agricultural Act of 1967 encouraged mergers of smallholdings up to 100 hectares, investment on farms suitable for development, and sales promotion. In 1978, the upper limit on mergers was brought down to 75 hectares (Ministry of Agriculture, 1978). This is reminiscent of French emphasis on reaping the economies of scale on the land while encouraging cooperatives and discouraging size for its own sake.

The corporatist nature of agricultural export policy presupposes a strongly structured farm community. The Agricultural Council (*Landbrugsraadet*) is the result of a merger as far back as 1919 between the federations of cooperatives and farmers; which the federation of smallholders joined in 1976. The Agricultural Council now represents all farmers' interests in dealings with the government, the food industries, and foreign trade associations. Yet, despite the coincidence of national and farm interests in food exports, Danish political support for the farmers has often been moderate by the standards of most EC countries. This is partly because the Social Democrats, mainly representing urban interests, dominated all governing coalitions until 1978; and partly because of traditional understanding of the need to be competitive abroad. Urban opinion has, if anything, been moving away from the farmers on some issues, such as factory farming and pollution.

CRITICAL FACTORS

The Institute for Future Studies in Copenhagen began in 1977 a study dealing with the trends of Danish agriculture till the year 2000. Two scenarios were developed, one for a long-term annual growth of 3 percent a year, the other, much more pessimistically, for a 0.5 percent annual decline in output. The scenarios suggest the strengths and weaknesses likely to emerge in either case. For instance, in both scenarios crops are expected to increase; the main variations come in the export markets for animal products. Both scenarios, though, conclude that a small number of farms with a relatively large share of total production will constitute the core of Danish agriculture towards the end of the century (Ministry of Agriculture, 1978). Full-time farm operators might progressively fall to between 35 and 40 thousand (excluding family and hired labor) by the year 2000 as against 80 thousand in 1977. Each farmer would on average hold 60–70 hectares (the British average of the late 1970s), with a total output much more adjustable to demand than is now the case for the smaller farms.

A high rate of agricultural growth is of course the hope, so that price increases in the CAP have Danish support. At the same time, it is realized that export markets, especially for pork, will be crucial. Pork (with the barley fed to the pigs) accounted for some two-fifths of Danish farm output in 1980. Trade in pork with the EC between 1974–76 and 1979–81 grew at 4.8 percent per annum on average, enough to fuel expansion plans of 5 percent per annum for 1979–84 (*Financial Times*, 14 December 1978; and *ASC*, various years). Dairy and beef accounted for another two-fifths of Danish output, and butter exports to Britain are important. The steadily growing British self-sufficiency in butter does not offer much hope in this area.

The Danish College of Agriculture calculated that the dairy herd could be reduced from 1.15 million head in 1978 to 0.68 million in 1990, that is, by 40 percent (*Financial Times*, 6 February 1979). Increasing yields (already very high) would mean that dairy products, in milk equivalent, might fall only about 30 percent, from 5.13 million tons to 3.62 million tons. This drop is roughly equal to the total export surplus of all Danish milk and dairy products. It is clear that the Danes, like the Dutch, favor a gradual cut in cattle numbers, not cuts in prices.

In the calculations of the Institute for Future Studies, the sector expected to grow in both scenarios is vegetable products: feedgrains to match the growth of pork output, and sugar, vegetables and fruit, to edge towards self-sufficiency. Denmark virtually achieved this for sugar by 1981 but is not and cannot become self-sufficient in fruit and vegetables (Jørgensen, 1978).

Danish attitudes to the CAP are positive but to the EC more critical. The CAP has fulfilled the Danish need of direct access at once to the British and German food markets. This may prove an illusion to the extent that both countries increase their self-sufficiency. Nevertheless, the Danes will support any CAP they identify with their agricultural export earnings, inside and

outside the Community. The Danes are, after all, among the main beneficiaries of the Community farm budget.[23] At the same time, as in Britain, there
is a strong suspicion of mainland Europeans and all their works. This is
reflected in a sizable "People's Movement against the Common Market" and a
powerful "watchdog" committee of the national Parliament on the EC, which
is an expression of democratic traditions but also of the Danes' vigilant care
for their national sovereignty. The Danes are among the most vociferous
opponents of any formal delegations of national authority to supranational
institutions.

Greece

MAJOR ISSUES

Since the end of the civil war in 1949, and until 1975, the growth of
agriculture averaged 4.1 percent per annum, in step with consumption. This
has implied an impressive rise in labor productivity on the farms—as much as
10 percent a year between 1971 and 1977. Yet the share of agriculture in Greek
employment and national product are both typically "Mediterranean"—much
higher than in the countries of the north, except Ireland: in 1980, they were
28.5 percent and 15.5 percent respectively (against EC-9 averages of 7.4 percent and 3.5 percent). Agriculture accounted for 26 percent of exports
(OECD, 1983b, p. 121).

Approximately 40 percent of cultivated land in Greece is in mountainous
and hilly areas. Sun is abundant, and water is scarce. Thus, the first issue is
irrigation. One-quarter of the cultivated land is irrigated and produces nearly
one-half of all crops. A further 20 percent of cultivated land can be irrigated in
the long run. Surface irrigation is the most widely used method (92 percent of
total irrigated area). In the early 1970s, more efficient techniques of spray and
drip irrigation were introduced, but have proved too costly for most farmers.
The Ministry of Agriculture now awards a 25 percent subsidy towards
purchase and installation costs for irrigation.

Greek agriculture consists of an excessive number of very small, highly
fragmented farms. In 1980, Greece had as many people working on the land as
Britain and the Benelux trio combined—over one million (*ASC 1982*, p. 285).
In 1971, nearly 22 percent of all farms covered less than one hectare, and only
5 percent exceeded 10 hectares. Such small holdings are not economically
viable, and their owners regard them mainly as a supplementary source of
income. Farmers also tend to be old: about two-thirds are over 45 years old,
and one-fifth over 65. This is largely the result of high rates of emigration,
especially in the 1960s. Paradoxically, shortages of agricultural labor are also
common in Greece, because of seasonal employment in tourism. This suggests
that no surplus labor exists in Greek agriculture, in the sense of labor that can
be turned away from agricultural pursuits without reducing output. Thus,
Greek efforts aim both to increase productivity and to keep agricultural

workers better occupied the year round. This implies (1) restructuring production in favor of non-seasonal crops (in hothouses, for example); (2) placing greater emphasis on livestock; and (3) promoting a more equal spread across regions and sectors.

The changing size and pattern of food consumption are also a source of policy issues. Food consumption in Greece increased at about 4 percent per annum between 1950 and 1975 (parallel to the growth of domestic production) but shifted towards meat, fruit, and vegetables and away from grains, legumes, oils and fats. Domestic production did not match these shifts. Greece in the mid-1970s became very deficient in meat and dairy products. Efforts are being made to increase the size of breeding herds despite pastures of poor quality, and to reduce dependence on imports of feeding stuffs, by such means as raising the price of maize.

The final set of policy issues concerns food processing and manufacturing, whose share in agricultural exports was around 15 percent in the mid-1970s. In 1973, there were about 11,000 food-processing units, so that, like the farms, they are far too small. This goes with a low level of technology and underutilization of capacity, lack of coordination between primary production and industry, and low quality products. Yet the production of canned fruit, vegetables and juices is one of the dynamic activities in the food industry and now heads the list of export products, having displaced wine and currants.

POLICY APPROACHES

Until the mid-1970s, Greek agricultural policy was formulated and carried out under the shadow of a general economic strategy which attached primary importance to the export-oriented industrial sector. It could be argued that no deliberate agricultural policy existed (Pepelasis, 1980, pp. 53–54). With the prospect of joining the Community, the approach changed. In 1978, indicative planning, on the French model (see Glossary) was for the first time envisaged for agriculture.

The 1978–82 plan was not met in quantitative terms (*ASC 1982*, p. 199), but the goals were also qualitative: to raise farmers' incomes; maintain the rural population in some sensitive regions; lift productivity through the increase in farm size and a more efficient use of inputs; encourage the adoption of new technology through better education and improved research and advisory services; and adjust agricultural production, in quantity and in quality, to domestic and external market demand.

The recommended guidelines in the five-year plan for 1983–87 under preparation in 1982–83 concentrated on (1) the production of higher quality foodstuffs in deficit in Greece (especially beef, dairy products and processed foods); (2) the development of exports; and for these purposes (3) irrigation and (4) the development, particularly for better marketing, of the farm cooperative movement, which already plays an important role in the country. For the same reasons, a bill on cooperation in the food industry was also under preparation (OECD, 1983b, pp. 29, 31).

A comprehensive effort has been made by government to provide farmers with production, marketing, and investment credit at low interest rates. Credit is given mainly to raise productivity, promote cooperatives and modernize and expand food processing and manufacturing. In 1977, the total amount of public support to Greek agriculture seems to have reached one-third of GAP, as against 39 percent in the EC (Pepelasis, 1980, p. 59). Aid included market intervention expenditure, income and input subsidies (48 percent of the total), expenditure on structural measures (29 percent) and government contributions to farmers' social security and insurance (23 percent). The structure of expenditure was thus characterised by the predominance of short-term measures over long-term ones. Although there is no strong farmers' lobby in Greece, an individual farmer can often obtain a personal favor if he can ensure his parliamentary representative of a certain number of votes. So far, no government has been prepared to take radical measures, the benefits of which would accrue only in the long run.

CRITICAL FACTORS

The most immediate and obvious critical factor is the rapid appearance of a major trade deficit in agricultural products with the EC since Greece's entry in 1981. Greece, unlike all the other Mediterranean countries, still had a healthy surplus on her farm trade in 1980 on the eve of entry into the EC. The coverage of imports by exports that year was 143 percent. But in 1981 it fell to 112 percent and in 1982 to 99 percent. In two years, the surplus had melted away. This was almost entirely due to agricultural imports from the EC, as the export-import coverages in Table 3.2 demonstrate. The impact of the surge in imports from EC member states can be gauged from the fact that between 1976 and 1982, the EC rose from supplying 30 percent to 72 percent of Greece's agricultural imports. This poses for Greece, in a more acute form, the same problem that exercised Italy in the 1970s, of becoming heavily dependent on expensive food imports from the EC.

However, 1983 has brought some alleviation on trade (Appendix Table 7), and both farm prices and budget payments have been much in Greece's favor. Greek farmers' prices have risen. Greek figures for 1977, four years prior to entry into the Community, suggest that Greek farmers at the time obtained some 20 to 30 percent less income from livestock than they would have done at the same time inside the EC. The CAP increased pre-accession returns for durum wheat, sugar, olive oil, citrus fruits, and wine, all of which are important to Greek farming and, except citrus fruits, in surplus in the EC (Pepelasis, 1980, pp. 38–39, Table 25).

The shift since 1978 to more intensive support of Mediterranean products, promoted by Italy, has greatly benefitted the Greek budget. It is estimated that in 1983, the Greek net surplus on the Community budget came to one billion ECUs.[24] This is an enormous sum when one reflects that total Greek GDP in 1982 was under 40 billion ECUs, and total export earnings came to less than 5 billion ECUs.

Table 3.2   Greece's Food Trade with the EC-9 and the Rest of the World, 1980, 1981 and 1982 (as the percentage ratio of exports over imports)

Year (food trade)	Greek Trade with EC-9	Greek Trade with Rest of the World
	(exports ÷ imports, percentage)	
1980 (before entry into EC)	152	135
1981 (1st year in EC)	74	201
1982	69	176

Source: Com-EC, Eurostat, *Monthly External Trade Bulletins.*

In this situation of contradictory extremes, the Greek government is seeking, in ways already familiar in other countries, to concentrate on structural reforms and on exports. As regards structures, plans place priority on increasing self-sufficiency in the deficit sectors, mainly in livestock and feedgrains (on the lines of sugar in the past). On exports, efforts to exploit comparative advantages in fruit and vegetables will be all the more determined in the light of the bad turn in the food balance. Drip and sprinkler methods of irrigation in Crete and the Peloponnese, with aid from the World Bank, could quintuple yields of relatively high-value, out-of-season vegetables, such as cucumbers, eggplants, and peppers, for export not least to the EC. However, since the entry into the Community, Greek export efforts have been particularly successful with the Arab world and North Africa; and the EC, though still the dominant outlet, has tended to decline in the total picture.

Conclusions

The surveys of the individual situations and policies of the Community's member states lead to one overwhelming conclusion. This is the pursuit by each nation of policies which expand food production. If a country is a net importer of food, it must close the gap and balance the national books whether or not the Community as a whole is in surplus (Belgium, Britain, and Italy) and even irrespective of whether it has a favorable balance of general trade (Germany). If a country is already a net exporter, this is a sign of its right to expand further, either because it is poor (Greece, Ireland) or more competitive (Denmark, Ireland, Netherlands) or by productive potential (France). Even the Danes, one of the two countries with the most export- and market-oriented agricultures in the Community, have nevertheless sought self-sufficiency in sugarbeet (a deficit item) and, by 1981, well ahead of schedule, seemed to have attained it. The EC's member states are unanimous on one point only: expansionist zeal for national agriculture. In the circumstances, the CAP can hardly fail to be expansionist also. To ascribe expansionism to the CAP as such is to put the cart before the horse. In fact, the Community institutions alone have shown some anxiety to control the process of growth. This is natural, given the potential for damage to the Community in a failure to balance agricultural demand and supply.

Expansionism is too general to be an accident. It is hard to be categorical, or exhaustive, about the many forces behind it. Some are obvious, such as the desire to improve the trade balance. Others are controversial, but probably powerful, such as the underlying thrust of technology in postwar agriculture. But some, and perhaps the deepest, seem to be social and political. These are rooted in the very nature of the corporatist systems of agriculture which prevail in every member state.

Details vary, but the broad picture is nearly always much the same. There are diverse forms of horizontal organization (between actors in a single sector) and of vertical coordination (between sectors at the different stages of a single chain, such as milk and dairy products), and all tend to place the individual farmer within an elaborate administrative context. Systems of credit often tend to encourage both borrowing and expansion, so that, especially in countries like Denmark, France, Germany, and the Netherlands, where farm debt is often high, the machinery of growth can only with difficulty be put into reverse. Often, also, the institutions which cap the various regimes are able to act virtually as monopolies and to structure their sector well away from any public gaze, including, to a considerable extent, the gaze of the Commission in Brussels. The proliferation of state aids, said by one well-informed observer to be "totally out of control," is only a symptom of a bias earthed in the structures themselves.[25] Agriculture is not an isolated phenomenon. It is woven into all the other activities of the economy of most of the member states. Regional, manpower, educational, labor, environmental, even industrial policies are all caught up in it, and plans and funds allocated within one or another of these sectors can have major effects on one or more of the others.

In these conditions, nationalism is built into the very texture of systems extending far beyond agriculture. This or that authority may pursue national purposes with greater or lesser indifference to Community goals and precepts. But in essence the opposition is rooted less in political motives of a general kind than in the structure of nationally based systems which cannot be fused merely by putting markets within easy access of each other, as in the CAP. It is a little like instituting free trade between nationalized industries. In practice, national hierarchies, networks and ways of carrying on business generate their own purposes (and, unless the issue is squarely faced, can hardly fail to continue to do so), within a Community that is thereby prevented from behaving consistently in pursuit of common goals.

Moreover, corporate systems are sooner or later captured by their constituency. Governments are supposed to regulate matters in the general interest from above. In practice, the interpenetration of rulers and ruled is such that an administrator has to be very strong indeed to lead the profession he administers. This is clearly the case in agriculture, nationally as in the CAP. The system of price supports is liked by farmers because it is not too directly felt by taxpayers and consumers and it is liked by large farmers even more because they make disproportionate gains from prices fixed to keep inefficient colleagues in business. The contrast with the difficult social and political adjustments that high productivity is bound sooner or later to force on a "declining" industry—declining, in the specific sense that demand is sluggish for long–term, not cyclical, reasons—makes it all too tempting to postpone issues and gain time. Governments and politicians, with the "risk aversion" specially marked in the representatives of elected regimes, would like to see agriculture, socially speaking, shrink quietly by natural wastage rather than face the odium and upheavals of speeding up the process. This kind of caution would be strong at the best of times—as in the 1950s and 1960s—and it is stronger still in a recession. The paradoxical result is that agricultural expansion in the CAP is only dynamic in a technical sense. In the broader political one, it is in the last resort highly defensive. It is rooted in the inability of governments to see their way through the social and political problems of the countryside.

The dilemma is quite evident in the various structural measures created to deal with those problems that play a large part in most countries' agricultural policies. A few countries give less emphasis to this aspect than others. The British, for instance, with relatively large farms, do not give so much formal stress to structural policy. They have nevertheless introduced an important innovation into the Community with the hill farmers' schemes since 1975. The countries which place the most obvious stress on structural policy are probably the French and Danes, whose legislation offers some striking parallels. Both place de facto ceilings on the size of farms public bodies propose to help, either by favoring purchase or by subsidizing young farmers. Both aim at reinforcing viable family farms. The assumption is that such farms can be prosperous and exploit sufficient economies of scale so long as producers cooperate together in various ways, either to operate their farms or sell their goods; and that a spread of smallish farms is better for the health of the countryside than the development of large farms on the British model. The Germans encourage part-time farming. In Italy, special efforts to develop the Mezzogiorno have evolved into substantial national and Community schemes.

The attractions of such policies for social, regional or environmental reasons are obvious. But, by their very nature, structural policies which are designed in each country to make individual farmers more viable cumulatively tend to make them all more productive and finally to raise the average of what is a minimum "competitive" performance. Given the fact that in modern farming, it is the productivity of the minority of farms that matters, not the numbers of the less than average ones, this often encourages people to invest in lines with little future in terms of markets and ultimately compounds the Community's problem of surpluses.

There is of course an uncomfortable awareness that the room for expansion may not be infinite. As Edgard Pisani notes, "no society can tolerate the indefinite production of structural surpluses."[26] Signs of this differ in the national surveys, in ways that may owe something to the outlook of individual experts but also reflect conditions in each country. The Dutch and Danes express some readiness to restrict, for instance, the numbers of dairy cows but not to reduce prices to producers. By implication, they prefer to see the numbers of producers fall than to lower the profitability of those that remain. It is also noticeable that the Danes seem more ready to envisage cuts in the total output of agriculture than are the Dutch. In Britain and Germany, official and quasi-official reports have brought out the extent to which production is likely to increase at rates well above those of domestic demand even if real prices fall quite substantially and regularly. Some French and Irish experts speculate that their countries could gain from lower prices and more "extensive" methods of production because their Community partners would have greater difficulty in following suit. It is doubtful whether farmers in either country would gladly adopt such strategies.

In all these glimmerings, there is a strong sense that each country is still inclined to point out how its neighbors might mend their ways the better to retain its own. The hints of national realization of the need to change course seem still far from crystallizing in a new consensus. This could be part of the normal bargaining process. Insofar as it reflects fears of reactions on the land when it is evident that the sectors with growth prospects are small compared to those where outlets are stagnant, and still smaller against the trends of output in virtually every field, the obstacles seem more fundamental. The impression conveyed is that reform will only come in response to the *force majeure* of circumstances, that is, when all other avenues, real or false, have been explored and it is painfully clear that the costs of carrying on massively outweigh those of opening up new routes. Yet the costs of carrying on are not the same for all the member states. That is one basic political factor in a situation made tense by the cumulative expansion of three decades. Ireland, for instance, is outstandingly vulnerable. The other is that the expectation of a single "crisis" is probably too simple for what is likely to be a long and turbulent passage from one kind of system and equilibrium to another. What that other balance will be cannot be foreseen at the outset. It will be the outcome of the patterns in which the pieces fall after a series of conflicts, negotiations, and partial adjustments, the cumulations of which are less likely to be logical than geological.

Notes

1. Consult the Preface for the major outside contributions made to the National Surveys.
2. French exports to others of the EC-9 (in millions of tons):

	Cereals	Sugar
1974	11.8	0.9
1980	9.3	0.5

3. Bergmann, 1983; for instability, OECD, 1980b; and OECD, 1983a.
4. Delorme and André, 1983, p. 357; Bergmann, 1983a, p. 275. The figures exclude grants for farm investments, which are in the capital not current budget accounts.
5. K. P. Riley, 1982, senior agricultural economist to Pauls Agriculture Ltd., pp. 59–69, and same source's memorandum, "Aids to agriculture in the EEC," pp. 45–59.

6. *Ibid.*, p. 54, fn. 4, quoting P. Guillot, *Typologie des Interprofessions*, Paris 1980; Delorme and André, 1983, pp. 301–63.

7. *Financial Times*, "National aid undermines common farm policy," 15 May 1981, quotes Pierre Mehaignerie, then French minister of agriculture, when French lamb policies were condemned by the European Court, as saying: "it is true I have suffered two judgments against me, but I am still well, I still breathe."

8. There is a wide range of institutions framing structural policy. They include the CNASEA; the SAFERs; the Fond d'Action Sociale pour l'Aménagemenent des Structures Agricoles; Groupements Agricoles pour l'Exploitation en Commun; Groupements Financiers Agricoles; and so on, N. Hicks, 1978; Bergmann, 1983b.

9. *ASC 1982*, p. 207, shows that from 1973 to 1981 the value in constant terms of final production rose in the Netherlands by 34.6 percent (next best, Greece 23 percent) and gross value added in agriculture by 37.8 percent (next best, Greece 19.4 percent), even though the Netherlands was one of the countries where agricultural prices fell the most compared with other prices (*ASC 1981*, p. 180; *ASC 1982*, p. 199).

10. In 1979, Dutch exports to all destinations, of food and feedstuffs, amounted to $14.2 billions; those of Brazil to $7 billions. (FAO, *Trade Yearbook 1980*, covering SITC categories 0 (except 03 Fish) + 1 + 22 + 29 + 4.) But three-quarters of Dutch exports are to EC partners.

11. Eurostat, *Analytical Tables of Foreign Trade, SITC. Rev. 2*, (annual). In 1980 Dutch unit prices of exports within the Community were about 1.75 those of Italian tomatoes (both in and out of season) and about 1.5 times for exports to the rest of the world (1.6 for out-of-season, 1.49 for in-season tomatoes).

12. See note 20, Ch. 1, supra.

13. See note 6, Ch. 1, supra.

14. Com-EC, 1983a, pp. 28-29; *ASC 1982*, pp. 194-95. See also notes Ch. 4.3 below.

15. House of Lords, 1978, pp. xxiv, paras. 83–84; and Com-EC sources. Regional aids to agriculture are estimated at 5 percent of national aids in Belgium and 5 to 10 percent in Germany.

16. Com-EC, 1981c, pp. 20–23; *ASC 1981*, pp. 33, 88–89; *ASC 1982*, pp. 15–16, 98, 164; Com-EC 1983a, p. 19: "if the Community is to find enduring solutions to these problems, it must put relatively more emphasis on longterm structural action, rather than on market intervention and price support."

17. *ASC 1981*, p. 267. British average farm size of 65 hectares about 2.5 times that of France, with the second biggest average in the Community.

18. Peter Walker, then U.K. minister of agriculture, in *Financial Times*, 6 July 1982, "Cresson stands firm," is quoted as saying, "if you are a 25 percent food importing country, you are entitled to fill that gap." Also *Financial Times*, "Thatcher urges higher food exports," 17 February 1983, Mrs. Thatcher sent a message to the Food from Britain conference of 16 February saying Britain "must greatly increase" food exports, with a greater share of the home market and replace as much as possible of the $4 billion of temperate zone food imports.

19. *ASC 1982*, p. 191. The exact figures for 1980 were:
Gross value added at factor cost—11.3 percent
Agricultural employment—18.9 percent

20. Ryan, 1983; *ASC 1981*, pp. 279, 282. Agriculture and the industries upstream and downstream from it in the food system accounted for 27.5 percent of GDP in 1970. Agriculture and food manufacturing employed 30.7 percent of the active labor force n 1970–72.

21. Corrected for the populations of the EC-9, the sums paid out by the EAGGF in 1980 came, in ECUs per inhabitant, to the following in each member state:

Ireland	166	France	53
Denmark	121	Germany	40
Netherlands	110	Italy and Luxembourg	32
Belgium	58	UK	16

22. *ASC 1982*, p. 303. A larger proportion of produce is sold through cooperatives in Denmark than in any other EC country. In particular, this is the case for over 90 percent of pork and nearly 90 percent of milk.

23. See Note 21, supra.

24. Scotto, 1983 *(Le Monde)* reports this is mainly due to production aids for tobacco, olive oil, hard wheat, cotton, fruit, and vegetables. In 1981, the Greeks received 140 million ECUs.

25. See Note 5, supra.

26. "Aucune société ne pourrait supporter de produire indéfiniment des excédents structurels."

4 Structures and Cross-Currents

Introduction

The politics of agriculture in the Community are not simply the balance-sheet of the individual situations and goals of the member states. As in all collectives, the behavior of the whole is more than the sum of the parts. Patterns of interaction have a life of their own. The very features which divide the members of the Community in policies based on the quest for larger national market shares can unite them in a genuine internal free-trade system where these shares are decided by comparative advantage. In the first case, each state will watch anxiously to see how its own "national interest" is advanced or sacrificed against those of other states. In the second, trade patterns (to ignore the problems of monopoly for the moment) will be determined by the most effective competitor, the farmer or food processor, not the nation, to the presumed advantage of the individual consumer buying cheaper food. The very causes of conflict under one set of policies can become the groundplan for cohesion under another.

Moreover, policy choices do not fall upon the member states as an undifferentiated mass. Because of the varying endowments, structures, traditions, and policy choices of the national agricultures, regions, and branches of farming, issues will affect them at different times, at different rates and in different ways. This influences the similarities and contrasts between member states, regions or branches of farming which have in the past, or may in the future, cement coalitions or define oppositions in the Community in the face of changing conditions. It is therefore necessary to look not only at the parts of the Community but at the ways in which it has been agreed to fit them together.

By definition, the compromises expressed in the CAP must at some time have satisfied, or satisfy now, a common will of some kind even if one of second-bests. If that were not the case, the CAP would not exist. When the Community was set up, the governments of the founding states must have placed such a high value on integration, or on using the EC to finesse their farm problems, or both, that they were all willing to change the traditional systems to make way for the CAP. Later entrants also had to pay this price, once they decided that in general the costs of staying out of the Community outweighed those of going in. Further, the form the CAP has taken, with high farm prices and mutual preferences on the markets of the Community states against all outsiders, has been such as to satisfy, or at least buy off, the farm lobbies in all the member countries. The CAP has helped to take agriculture, as a declining sector, off the agenda of serious social, economic, and political disturbance in each country. It would not necessarily have been on the agenda in any case. General prosperity, until the late 1970s, made the drift from the land relatively easy. Nevertheless, the CAP stilled anxiety in a large section of society. When one considers the hints of violence in the farm community, certainly in France, the peaceful way in which the old-style peasant agriculture has largely bowed itself off the scene during the course of a single generation is something for which policy-makers and the rest of society can reasonably feel some satisfaction. A huge social shift, involving almost a quarter of the population of the founding states, has passed off virtually without incident.

But times have changed. The CAP has essentially bought off trouble by expansion; and as the costs of expansion grow, this becomes a less and less effective strategy. The contradictions concealed in the compromises underlying the CAP are bound to surface again every time circumstances call established bargains into question. The tensions are potentially the greater because the member states seem less wedded to integration than in the 1950s. France has passed through the prism of de Gaulle. Germany is less constrained by her overwhelming postwar need to re-establish her international credentials. Britain accepted the present CAP because she had to and might be delighted to revise some of it. Italy seeks transfers to the south which ultimately add to the financial tensions and surpluses in the Community. In these circumstances, it is important to have a clear idea of the compromises and contrasts embedded in the CAP and of their potential effects in the coming years.

This chapter therefore seeks to prepare the discussion of policy options considered in the final chapter by looking at some of the major cross-currents which may shape future policy coalitions and conflicts. It examines three major fields of tension. The first arises from the differences between the dominant agricultures in the various member states, which themselves reflect broader political and economic conditions and national histories. They have had, and are likely to have, considerable influence on future policy outlook. The second concerns the issues raised by the evolving market shares of the member states. These can be approached through (1) the contrast which has already been crucial, between food exporters and importers within the Community; and (2) the conflicts over agricultural "green rates" which are often held to have favored the strong currency countries in the Community led by Germany. The third set of issues differs from the other two in that the focus is not on politics between nations so much as between classes of people and more particularly farmers and the rest of society. For demographic reasons alone, the agricultural population is bound to go on falling more or less rapidly to the end of the century. Will this affect the power or purposes of the farm community, or of society towards it, and the support which agriculture has hitherto enlisted?

Contrasting Agricultures

From the outset, the CAP has juxtaposed rather than fused at least three distinct types of agricultural tradition—three choices of economic orientation—to which British accession in 1973 added a fourth. Each type has generated its own characteristic patterns of interest and attitude, and the divergences among them are reflected in the CAP. The first type is northern agriculture as a transforming industry, with a concentration on intensive livestock production. This type is based on imports of cheap animal feed and aims at production and exports of high-value dairy products and meat. The Netherlands and Denmark best exemplify this mercantile and specialized farming, which has its roots in the last two decades of the nineteenth century, when cheap grains began to arrive from the Americas, Australia, and Russia. The Netherlands gave up cultivating cereals, and Denmark, though growing its own barley, came nearest to free trade in agriculture in Europe (and indeed, with New Zealand, in the world). Both prospered on exports to Britain and Germany, then the major food markets. Characteristics of this type of agriculture are high imports of animal feed and inputs of capital and technology; high yields and production; an educated workforce and good advisory services; high incomes for relatively few farmers (though still not as high as average incomes in other walks of life in their own societies); and a substantial export surplus, traditionally with Europe (Appendix Table 7). It is commercial and industrial in outlook and organization and, of late, through "factory farming," decreasingly tied to indigenous land resources.

The second agricultural tradition, also mainly northern, but autarchic, at least in intent, came as a result of the protectionist reaction by dominant cereal-growing interests to the influx of cheap grains from the new continents in the last century. It is, therefore, the outcome of the opposite reaction to the Dutch-Danish strategy. In the 1950s, it was most clearly represented by the two giants of the EC-6, France and Germany. Both had reacted to cheap grain imports in the 1880s by high tariffs and attempts to buttress their own traditional basic crops and dominant landowners, the cereal growers of the Paris basin and the Junkers in eastern Germany. Those attempts failed to the extent that France, though an exporter of wheat, and thought of as a largely agricultural country as late as the 1950s, in fact had a deficit in food trade as late as 1970! (Appendix Table 7). Both countries still had a numerous peasantry in 1945. Even Germany, generally thought of as powerfully industrial, had proportionately (and of course absolutely) more workers on the land in 1951 than England had had a century before.[1] Their farming was less specialized than that of the mercantile exporters of high-value products; inputs and yields were lower; the labor supply was larger; methods were generally less advanced and incomes were correspondingly low. Though both in France and in Germany, labor on the land has fallen steeply in the past thirty years, incomes from farming are still low compared to the national average. On a comparative European farm scale, this gives French and

Germans middling farm incomes (Table 4.3 and Appendix Table 17). There are great variations, however. The big cereal growers of the Paris basin or in Schleswig-Holstein have some of the highest agricultural incomes in the Community.[2]

The third type of farming represented in the original Community, the southernmost and poorest, is that of the Mediterranean zone. In the original EC-6, it was represented by Italy, especially the underdeveloped south, the Mezzogiorno, and to a much lesser extent by the French Midi. In an EC of twelve countries, it would extend to Greece, Portugal, and Spain and so cover four countries and the French Midi.

The southern nations have been at a disadvantage in at least three ways. First, numbers working on the land are far higher than elsewhere—proportionately about as high as in France and Germany in the 1950's, except in northern Italy which, in this as in other respects, is closer to northern than to southern standards (Wade, 1982). Farm incomes, except in the French Midi, are correspondingly low. The ratio, at the extreme, in 1977, between average farm income per head in the Netherlands and in Portugal was over 7 to 1. Second, because climate and generally less advanced economic conditions work against livestock production, crops account for some 60 percent of gross agricultural output against 15 to 35 percent in the rainier areas of northern Europe (Table 4.1). Yet, because demand has grown less rapidly, specially during the 1970's, for fruit, vegetable, olive oil and wine than for meat or cheese, the Mediterranean countries tend to be specialized at the vulnerable end of the product range. This has been underlined by the big increase in meat consumption in southern societies which led to food trade deficits in all of them, even ultimately in Greece, which held out the longest. Third, until 1978, southern products gained much less than northern ones from Community finance, so that the poorest regions received least help.[3] Attempts since then have tended to generate new surpluses in commodities not previously plagued by them. Such problems must acquire added significance once the Community is enlarged to include not only Italy and the French Midi, as was the case until 1981, and Greece, as it has done since that year, but also Portugal and Spain, which might join, in or after 1986.

The original contract in the Community was largely an agreement of coexistence between these three constituent agricultures of the CAP. The situation was further complicated when Britain joined in 1973. Like the Netherlands and Denmark, Britain was receptive to cheap food imports from the new continents a century ago. But unlike them, she had already shed a large part of her peasantry, and the interests of the towns and manufacturers predominated. During the first half of the century, Britain was far and away the world's greatest import market for food, the magnet for Danish, Dutch, and Irish exporters alike. Though since the 1930s and particularly since World War II, Britain began to build up home farming again, 40 percent of food consumed was still imported on the eve of entry into the common market. The danger of this system for Britain, once an EC member, was that her agriculture was under-sized compared to Britain herself. This created the fear that

Table 4.1   EC-12 Patterns of Production, 1980 (percentage GAP)

	Livestock Products[a]	"Mediterranean" Crops[b]	Cereals, Potatoes, Industrial Crops
Northern			
Luxembourg	84.6	7.6	7.4
Ireland	83.4	3.2	11.5
Denmark	70.9	2.1	17.9
Germany	69.1	11.6	14.8
Belgium	66.3	12.8	12.7
Netherlands	66.0	18.4	8.2
United Kingdom	61.3	9.3	25.3
Intermediate			
France	51.3	20.1	23.0
Southern			
Spain	40.1	34.5	23.6
Italy	39.0	40.5	14.6
Portugal	37.6	48.2[c]	10.4
Greece	31.1	47.4	18.8

[a] Meat, dairy, eggs.
[b] Fruit, vegetables, wine, olive oil, tobacco, rice.
[c] Includes root vegetables (e.g. potatoes).

Source: Com-EC, *ASC 1981*, pp. 174–75; *Anuario de Estadistica Agraria 1980*, Madrid, p. 610. For Portugal (date unspecified), J. Bourrinet and R. Stioui, *Problèmes Agricoles d'une Communauté Européenne à Douze* CERIC, Aix-Marseille III, 1982, p. 2.

higher food prices, for a big food importer, would have crippling effects on a weak trade balance and on manufacturing. And, since the Community was three-quarters agriculture in financial terms, Britain, who paid into it as a major member, benefited only as a minor one and sustained heavy losses. These two factors have had a great deal to do with prolonging Britain's traditional dislike of the CAP.

CONFLICTS BETWEEN AGRICULTURES

The experience of common life in the CAP has not made the various types of agriculture dovetail in greater harmony. The disparities have, if anything, grown sharper as surpluses have increased the pressures on the system as a whole. In the CAP, there are several sources of contention affecting the relations of each type of farming sector with one or more of the others.

Imported Feed and Cereal Surpluses. At the present time more than three-fifths of the cereal grown feeds farm animals, not people, and surpluses are persistent.[4] The conflict arises between mercantile farming, which has prospered on a regime of imports of cheap feed for livestock, and the autarchic forces in the Community which seek to establish a preference for home-grown but high priced Community cereals. When the CAP was set up, the cereal interests seemed to have settled the matter in their favor. The Germans saw to it that cereal prices were fixed near their own levels, not those of the French which, in 1958 were below the American.[5] The Dutch accepted this increase in the cost of the raw materials for their dominant livestock so long as milk producers obtained correspondingly high prices for their own output. But the loopholes in the system soon proved to be far wider than its authors realized and, the breach once made, they widened further. Imports of animal feed have become a classic example of the difficulties of protecting a product if there are loopholes for consumers—in this case the importers who manufacture feed for livestock.

There have been two substitutes, or partial substitutes, for cereals in the provision of animal feed, both largely imported. The first is a whole range of energy foods, especially for pigs and poultry, to which the label "cereal substitutes" is applied. Imports are low-duty or duty-free, either because they were bound in GATT when the CAP was set up and mainly supplied by developing countries to whom it was thought expedient to make tariff concessions; or because they are waste products of industrial processes, notably in the United States, unknown 20 years ago. The range is very wide. They include tapioca (the root crop, manioc or cassava), molasses, citrus pellets, cereal brans and maize gluten feed (a by-product of isoglucose manufacture) and others (European Parliament, 1982, pp. 67-84, especially Table p. 70).

The second partial substitute is oilseeds, particularly soya-beans imported mainly from the U.S. Soya-beans provide a high-protein feed for dairy cattle. The oil is a bonus. The Community has, and for climatic reasons probably always will have, a major deficit in oilseeds. Accordingly, oilseeds are imported free of duty, while home production is aided by direct production subsidies ("deficiency payments") to growers. This was the main price paid for getting GATT to accept high EC cereal prices. But the result is a market price for oilseeds which is too attractive compared with that of the cereal prices supported by CAP. In the EC, prices of soya-beans oscillate around 1.2 times the price of maize, the main cereal for animal feed, after the levy of import duties. In the United States, where maize prices are much lower than in the EC and where grains and oilseeds are freer to establish a natural market balance, soya-beans are around 2.5 times dearer than maize.[6]

The result has been a marked decline in the demand for cereals for animal feed in favor of cereal substitutes and oilseeds. At the extreme, in the Netherlands, the proportion of cereals in the mix for compound foodstuffs for livestock fell, from 63 percent in 1960–61 to 17 percent in 1978–79 (Debatisse, 1981; *ASC 1981*, p. 413), an amazing record of decline for a dominant product. Instead, "the Community has become the importer of the 'industrial offals' of the world," as regards cereal substitutes, and has pushed the consumption of oilseeds well beyond what would otherwise have made sense (European Parliament, 1982, p. 68). Thus, milk paid for at high CAP prices is produced with "cereal substitutes" at low world prices. Further, since protein feeds encourage high yields, notably of milk, the artificial emphasis on oilseed consumption has played a significant part in creating the largest and most intractable of the Community's surpluses, that for dairy products.

What has long been an anomaly has turned into an acute issue since the Community became a net exporter of cereals. Between 1970 and 1980, an EC net import of 18 million tons of grain turned into a net export of 1 million tons, despite an increase in domestic consumption and stocks of 9 million tons. (The total output in 1980 of the world's second exporter of cereals, Canada, was 40 million tons.) The French, as the main EC producers and exporters of wheat (the grain most in surplus in the Community) have long argued that the Community should cut out foreign imports of feed in favor of Community-grown cereals. As the CAP preference is not observed, the French argue, it is not their fault that exports have to subsidized. They denounce "factory farming" and the *scandale permanent,* as Edgard Pisani has called it, of the transformation of soya into milk, the drying of this milk at high energy cost, and the heavily subsidized sale of the dried milk to feed calves and pigs (Pisani, 1983, p. 38).

The importing lobby throughout the Community is predictably unenthusiastic. The impact of cheap feed and oilseed imports is enormous. According to Thiede's estimates, imports of animal feed into the Netherlands were equivalent in 1981 to an agricultural area 13 percent larger than that of the country itself. Belgium and to a lesser extent, Denmark, Germany and Italy, are also notable importers (*ASC 1981,* p. 293). Specialist farmers even in some of the countries least reliant on feed imports, such as Britain and France, buy significant amounts. The lobby against any cessation of feed imports is a powerful one, and widespread. It is reinforced by the fact that the main supplier of most forms of feed turns out to be the United States, which has a major stake in the flow and is already embattled over the trade effects of the Community's agricultural expansion. At this point, of course, the problems of farming spill over into the wider politics of the Atlantic alliance.

Oilseeds and the southern tier. Oilseeds pose a further set of problems. The fear of excess dependence on the American soya-bean crop, the *locus classicus* of which was the abrupt and short-lived American export ban of 1973 (to combat inflation at home), has led the Community to subsidize heavily the domestic production of oilseeds.[7] The phosphorescent yellow of ripening rape now cuts a swathe across the general green over wide stretches of the Community. Once again, the ramifications are complex. Rapeseed (colza) and sunflower seed, the two oilseeds with the best prospects in the Community, produce protein for animal feed but, as their name suggests, also vegetable oils. Rapeseed in particular is not highly rated in the trade (European Parliament, 1982, pp. 87,

89). Problems of disposal arise; and aggravate those of competing olive oil, which is the quintessential Mediterranean crop.[8] Importer–exporter conflicts thus spill over into contention between north and south and between rich and poor.

Olive oil is a high-grade, even luxury oil commanding a price premium of at least 60 percent against other vegetable oils without losing market share. The Community has pushed the sense of its qualities, or of the needs of olive-growers, so far as to price it 2.5 times higher than other oils, and even at some periods three times, though producers also get direct subsidies for their output.[9] In the Community of Nine, this was acceptable as a form of subsidy to the Mezzogiorno (especially Calabria and Apulia), because there was no prospect of Italy, the sole producer, supplying more than the Community could consume. With the enlargement to include Spain and Greece, after Italy the world's second and third largest producers, respectively, the picture becomes much more complicated. It is not certain that surpluses will be so huge as it appears they would be, because nobody knows exactly what Italy really produces—it is suspected that the statistics of production are fraudulent. Whatever the real situation in Italy—assuming anyone knows—the claims put forward to obtain production aids are over three times the sales on which consumer subsidies are paid.[10] Greek production also rose suspiciously on entry into the EC.

Nevertheless, even on the official production figures of 1975–77, which give a fairly modest account of Italian output, the Community's self-sufficiency in olive oil would move from 88 percent to 121 percent with both Greece and Spain included (Com-EC, 1981b). However, Greek and Spanish prices are much lower than Community (that is, Italian) prices, and it will be difficult to counter the incentives to raise output (Tovias, 1979, pp. 42–43; Pepelasis, 1980, Table 25, pp. 38-39). Olive oil subsidies added to those for rapeseed and other Community oilseeds, could turn vegetable fats into one of the two or three major items on the Community budget. Fats could rise (at 1981 prices and budgets) by 1.5 billion ECUs or more, to the equivalent of 14 percent of the farm budget, an amount inferior only to dairy products and cereals. The irony is that, after all this, Community self-sufficiency in "proteins" (that is, in feed derived from oilseeds) will have risen from 20 percent only to 24 percent, an almost negligible change (Com-EC, 1981a, p. 38; European Parliament, 1982, p. 93).

Olive oil is perhaps the exemplary product for gauging the difficulties of meeting the problem of poverty in the Mediterranean by the dominant means open to decision-makers operating through the present CAP: the subsidizing of agricultural development or of particular products. To subsidize the product leads to unsellable surpluses: tinned fruit and vegetables, wine, and olive oil are all cases in point. It encourages fraud, especially glaring in Italy. It may reach poor areas, but not always the poor in these areas. Rather, it tends to enrich middlemen, including, as some suspect and recent revelations seem to have confirmed, the Mafia and Camorra, more than the small producers themselves.[11] And subsidies are not confined to small producers: the Italian Government has resisted attempts to put an upper limit of 10 hectares on production aids for hard wheat. Moreover, aid to peasants clearly would not meet the problems of seasonal labor peculiar to the *latifundios* of Spanish Andalusia.[12] It concentrates efforts on lines of production which have little future prospects of expansion and diverts attention from broader-based development programs. Surpluses of olive oil could also vitally damage close associates, like Tunisia.

Olive oil, therefore, poses many of the wider issues that recession has made increasingly urgent regarding the role of the Mediterranean in the policies of the Community and especially of an enlarged Community, including Iberia. With Spain and Portugal, the poorer states and regions would account for over 60 percent of the Community's farm labor and half the cultivated area. Given the generally lower levels of prices for southern products in the Mediterranean countries, surpluses are virtually certain to arise for such products, which have not in the past constituted major problems for the Community. Olive oil, wine, and tomatoes are likely to be among the more troublesome commodities. In any case, budgetary costs will rise. A Commission study prepared in Spring 1982 estimated that (at 1980 prices) it would, in a Community of Twelve, have been necessary to raise VAT contributions to 1.05 percent or even 1.14 percent, instead of the 0.73 percent that obtained in the Community of Nine that year. The proportionate increase would not be enormous: an extra 1.6–2.5 billion ECUs at 1980 prices, or 10 to 15 percent.[13] But by this alone, enlargement would break the upper ceiling set on Community VAT revenues by the Luxembourg decision of 1970 and would pre-empt a great · deal of any increase in the VAT ceiling to 1.4 percent.

Southern interests will have to be taken into account much more than they have been in the Community. This needs to be emphasized because of the relatively slight leverage exerted so far by the southern coalition of member states—less, for example, than the United Kingdom. Britain, as a big creditor of the budget and a net importer from the other member states, has been in a strong position: threats to refuse to pay dues into the budget have carried conviction. This is not the case with the new Mediterranean countries, in particular. The southern states are smaller economies than the British and have proportionately far larger agricultural sectors. Some of the most vulnerable sectors (olives, tobacco, and so on) obtain, and presumably would continue to obtain, large Community subsidies. The southern states are likely, therefore, to be net beneficiaries of the budget. In such conditions, the southern member states will have less will to emulate Britain and fewer cards to play.

However, this takes no account of the long-term strategies and influence of a group potentially in difficulties and with strong claims upon the support of their richer partners. As a substantial coalition with net import deficits; an agricultural sector of more than average Community importance; and relative poverty to give urgency and appeal to their special preoccupations; it is hard to believe that four southern members of an enlarged Community, backed by France in some respects, would fail to make a cumulative impact on the Community.

First, southern states are likely to be reluctant to reduce real prices for northern products. This is consonant with attempts to become as self-sufficient as possible in their high-cost (but important) cereal, sugarbeet, and livestock sectors. It is also important for social and political reasons. Some of the most densely populated and poorest farming regions, as in northwestern Spain, depend on cattle, not on Mediterranean crops.

Second, southern states will seek to shift the balance of farm spending to southern products. Because the markets for these do not seem too promising and there will be resistance from the North, they are likely to emphasize other forms of transfer, such as straight subsidies or general development and social programs.

Third, as far as agriculture itself is concerned, such programs could well stress "structural" improvements, in the wake of the Mediterranean program of 1978. Such operations increase production capacity and the risk of surpluses.

In short, there is an evident incompatibility between the southern desire for parity, when pursued primarily through the CAP, and policies to control agricultural output. If the problems of the south are to be dealt with, policy will have to break out of this straitjacket. The Commission has already been moving in this direction, seeking to integrate agricultural, regional, and social policies in broader development strategies.

In this, as in other ways, the Mediterranean raises the stakes in the CAP. Southern influence may retard restraints on agriculture; it may, by adding to the tariff of claims on the CAP, increase the sense of urgency for new balances and policies in the Community; or it may even break the apparently fragile frame of compromises on which the CAP rests. Whatever the outcome, the Mediterranean heightens the pressure behind the issues.

Trade and budget deficits. Southern countries are in the thick of this problem too, though it is not confined to them. Exporters in the Community have tended to gain both through trade and through the budget. The opening up of markets, first in Germany and Italy and later in Britain and Greece, has favored them. The financial system of the CAP has also tended to reward countries (or more precisely farmers, processors, and traders in the member states) generating surpluses to put in store or export at Community expense. The importers have paid. Germany was both the major importer and the paymaster of the EC-6 farm fund. She was not exactly glad to pay, but resigned to her contribution as a tax on the richest member state and as the price of being accepted again as a member of the club and being reconciled with her neighbors. This attitude had worn thin by the advent of recession in 1973 and a decade later, the Germans were beginning to dig in their heels over the budget, despite their search for higher farm prices.

German attitudes were almost certainly influenced by those of Britain and Italy. Far from being the strongest economies in the Community, Britain and Italy in the 1970s suffered from the most spectacular economic disorders and were, or appeared to be, among the poorest.[14] Italy did nothing about her increasingly adverse balance of agricultural trade during the boom years when consumption ran so rapidly ahead of domestic output. She made an issue of the matter only in the depressed 1970s when her self-sufficiency was in fact rising again (Appendix Table 2). Britain, which had always recognized the farm balance would be unfavorable, found that the promised "dynamic" benefits of the common market for her manufacturing industries failed to materialize. This outweighed the fact that the trade gap in food itself was being narrowed quite unexpectedly fast (Appendix Table 7). More recently, Greece, on entering the Community, has seen a sudden and relatively huge trade gap open up even in her food trade with the other member states.

Deficits in both Italy and Britain have also led to budget problems. Britain, the extreme case, pays into the Community as a big country and receives funds as a relatively small agricultural producer. In 1980 (though not 1981), the Netherlands were paid 75 percent more by the Community farm fund than Britain was. This was galling, since the Netherlands were not only much smaller but much richer. Italy might have faced similar problems, but her agriculture was larger and it has become an unwritten rule that, as the poorest of the founding states, she should not suffer deficits on the Community budget. There was only one significant slip-up, in 1978, and it was immediately corrected (Com-EC, 1979b, pp. 14, 17). The high subsidies for olive oil and tobacco are a direct reflection of this solicitude (Appendix Table 12). Much the same guarantee has been given to Greece for her transition period to full membership of the Community and will no doubt be confirmed beyond that time.

Mrs. Thatcher, in threatening not to pay Britain's dues to the Community, from 1980 onwards, in effect sought a similar, though not so complete, concession on behalf of Britain. There is, however, a significant difference of principle as well as of degree between the compensation Italy and Greece have gained and that sought by Britain. Because they have relatively much larger farm sectors, it has been possible to make transfers in a pragmatic way without raising questions of principle. Britain, anxious to limit domestic budgets in general, as well as her CAP deficit, tried to introduce a precedent. Whatever the Community agreements, prompted by article 201 of the Treaty of Rome, may imply, Britain would like to establish a formal ceiling on how much one country may be asked to contribute to common funds. This would introduce overt quotas, which have previously been avoided, into Community policy and financing.

Thus, between every major type of agriculture there has persisted a latent problem which, in most cases, has become active. Between the autarchic and mercantile agricultures rears the huge disputed market for animal feed (though all countries have their mercantile farmers). Between northern and southern agricultures lie a whole range of issues, at the root of which is the problem of attitudes on transfers between rich and poor. Finally, there are strains, which have so far taken a mainly budgetary form, between surplus agricultures and deficit ones, the most extreme example being Britain, which has not yet admitted to feeling comfortable in a CAP designed by and for others. In short, structural and policy differences between the types of agriculture of the Community have not been merely theoretical. They have precipitated clearly discernible controversies between equally defined camps, which have already influenced the development of the Community itself.

EXTENSIVE AND INTENSIVE PRODUCTION

Interestingly, most of the differences between types of agriculture are more closely connected with traditions of policy and social constraints than with preordained "structures." Even the problems of southern agriculture have had more to do with, first, social backwardness and, more recently, the process of catching up, than with, for instance, climate. There is, however, one structural feature that influences policy attitudes and is so obvious that its implications can sometimes be overlooked. This is the simple fact of countries' (or regions') different natural endowments. It is notable, if not altogether surprising, that four of the five exporting agricultures (Appendix Table 2) in the Community of Ten (Table 4.2) rank at the top in the amount of agricultural land available per head of the *total* population. The fifth food-exporting country, and in many ways the bellwether for agriculture in the Community, the Netherlands, has *less* land per head of total population than any other member state. It has largely made up for this handicap, however, by exploiting huge imports of animal feed.

The amount of land relative to the labor used on it is usually taken as the measure of intensive and extensive farming. Countries with limited land try to increase its productivity, in value and volume, and tend to stress high prices: the extreme example is perhaps Japan. Countries with relatively more land emphasize the productivity of labor rather than of land and can more easily afford to envisage price competition.

Compared with the traditional exporters of grains of the Americas and Australia, all Community countries are in this sense intensive producers. The Community country with the highest land to farm labor ratio (as distinct from

---

Table 4.2   Hectares of Agricultural Area (including pasture) per Head
of the Total Population in Each Member State of the EC-10 (mid-1979)

Ireland	1.75
Greece	0.97
France	0.59
Denmark	0.57
United Kingdom	0.33
Italy	0.31
West Germany	0.20
Belgium-Luxembourg	0.15
Netherlands	0.14

Source: FAO, *Production Yearbook, 1980.*

---

total population) is Britain, with 13.3 hectares cultivated land per farmworker in 1980. Compare this with 26 hectares per farmworker in Argentina, 86 in Canada, and 87 in the U.S. Yields per hectare in these countries are low to very low by European standards, but the costs of raising crops are usually cheaper all the same because of the highly efficient use of labor and capital made possible by plentiful and relatively cheap land. (FAO, 1980b, Tables 1 and 3, pp. 45–71).

However, even within the Community, there are significant differences in land–labor ratios between different sectors of farming, regions, and member states. To simplify by looking at only the differences between member states, the data (see Table 4.3) show that they fall into two distinct groups:

1. Countries with over 13 persons per 100 hectares of utilizable agricultural area (UAA): Greece 29, Portugal 24, Italy 19, Netherlands 16 and Germany 13.[15] This is land intensive farming by any standard.
2. The other member states, with eight or fewer persons working per 100 hectares of UAA, ranging from Britain with 4 to Belgium-Luxembourg with 8. By Europe's not very exacting standards, these are countries which practise, in relative terms, land-extensive farming.

Of course, national averages tell only part of the story. Cereals in East Anglia and the Paris basin tend to be produced extensively on large mechanized farms (that is, they are capital but not land intensive). Cattle and dairy farms tend to be smaller and to vary considerably by region. Fruit, vegetables, wine, pigs, and poultry (the last two being the most profitable lines in Community farming) tend to be produced intensively on small areas, and sometimes off the land altogether.[16] The poorest areas are often those of extensive animal farming, as, for example, in the French Massif Central and Sardinia, where little capital and technology are applied. Because of such differences, regional variations in a single country can be wider than those between countries. This is particularly true of Italy and Spain, which both have a multitude of tiny farms contrasting with a small minority of holdings extending over huge, sometimes barren, landscapes (see Table 4.4).

Of course land–labor ratios alone do not account for the dispersion of productivity across the Community (Table 4.3). Assuming that land constraints imply comparatively low labor yields but high ones of land, only Italy conforms to the ideal pattern. Similarly, only Britain and France, with comparatively plentiful land, conform to the model of relatively high labor but low land yields. For the rest, Denmark, Germany, and the Netherlands have high productivity of both land and labor, irrespective of land-labor ratios; and at the other end of the scale, Greece, Ireland, Portugal, and Spain all have low-land and labor ratios. Taking yields of milk and wheat as the yardsticks of technical efficiency: (1) Four northern countries (Britain, Denmark, Germany, and the Netherlands) all have high yields; (2) France and Belgium have high wheat but rather low milk yields; and all four southern countries plus Luxembourg have low yields of both wheat and milk while Ireland (not a significant producer of wheat) has low yields for milk.[17] Fairly predictably,

Table 4.3   The Structure of Agriculture, EC-12, 1977

	GAP (millions of dollars)[a] (1)	Employment in Agric. (thousands) (2)	GAP per Pers. Empl. (dollars) (3)	Utilized Agric. Area (UAA) (thousands cf ha)[e] (4)	GAP per hectare UAA (dollars) (5)	Employment per 100 ha UAA (6)	Farm Number (thousands) (7)	Average Farm Size in GAP ($) (8)	Average Farm Size in Employm. (persons) (9)	Average Farm Size in UAA (ha) (10)
France	17,816	2,034	8,759	29,250	609	7.0	1,149	15,240	1.74	25.5
Italy	14,840	3,149	4,713	16,271	912	19.4	2,192	7,228	1.53	7.4
W. Germany	14,452	1,655	8,732	12,344	1,171	13.4	859	16,256	1.86	14.4
Spain	10,703	2,568	4,168	31,516	340	8.1	1,939[g]	5,520	1.32	16.3
U.K.	6,014	735[c]	8,182	17,171	350	4.3	262	22,357	2.73	65.5
Netherlands	4,990	320[d]	15,594	2,053	2,431	15.6	137	35,390	2.27	15.0
Greece	3,866	899	4,300	3,125	995	28.8	732	4,767	1.11	4.3
Denmark	3,143	219	14,352	2,926	1,074	7.5	124	24,748	1.72	23.6
Portugal	2,140	972[d]	2,202	4,130	518	23.5	500[f]	4,280	1.94	8.3
Belg-Lux.	2,017	132	15,280	1,576	1,280	8.4	104	18,676	1.22	15.2
Ireland	1,314	236	5,568	5,068	259	4.7	225	5,054	0.91	22.5
EC-12	81,295	12,919	6,293	125,430	648	10.3	8,223	9,835	1.56	15.3

	GAP As % GDP[a] (11)	Agric. Empl. As % of Total Empl.[b] (12)	Inter-Sectoral Income Parity Index[i] (13)	Labor Productivity Index[k] (14)	Land Productivity Index[m] (15)	Labor/ Land Ratio Index[n] (16)	Percentage Distribution of EC-12 Total:			
							GAP[p] (17)	Agric. Employ- ment[q] (18)	Utilized Agric. Area[r] (19)	Farm Numbers[s] (20)
France	4.7	9.7	48	139	94	67	21.9	15.7	23.5	14.0
Italy	7.6	15.9	48	75	141	157	18.3	24.4	15.5	26.7
W. Germany	2.8	6.8	41	139	181	127	17.8	12.8	10.1	10.4
Spain	9.3	20.7	45	66	52	77	13.2	19.9	25.9	23.6
U.K.	2.5	3.0	83	130	54	65	7.4	5.7	8.8	3.2
Netherlands	4.7	7.0[d]	67	248	375	235	6.1	2.5	1.1	1.7
Greece	14.7	28.4	52	68	97	143	4.8	7.0	4.9	8.9
Denmark	6.8	9.1	75	228	166	51	3.9	1.7	3.4	1.5
Portugal	13.1	28.3[d]	46	35	80	167	2.6	7.5	4.5	6.1
Belg-Lux.	2.5	3.3	76	243	198	91	2.5	1.0	1.1	1.3
Ireland	14.0	23.1	61	88	40	147	1.6	1.8	1.2	2.7
EC-12	4.7	9.8	48	100	100	100	100	100	100	100

a UN Year Book of National Accounts Statistics 1978 (Current price data)
b OECD Annual Review of Agricultural Policies, 1979
c Estimate including spouses
d FAO Production Yearbook, 1977
e Commission of the EC, Agricultural Situation in the Community, 1981
f 1970 Estimate
g 1972 Data
h 1974 Data

i Col. 11 divided by col. 12
k Derived from col. 3
m Derived from col. 5
n Derived from col. 6
p Derived from col. 1
q Derived from col. 2
r Derived from col. 4
s Derived from col. 7

Note: 1977 is the last year for which details on UAA (col. 4) and farm numbers (col. 7) are available for all EC-12.
"Agriculture" includes agriculture, forestry, hunting and fishery.
"Farm number" excludes farms smaller than 1 hectare.
"Utilized agricultural area" (UAA) includes arable lands, pasture, and permanent crops. For Greece, "cultivated area" has been retained for reasons explained in note 15, Ch. 4.

Table 4.4   Farms Over 50 Hectares in the Agriculture of Italy, Spain, France, and UK

Category of Farms	Italy	Spain[a]	France	UK
Farms of 50 hectares as				
Percent all farms	1.7	4.7	12.5	31.1
Percent UAA	30.5	68.0	43.0	81.0
Average area of farms over 50 hectares (in hectares)	130	260	88	171
No farms over 50 hectares (in thousands)	38	120	143	81

[a] Includes forests.

Source: Com-EC, *ASC 1981*, pp. 266–67, data for 1977 (only ones available for Italy); and for Spain, *Anuario de Estadistica Agraria 1980*, p. 38, data for the census year of 1972.

one finds here a close concordance with ranking according to purchase of factors of production as an indicator of the intensity of capital in farming (Table 1.9). The only recent change of significance has been the rapid increase in the proportion of factors of production bought in Ireland. Thus, in general, as common sense would suggest, the broad level of development of an economy has at least as powerful an effect on yields as the special characteristics of this or that national, regional, or sectional agriculture.

Nevertheless, policy attitudes taken up in the past suggest that such patterns imply latent convergences and divergences of interest between countries (particularly on individual products) which could produce possible future alliances. Land–labor ratios hint at which countries might sometimes serve as "models" to others developing in their wake (see Figure 4.1). If Britain were to approach self-sufficiency, as it has already done for cereals, the degree of correspondence, say on prices, with France might surprise those judging only by conventional assumptions. To take another example, it is a common view in Britain that milk production should be concentrated in Ireland, Britain, and parts (presumably the west) of France—that is, in the maritime areas of the Community (House of Lords, 1980b, pp. 12, Q.27). From this point of view, Germany, in particular, is not a "natural" milk producer. It is equally consistent that (as Chapter 3 shows) both in Ireland and in France voices have been raised advocating extensive cattle rearing (and in the case of France, cereal-growing as well). Along the other axis of development, too, the various coalitions in the past between Germany, Italy, and Belgium seem easily explicable. While this is not an infallible signpost to policy, contrasts between extensive and intensive farming have to be kept in mind as indicators of potential national attitudes, once the pressures force decision-makers to fall back from preferred positions and take care of basic needs.

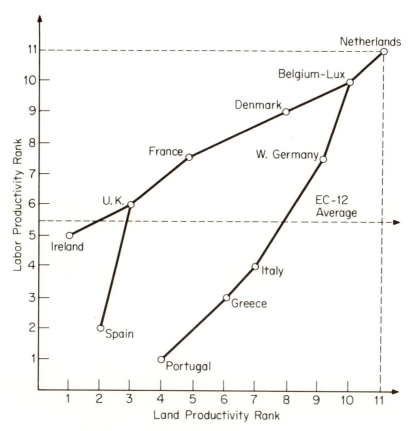

NOTE. The rankings do not refer to actual productivity of Land/Labor,
but to the rank of each country (from 1-11) on the yardstick chosen.
Luxemburg is included with Belgium.

Figure 4.1.
Labor and Land Productivity Ranking, in EC-12, 1977

Market Shares

One of the principal causes of the strains between the different agricultural
structures and traditions of the member states of the Community is their
common struggle for larger market shares. Market shares are, of course,
related to the structural features just discussed. But they were also inherent in
the decision, mainly but not only imposed by Germany, to pursue a high price
policy. High guaranteed prices are a form of protection, as is evident from the
politics of the establishment of the CAP. It was confirmed by the introduction

of minimum prices for trade between states in the Community during the wine war between France and Italy. It is reflected in similar suggestions for dealing with problems of the enlargement of the EC to include Spain (Harris, Swinbank and Wilkinson, 1983, p. 148). By the same token, while high prices remove market balances as the arbiters of competition, they have to be replaced by something else. In practice, given the general expansionism to which high prices have led, market shares have tended to become a criterion of national success. Market shares become more than a standard of success once the growth of the market and the replacement of outsiders in the preferential area of the Community cease to be relatively costless. Market shares become an issue of negotiation, even when not acknowledged as such.

It is not, then, surprising that the different outlooks and presumed interests of exporters and importers have dominated the entire history of the CAP. They shaped its very conception, given the high price policy adopted to persuade the countries that were ostensibly weaker in farming—Germany at their head—to open their markets to their expectant exporting partners. Trade interests have also conditioned the controversies of the CAP, especially in the recession-ridden years since 1973, more perhaps than any other single factor.

EXPORTERS AND IMPORTERS

Among importing countries and especially in Britain, where a strong constituency has always deplored the CAP and seen it as a convenient stalking-horse for general opposition to the Community, a popular judgment was that the CAP constitutes daylight robbery by the exporting nations. Certainly, the exporters, especially France and the Netherlands, gained greatly from the new outlets offered by the CAP until around 1972. But the clear divide between exporters as beneficiaries and importers as losers from the CAP has been blurred by later developments. In particular, the general rise in the levels of self-sufficiency in food in the member states has produced a distinct change in bargaining power in the CAP. As the traditional importers, especially Germany and Britain, have increased their self-sufficiency, the potential value of their markets to others has declined. The importer now holds the whiphand. The producer in the importing country has nothing to lose by expanding the national farm product and the treasury gains an improved balance of trade, whatever surpluses may weigh down the Community as a whole. The net exporter has no weapons with which to retain the Community markets gradually being whittled away by the producers of the importing country. In this context, it is perfectly logical, if hardly *communautaire*, for importers to concentrate on cutting budget commitments to the Community, while expanding domestic output and cutting obligations, as well, in trade.

In these conditions, the obvious option for the exporting country is to look elsewhere and sell onto the world market. This is not an easy operation, nor one that can be exploited rapidly. Developing new markets requires time.[18] The strategy is also less secure than the Community preference seemed to be, yet many of the budgetary advantages of the earlier operation can be recouped, given present CAP rules. CAP prices being what they are, exports can only take place, for the major traded products, with subsidies paid out of the funds of the Community. The countries exporting least onto the world market contribute comparatively most to the subsidies for the exporter. France, for one, has been pursuing a policy of exports heavily subsidized by the Community. Since 1969, she has provided much the biggest proportion of the increased EC-9 exports of food to the outside world, enlarging her contribution between 1978 and 1980 to fully one half.[19] This strategy, then, may not have been spurred after 1973 by the idea of *pétrole vert*, a later accretion. France dominates Community farm exports to the world (see Table 4.5) and at the same time, since 1972, has been losing much of her preponderance within the Community. Her lead is particularly marked in the commodities which the Community's farm budgets most heavily subsidize. If one looks at rates of growth, however, German performance on world markets has been more expansive than French for two decades and in the 1970s those of Belgium and Ireland even more so. Denmark and the Netherlands, on the other hand, have been relatively backward in this area, like Italy and Britain, the last of which seems to have concentrated on the Community market (Appendix Table 8). In many ways, it looks as if a new area of competition is opening up.

In short, great changes are taking place in the commercial conditions of the CAP. Twenty years ago, there was a clear notion of who were food exporters and importers and rather summary ideas of the future division of labor

---

Table 4.5 Proportions of Extra-EC Farm Exports Provided by Each Member State (EC-9 = 100), 1974 and 1980.

	All Food Exports (Nimexe Chapters 0–24)		Main Exports Subsidized by EAGGF (Nimexe 2,4, 10, 11 and 17)	
	1974	1980	1974	1980
Belgium-Luxembourg	4.4	5.1	7.5	8.6
Denmark	10.1	7.7	8.6	7.5
France	27.7	29.9	42.2	40.3
Germany	13.8	15.2	10.5	14.7
Ireland	2.1	3.2	3.6	3.0
Italy	9.4	8.5	5.2	5.6
Netherlands	15.8	15.5	15.4	14.2
United Kingdom	16.8	15.0	6.9	6.1

Source: Com-EC, Eurostat, *Analytical Tables of Foreign Trade*, Nimexe series, 1974 and 1980. Nimexe Ch. 2—fresh meat; Ch. 4—dairy products; Ch. 10—cereals; Ch. 11—flour; and Ch. 17—sugar and products. For the two internationally accepted ways of establishing trade statistics, see Chapter 1, note 19.

between them. Today, importers have become more self-sufficient and in some cases formidable exporters themselves; while they and the exporters of the past have almost equally come to look, in recent years, to external markets. Old recipes do not apply to the politics of the emerging commercial geography. The new landscape needs to be explored in its own terms.

The most comprehensive base for this is probably the detailed and largely comparable supply balances now available from the Commission for the years 1973–81.[20] The various constraints on Community supply and demand offer some scope for extrapolation—not to prophesy but to look for thresholds of impossibility that provide the latest dates by which change becomes imperative (if price and other effects have not already made it so). To this extent, extrapolation can help to switch on warning lights and illuminate zones of risk. If, for example, the trends of 1973–81 persist to 1990, the self-sufficiency ratio of the Community will rise from 110 in 1981, to 125 in 1990, and 143 in 2000.[21] Given the difficulties already arising, such a rate of expansion is obviously unsustainable.

This is the obvious, dominant fact. At the same time, for concrete situations, one has to look at individual commodities. Four commodities immediately suggest themselves—cereals (both breadgrains and feedgrains), sugar, milk, and beef—because these account (in value and in 1980) for half the gross agricultural product (GAP), three-quarters of the common farm budget, and nearly nine-tenths of the food export subsidies of the EC-9 (*ASC 1981*, pp. 174-75, 244-47). Yet, dominant as they are, they represent only northern products. Future policies, assuming they lay more stress on the south, will have a broader range. Unfortunately, it is impossible, without detailed figures for the 1970s for Greece, Portugal, and Spain, to pin down the trends; and price changes could affect them anyway. A shift of emphasis to southern products has to be kept in mind, as it will probably amplify the figures to which other calculations lead.

Were the trends of 1973–81 to persist (Table 4.6), the net import needs of the member states of the Community would shrink steadily and rapidly (reflecting, of course, the fact that this is what they did during the 1970s). This is plain when we relate the sum of the net imports of the member states with deficits to the sum of the net exports of their Community partners with trade surpluses for 1973, 1981 and 1990 (Table 4.7). Net imports would disappear by 1990 for each of the products. Actual imports would be insignificant except for feedgrains. Fewer and fewer countries would be in deficit on any product and more and more would be in surplus.

It is politically significant to note, for each product and member state, when the watershed is crossed from a net deficit into a net surplus. In Table 4.8, a plus sign indicates that a country was already in surplus for the commodity in question in 1973; the dates thereafter indicate when a country, on the conditions assumed, would move from deficit to surplus; and blanks indicate a continuing deficit in 2000. Of the 40 slots in Table 4.8, 17 already indicated a surplus in 1973; another 15 surpluses would appear before 2000; leaving only 8 still open at that date, three of them—for wheat, milk and beef—in Italy.

Table 4.6 Production and Consumption of Major Commodities in EC-9, 1981, and Projections of 1973–81 Trends to 1990 and 2000 (in million tons of grain equivalent)

Commodity	1981			1990			2000		
	P	C	P–C	P	C	P–C	P	C	P–C
Wheat [a,b]	52.0	43.1	9.0	68.1	44.0	24.1	91.9	45.0	46.9
Coarse grains [a,b]	67.6	71.9	–4.3	75.4	72.2	3.2	85.1	72.6	12.6
Total cereals [a,b,d]	119.6	115.0	4.6	143.5	116.2	27.3	177.0	117.6	59.5
Growth production	100			120			148		
Growth consumption		100			101			102	
Surplus as % prodn.			3.8			19.0			33.6
Sugar [c,d]	11.2	9.2	2.0	20.2	8.3	11.9	31.8	7.7	24.2
Milk prodn [b,d]	80.6	70.2	10.5	97.7	77.3	20.4	120.9	86.1	34.8
Beef & veal [b,d]	55.2	52.1	3.1	72.7	54.3	18.4	98.6	56.8	41.8
Total sugar, milk, beef	147.0	131.5	15.6	190.6	139.9	50.7	251.3	150.6	100.8
Growth production	100			130			171		
Growth consumption		100			106			115	
Surplus as % prodn.			10.6			26.7			40.1

[a] Including animal feed etc.
[b] Base 1973–81.
[c] Base 1973–78 only. Data for sugar for 1980 and 1981 include molasses (unspecified), which are excluded from data 1973–78.
[d] Cereals = 1 times weight in grains, Sugar = 1, Milk = 0.8, Beef = 8.

P = Production (Final Agricultural Production).
C = Consumption (Utilization for Food and Industry).

Source: Com-EC, Eurostat, Günther Thiede, Agricultural Statistical Studies, No. 22, *Overall Accounts on the Community Supply Situation Based on Grain Equivalents* (1980); and *Crop Production 1–1983*, updated figures for 1979/80 (1980) and 1980/81 (1981), pp. 129–53.

The others would be wheat in Ireland, feedgrains in Belgium, Germany, and the Netherlands (all confirmed purchasers of imported feed for their livestock), and dairy products in Belgium. That is all. The tendency to high self-sufficiency was clear in Germany during the 1970s; and in Britain for grains in the 1980s and for everything else in the 1990s. This table gives statistical expression to the passing of an era.

The pressures of such a change will inevitably find expression in more exports to the world, which will have economic, and therefore political, consequences. Were one to assume that Community export subsidies per unit were the same as the average for the four years 1978–81 (which encompass years when export subsidies were high and others when they were low), the costs would increase by 6.3 billion ECUs a year by 1990 (at constant 1981 prices) and by a further 9.7 billion ECUs by the end of the century. Export refunds for the commodities under review accounted for a quarter of the total Community budget in 1981.[22] Yet based on these results, the subsidies to sell the four commodities alone would increase that entire budget by a third by 1990. Given the reliance of the budget on VAT revenues, this would be the equivalent of a value added tax of 1.29 percent in 1990 and 2.07 pecent in 2000, as against 0.79 percent in 1981. This is independent of the 0.26 to 0.35 percent extra VAT needed (on static assumptions) for the enlargement of the Community[23] and the unpredictable subsequent costs for the CAP to deal with growing Mediterranean production and claims. It ignores pressures for more nonfarm spending, as well as the likelihood that large quantities of Community exports would probably push international prices down and—therefore— subsidies up. The 2.5 percent VAT which the McDougall report saw as the minimum "federal" budget to reduce by 10 percent the income gap between the richest and poorest regions of the Community heaves into sight (McDougall, 1977); but the goals and effects of the expenditure would be of an entirely different order. It is hard to imagine the governments being willing to pay up during a recession or its aftermath when governments have reverted to habits of extreme financial caution.

The extrapolations also point to marked relative shifts between the member states in trade. For crops, France, the sole major net surplus producer in

Table 4.7   Net Imports of Deficit States in the EC-9 Compared to Net Exports of Surplus States in 1973 and 1981 with Projections to 1990 (based on trade to all destinations and volumes in grain equivalents; net exports = 1.0)

Commodity	1973 (actual)	1981 (actual)	1990 (extrapolated)
Wheat	1.16	0.33	0.12
Feedgrains	2.22	1.46	0.72
Sugar	1.42	0.46	0.05
Milk products	0.67	0.32	0.12
Beef and veal	2.99	0.66	0.13

Source: Com-EC, Eurostat, *Overall Accounts on the Community Supply Situation based on Grain Equivalents*, Agricultural Statistical Studies, No. 22, 1980 (for 1973–78); supplemented by Günther Thiede, *Mengenmaessige Gesamtrechnungen zur EG-Versorgungslage*, Agrarwirtschaft, Bonn, March 1981 (for 1979); Com-EC, Eurostat, *Crop Production*, 1–1983, pp. 129–53 (for 1980–81).

Table 4.8   Deficits and Surpluses per Country and Commodity in EC-9 with Dates of Shift from Deficit to Surplus under Assumed Conditions between 1973 and 2000 (+ = surplus in 1973)

	Wheat	Feedgrains	Sugar	Milk Products	Beef
Belgium	1992		+		1977
Denmark	+	1991	+	+	+
France	+	+	+	+	+
Germany	1979		1974	+	1978
Ireland		1985	+	+	+
Italy		1993	1984		
Netherlands	1990		+	+	+
United Kingdom	1983	1984	1999	1990	1987

Source: As Table 4.7.

1981, would be joined, in each commodity, by one or more important surplus producers. The most prominent would be Britain in cereals, especially wheat, and Germany, which would actually surpass France, in sugar. For milk, the main expansionary forces would again be in Germany and Britain, though proportionately they would be still more intense in Ireland and the Netherlands. In beef, expansion would be universal, but strongest in Germany, France, the Netherlands, Britain, and Ireland. The net effects of these developments would be that France's dominant position in Community agriculture would be further eroded in favor of Germany and, almost equally, Britain. The small countries would remain in much the same position as they are. In terms of the increase for all the four commodities combined (in grain equivalents), the most expansionary of the member states would be the United Kingdom, with the stress on cereals, and the Netherlands. Of course, all this simply reflects, in a magnified way, what actually happened between 1973 and 1981.[24]

Such shifts in the balance of supplies are bound to have consequences also for the financial balances between member states, though these seem more moderate than one might imagine. Germany's budget deficit of 1981 would be moderately increased by 1990, but that of Britain reduced by as much as two-thirds. Italy's moderate surplus and France's almost exact balance of 1981 would turn into limited deficits, neither being as big as the relatively considerable one of Belgium (which, however, gains from Community spending in Brussels). On the other hand, Ireland's large surplus would become half as big again and so would Denmark's modest one.[25]

When one considers these possibilities, the 1970s cast an interesting light on the 1980s and beyond. There are four directions of potential change. The first concerns the effect of expansion on the overall attitude of the member states toward the CAP. All, with the possible exception of Italy, will soon become net exporters of the commodities under review. When one considers the diversity of products, there is, or will shortly be, no country, not even Italy, which can be regarded as a systematic importer. All will have taken a stake in the continuing existence of the CAP by seeking outlets for export. In the past, this would have meant dependence on the preferential markets of the Community. But now the internal Community preference will mean less and less in practice, whatever claims are made for it in theory. This is not to say that its attractions will disappear. Community food trade is still worth nearly twice as much as exports to the world (Appendix Table 6). Specialized trade channels, like the conveyor belt for milk from Bavaria to northern Italy, will remain important.But retaining the preferential market will be defensive. It will not offer new frontiers; on the contrary, horizons will tend to shrink. Open trade inside the Community, which has been crucial in the commitment to the CAP, will lose part of its force. So long as they provide a margin of new gains, export markets will interest the decision-makers more.

Thus, a primary preoccupation with world exports, to the extent it has not already appeared, will constitute the second change. The politics of world exports are quite different from those of the preferential home market. Trade is more heavily concentrated on basic products, such as grains, reflecting worldwide protectionism which reserves domestic food markets for the home industry. The relative strengths and weaknesses of the member states are also very different in world markets than in European ones. The Netherlands, for instance, have dominated internal Community trade but are much less well established outside. All the smaller producers, precisely because they have been so successful as specialist exporters to European markets, will have to make a correspondingly greater effort to convert to international markets (Appendix Table 9). Denmark has already suffered considerably from the shrinkage of relative food markets in the 1960s (Appendix Table 8). The role of the Community, too, is likely to change. It may well continue to be of great importance, but its value will not be so deeply rooted in the preferential European market. Its advantages will be much more like those of an export cartel. This is much more uncertain than a preferential area.

A third potential line of development concerns the impact on the budget and the member states' political attitudes toward the CAP. At least two major pressures should affect the Community budget: the obligation to help the poorer countries—the Community budget has been very favorable both to Ireland and to Greece—and the growing costs of disposing of surpluses abroad. Since the Community budget depends increasingly on VAT, barring reforms, the weight of payments for expansion to Iberia will fall mainly upon the larger and richer countries providing most of VAT revenues. If that is reinforced by trends in exports to the world, one could find France becoming a significant net funder of the Community, while Britain's relative contribution might shrink slightly. By this time, the flow of net funds in the Community might be settling increasingly into a channel from the large (Germany, France and Britain) to the poor—to Ireland and member states in the Mediterranean area. This would constitute a de facto step towards the kind of Community, stressing social transfers to the poor, which the Commission showed signs of defining in the Jenkins presidency. The country most likely to cut across this pattern would be Denmark, rich but in surplus, and she could come under pressure to drop into line. (The Netherlands are, and would be, more or less in balance.) This change, in turn, could be part of a wider movement to revise the Community's finances.

The fourth, and related, shift implicit in recent trends of the CAP would be quite simply the growing visible cost to society of supporting a shrinking number of farmers producing more and more. If the costs to the Community of growing export surpluses and other items increase by 4 to 5 percent per annum or more (export refunds alone 3.5 percent per annum), while European economies on average grow between 1 percent and 3 percent per annum, one can expect little relief in political tensions over the budget. The costs would become more visible as surpluses brought about a shift in the proportions of funding from the consumer in the shops to the taxpayer through the farm funds. The shopper has some sense of choice, however illusory, and costs of food tend to be influenced at least as much by manufacturing and distribution as by farmers' prices. When budgets and taxes grow, the pain is infinitely more direct: the process is far more contentious and likely to arouse opposition. There are the makings here of a greater cleavage between farmers and society than there has been in the past 30 years when consumers paid the bulk of farm supports.

INFLATION AND MARKET SHARES

On examination, market shares are also an important ingredient, though not the only one, in the problems raised in the Community by high inflation since 1969. In its full but pristine form, which lasted only from July 1967 to August 1969, the CAP provided the frame for a preferential, internally open European market resting on the assumption of a virtually single monetary area. One of the arguments at the time for further economic integration leading ultimately to political federation was that any reversion to national economic patterns would kill the CAP. There was assumed to be an absolute incompatibility between its existence and that of radically different national economic policies and performances. Yet this potentially lethal environment has been precisely the one in which it has managed to survive since its second year of existence.

The flaw in the initial assumptions of the CAP emerged almost at once when the upheavals of 1968 were followed by high rates of inflation, which accelerated in all countries, even in Germany, but at radically different speeds. The societal and political divergences within and between countries, of which these disorders were symptoms, rapidly reversed the CAP's convention of a potentially single monetary system. Frequent changes in exchange rates, followed by floating rates, played havoc with the main policy instrument of the CAP—common prices. During most of the 1970s, price differences between member states were often much larger than before the CAP was set up.[26] The fact was that devaluation (and revaluation) as the normal device for compensating differences in the international economic performance of countries proved in practice incompatible with common prices.

If prices are indeed common, that is, expressed in a European currency, as the CAP requires, the effect of a devaluation, say of the French franc, should be to raise French farmers' prices *immediately and automatically* by the full extent of the devaluation, since the European ECU is now worth that much more than before in French francs. This is more radical than a devaluation in the traditional interstate system. In the usual national devaluation, the franc is worth less than before, but price rises work their way gradually through the economy under the pressure of increased costs of imports which represent, of course, only a proportion of total costs. With agricultural prices denominated in a European currency, all French-produced farm goods rise at once in francs by the full extent of the devaluation. Given the importance of food prices in public consciousness, this abruptness is an unwelcome shock to a government trying to tame the inflation which forced the devaluation in the first place. An administration trying to damp down inflation will seek to gain time. The French government, after the events of May 1968, felt specially vulnerable and nervous. Accordingly, when the French were forced to devalue the franc by 11.1 percent in August 1969, they refused to raise farm prices automatically as the common European price system should have implied.[27]

Three months later, in October 1969, the Germans, after a long resistance, for fear of the harm to their exports, were forced to revalue the DM upwards by 9.29 percent; and their attitude was the mirror image of the French. According to the CAP rules, an increase in the value of the DM against foreign currencies meant that the European unit of account was worth less in DMs than before. Consequently, prices paid to German farmers in these units must come down at once in DMs. Germany's refusal to reduce her farmers' incomes in just this way had been the major sticking-point in the long and arduous negotiations to set up the CAP in the early 1960s. It was unlikely that the Germans would bow for technical reasons to constraints they had stubbornly resisted through a number of political crises. And so it was. The Germans first refused to lower their farm prices and then, when they did, after three months, compensated their farmers with a nationally funded subsidy (endorsed by the Community) of 1.7 billion DM a year for three years from 1970–73, a sum equivalent in 1971 to 4.8 percent of the value of the total farm output of the country.[28] This was at least equal to the net income presumed lost as a result of the revaluation of the DM.

Thus, when it came to the pinch, neither the French nor the Germans were prepared to live with the domestic consequences of the rules to which they had subscribed in setting up common basic prices only a few years before. What they actually did when the crisis burst not only violated the rules of the CAP. It also restored national prices.[29] These were bound to have consequences for traffic across frontiers. Since French farm prices in francs were the same as before but the franc was worth less in DMs, French exports would undercut German farm sales everywhere, including Germany itself. Again, that was exactly what the Germans had, with great effort, averted by negotiating high prices across the whole Community when the CAP was set up. One extreme solution was, of course, always possible. This was to protect national markets in the traditional national way. But it would destroy the whole rationale both of the CAP and of European integration, with all the political hopes and interests vested in them. This was the period of the Pompidou-Brandt relance of the Communities. A less extreme way had to be found that would reconcile the reality of different national prices with the principle at the root of the European economic communities, that there be equal treatment—that is, no discrimination—between members of the Community on the territory of each member state. Community farm produce, whatever its provenance, should sell at the same price in each country, even though prices differed from country to country. This result was attained by a system of communication through locks. Any agricultural traffic moving upstream from a low to a high farm-price country would go through a lock raising the price level to that of the country in which the sale was made; the Community would in effect tax it, as by a customs duty, to bring the price up to those in operation in the importing country. In reverse, any traffic moving downstream from a high to a low price country would go through a lock reducing its price level; it would receive an export subsidy from the Community to diminish its price to that prevailing in the importing country. These taxes and subsidies on trade were called "monetary compensatory amounts" (MCAs), presumably to avoid saying clearly that they were taxes and subsidies. The first breaches of the CAP by France and Germany were, of course, sworn to be temporary. But with the increasing chaos on the exchanges, the *provisoire* proved once again to be lasting. MCAs reached their peak in 1976, and though they have played a reduced role since 1979 when parities became more stable, only Denmark has avoided them altogether (Strauss, 1983, pp. 264-65; Com-EC, 1979c, pp. 8-9).

So were born the "green rates," which insulate farm goods, in most member states, from the international exchange rates that applied to all other goods; and the export taxes and subsidies, or MCAs, imposed by the Community in order to raise or lower the prices of farm goods as they cross frontiers to the levels obtaining in the country where they are to be sold.

Free and equal access by Community farmers to all markets in the CAP system was in principle maintained even though common prices had in fact gone. This was not negligible considering that in 1975 the range of inflation between member countries reached the extremes of 6.4 percent per annum in Germany and 26.9 percent per annum in Britain, and that between 1977 and 1979 the top and bottom "green rates" diverged by 40 percent (between Germany and Britain) (Strauss, pp. 264-65; Com-EC, 1978-79, pp. 8-9). But if MCAs averted the formal closure of frontiers, they introduced other distortions, or presumed distortions, in the development of the CAP and of the different national agricultures. When "prices in the agricultural sector, in contrast to other sectors, are protected from the effects of the currency adjustment," the whole process of adaptation is falsified.

Essentially, farmers in one member country are in competition not only with farmers in other member countries, but with the rest of the economy in their own country. Relative inflation rates really reflect the performance of the rest of the economy, rather than that of the agricultural sector. A country with a low rate of inflation is really a country with a highly efficient economy and in that situation farming, it can be argued, should decline rapidly in importance. In contrast, a country with a high rate of inflation has an inefficient manufacturing sector and farming should probably increase in importance [European Parliament, 1982, p. 25].

Adjustment of this kind is, at least in theory, frustrated by MCAs, because they change the incentives of farmers in the strong and weak currency countries to produce and to export or import.

Farmers in a country with a strong currency should, inside a single-price European system, feel a constraint on their incomes because revaluation reduces producer prices at home (a loss partly, but only partly, compensated by lower prices for imported inputs). This tends to hold back their expansion. Alternatively, in the normal, interstate system, they would face greater difficulty in exporting at what are now, in foreign currencies, higher prices. But neither the one nor the other occurs with green rates and MCAs. Producer prices do not fall, because the whole system is designed to prevent their doing so; and exports are no dearer than before because they are subsidized to preserve equal access for all Community producers on all Community markets whatever the price levels of these.

Reciprocally, farmers in a weak currency country in a European system should find their incomes increased by higher producer prices (partially but only partially reduced by higher prices for imported inputs). Alternatively, in the interstate system, they should find they are more competitive and profitable in their exports. With MCAs, they obtain neither of these benefits of increased earnings at home or abroad, because their exports are taxed. They only suffer losses from the higher costs for imported inputs, which are governed by the general exchange rate. It is true that since consumer prices for food in the weak currency country may be presumed to rise more slowly than they otherwise would, demand may be larger than it would otherwise be. But there is nothing to stop the strong currency neighbor, with his subsidized exports, from freely sharing in the market and perhaps even pre-empting it.

Clearly, these anomalies run directly counter to the very purpose exchange rate changes are supposed to serve. Parity changes are designed to give a boost to production and exports in the weak currency country and damp them down in the strong currency country and so restore a measure of balance in payments between states. With green rates and MCAs, there is, at least in principle, a tendency for the exact opposite to occur. The imbalances, far from being corrected, are reinforced. Farm exporters in the strong currency country now buy their inputs cheap and yet are in no way penalized in the production or export of their outputs. Their net income, far from being restrained, is increased. Farmers in the weak currency country buy their inputs dearer and yet receive no encouragement to produce more or earn more through exports. Their net income, far from being increased, is cut. The logic of parity rate changes has been stood on its head. The strong, at least in principle, are reinforced, and the weak are weakened.

Naturally, this has led to considerable criticism of the effects of green rates and MCAs in distorting competition inside the common market. The Commission has stressed repeatedly that different price levels tend not only to convey "wrong signals" to producers but to break up the common market.[30] The French have argued, with some statistical backing from the Commission, that MCAs have distorted competition, or more precisely, favored the expansion of agriculture in the strong currency countries, especially Germany as the strongest of all, at the expense of the weak currency countries, including France, whose CAP benefits are thus frustrated by a distortion of the rules. On at least three occasions—in the establishment of the European Monetary Scheme (EMS) in January 1979; during the negotiations over the devaluation of the franc in March 1983; and again in the negotiations over the future of the budget and the CAP in 1983–84—the French government has tried (so far largely in vain) to persuade Germany to reduce her farm prices by substantial cuts in the DM "green" rate against the ECU. French farmers, especially in their denunciations of cheap imports of pork from Holland and Germany in the winter of 1984, have repeatedly attacked the effects of this system on their incomes. In Britain under the Labour government from 1974–79, MCAs were attacked for discriminating against British pig farmers in particular. In these and other instances, the system has aroused a substantial amount of political heat.

Yet when these allegations are investigated to assess their general importance, they prove difficult to substantiate. Some economists have argued that MCAs, by partly holding down the CAP's high price levels, have actually *reduced* distortions in incentives to Community producers (not vis à vis each other but to producers in the rest of the world). Others argue that they have reintroduced into the CAP some of the flexibility needed to cope with very different national inflation rates.[31] Countries with weak currencies have raised their farm prices gradually (as they would in an ordinary change of parities) by "devaluing" their currencies when it suited their purpose against the European unit of account. This was a way of giving farmers more income when the pressure for higher prices became too strong to resist.

It is also surprisingly difficult to link the forward march of German agriculture closely with MCAs. The Commission has brought out figures showing that in the 1970s there was indeed a forward surge of German exports within the Community (Table 4.9). The increase in German market shares, especially for wheat, sugar, milk, and butter, often at the expense of France, is indeed striking. All the same, it is very difficult to establish a chain of cause and effect with MCAs. Links with individual developments can be detected. It is alleged that MCAs amplified the recourse to cereal substitutes for animal feed through Rotterdam. States have subsidized sectors on several occasions

Table 4.9   Shifts in Export Market Shares in Intra-EC Trade in Some Basic Commodities between 1971 and 1977 (percentage; EC-9 = 100)

	Fruit	Wheat	Barley	Sugar	Fresh Milk	Butter	Cheese	Beef
Germany	+1.6	+10.0	+2.8	+21.2	+23.6	+17.1	+7.2	+6.0
France	−15.7	−5.2	−15.7	−26.8	−19.6	−3.8	−3.7	+2.4
Netherlands	+0.4	−8.0	−2.1	+2.6	−12.7	−3.8	−6.6	+0.8
Belgium–Luxembourg	−1.1	−2.2	+4.2	−9.0	+5.3	+1.6	+1.3	+0.1
Denmark	+0.5	+2.9	+1.7	+9.2	+2.4	−11.0	+2.2	+2.6
Ireland	−0.1	+0.1	+1.5	+3.5	−0.6	−1.6	−0.5	−14.8
United Kingdom	±	+2.3	+7.6	−0.7	+1.6	+1.5	+0.9	+2.8
Italy	+14.4	+0.1	±	±	±	±	−0.8	+0.1

Source: Com-EC, *Economic Effects of the Agri-Monetary System*, Com(79) 11 final, 14 March 1979, tables 31–68.

when they thought the operation of green rates was undermining them: for example, Germany, in the case of fruit and vegetables, in 1972; Britain, with pork in 1977. Parts of the food industry in Britain seem to have been stimulated by green rates and to have harmed the Irish industry when the two currencies adopted different parities. Pigs have been moved back and forth across the Northern Irish frontier to make fraudulent profits (Com-EC, 1978–79, pp. 8, 10). The list could be lengthened. But to move from precise observations to general conclusions is another matter.

In particular, Table 4.9, showing shifts in market shares in food trade within the Community between 1971 and 1977 (the years of worst disparity in inflation), is not as unambiguous as it looks, despite its polar contrast between a German advance and French retreat, both of major proportions. If strong and weak currencies were a sufficient reason, one would have to explain why the Netherlands, with a strong currency, shows a range of setbacks second only to France, while Britain, with Italy the outstanding example of a weak currency until 1980, on the whole, though modestly, made progress. One would also have to explain why, in fruit, Italy, already the dominant exporter in 1971, made further substantial progress. On the basis merely of the figures, it is possible to put foward an alternative conclusion which fits the patterns more comfortably than do green rates. This is that, on 15 major commodities and with the sole exceptions of fruit (Italy) and fresh milk (Germany), the dominant exporter within the Community in 1971 lost part of its market share by 1977, sometimes a large part.[32] France and the Netherlands were each dominant in five sectors and lost market shares in every case; so did Belgium in eggs, Denmark in pork, and Ireland in beef, each of which was market leader in 1971. This seems to square with the general trend in Community trade towards the reduction in the dominance of the original major exporters as self-sufficiency rises in all countries.

Similar difficulties are encountered with the evidence on output and incomes. Germany is certainly in the group of countries where self-sufficiency in quantitative terms increased most from 1973 to 1981, but is by no means the most dynamic of these (Appendix Table 2). Britain and Italy, both of them weak currency countries, grew faster. If one looks instead at value, production rose faster between 1973 and 1980 in the Netherlands, as well as in two high inflation countries, Italy and Ireland (*ASC 1981*, pp. 184–85). As regards the growth of income per head of people employed in agriculture, Germany comes near the bottom of the list in 1981 compared either with 1973–75 when recession started or with 1967–69, the only period when the CAP existed in a pure form. Italy, which has consistently had high inflation and a weak currency, belongs, with Denmark and Benelux, to the group of countries at the top.[33] The conclusion of the various studies the Commission has made of the question is negative but clear:

> it does not appear that a higher than average rate of inflation has been associated with a lower than average rate of increase in agricultural incomes . . . many other factors, including the adjustment of green rates and improvements in productivity and agricultural structure, influence the longterm development of incomes in agriculture [Com-EC, 1982a, p. 37].

Such results, far from proving that green rates favor strong currencies, seem if anything to hint at two somewhat different conclusions. The first is that in the medium-term, countervailing forces re-establish a rough equilibrium between the domestic rate of inflation and farm prices in the different countries. The pressure of inflation cutting into farm incomes leads governments to the gradual devaluation of green rates back towards the level implied by the general exchange rate. They provide, in fact, more or less the gradualness in the CAP that a devaluation in the interstate system normally provides. Second, there is more than a suggestion that the forces behind the expansion of one country's agriculture against another's are much wider than the mechanism of exchange rates. The effectiveness of the German economy in general and of its organization of food exports in particular might have given it the edge with or without MCAs. Its export shares have grown more steeply than those of any other member state in both the 1960s and the 1970s (apart from the UK in the 1970s—see Appendix Table 8). Similarly, the Netherlands had easily the highest rate of growth of value of production during the 1970s despite the fact that her farm prices moved rather unfavorably against farm input costs and more unfavorably against inflation than anywhere else (Com-EC, 1982a, pp. 65–68). It seems, then, that divergent rates of inflation have been less destructive, and of MCAs less fundamental in bringing about structural changes between the member states, than the political concentration on this issue would lead one to suppose. If, as is possible, inflation plays less of a role in the international economy in the next decades than it has in the 1970s, this particular feature of discord could even recede.

Yet, if symptoms change, underlying problems do not disappear. The conditions prevailing at the turn of the decade, as the dollar strengthened and its mirror image, the DM, correspondingly weakened, meant that exchange rates in Europe steadied and green rates for a while all but disappeared. Whereas in 1977–79, the monetary gap between member states in the CAP reached 40 percent, by March 1982 it had narrowed to 10 percent. French inflation rates, however, were nevertheless nearly three times the German rates (OECD, Main Economic Indicators [monthly]). Production costs, under the pressure of inflation and the second oil shock, were rising rapidly. French farm incomes suffered worse than those of any other member state, except for Ireland, in 1980 and fell again in 1981. They were not relieved by the Commission which, alarmed about booming output and budget costs in the EC, was trying to make its "prudent price policy" stick. French farmers threatened trouble, elections (in Giscard's case) were impending, the government felt the need to give them more than the Community provided and to give it fast. The national subsidies unilaterally provided in each year—without prior consultation of the Commission—amounted to some 5 percent of gross agricultural value added in France. From this point of view, the Commission's anxiety to eliminate MCAs is less an economic concern with "distortions of competition" than a political fear of the renationalization of the CAP of which the MCAs have been one, but only one—and not necessarily for the Community the most dangerous—expression.

In a longer perspective, the tensions behind divergent economies and an agricultural system presupposing a single economy are clearly linked to changing perceptions of the agricultural balance of power. In the past, the issue has arisen almost invariably over claims that an industry, such as pig-raising in Britain, or farm exports to the Community from France, may be losing ground. The argument is about the equity of the system, but the passion is provided by the loss of ground. Whether differences in inflation, or green rates and MCAs, are or are not responsible for such a loss of relative weight, the politically important issue is the loss itself. This could be the case even if inflationary differences between the countries lose their virulence. The problem could become the more serious as the growing difficulty of finding outlets for surpluses begins to limit the room for maneuver of each national agriculture. So far, changes in the relative weight between nations have been significant but not overwhelming, as Table 4.10 demonstrates. The increase in the relative weight of Italy is not perhaps surprising since domestic consumption has risen considerably faster there in the quarter century than in other member states. The big gainer, therefore, is really the Netherlands, which emerges as much the most dynamic of the Six; and the principal losers are France and (proportionately) Belgium. Germany's position is not much changed. Shifts, in any case, have been rather slow. In the circumstances, this suggests the sensitivity of countries to even quite small changes in market

Table 4.10   Share of Each Member State in Gross Agricultural Output of EC-6, 1953–56 and 1980 (percent)

	1953–56	1980	+ or −
Belgium-Luxembourg	5.7	4.5	−1.2
France	37.1	34.3	−2.8
Germany	25.3	24.3	−1.0
Italy	24.0	26.8	+2.8
Netherlands	7.9	10.1	+2.2
EC-6	100.0	100.0	±0

Source: 1953–56 — Com-EC, *Report on the Economic Situation in the Countries of the Community*, September 1958, Table 12, p. 69; 1980 — Com-EC, *The Agricultural Situation in the Community, 1981*, p. 178.

shares. It may well be that, for the next two decades, this will be one of the most important political lessons of the experience of MCAs.

Farmers and Society

The issues analyzed so far tend to pit state against state. States, however, crucial as they may be, are mainly intermediaries. The ultimate gainers and losers in the system are various social and geographical groupings inside and outside the Community. It is natural that these groups themselves might potentially form significant poles of tension inside the Community and CAP. The distinctions between rich and poor farmers or between rich and poor regions have already been referred to in Chapter 1. Others could well arise between producers and taxpayers or consumers (including food manufacturers as well as housewives). The CAP has to some extent recognized these polarities. The high support for olive oil, tobacco, and fruit and vegetable canning seeks to transfer incomes to poorer regions. But it still operates within a system which basically benefits richer individuals and regions capable of exploiting the superior opportunities guaranteed prices offer to those who already produce abundantly. The Commission has certainly been trying to edge towards giving a higher priority to transferring incomes inside the Community. This issue, always latent, could ultimately emerge as a major factor in any reform of the CAP.

Before any such question can be broached, the prior question to be answered is whether the political forces behind the present system are likely to change. In part, this involves a general accounting by society of the gains and costs of the CAP. It also depends on the effective demands of the farmers themselves: both what the farmers' lobbies want, and their power to influence governments to endorse it. What farmers want and how this may change are bound up to a considerable degree with what kind of farmers they are. In the 1950s, they constituted a mass constituency with low incomes for whom price supports seemed axiomatic. By the 1980s, a minority of relatively large farmers exploit a major proportion of the agricultural area. If the present trend were to continue in the next twenty years, would the interests, outlook, and relative incomes of farmers change enough to modify their goals? The leverage farmers can exert with governments and society are also linked to this development. It depends, however, not only on farmers themselves but on how they are perceived by other political forces. This section addresses both these problems: how changes in farming may affect farmers' aspirations; and possible developments in relations between farmers and the rest of society.

THE DRIFT FROM THE LAND CONTINUES

One of the few prospects for the next two decades which is reasonably certain is that the numbers of farmers can hardly avoid continuing to fall. The age structure of the industry today is such that, barring the assumption of unprecedented levels of return to the land, one can establish plausible levels of drift out of farming. Table 4.11 offers two alternative projections of the agricultural labor force in EC-12 until the end of the century. Based on ILO demographic projections, they concentrate on the effect of the age structure in farming in 1977 on future agricultural employment. Alternative *A* assumes that the proportion of 14 to 24-year-olds in the projection year, 1997, will be the same as in 1977 when it was higher than in the earlier boom years. Alternative *B* has been calculated to take into account the fact that fewer children are being brought up on the farms as a result of earlier migration. In the ten years before 1977 the fall in the reproductive age group relevant to the number of farmers' children entering agriculture between 1977 and 1997 reached 60 percent in Germany and Italy and not much less in other countries, except for the Netherlands and Britain where it only amounted to 30 percent. No allowance has been made in either alternative *A* or *B* for migration. The figures nevertheless suggest that, on demographic grounds alone, one should expect by 1997 a reduction of the labor force (12.9 million in 1977) of 40 percent for alternative *A*, and 50 percent for alternative *B*. The rate of decline in the 1990s would be rather more rapid than in the 1980s. The reduction from 1960 to 1980 was of 55 percent (Read, 1979; *ASC 1982*, p. 285).

The degree of reduction will, of course, vary between countries. The U.K. and the Netherlands are projected to experience the smallest amount because the long decline in the agricultural labor force seems to be approaching an end and the labor force is relatively young. Close to them is Ireland. At the other end of the spectrum, the largest decline is projected for Italy, where the agricultural population is one of the oldest (57 percent in the over-45 age group). Denmark and even France and Germany are not far behind. Italy's relative share in the EC agricultural labor force should diminish, that of the

Table 4.11   Projections of Agricultural Employment in EC-12 for 1997

	Employment 1997 (thousands)		Decline 1977-1997 (percent)		EC-12 Total (percent)		Employment per 100 Hectares of Cultivated Area		
	A	B	A	B	A	B	A	B	1977
Italy	1635	1370	48	56	21.2	21.0	13.2	11.1	25.5
Spain	1700	1370	34	47	22.0	21.0	8.2	6.6	12.4
France	1130	970	44	52	14.7	14.9	6.0	5.2	10.9
W. Germany	940	825	43	50	12.2	12.7	11.7	10.2	20.6
Portugal	590	470	39	52	7.7	7.2	16.4	13.1	27.0
Greece	540	440	40	51	7.0	6.7	13.9	11.3	23.1
U.K.	598	534	19	27	7.8	8.2	8.6	7.7	10.5
Netherlands	222	211	31	34	2.9	3.2	26.3	25.0	38.0
Ireland	160	150	32	36	2.1	2.3	16.1	15.1	23.8
Denmark	115	110	47	50	1.5	1.7	4.3	4.1	8.2
Belgium-Luxembourg	80	70	39	47	1.0	1.1	8.9	7.8	14.7
EC-12	7710	6520	40	50	100.0	100.0	9.7	8.2	16.2

A: Alternative assumes that the 14-24 year old persons employed in agriculture in the projection year will form the same proportion of the total labor force in this age group as in 1977.

B: Alternative assumes that the 14-24 age group employed in agriculture will decline at the same rate as the corresponding parent generations have done.

Source: Demographic projections (1977-97) based on ILO, *Labour Force and Labour Force Projections*, 1975-2000, Vol. IV, 1977, without inter-sectoral population shifts.

U.K., the Netherlands, and Ireland slightly increase. The shares of the other countries would not be seriously affected.

By 1977, there should be four groups of member states as regards the proportion of the workforce on the land, using the year 1980 as a yardstick, which is necessary, since one cannot predict the total workforce in 1997 (Eurostat, 1981a). The first group, comprising Belgium and Britain, might, on this criterion, account for around 2 percent of the workforce on the land (among the world's lowest proportions). The second group, Germany, Denmark, the Netherlands and, at the top end, France, would have 3 to 5 percent. Third, Italy would be close to this group (with perhaps 6 to 7 percent on the land), somewhere between Germany and France today. All these would be small by Europe's historic standards and, for most of them, the transition from the agricultural to industrial—or post-industrial—society could be considered as more or less achieved. This would still not be true of the last group, comprising Spain, Ireland, Portugal, and Greece (in rising order of proportion of the workforce on the land): they would remain close to the present position of Italy, with 13 to 15.5 percent according to alternative *A*, and 10.5 to 13 percent according to *B*.

Further hints can be gleaned from extrapolating 1970s changes in farm structures, and more particularly the recession years 1975 to 1980, to the end of the century. This projection is not nearly as firmly based as the demographic projections, since conditions in the next decades will vary from those of the second half of the 1970s (indeed, have already done so). Yet, since recession has slowed up the drift from the land, arguing from this period is more likely to understate than overstate longer term trends if there is any marked recovery. Figures for 1980 exist only for Belgium, Britain, Denmark, France, Germany, and the Netherlands. Since they do not exist for Greece, Ireland, and Italy, the results apply essentially to the richer and more northern countries. The figures can be seen from two points of view, numbers of farms of a given size and, in many ways more significant, the area of land occupied by the various sizes of farms.[34] If this table is indicative, the proportion of farms over 50 hectares in the Low Countries, Denmark, France, and Germany will double by the year 2000, but still be little over half of that of Britain in 1980. The largest group of farms would still be holdings between 20 and 50 hectares, which suggests that the numerical stress will remain on quite small family farms even in the Community's more prosperous member states. The category of very small farms, under 10 hectares, though falling substantially from the levels of 1980, would still, by number, be easily the second largest. This suggests that changes will be substantial but far short of revolutionary.

The other, and more fundamental way to measure the distribution of farms by size is to consider the total agricultural area they cover. The picture here is quite different. Farms over 20 hectares and 50 hectares already occupied most of the agricultural area in 1980. Nevertheless, once again, the contrast with

---

Table 4.12   **Distribution of Farms of Different Sizes in Five EC Countries—Belgium, Denmark, France, Germany, Netherlands—in 1980, with Projections to 2000, Extrapolated from 1975-1980, Compared with the UK in 1980**

Category of Farms (hectares)	1980 (percent)	2000 (percent)	UK 1980 (percent)
1–less than 10	41.4	32.3	24.3
10–less than 20	22.6	16.8	16.0
20–less than 50	27.0	33.1	27.1
50 or larger	8.9	17.9	32.6
Total (in thousands of farms)	2,269	1,695	249

Source: Calculated from Com-EC, *Agricultural Situation in the Community 1982*, pp. 290–91.

Table 4.13   Distribution of Agricultural Area Among Different Sizes of Farms in Five
EC Countries—Belgium, Denmark, France, Germany, Netherlands—in
1980 with Projections to 2000, Extrapolated from 1975-1980, Compared
with the UK in 1980

Category of Farms (hectares)	1980 (percent)	2000 (percent)	UK 1980 (percent)
1–less than 10	9.0	5.2	1.8
10–less than 20	15.9	9.5	3.4
20–less than 50	39.1	41.0	13.0
50 or larger	36.0	44.3	81.8
Total (million hectares)	47.3	45.5	17.1

Source: Calculated from Com-Ec, *Agricultural Situation in the Community 1982,*
pp. 290-91.

Britain is striking (see Table 4.13). Even in 2000, the weight of farms over 50 hectares is little over half of that in Britain in 1980. For the countries other than Britain, the emphasis on quite small holdings (20 to 50 hectares each) remains very strong. On the other hand, the area held by farms under 20 hectares is cut by over 40 percent and becomes almost residual, especially if one takes account of horticulture, orchards, vineyards, pigs, and poultry, where smallholdings in terms of area are often sizeable businesses in economic terms. Non-specialist farms below 20 hectares, and particularly below 10 hectares, will have become almost negligible. Comparisons between farms with large versus small turnover—that is, as businesses—give results that stress the concentration of productive power even more. The weight of medium and larger farms can be expected to grow markedly in the Community.

One cannot draw policy conclusions with any confidence from structural developments. Nevertheless, there are implications in such changes in the system. One relates to incomes. Hitherto, the big farmer has been able to merge his public identity in part with the poor peasant. The CAP itself pursues its price supports officially to raise farm incomes to national averages. But in an employment sector within which incomes vary so widely averages have little value. Even today, it is clear that farms over 50 hectares, which are not necessarily very large, nevertheless produce incomes which have little relation to those of average farms (Appendix Table 17).

Unfortunately, farm incomes are difficult to assess because of the difference between incomes earned by farmers on the land and those many of them obtain from sources away from the land. In general, the conclusion is that many holders earn more, but that some are as poor, as the agricultural returns suggest.

Even in a country such as France, where farmers are relatively poor, a mere

17 percent of farms in 1980 were responsible for 60 percent of final output. The European Commission's *Agricultural Situation in the Community 1982* points out that in 1979–80 (a bad year for farm incomes), 18 percent of French farmers enjoyed incomes per head over 120 percent of the average of all earnings in their local region (*ASC 1982*, p. 119). Here is a striking concordance. Of course, not all the farmers in the first list are to be found in the second. But given the close relation, in the CAP system of price supports, between output and production, it would be astonishing if the large majority were not identical. If so, the larger farmer has ceased in France even in a bad year to be a poor relation. It is unlikely that the situation will be very different in any of the richer Community countries.

If concentration continues in the next two decades, the phenomenon is likely to color the total agricultural scene more and more. This would only fail to happen if either the trend to concentration, against all likelihood, were to be reversed or there were a steep fall in real prices for farm goods, or a combination of both. One should assume, therefore, that the dominant producers in the Community will increasingly be seen as enjoying average, or more than average, incomes. The real small farmers, the poor peasants of tradition, though still numerous, especially in the south, will tend to become localized.

Farmers also have other assets that salaried workers do not enjoy, or not to the same degree. The farmer gains from increasing land values (and loses by falling ones). In the 1970s, land values rose sharply in real terms in some countries (Germany and Holland, for example) and in others have generally kept their value, a reflection of guaranteed prices, which have made land a good investment in recession.[35] Holders of land have profited. The larger their holdings, the greater the capital gain. A medium to large farmer has become a sizeable capitalist. The trend has been strong enough to arouse anxiety about the access to land of aspiring young farmers with no money of their own. This is behind most of the legislation designed to reduce the cost of purchase of land. In addition, in most countries, except in Britain, Denmark, and the Netherlands, farmers have substantial tax advantages.[36] In any case, the farmer can, like other businessmen, but not employees, conceal private assets in business expenses. In aging societies, however, with possibly more unemployed and increasing tax burdens to finance welfare, there may well be less tolerance of tax privileges than in the past.[37] They will become politically more noticeable and harder to justify.

Farmers are also privileged as regards employment. It is true that the poor farmer can have very low earnings and accept a standard of living most urban people would reject. On the other hand, farm bankruptcies and loss of employment, though far from unknown, are still relatively rare. Employment in the industry has declined mainly at the rate of demographic change, as children fail to follow their parents, not as a result of positive loss of jobs. If unemployment in the cities persists, and still more worsens, farming may become an object of envy and not, as in so many places in the past century, of condescension. "A generation ago, the farmer cut a very poor figure" (CNA-

SEA, 1980).[38] In the next decades, the farmer could acquire a new air of privilege. As with all questions of perception, the rate, intensity and even fact of its emergence are quite unpredictable. Nevertheless, it is hard to gainsay that from a farmer's point of view, his occupation appears to be entering a period of greater risk in relations with the rest of society.

Incomes are only one aspect of an increased emphasis on larger farms. Larger farms are apt, of necessity, to be more commercially and technologically oriented than small ones with limited access to capital. To this extent, they should be more flexible in changing the composition of output. Flexibility will also be enhanced insofar as a larger proportion of the remaining small farms will, by elimination, be ones where limited land is compatible with high incomes or be held by part-timers who can to some extent shift their sources of income.

On the other hand, the greater degree of capitalization and recourse to credit makes farmers more vulnerable to changes in macroeconomic conditions. The rash of bankruptcies in Danish farming between 1979 and 1983, due to speculative overinvestment in expansion, provides a rather dire example of the risks. The Danes undoubtedly overexposed themselves. They were unique in that interest payments as a percentage of gross value added, which was already higher than in any other OECD country in 1975 at 23.4 percent, virtually doubled again to 46.3 percent by 1980. (OECD, 1983b, p. 134). In these circumstances, crisis on the land in Denmark was hardly surprising. But elsewhere too, the burden of credit rose in the 1970s, doubling in Germany, for instance from 6 percent in 1965 to 12.8 percent in 1980. Farmers with such debts are eager to expand production in order to obtain returns on their capital. They will even wish to expand to maintain the value of the capital itself. Just as rising prices tend to inflate land values, so falling ones tend to deflate them. The solution of these problems could assume considerable economic and political urgency if real returns on production were reduced.

A smaller, but more productive agriculture run in larger units can also have implications for relations between farming, food processing, and manufacture. Larger farms are necessarily more commercial than small ones, and more intensively managed because they have to be in touch with all developments which might affect their markets. They produce for downstream sectors which, in distribution even more perhaps than in the food industry, have become increasingly concentrated and demanding. As a result, there has been an increase in contract farming, where the industry, not the farmer, tends to determine the amounts, standards, and to some extent the prices of produce. To cope with this invasion of farming by industry and distribution, the farmers themselves have been building up cooperatives, especially in dairies, which can compete with joint stock companies based in manufacturing. Wherever the ownership and control may lie all these tend to tie the producer in with markets and the downstream industries.

This is not to imply that there is incompatibility between the different stages in the food chain. For all practical purposes, agriculture and the food industry have become increasingly symbiotic, and the CAP has contributed to this development. The managers of the CAP, for instance, use the sugar factories, dairies, grain dealers, and meat packing plants as their agents in the fixing of farm prices. Farmers are rarely paid direct. Prices include a component specifically designed to cover the processor's margin. Tariffs and duties are higher on processed foods than the raw product. Consequently, *effective* duties on manufactured food are relatively high (Harris, et al., 1983, p. 242). The food industry is in effect a beneficiary of the protection afforded by the CAP and a part of the system. There are conflicts of interest—manufacturers complain that export subsidies on their produce do not take sufficient account of their extra costs due to the CAP, firms reliant on imports from outside the EC object to the CAP raising their raw material costs, it is sometimes claimed that processors do not fully pass on prices to producers, and so on—but these operate within the system, not to break it up (Delorme and André, 1983, pp. 346–47).

Nevertheless, the growing linkage between farming and the food industry does have potential for substantial change. For one thing, the "chain" in milk or grains may become more significant than the milk or grains themselves. If the growing demand is for yogurt or poultry, the health of the farmer at the back of the productive chain is dependent on the success of the broiler factory or the dairy. In 1981, processors and manufacturers took about 75 percent of farm output (*ASC 1982*, p. 27). Success at the most dynamic points is therefore what matters to all the producers in the chain. It may make more sense to subordinate policy, or subsidies, to the success of the chain at that point rather than in farming itself. This is the most concrete insight in the fashion for food policy as against farm policy which began to be evident around 1980 (OECD, 1981d). It does not renounce support and protection of the CAP type, but could displace the focus. Though some countries have been more deliberate in articulating this approach than others, all seem to be moving in much the same direction.

An examination of the food chain clearly reveals the real size of the food system. Agriculture has begun to figure in advanced societies as a rump activity. The food chain corrects this impression. If one follows it through from the firms supplying inputs to agriculture, via farming itself, the first-stage processors such as the meat-packers and sugar factories, and the second-stage manufacturers—of chocolate, for example—to the product the consumer usually sees in the supermarket or restaurant, the food system in most countries accounts for between a quarter and a fifth of employment in the economy.[39] To the extent that these activities coinhere, they are not easy to tamper with.

At the same time, agriculture seems only a small part of value added even in the food system. Value added per employee is three times as high in the food industry; and employment has been shrinking much less in processing and manufacturing than on the land. It is already almost as large in the industry as on the farms in Belgium and Britain, and by the end of the century that will probably also be the case in Germany (*ASC 1980*, p. 38; *ASC 1981*, p. 282). Governments are becoming increasingly aware of their trading interest in the processing and manufacturing ends of the food chain. There is, then, a potential question of where it will in future seem to make sense to concentrate government support: on the farms, which provide the raw materials, or the industry which sells most of the items consumers buy, or on the exporters, irrespective of their place in the chain, who bring in new markets and foreign exchange. It is, in a new form, the same question agriculture faced a hundred years ago in deciding on whether to continue protecting grains or switch to feeding livestock from the cheapest sources, at home or abroad.

None of the structural changes here discussed is revolutionary; all of them are essentially extensions of what has been occurring for the last twenty and even thirty or more years. Yet, cumulatively, one cannot help feeling that, in a number of important senses, a watershed is being reached and that, though no point on the journey can be called decisive, the journey as a whole transforms the situation. All that is mercantile, highly technological, and productive appears to be reinforced, while all that is in the peasant tradition becomes more peripheral. As a result, some of the issues that have marked farmers off from the rest of society—poverty, lack of integration and immobility—tend to become anachronistic. Questioning of received solutions is therefore liable to become more intense in the next two decades.

One would expect this to emerge first in the regions where the changes have been profound, not in those where the requisite thresholds have still to be attained. This again tends to mark off the south from the north. The developments of the past 20 years provide little evidence, for instance, that the patterns of distribution of sizes of farms characteristic of the northern countries will apply in Italy. The changes likely to take place in the northern countries could add another touch to the all too heavily delineated catalogue of contrasts between north and south. The gaps might close again subsequently; but on present indications this would occur in the first two decades of the twenty-first century rather than in the last two decades of the twentieth.

FARMERS AND POLITICS

Implicit in this, as in all discussion of the reduction in the size of agriculture as a part of society, is its political significance. In the past century, it is the political power of farmers which has compensated for their economic weaknesses. The power of farm lobbies is legendary, and in many ways the CAP is a monument to it. But this in itself carries risks of overexposure. What if numbers of farmers drop by half—or nearly that amount—and in several countries fall to proportions below those current in Britain and Belgium today? It has been pointed out in America that most of the new issues which have affected the food system in the past decade have—perhaps for the first time—come from outside the sector and forced it on the defensive (Paarlberg, 1980, pp. 59–64). In Europe, too, urban and ecological preoccupations have been putting pressure on the farm community: consumer protection, pollution, conservation, factory-farming, health foods, subsidies to agriculture, opposition to farmers' tax exemptions, and so on, are most of them urban-based, or at least not farm-based, concerns. The reduction in numbers on the land could, we have seen, be associated with the increasing visibility of the richer farmers. If so, the claim of poverty which has always been implicitly conceded to the "peasant" in continental Europe will begin to wear thin. Especially if mass unemployment persists, it could well be replaced, at least in part, by envy of the big farmer. The future of farming's political influence needs at least to be re-examined, if only because the industry has ceased to represent a third or more of society, as it did in many countries only a generation ago.

A cautionary tale is to be found in the example of the fishing industry. Fishing represents an infinitesimal part of both the GDP and the workforce of the Community, about 0.45 percent in each case—that is, far less than farming is likely to account for, even in 2000 and in Belgium and Britain (Rosemarie Allen, 1982). Yet it took over a decade to establish a very limited common fisheries policy, despite urgent pressures to agree on conservation; and in 1983 the wrangles were continuing in the old style on herring quotas. (*Guardian*, 27 July 1983). Fishermen, however few, were able to exert marginal but not negligible electoral muscle. They made claims on national solidarity as a social problem, and fishing became identified with the national interest.

Farmers have far more electoral muscle than fishermen. Reduced in numbers though they may be by the standards of the past, nevertheless compared with other professions they remain in almost all cases easily the largest. They are also widely dispersed, often in electorally strategic ways, in key constituencies. In Britain in 1974, in elections won by Labour, 74 of the 100 constituencies where farming occupied 7 percent or more of the workforce (up to 30 percent in one untypical constituency), went to the Conservatives and a mere 6 to Labour (Butler and Karanagh, 1975, pp. 299-323). Seven percent is not a very large proportion of the workforce, and farming may not have been the key to the allegiance of these constitutencies; but one has yet to meet politicians who would make scientific experiments to find out. Similarly, in France, in the presidential polls of 1974, farmers handed a million net votes to the victor, Valéry Giscard d'Estaing, who had a majority over his rival, Francois Mitterrand, of only 400,000 (Lancelot, 1975, pp. 175-206).

That the right, which is usually in power, has to nurse the farm interest, is a familiar rule of thumb of politics. Matters become more interesting with governments which are mainly urban-based. One of these was the SDP-FDP coalition which ruled Germany for thirteen years, from 1969–82. The minister for agriculture, the formidable Joseph Ertl, was a member of the Bavarian FDP who has since become president of the farmers' union (and been replaced in the CDU-FDP government by a Bavarian official of the same union). Victory at the polls in 1980 depended on the FDP pulling above the 5 percent floor for representation in the Bundestag. A handful of constituencies in Bavaria and Schleswig-Holstein were thought to be influenced by the farm vote. As a result, although Chancellor Helmut Schmidt's criticisms of the CAP were said to be abrasive, they were not reflected in the policies of the government he led. The more precarious the balance of the majority behind a coalition government, the more powerful marginal interests become. In 1964, the Belgian minister of agriculture, M. Héger, played a crucial role in the decisions to impose high milk prices for the CAP. On the face of it, this seems surprising, or at least unnecessary. Belgium has few farmers and M. Héger came from industrial Liège. But he was a Walloon in the Social Christian Party, most of whose members came from Flanders, where the agricultural interest is strong. His standing in the party depended on effective representation of that interest. The crucial fact is that coalition government is the norm in most European countries most of the time.

The question becomes more problematic when a predominantly urban party holds power alone. It is therefore specially interesting that in the U.K., the White Paper of 1975, in the early days of Labour's tenure of office, when the Government was trying to hold farm prices down to limit inflation, was almost as expansionary as regards ambitions for output as the subsequent policy of the Conservatives after 1979. In other words, farm policy cannot simply be reduced to the successful exercise of lobby pressure from below. Influence is related to the perceptions in government and the polity as a whole of the congruence between the sectoral and general interests.

The balance of payments is clearly a major factor in several states in the belief that what is good for farming is good for the country. Labour's White Paper in Britain, or the *Piano Quadrifoglio* in Italy, both aimed openly at maximum national self-sufficiency. In France, the country of *pétrole vert*, the responsible ministry noted that, in 1974, agricultural exports had an import content in their production of under 11 percent against over 18 percent for capital goods or vehicles and 24 percent for semi-manufactures.[40] This consideration is especially important for Ireland, where farm and food products are much the largest export sectors. Exports are not the only consideration which predisposes policy-makers in favor of the farms. To maintain workers on the land keeps them off the streets in recession. Regional balances in wide areas of the country can also be served by farm policies. The Danes and French hope to promote a broad class of moderate-sized but economic farmers as part of the cement of rural society. The Germans regard part-time farmers as essential to the balance of the countryside and as contributing to the healthy decentralization of economy and society. The Community itself, taking a leaf out of the British book, encourages farmers in hill or disadvantaged regions.

In a Community with national vetoes, or near vetoes,[41] all farmers to some extent enjoy the bargaining power of the main country, or group of countries, with high stakes in agriculture. They are already numerous in the Community, and southern enlargement will increase their number. There is also the reluctance of any government, in an international negotiation, to be seen giving up more than it must, or than another government does or may claim to do. In systems where every decision is politicized—as inevitably each is in the CAP—it becomes a contest for advantage where all groups know that political will may shift the final outcome. There is a strong incentive, in some cases amounting, subjectively, to a duty, for each interest and nation to carry advocacy or resistance to the limit of determination. This is not a recipe for prompt and rapid adjustment to changing conditions.

Indeed, such conditions seem almost ideal for the effective operation of powerful lobbies. The greater cohesion, resources, and improved organization of modern agricultural lobbies seem to make up for any loss in numbers. In countries with a large and backward agriculture, a small number of large farmers tend to fill the vacuum created by the passivity of the majority of farmers. Organizations tend to be weak, or dominated by minorities, as in France after the war and Spain at least until the death of Franco, or else clientelist as in Italy. Groups such as the cereal and sugarbeet growers of the Paris basin or the latifundists of Andalusia tend to push their own concerns in the name of farming in general.[42] In countries where farmers have shrunk in numbers, the organization becomes much tighter and more representative but also imposes controls on the individual member. The Netherlands and Denmark are excellent examples. In Denmark, some of the functions elsewhere assumed by government, notably in foreign trade negotiations, have at times been largely delegated to the *Landbrugsraadet*.

There also seems to be a basic psychological cohesion among farmers vis à vis the rest of society which is a major political asset. It is, for instance, intriguing that farm associations, 72 percent of whose members have incomes below 80 percent of the average for their region back a system like the CAP which favors larger farmers with incomes 20 percent above the regional norm (ASC 1982, p. 119). Do they give higher priority to the minimum security the CAP affords them? Are they too hard-worked, too passive, or too isolated to make themselves felt? Do they distrust all non-farmers? Whatever the reason, there have been few revolts within the farm community and none against price support systems.

There is one interesting cultural divide, between the northern lobbies and the French and Italians. While the northern farmers are determined promoters of their interests, they are ostensibly susceptible to market arguments. This is much less the case in France and Italy. One of the favorite arguments against income aids in France and Italy is that they demean the farmer's dignity and that it is an insult to treat a producer as a pensioner. On the other hand, to pay high prices unrelated to the market is a just reward for honest toil, a right the farmer has earned by the sweat of his brow, and in this sense only a fair price. Certainly in France this is a view often held with some passion. The distant analyst might be tempted to look on this cynically as self-serving, which indeed it is. But this might miss the emotional force of the phenomenon. There seems to be considerable depth to it: a lack of historical experience of open markets and an equally long history of the politics of patron-client relationships might go some way to explain this attitude, which may at times be associated as in the French agrarian history of the past century, with violent protest (Delorme and André, 1983, p. 333). Its importance should not be underestimated.

It would, in short, be surprising were declining numbers alone to reduce the power of the farm lobbies in the next twenty years, or greatly to change the policies farmers, when free to choose, would prefer. The pressures for change are more likely to have their source where common sense would in any case suggest: the degree of convergence or divergence between general and agricultural policy priorities. One of the reasons the fishing lobby has had influence out of all proportion to its numbers has been the perceived congruence between its own sectoral and wider national interests. Agriculture is quite different, since it has begun to flout the unanimous will of the governments to cut budgets, on the one hand, and "restructure" industry from the declining to growth sectors, on the other.

The pressures for policy change will reflect two basic considerations. One is a weighing of the rising costs of continuing the system as it is, as against the costs—political and otherwise—of doing something to change priorities. It is clear that the costs of simply carrying on the CAP along present lines are likely to increase intolerably in the not-too-distant future. The other consideration is the changes that may take place in perceptions of priorities among both the public and governments. The potential conflicts between farmers and ecologists, or taxpayers or various claimants on public funds in a period of greater strains are likely to put farmers more at odds than they have been with urban-based outlooks and interests. There is evidence even in countries where farmers are commonly reputed to be sacrosanct that governments may at times put other priorities higher on the scale. It was the French government which refused in 1969 to give farmers instant price increases through devaluation, fearing the reaction of the rest of society to a sudden increase in inflation rates.

Conclusions

As the policies of agricultural expansion bear fruit, traditional differences of structure between parts of the European Community—differences which in other circumstances and under other policies could lead to complementarity and integration—have become sources of strain and conflict.

Some are more important than others, of course, and by far and away the most important has been the complex of issues revolving around trade and the budget, the two being intimately linked. Most of the controversies of the CAP, from its very inception, have involved the different outlooks and interests of exporting and importing countries. The form in which it was established was itself a compromise between them. Free access across borders within the Community was provided to satisfy the thirst for preferential markets of the exporters. Common prices were set high to protect the high-cost producers of the importers. At first, the exporters' interests appeared paramount. They gained most of the extra trade in Europe at the expense of overseas suppliers of cheaper food. They also won Community funding to subsidize their exports to the rest of the world. This was a major privilege, since subsidies are often worth more to European exporters than the prices paid for their sales overseas.

Even so, generally rising output meant that the importers gradually increased the proportion of their food grown at home. Little by little this limited the potential for cross-border food trade in the Community. Also, as surpluses built up, the costs of disposal weighed more and more on the Community budget. By 1983, the funds provided by the Luxembourg agreement of 1970 ran out. This gave the importers (who were also, given the system, the main funders of the budget) the chance to call the initial model of the CAP in question. The balance of power inside the CAP shifted to the importers and bankers. This shift in the balance is the essence of the crisis of 1983–84.

If expansion continues, all Community countries will become exporters in most or all commodities. The balance will shift again and influence prospects accordingly. Developments can lead down one of two broad avenues. Importers can continue to increase home output until they reach national self-sufficiency across the board, while limiting their budget payments. If so, they will force the exporters more and more onto world markets and to pay their own export subsidies. In this case, the CAP will probably disintegrate in the resulting scramble. Alternatively, importers and exporters can cooperate to control farm production. In this case, the CAP continues, but within limits, which also breaks with the past.

The changes in the Community's budget which have accompanied, or could accompany, these developments also contain political implications. One of the consequences of the repayments that have been made to Britain since 1980 has been to change the patterns of profit and loss on the Community budget. Previously, these tended to be tied to the importing and exporting character of the various member states. But in 1981, for instance, the clear beneficiaries of the budget were Denmark, Greece, Ireland, and Italy. With the sole exception of Denmark, the unifying factor in this group was its relative poverty. In the future, if Spain and Portugal were to behave according to form—Greece seems to have done so on the budget— the list of beneficiaries would include all the Mediterranean countries plus Ireland. Apart from the anomaly of Denmark, the Community would de facto be practicing a kind of progressive taxation as between rich and poor states. (Rich and poor recipients are another matter, as in some poor countries middlemen often seem to do much better than smallholders.) In short, the interest the poorer countries undoubtedly have in the Community as a source of funds is beginning to take a substantial form, not only for them but for the Community as a whole.

Budget transfers are only one aspect of deep-lying contrasts between north and south (or, rather, including Ireland, rich and poor countries) in the Community. Henceforth, most of agriculture in the north conforms to the "industrial" image of a sector integrated into the general economy. This is still much less the case in the south. In the south there will still be more people on the land. Rural areas suffering depopulation will find it hard to generate alternative employment. The governments themselves will be poorer than in the north. They will tend to press for high prices to raise national self-sufficiency in basic crops, which tend to be "northern." Southern agriculture will no doubt gradually move toward patterns closer to "industrial" ones, but the watershed is likely to lie the other side of the year 2000. Til then, what to do about the north-south divide will be one of the deepest problems of a Community balanced much more equally between rich and poor countries than when originally conceived.

When reforms are debated, other cleavages of outlook come up again and again. There is a very sharp difference between countries, and more particularly governments, of different political shades of opinion, who stress the difference between smallholders and large farmers, and those who resist all such distinctions. Thus, in 1983, the French, Belgians, and Irish were in favor of income aids to smallholders. The Germans and, perhaps more surprisingly, the Italians were neutral, though tractable. But not surprisingly at all, countries such as Britain, Denmark, and the Netherlands, with a big preponderance of economically large farms, were very determinedly against such aids.

Another cleavage arises between the small and the large countries. Small countries are much more committed to the CAP than the large ones seem to be. The small countries are extremely conscious of their dependence on exports, traditionally concentrated in Western Europe. They have tampered relatively little with the CAP even when, as in Denmark, there is strong anti-Community sentiment in society at large. Not so the large countries. The British, the French, and the Italians have all at some time or other closed their frontiers for some product within the CAP (for example, poultry, pork, wine, and eggs). The Germans and French have handed out income aids to their farmers in lieu of Community price increases without effective reference to the Commission. Mrs. Thatcher's legendary eloquence about "my money" in her budget demands of 1980 seemed to all the other member states symbolic of the British outlook. If "re-nationalization" is to occur, it will come from the big, not the small, countries—and from the north not the south. That means, in effect Britain, France or Germany.

Third, there is a significant potential difference between the extensive agricultures, typified by Britain, France, Ireland, and, among the candidates, Spain, and the intensive agricultures of which the most extreme are the Netherlands and Belgium, but also include Denmark, Germany, and Italy. Though all the countries and a fortiori the farm lobbies in the Community member states resist lower prices, there is nonetheless a difference between those which could expect to perform relatively better and those who fear they would perform relatively worse if prices were substantially reduced. This distinction is probably well below the surface of policy-making, because big price cuts would be the last resort in most commodities. But it does mean that some countries are even more attached to a high price policy than others.

Finally, there is the contrast in outlook between the big crop producers and the transforming (livestock) sectors and agricultures exploiting intensive methods of feeding and selling. It comes last, perhaps, because it is so important that it may well not be susceptible to profound policy changes. This is clear in the problem of imported animal feed. The differences of interest between the grain exporters especially from France, Britain, and Germany and the importers of low-cost feed—including in those same countries—are so great that it is hard to see the present deadlock being broken. The stalemate is reinforced by the fact that the United States sets particular store on its export to the Community of oilseeds and maize byproducts for feed. Changes are more likely to take place, therefore, on the periphery of the problem than in ways which affect it at the core. Supposedly voluntary export restrictions imposed on the east Asian suppliers of cereal substitutes; a tax on all vegetable fats designed to fund the expected cost of olive oil surpluses—various measures of this kind have been put forward and some of them (the fats tax, for one) are highly controversial. To move beyond partial or stop-gap solutions to a root-and-branch change of the system of imports of animal feed would imply agricultural and also political changes beyond present horizons.

When all these contrasts are laid out, the differences of interest of the member states in the CAP still do not seem inherently irremediable. They are of a kind which in favorable circumstances could probably well be drawn in the wake of a bold policy. However, there are at least two factors which seem to explain why they are in practice so difficult to overcome in the Community. The first is the nature of decision-making between ten countries. The member states are no doubt under greater pressure to come to agreement in the Community than in an intergovernmental organization of the classic kind. The Community nevertheless suffers from many of the traditional disadvantages of such an organization. The fundamental problem in the CAP is not so much agriculture as such, but that while the delegation of powers over policy has been formally agreed in part, the priorities which determine attitudes are still situated stubbornly in the capitals of the states. The doubt about the CAP is ultimately over the question whether the national governments think there are overriding reasons for reaching common decisions at all; and if so, in what areas and at what cost. This is the sort of issue that has rarely been decided in history by rational argument; the answers are the results of compromises reached in crisis. The outgrowing of the original difficult bargain over the CAP does not merely imply crisis. It actually calls for one.

The second difficulty is that unless ways are found to turn agriculture into a dynamic industry—which is, in effect, what the CAP tried to do through the European preference for twenty years—there is no escaping the social strains that stagnation of demand must sooner or later impose on the countryside. The problems of adjustment are the more difficult because agriculture has always been protectionist (in all but a handful of countries) and farmers have in most countries been accustomed to thinking of themselves as underprivileged. This has created dependency and outlooks which resist adaptation to markets. Such adaptation is not easy in any sector, at least in European conditions, even when general growth is rapid. It is doubly difficult in a sector like agriculture during recession. In some ways, the CAP is suffering from the fact that the governments managed to postpone during the fat years some of the adjustments that are becoming impossible to avoid during the lean ones.

BEYOND CRISIS

All the features discussed so far relate to the central current issue of the CAP, the appropriateness or not of its market support system or, more precisely, of the price levels at which support is provided and the effects on the balance of demand and supply. Like all major issues capable of affecting the political balances in a regime and potentially the system itself, they are apt to become obsessional and fill the horizon, particularly when they reach crisis proportions. There is always a danger in such circumstances, however of assuming that conditions will always reflect these priorities and that temporarily less salient features are of lesser importance. The very fact that the CAP, and by implication also national agricultural policies in the Community, are in crisis suggests that a turning point may be reached sooner rather than later and that once the corner has been passed priorities will begin to change. Of course, the issues today may linger and dominate the scene for some time to come. Nevertheless, other manifestations of change, less dramatic, perhaps, but shaping influences too, have become very evident and suggest different emphases in future. Three of these seem of special importance.

First are the tensions between the traditional values of agriculture and the new preoccupations of post-industrial, largely urban (or suburban) society—even in large stretches of the "countryside." Some of these tensions are rooted in technological and economic change. The growing use of fertilizers and pesticides, the burning of stubble, the encroachment on recreational areas, and so on, affect the environment in a way an earlier kind of farming would not. Others are connected to values changing in suburbia faster probably than in rural areas. Indifference to animal welfare, factory farming, the cutting down of trees, chemically treated produce, and so on offend increasing constituencies of middle-class people, most of them a shade greener than they used to be whether they vote "green" or not. Still others are a result of the changed economic status of some if not all farmers relative to the rest of the community. The traditional image of a farmer, as distinct from a landowner, was of a poor man, deserving and worse off than most. This is changing in the northern member states and around the big cities where the main markets are. Farm land is expensive, giving farmers relatively large capital; they do not have to be unemployed unless they choose to leave the land; the larger among them have businesses to which much of their living expenses can be charged. In such a situation, tax concessions and subsidies seem consistent not with poverty but with privilege. Admittedly in a society with a growing amount of leisure and services, the farmers will not have the problem many others have, of convincing themselves and others that their job is vital. Farmers also have "un-social hours." Nevertheless, they may not automatically touch the old chord of sympathy, and they could increasingly find themselves at odds with the values of the day.

Another set of issues concerns the place of agriculture in the economy and society. All sorts of balances—of human society in nature, of the countryside against the towns, of some regions as against others, and even of employment as against unemployment—were automatically cared for by an often poor but populous agriculture occupying nearly the entire territory. Once this cover is withdrawn, all sorts of social and economic balances once taken for granted, or ignored, begin to demand attention. Policies dealing with such situations cannot be confined to agriculture, even though this remains in the most remote areas almost the only major activity. Agriculture, as a declining sector, cannot provide enough activities to replace the old. Agricultural policies have to be tackled in a larger setting. Hence the increasing tendency, in the European Commission and elsewhere, to look beyond agriculture and the CAP to "integrated development programs." These are particularly important for Ireland and the Mediterranean, and can constitute an alternative framework for policies aimed at compensating poorer farmers for loss of employment and income resulting from economic change. There are indeed areas of Spain, especially Andalusia, with its large pool of landless laborers and unemployed, where a CAP based on price supports to producers is largely irrelevant.

The third set of issues concerns the priorities for policy implied by the increasing interaction, amounting at times to virtual integration, between the various stages in the food chain: farming proper, first-stage processing, food manufacture, and distribution (Appendix Tables 19 and 20). Because value added is higher in food manufacturing than in agriculture and three-quarters of farm output is processed, governments seeking to raise the value of exports think more and more of selling increasingly elaborated food products. They therefore come to consider agriculture less as a separate entity than as one point in a thread of production in which the decisive profits can be made at any point, not necessarily on the land itself.

This is linked to another phenomenon: the greater concentration of food production, in farming but still more so in manufacturing and distribution. For instance, in Britain, one processor supplying a major distributor has contracts with farmers for the meat of a quarter of a million pigs per year (House of Lords, 1982, K. P. Riley, p. 60, Q. 154; Pisani, 1983). To obtain increased bargaining power against such competition, farmers—especially small holders—are encouraged in some countries to form cooperatives. These farmer organizations have a long history in Denmark and the Netherlands and are now common in France. In some cases cooperatives become major powers in manufacturing and buy their way into distribution, as the Union Laitière Normande has done. When farming was very distinct from downstream activities, it was a relatively simple matter to bring political power to bear in increasing agriculture's economic power against the manufacturers. When the two become intertwined at many points, and politically manipulated prices become more difficult to sustain, there is a tendency for the more concentrated and powerful firms, wherever they are situated along the chain, to gain power of decision over the smaller and weaker ones. This will usually be in distribution or manufacturing rather than farming; so that whoever controls the main centers of decision, irrespective of whether their origin was originally in manufacturing, distribution, or farming, tends to gain more influence over policy. This means that if the erosion of the political power of agriculture is accelerated, say by reducing public support to farmers, the tacit practical transfer of decision-making power over farming to more concentrated upstream and downstream sectors will be hastened. This, in turn, feeds in to another set of problems. In some countries, especially Britain and the Netherlands, food manufacture in some sectors is heavily concentrated in a few firms. This raises all the potential problems not only of cartels or abuse of monopoly power but also of strikes, as in the British bread-making industry, where only two firms control the bulk market. These could affect customers far more directly than farmers' demonstrations.

It has therefore become a common contention that farm policies should give way to food policies, taking account of the inputs the entire length of each food chain (cereals, dairy products, meat, and so on). It is likely that the trends of the past twenty years will indeed continue to move in this direction. There is nevertheless difficulty in presenting these priorities as really new. Some governments have for some time been promoting such policies, in some cases in the framework of a plan, in others haphazardly. In France, for instance, food policy in this sense has been pursued since the 1960s (Delorme and André, 1983, pp. 346–47). For countries like the Netherlands and Denmark, the priority is much older still. In any case, far from being deeply divided over the CAP, farmers and manufacturers are in effect joint beneficiaries of the direct and indirect protection it affords (Harris, et al., 1983, pp. 235–51). This is pleasant for the interested parties in Europe. From the point of view of foreign trade, however, the protectionism evident in agriculture throughout the world tends to restrict the new gains a food as against a farm policy is likely to make. The best markets for high-grade food products are potentially the developed ones. In many cases, such as Japan or the U.S., they are also highly protectionist. Every developing country is trying to build up its own food industries, often by bringing in multinational corporations when it does not already have them. In these circumstances, it is easier to export basic crops than patented foods. It is striking that the food exports of the United States, which has something like half the world's large food corporations, are still concentrated on basic commodities.[43]

There are, then, two sets of overlapping and interconnected but not identical "structural" developments in Community agriculture: the major immediate issue for the system—surpluses as a symptom of a deeper problem in readjusting from traditional to new balances and policies in the sector; and longer-term changes that are likely to assume greater importance as the difficulties of the transition are mastered. The problems of which surpluses are symptomatic are, for their sector, epic in proportion: they entail major changes of outlook and policy affecting not only agriculture but the wider arena of the European Communities, integration, even international "agri-power." Other developments—such as the invasion of traditional country values by those of the suburbs, the health of regions where the old cover of peasant population has been suddenly withdrawn, or the concentration of economic power in food chains as in other industrial sectors, and so on—may seem more diffuse and of less interest to the non-specialist. They are nevertheless likely to be longer-lasting in their impact. They will tend to define the politics of food beyond the critical transition.

Notes

1. In 1851, 20.9 percent of the working population in England and Wales and 22.7 percent in Scotland (as against 48.4 percent in Ireland) was engaged in agriculture (excluding fishing, another 0.2 percent in England and Wales). Best, 1971, p. 99, using the *Journal of the Royal Statistical Society*, xlix (1886), pp. 314–435. In 1950, in the Federal Republic of Germany the corresponding rate was 25.3 percent. Com-EC, 1958b, p. 62.

2. *ASC 1979*, pp. 248–49: in Italy gross value added per agricultural worker was 3.1 times in Lombardy what it was in Molise, in 1978; in France Ile-de-France (Paris basin) 5.8 times the Limousin (gross farm income per family worker). In Britain the gap was much lower (Eastern region and Wales, 1.4) and in Germany still lower (Schleswig-Holstein and Hessen, 1.3).

3. Table 4.A gives some idea of the changes that have taken place between 1978 and 1983 in EAGGF payments in Mediterranean products—as well as to oilseeds and sheepmeat (the two other products to gain more than proportionately in support). The increases in column 2 are based on constant prices. Even after the increases, the share of Mediterranean products in EAGGF outlays seems roughly in line with their weight in total Community farm output (assuming this is a relevant criterion, which is debatable).

Table 4.A

	% of value EC-10 farm output 1980 (1)	Increase in value EAGGF spending 1978–83 (2.0 = twice, etc.) (2)	Percentage of EAGGF spending	
			1978	1983
			(3)	
Rice	0.2	2.9	0.2	0.5
Olive oil	1.4	2.4	2.1	4.2
Fruit and vegetables	12.7	7.0	1.2	6.8
Wine	4.8	6.5	0.7	4.0
Tobacco	0.6	2.0	2.5	4.2
Total Mediterranean, products	19.7	3.5	6.7	19.7
Oilseeds	0.6	4.4	1.6	6.1
Lamb and mutton	1.8	—	—	2.2

Source: Com-EC, 1983a, pp. 26–29; *European Economy*, November 1983, Table 17; *ASC 1981*, pp. 174–75.

4. *ASC 1981*, p. 311. Out of total demand for cereals of 120.3 million tons in 1979–80, 72.9 million were for animals, 10.7 million for the food industry, and only 30.7 million for direct human consumption.

5. In 1957–58, the comparative prices received by farmers in Germany, the Netherlands, U.K. and the U.S., on the basis of France = 100, were as shown in Table 4.B. These ratios have been calculated from Marsh and Ritson, 1971. See also Lindberg, 1963, p. 225.

Table 4.B

	Germany	Netherlands	UK	USA
Soft wheat	143	104	110	101
Sugarbeet	155	107	143	136
Milk	139	126	154	157
Beef	107	117	99	99

6. Johnson, 1973, p. 102. The same ratio has been observable from 1980–82, though in 1976 it fell just below 2 and in 1977 rose just above 3 declining again by stages to 2.5 in 1980. USDA, ERS, 1982b, p. 5.

7. Community subsidies for oilseeds rose from 91 mn ECUs in 1977 to 721 mn ECUs in 1983. Com-EC, 1982b, p. 26.

8. In 1980, 99 percent of world production of olive oil, a unique proportion for any product, came from the Mediterranean basin. FAO, *Production Yearbook 1980*, pp. 138–39.

9. Com-EC, 1981b, para. 3, states that "the relationship at the consumer level between the price of olive oil and of the competing seed oils should not exceed 2:1." This still seems too high. The Spanish have established a ratio of 1.6:1.

10. *Financial Times*, "Olive oil 'fraud' in Italy may cost EEC $230m a year," 20 December 1982. From the article, it seems that producer aid demands are based on claims to 800,000 tons of production of oil, whereas demand for consumer aids on sales through wholesalers only come to 250,000 tons at most. It is assumed that the EEC's 1 million olive growers and their families consume 100,000 tons and sell another 100,000 tons locally. (Fears of a glut are based on estimates of Italian production in 1975–77 of 450,000 tons.) Estimates of alleged Greek production also jumped 100,000 tons in a single year on entry into the Community.

11. See note 10, supra.

12. Spain, apart from Britain, is the only country in an EC-12 to have a substantial proportion of paid farmworkers—i.e. landless laborers—about 30 percent of the workforce on the land. *Anuario de Estadistica Agraria*, 1980, p. 17.

13. Costs would rise 3.8 to 5 billion ECUs, while receipts from Greece, Portugal and Spain would rise (at full 1 percent VAT) by 2.2 to 2.5 billion ECUs. Bourrinet and Stioui, 1982, pp. 35–39.

14. Britain and Italy, relative to the average of the Community, both seem to have become poorer during the 1970s, even when one takes account of their lower domestic prices by adopting "purchasing power parities":

	1970	1979
	(EC-9 = 100)	
Britain	95	91
Italy	81	78

Com-EC, Eurostat, *Review 1970–80*. A number of studies suggest that Italy's "black economy", not registered in the official figures, adds substantially to the country's real income.

15. Greece and Ireland pose problems for the choice of yardstick for land surface. This can either be the arable (cultivated) area mainly used by FAO, or the utilized agricultural area (UAA), including pasture and permanent crops, such as olive trees, orchards, and vines, mainly used by the Commission of the European Communities. The standard of cultivated area gives Ireland a misleading air of being an intensive agriculture, because it leaves out pasture land, which constitutes 82 percent of UAA, and this is vital to output. If, however, one takes UAA, including pasture, this makes Greece appear an extensive farm producer, which is equally misleading because in her dry climate, pasture, though covering 57 percent of UAA, provides only a small fraction of value-added in agriculture. For this reason, UAA has been taken as the criterion, since pasture is important for most "northern" Community farming, except for Greece, where cultivated area, which brings out the tiny average holdings, has been taken into account. For Italy, oddly enough, it makes little difference, in comparisons with other member states, whether one takes UAA or cultivated area, so UAA has been retained.

16. Differences between agricultural enterprises measured by average acreage and turnover can be very great. See Table 4.C, for example (*ASC 1981*, pp. 294, 297).

Table 4.C

	Land	Turnover
	(EC-9 = 100)	
Horticulture	21	294
Vines	28	62
Pigs	35	197
Poultry	35	214
Beef	158	71
Sheep, goats	224	57

17. The yields in "1980" (i.e., the average of 1979–1981) of wheat and milk in the member states are shown in Table 4.D. The figures are taken from relevant Com-EC, ASCs.

Table 4.D

	Wheat	Milk
	(in tons/annum per)	
	ha.	cow
Belgium	5.0	3.9
Denmark	5.1	4.8
France	5.0	3.6
Germany	5.0	4.5
Greece	2.8	2.4
Ireland	5.1	3.3
Italy	3.3	3.4
Luxembourg	3.4	3.9
Netherlands	6.3	5.1
United Kingdom	5.6	4.7

18. Jørgensen, 1978, pp. 310–11: "It should be emphasized that shifts from one market to another, according to Danish experience, are difficult, as the attempts to acquire a foothold in the original EEC countries after Danish entry into the Common Market have shown."

19. In constant prices of 1960, France accounted for half the increase in EC exports to the rest of the world from 1978–80, while her exports inside the Community declined. In 1981, the rate of increase in exports to the rest of the world was not maintained.

20. See note 5, Ch. 1, supra.

21. These and subsequent figures (e.g. below) are based on supply balances in grain equivalents (see note 5, Ch. 1, supra), but for comparability exclude sugar, fresh fruit (except citrus), and vegetable fats and oils, since the bases for calculating these changed in 1980. As a result, the proportions are marginally different from those given in Appendix Table 2.

22. Taking the four commodities together, export aids varied as follows (1978 = 100): 1979—96; 1980—88; 1981—72. In the budget of 1981, export subsidies came to 4939 million ECUs, of which 4,327 went for grains (except rice), sugar, milk, and beef (*ASC 1982*, pp. 268–70). The total Community budget ("payments effected") in 1981 was 16,712 million ECUs. Each point of value-added tax (VAT), i.e. 0.01 percent, would have brought in about 125 million ECUs in 1981.

23. See note 13, supra.

24. Comparing production (Final Production—see note 5, Ch. 1, supra) and consumption (Utilization for Food and Industry), for 1973 and 1981, state by state, one finds that net availabilities (production less consumption) rose between the two chosen years (million tons of grain equivalents) as shown in Table 4.E. The necessary exclusion of sugar, vegetable oils and fruit (note 21 supra) falsifies the results for Italy. If these are included, Italian net availabilities seem to rise to 7.0 million tons—but 1973 and 1981 are non-comparable.

Table 4.E

	Increase in million tons	Percent Increase[a]
Belgium-Luxembourg	−0.4	−3
Denmark	1.1	9
France	9.5	11
Germany	5.2	9
Ireland	1.5	21
Italy	1.5	3
Netherlands	5.1	25
United Kingdom	9.3	24

[a]Over final production 1973.

25. The results of the financial review of the four commodities—grains, sugar, milk and beef—are shown in Table 4.F. (The second column can be added to the first, i.e., is not included in it.)

Table 4.F

	Balance of budget payments at 1981 prices	
	1981 Budget[a] (ECU million)	1990 Export Refunds
Belgium-Luxembourg	−412	−132
Denmark	221	90
France	−6	−136
Germany	−2555	−373
Ireland	558	359
Italy	287	−543
Netherlands	−2	251
United Kingdom	−752	490

[a]Excluding administrative and other costs which involve no direct payments to member states, but from which Belgium probably gains most. This explains the preponderance of deficits over surpluses.

26. Harris et al., 1983, p. 194: "The gap between the highest and lowest price was often greater than the price gap that had existed prior to price harmonisation in 1967." In 1977–79 British and German green rates diverged by over 40 percent compared with the parity between the mark and the pound in general. In 1957–58, before the EC, price divergences of over 40 percent between member states were also quite common, especially between France and Germany (soft wheat, barley, sugarbeet) or Italy (soft wheat and beef). See note 5, supra.

27. Strauss, 1983, pp. 261–81. There is a very large literature on "green" rates and MCAs to which this article refers. See also Harris, 1983, Ch. 8, "Green 'money' and Monetary Compensatory Amounts."

28. See note 32, Ch. 1, supra.

29. Strauss, 1983, points out that "the introduction of MCAs brought to light for the first time one element of national choice within the supposedly common Community price system. France used pre-devaluation Green rates for most but not all CAP products. As farm products could not attract differing Green rates, it became apparent that a country could decide it did not want the relative prices for products agreed at Community level."

30. E.g. Com-EC, 1978–79, p. 6, paras, 3.4 and 3.5; *ASC 1978*, pp. 95–97; Harris et al., 1983, p. 203, quote Roy Jenkins, president of the European Commission, Royal Agricultural

Show, Stoneleigh, U.K., 3 July 1978: "when national prices in francs, lire and pounds are affected more by green devaluations and revaluations than by the common prices, there is a process of renationalisation of the CAP."

31. Strauss, 1983; T. Heidhues, et al., 1978. Com-EC, 1982a, pp. 12–13, 32: Though green rates were introduced to put off the effects of exchange rate changes on agriculture, they postponed rather than prevented alignment on the new parities. "The part of the total increase in support prices in national money attributable to green devaluations has been very significant in the period 1973–81: Italy 73 percent, Ireland 56 percent, France 50 percent, Denmark 44 percent, United Kingdom 39 percent. For the countries where money has appreciated the percentage of the increase in common prices offset by green revaluations has been: Netherlands, Luxembourg and Belgium about 3 percent, Germany 36 percent."

32. Com-EC, 1978a and 1979c, Tables 31–68. Even the enormous exports of milk from Bavaria to northern Italy seem a special case. This trade alone accounts for almost all the increase of Germany's market share in fresh milk trade in the EC. German exports of milk to Northern Italy, relatively though not absolutely, rose almost as much in the 2 years 1970–72, *before* Italy adopted green rates in 1973, as they did afterwards in 8 years, from 1972–80 (the figures are in thousands of tons): 1970—71; 1972—284; 1973—422; 1980—1240. Com-EC, 1978a, para. 2.

Italian consumption grew faster than milk production during the period; French domestic consumption rose while German fell at a time when French milk production was actually rising faster than German; Bavaria is the nearest to Italy of the big milk producing areas.

33. Eurostat, 1982c, pp. 19–27, gives the results shown in Table 4.F.

Table 4.F. Per Capita Net Value Added at Factor Cost in Agriculture in 1981 Compared with 1967–69 and 1973–75

	1967–69 = 100 (start of CAP)	1973–75 = 100 (start of recession)
Belgium	144.1	105.7
Italy	139.0	103.3
Ireland	127.8	86.1
Denmark	121.9	107.3
Netherlands	115.0	104.5
France	106.1	75.8
United Kingdom	98.4	79.4
Germany	90.8	78.5

34. Data for Greece, Ireland, Italy, Portugal and Spain do not suffice. But for Ireland they suggest that farm sizes and structures may evolve more or less along the lines of the other northern EC countries. In Italy and Greece there was almost no change from 1970 to 1977 in the enormous preponderance of farms under 5 hectares. For Spain, between the censuses of 1962 and 1972 the number of farms under 5 hectares fell from 2 to 1.6 million. Farms over 20 hectares occupied over 80 percent of the agricultural area in 1972. This suggests that in Spain the number of small farms is more of a social than productive problem.

35. Between 1973 and 1979 land values rose in real terms in nearly all countries listed by OECD, 1983b, p. 136 (U.S., Japan, New Zealand, Belgium, Denmark, France, Germany, Netherlands). The only exception was the U.K. After the second energy crisis, prices in the U.S., Japan and Germany continued to rise till 1981. In the other countries, they fell, as much as 36 percent in Denmark.

36. *Ibid.*, p. 81; and House of Lords, 1982, pp. 102–3.

37. For example, the demonstrations against farmers' tax privileges in Ireland in the run-up to the elections of December 1979.

38. "Il y a une génération, l'exploitant agricole faisait pitié" (CNASEA, 1980, p. 32).

39. For France, see Klatzman, 1978, pp. 52–53; also *ASC 1981*, p. 282, shows that the proportion of GDP contributed by agriculture, the farm input and food industries together, came to a little over 10 percent at the end of the 1970s in the Community as a whole.

40. Direction de la Prévision du Ministère de l'Economie in Paris.

41. See note 1, Ch. 1, supra.

42. Lindberg, 1963, pp. 225–32; Holmes and Duchêne, 1981, p. 13; Delorme and André, 1983, pp. 305–7; in Italy, deficiency payments for olive oil are administered by the Producer Organizations, who thereby acquire powers of patronage.

43. Data assembled at the OECD show that in two global surveys of the food industry in 1974, about 50 percent of the largest food firms, by turnover, were based in the United States and about 20 percent in the United Kingdom. (This figure excludes Unilever.) The U.K.–Dutch enterprise and the largest food company in France accounted for 4 percent in one survey and 9 percent in the other; West Germany and the Netherlands for 3 percent (2 percent and 1 percent respectively).

5   Limits and Strategies

The Limits of Expansion

It is extraordinary today to re-read the language used by the experts of the European Commission when they drew up the Mansholt Plan a decade and a half ago.

> The Community is now saddled, for many commodities, with surpluses some of which have no prospect of outlets on saturated world markets. Where outlets do exist, surpluses depress prices so that they can only be sold at high cost to the Community's budget . . .
>
> It is therefore vital, in future, to adopt another policy for farm prices.
>
> Suggestions are sometimes put forward that producer prices should be cut to the consumer's benefit. This would have the advantage of stimulating consumption while reducing unit and global support costs . . .
>
> But cuts, apart from the fact that they would be difficult to achieve, for obvious political reasons, would have to be very substantial to meet the goal. More limited reductions would run the risk of farmers simply increasing their output to maintain their incomes.
>
> The Community can achieve a better balance of agricultural markets by a longterm strategy with annual adjustments within the framework of that strategy [Com-EC, 1969, pp. 34-35; translation by authors].

That an early text from the heart of the Community should still be apposite today, and that during the intervening period so little attention has been paid, in itself conveys a message. Ideas in this field have no weight unless they commit the political forces in play. Social pressures of immense power have determined the progress of the CAP, as they have the national policies before and since its inception. Only political counterforces of similar power are likely to divert them. Ideas for policies, however constructive, must respect the resulting tensions to have any relevance.

Since the war, agriculture has become a "declining" industry in the technical sense that the growth of demand has permanently slowed down, thus putting it in the category of "mature," or "traditional," industries with reduced prospects of expansion. But supply has been radically different, in fact diametrically opposed. The more advanced segments of farming have industrialized since the war as never before.

Seen in this perspective, the CAP is the heir to traditional forms of support geared to a relatively backward peasant agriculture. Sooner or later, the new industrialized agriculture, growing in the matrix of a political system geared to scarcity, or near-scarcity, was bound to lead to an *embarras de richesses.* Equally naturally, the beneficiaries have had no intention of giving up their cornucopia, especially as they could hide behind the large numbers of farmers (representing a small proportion of output) who continued to be impoverished. In combination, the new productive farmers and the old less productive peasantry constituted a formidable and historically entrenched lobby.

Even so, the perpetuation of the traditional system might have been impossible had the exporting countries failed to find new markets. During two periods, they did find the necessary outlets. In the 1960s, the old policy was kept going by the preferential exploitation of the markets opened up by the new European Community. Then, in the 1970s, Community exporters found they could profit from the decade's great expansion of world food markets and, starting largely unnoticed from a modest base, greatly increased their world market share in a number of major commodities (Chapter 2). By these means, a "declining" industry has for twenty years been able to operate like an expanding one.

However, the tour de force could not go on for ever. By the early 1980s, the filling of what might be called the semi-vacant spaces of the expanding food economy has been largely achieved. From now on, expansion has almost certainly to be closely related to the general rate of growth of demand at home and abroad. In practice, the modest prospects of growth in the Community put most of the weight of expectation on the expansion of world demand. World markets are likely to accommodate EC growth at the steady rates of the past fifteen years only in the most favorable circumstances (Chapter 2). At anything less, the further EC exports push forward in excess of external demand, the more the costs build up and the greater becomes other exporters' resistance to the outward thrust. The new forces, as they expand, themselves harden the opposition from the old forces behind the equilibrium they disturb.

Even when world market conditions are favorable, they are not politically insulated as were those of the Community. The world outside cannot be manipulated in the way that the preferential areas gained through European integration have been. Thus, world markets are both the most significant safety valve, or variable, for expansion, and, more important, the ultimate limit upon it. This limit of course is not absolute. World markets vary with the economic cycle and changing structures of demand. In the long term, they will certainly grow. Further, the strong can manipulate export markets to some extent by cartels, long-term contracts and other means. But even OPEC has discovered the limits of manipulation. Between two concepts, the one of more or less free trade between individual economic agents, the other of the political control of the economy by the state, the EC's growing dependence on the world implies a significant shift away from political control to markets. This fact alone undermines the assumptions on which postwar European agriculture and the CAP have been operating.

A BUDGET CRISIS OR SOMETHING MORE?

The warning lights of crisis have flashed a number of times in the past decade. The agricultural self-sufficiency rates of the six founder members reached high levels in 1972 on the eve of the first expansion of the Community. In 1980, the Community's budgetary crisis was widely thought to be imminent before the food trade boom of 1980–82 postponed the reckoning. By 1983, it seemed unavoidable, though in theory a miraculous recovery of world trade combined with a strong dollar could put it off yet again.

In the first instance, the crisis is a financial one. It arises because the tax base of the Community, fixed by the six founding states in 1970 in anticipation of British entry, had become fully exploited by 1983 (Strasser, 1977 p. 46). A further expansion of the tax base would require a new agreement of the ten member states—in effect a new treaty, since it would require parliamentary ratification. Such a basic review naturally opens up a broad range of issues to political discussion. Technically, it might be possible to avoid this by finding more funds in agriculture itself. Dairy producers fund about 10 percent of the cost of the milk regime, the sugar producers up to 70 percent of theirs. The Commission, in the wake of the French, has proposed a tax on vegetable fats (Com-EC, 1983a, Annex II, pp. 26 and 34). Another idea explored to try to satisfy British demands for a better balanced budget has been a tax on petroleum imports, which would be paid basically by the continental countries, except for Holland.[1]

Unfortunately, these proposals divide the member states. The tax on fats is highy controversial and may not be passed even in a general package deal. A tax on imported oil might placate the British, though even that is questionable; but the Germans, who also complain of excessive net contributions, would be among the main payers. Second, solutions for extra revenue do not meet the point which has become primary among the member states, not only Germany and Britain, that expenditure itself must be brought under control. In 1983, this had become European orthodoxy, even in France. One French motive in pursuing the CAP twenty years ago seems to have been to reduce the pressure of farm subsidies on the national budget by persuading Community partners, primarily Germany, to pay as much as possible of them (Delorme and André, 1983, pp. 348, 362–63). This gives more historic depth than might be expected to the French proposals of November 1983 for the stricter control of Community, including CAP, spending (*Financial Times*, 1983f). Third, it seems clear that the British, if no one else, probably want to have a Community crisis and to force the issues. For the first time ever, they have a strong bargaining position in the Community. What they really want to do with it is not so clear. They certainly want to save money. This may give them a real desire to bring the CAP under control. There probably is a wish to placate opposition at home (in Germany too the Social Democrats have been playing on fatigue with funding the Community). There may conceivably be a desire to see what chance there is of "re-nationalizing" the CAP. The British have never subscribed to the maximalist view of the Community that the CAP, however imperfectly, represents. To bring the CAP back to more intergovernmental norms of cooperation would represent a strategic victory against a conception of the Community which had at first to be swallowed hook, line, and sinker. It is not possible to isolate such motives clearly, because they are not mutually incompatible. Whichever predominate, they all argue against the resort to expedients which might short-circuit the basic negotiation. In a Community of vetoes, it is not possible to circumvent such opposition.

For all these reasons, then, the traditional postwar agricultural policy is coming up against limits which did not exist before. The limits are not fixed, because there are many imponderables. It is no accident that the crisis has come during two years marked by, first, stagnation and, second, regression of world food trade after a decade of average growth exceeding 5 percent a year in real terms. In that perspective, the crisis of 1983–84 represents an extreme and is almost certainly no more representative of the future than of the past. The limits are not those of a steady state, but the much more elastic ones of constant uncertainty. Uncertainty calls for flexible responses, which are not consonant with production rigidly set against even temporary phases of deceleration. Flexibility thus constitutes a limit in itself.

This is, of course, a key conclusion. It implies that governments, however unwillingly, must begin to espouse policies of flexible control, which is no less control for being flexible. To apply flexibility in practice would mark a watershed. Precisely because of this, and because the crisis of 1983–84 involves the political exploitation of an extreme swing in the economic pendulum, it is necessary to examine in a longer perspective whether there is room for expansion and what limits must be envisaged for the future.

DOMESTIC SCOPE FOR EXPANSION

There are three conceivable *domestic* European areas of demand into which Community output could expand. They are: home markets for animal feed, at the cost of the foreign suppliers who have so far captured a large part of them; (2) the preferential capture of Iberian markets in a Community of Twelve; and (3) growth of further demand in the Community, whether enlarged or not.

The Community's animal feed imports are very large. They represent, year in year out, some 9-10 percent of the total domestic consumption of agricultural products in the Community. Around 1980, they included about 14 million tons of cereal substitutes imported largely for their carbohydrate content and 19 million tons of oilcake for protein (Eurostat, 1983b, p. 148; European Parliament, 1982, pp. 69–102). The chief suppliers of cereal substitutes are in southeast Asia, while the overwhelming supplier of protein products is the United States. The Community, even with costly expansion programs (partly under way) cannot go much above 30 percent self-sufficiency in proteins (Com-EC, 1981a, p. 38; European Parliament, 1982, p. 93). The imports of cereal substitutes have already been subjected to "voluntary" export restrictions, but there is little the Community could do, politically or technically, to replace soya-cake. The working group on Europe for the Ninth

Plan of the French Commissariat du Plan has drawn the inference: "Since the threat of serious American reprisals makes it improbable that factory farming will be reined in by re-establishing duties on imports or soya-beans, policy will have to fall back on price supports . . . an approach which poses problems for farmers' incomes" (Commissariat Général du Plan, 1983, pp. 61 and 63). Clearly, the best hope of regaining the animal feed market, at least in part, would be to lower (or subsidize) Community cereal prices to compete with imports. Since the consumption of oilseeds has been artificially boosted by the high relative prices in the Community for cereals, this might reduce not only cereal imports but also regain some of the market from soya-beans.[2] Even so, the ultimate goal of expanding cereal sales to the Community feed market by even 10 to 15 million tons a year would be ambitious; and it would only buy three to five years (for this sector alone) at the average rate of growth of Community cereals output during the 1970s of 3 million tons a year.[3] Given the political importance of the cereal growers in the Community (often the same as the oilseed producers), this is not negligible. But it is no new frontier either.

The limitations of the Iberian market have already been stressed. The Spanish import market in 1980 was equivalent to about 14 million tons of grain equivalent, again, overwhelmingly in cereals and oilseeds bought from the Americas, North and South. EC-10 dairy markets in Iberia might be expanded, but would hurt highly populated, high-cost and low-income Spanish regions, mainly in the northwest, which, once in trouble, would have to be funded by the Community in other ways. Portugal's import market in 1980 was much smaller: about 2 million tons of grain equivalent. Whether this would add up to major market opportunities for the Community's present producers is open to serious question. An FAO study of the problem concluded that the 75 percent self-sufficiency in grains of Greece, Portugal, and Spain which obtained in 1975–77 would rise to 90 percent self-sufficiency by 1990 without the enlargement of the Community and to 100 percent self-sufficiency with enlargement (FAO, 1980a, pp. 123–26).

As for the domestic growth of the Community market, the French situation, somewhat more expansionary than the German or British, is a good instance of the limits of demand. Population will grow about 0.4 percent per annum to the end of the century; and the elasticity of demand for food is only some 20 percent of every unit of growth in consumption. This means that even with an average 4 percent per annum rate of economic growth, lower than in the 1960s but well beyond current expectations, future French demand for food would rise by only 1.2 percent a year (in value), less than in the 1970s. This slightly understates growth in the volume of demand, because of the declining prices farm goods are likely to fetch in terms of other products. Nevertheless, the low levels of growth of consumption of the 1970s are not likely to change substantially even if the general economic climate improves; and if it does not, they may even fall from the standards set in the recent past (Appendix Table 1) (Bergmann, 1979, pp. 5 and 5a).

In these conditions, the only relief of the domestic pressures of excess supply on the CAP would be substantial and unforeseen restrictions on output. The growth of production has been so steady for the past thirty years (Appendix Table 1) as to constitute a kind of standard of "normality." If one assumes its continuance, other things being equal, there are only four evident ways in which it could plausibly be discouraged, one of them being deliberate policy disincentives, which is precisely what the expansionary political forces in the Community would wish to avoid. That leaves, as alternatives: a change in climate unfavorable to European farming; an energy crisis which, unlike those of the past decade, hits supply more than demand; or a slowing down in the long-term rate of progress of productivity.

Reference has already been made to American expectations of a warming up of climate, though with what detailed effects cannot yet be foreseen. This might reduce the growth of European agriculture, or it might not. Short of nuclear winter, there would presumably be enough premonitory signs for adjustments to be made, given the leeway between supply and demand which exists for most products (Table 5.1). There is obviously room for slowing down the growth of supply without risking failure to meet demand. This applies even to those few products, like cheese, pork, and poultry, where domestic Community consumption has continued to grow with some vigor. There is as yet no discernible problem of food security on these grounds. The OECD is inclined to play down the relevance of general climatic change in the next decade (OECD, 1983a, p. 50, para. 123).

Table 5.1   Growth of Supply and Demand in the EC-9 for Selected Farm Commodities, 1973-1981

Commodity	Supply (percent)	Demand (percent)	Self-sufficiency 1981 (percent) [a]
Wheat	27	2	123
Sugar	57	0	129
Dairy (excl. fresh milk, cheese)	18	1	125
Cheese	38	27	107
Beef	28	4	105
Pork	25	24	102
Mutton	24	−2	77
Poultry	30	21	111
Wine	24	10	100

a $\frac{\text{Total production}}{\text{Total domestic use}} \times 100$.

Source: Thiede, 1980; Com-EC, *ASC 1982.*

In many ways, if one identifies food security with self-sufficiency, producers' reliance for high output on imported fuels, fertilizers, and feed could be a more acute source of vulnerability. All of them are directly or indirectly connected with energy. So far, the effects of the two energy crises on production have been outweighed by their depression of demand. Contrary to many fears, the tendency to surpluses in the CAP was intensified by the energy crises. However, this may have been due to the kind of crises that occurred.[4] In 1973–74 real energy prices rose over 4 times and in 1979–80 they doubled, but in both cases energy supplies hardly fell. A serious and sudden interruption of supplies, on the other hand, would not necessarily have the same consequences. Some American studies, now rather old, suggest that the price effects of even quite a moderate cut in energy supplies could have an altogether disproportionate impact on agricultural costs of production (Dvoskin and Heady, 1976, p. 5). Since the whole food chain, including manufacturing and distribution, uses about one fifth of all energy produced, it would, in a real supply crisis, have to take its share of cuts. This would not bring famine because human consumption accounts for only a quarter of Community grain production, and food would have priority. Yet the shocks to demand, to the pattern of output and to farmers' incomes could be enormous. Crop production would not be affected to anything like the same extent as livestock farming and greenhouse horticulture.

Like climatic change, an interruption of energy supplies is largely speculation. Unlike the effects of climate, it could be sudden. Both situations are hard to prepare for. Their potential, in the wide range of possibilities, is too idiosyncratic to make it easy to bend the middle run of policies to their special and very hypothetical needs.

As for the progress of productivity, the field, as always with technology, tends to be sharply divided between optimists and pessimists. Optimists point to extraordinary advances in the breeding of crops and livestock, and to the very large reserves of productivity which exist, without new developments, in countries like France and Ireland. The pessimists point to stagnation of maize yields in the past decade or the lack of fundamental discoveries so long as research on techniques such as nitrogen fixation does not produce results. This cannot, it is generally agreed, come before the 1990s at the earliest. The experts of the U.S. Department of Agriculture seem to plump for continuity in yield trends. The OECD tends to expect genetic progress to continue fairly strongly. The EC stresses the reserves of productivity available for grains.[5] Though forecasting is notoriously inadequate, in this as in other fields, there seems no strong reason for assuming a major change in the pace of growth of yields.

In short, despite inevitable and necessary reservations, there is little reason to expect that in the next two decades the pressure of supply of the last twenty years will diminish if policies stay the same. (The most obvious exception is an extreme and prolonged interruption in energy supplies.) Of course, this assumes that some time is available in which to react and that farming is sufficiently flexible to respond to price signals. All the evidence suggests that Community farming is in fact very responsive to stimuli for higher output.

There is nothing clear in the prospective development of either demand or supply in the Community to suggest any spontaneous remission of the pressures which make surpluses the major problem of the early 1980s. If this is so, the focus of attention for the future of the CAP has to be on foreign trade, which has provided much of the room for expansion of recent years, at least until the slump of 1982–83.

LIMITS AND WORLD MARKETS

World markets cannot be discussed as an indistinct whole. Each commodity has its own characteristics and its own environment. The contrasts are particularly marked in three exemplary cases. The first is where the traditional exporters with whom the Community engages in a potential struggle for market shares are strong. A second is where they are weak. And the third is where the Community is already the world's dominant exporter and is plugged in directly to the ups and downs of demand. Of the three commodities the Community exports most heavily, cereals illustrate the first situation, sugar the second, and dairy products the third.

Not surprisingly, as the world's leading food exporter, the United States is involved, directly or indirectly, in many important Community exports, and in none so much as cereals, where it has traditionally dominated world trade. It is no accident that the first active U.S. attack on Community food exports focused on wheat flour. The American preoccupation with cereals spills over into poultry, which professionals now treat virtually as a mobile bag of grain. French and Dutch exports of poultry have boomed in the past decade. In 1963, with American political support for European integration still near its height, conflict in this area led to the *opera buffa* known as the "chicken war." In practice, American farmers have done very well out of the CAP, because soya-beans have become the protein base of Community expansion in live-stock. The EC takes more than 40 percent of all American soya-bean exports. This makes the United States vulnerable to retaliation and is one factor explaining past caution in dealing with the CAP. While the expansion of European exports has caused the U.S. increasing nervousness, for several years the boom in world exports generally defused the European threat. Depression after 1981 changed the situation completely. Vigorous American warnings of a trade war turned into formal complaints in GATT, and complaints in GATT to pointed sales of flour and butter to Egypt, undercut-ting—by subsidies—a market the EC had earlier in the decade wrested—by subsidies—from the United States. Confrontation between the two great powers of world trade has been averted, but the possibility lurks in the background.

American protests at European farm practices, however well founded, leave cognoscenti less than deeply moved. The United States is itself, in agriculture, "an intensely protectionist country":

> Central to American protection is the right obtained in 1955 to "waiver" agreements under the GATT to continue import quotas and restrictions. Almost all dairy product imports are limited by quota as are imports of

cotton and peanuts. Imports of sugar are subject to a "fee" whch is similar to the EEC's variable levy. Imports of fresh, chilled or frozen beef and veal are subject to the Meat Import Law by which quotas can be imposed if imports exceed certain trigger levels. In fact, they rarely do so because voluntary agreements keep imports modest. Cattle and dairy products, peanuts, cotton and sugar account for about 40 percent of American agricultural cash receipts.

The same scepticism tends to greet American complaints about EEC unfair competition on third country markets. The United States charges that the EEC uses its export subsidies to win commercial sales . . . America is worried about two new policies being discussed by the EEC: longterm export contracts between the EEC and customers (the North African countries are most frequently mentioned) and special export credit arrangements . . . The United States herself, however, has a panoply of measures which aid agriculture, though no export subsidies as such . . . (There is the longterm cereals contract with the Soviet Union.) . . . The Europeans also claim that the United States uses' its ability to make concessionary loans available to developing countries (Public Law 480) to develop new markets unfairly and that the Commodity Credit Corporation makes available the sort of export credit guarantee and insurance that is not available as such to the Community. To this litany of complaints the Europeans would add the DISC system which permits American companies to enjoy tax concessions on export earnings and which is regarded as an export subsidy; food aid under public Law 480; and government-to-government arrangements for dairy products [Curry, 1982a, p. 23].

Clearly, there is plenty of ammunition for a war of words.

In practice, both the Community and the United States are vulnerable in a number of ways, which sometimes seem to cancel each other out. As far as markets are concerned, the United States has committed a large hostage to the Community in the enormous exports, already noted, of oilseeds and maize gluten feed. On the other hand, it has the potential to disrupt Community exports of sugar and dairy products where, in contradistinction to cereals, it is the Community not the United States which now has established positions to defend. Finance also has to be taken into account, because the longer purse would be likely to win a war of export credits. The United States obviously has a major advantage in the divisions among the Community's member states. With Mrs. Thatcher to hamstring the Community budget, is there much the Americans need do? The U.S. also has the advantage in its lower cereals prices which means that per unit of sales it would have to lay out far less money than the Community. On the other hand, it also has some major weaknesses. Its volume of cereal exports is five or six times higher than that of the Community, so that unless the rivalry were confined to random sales, the cost to the United States could be high. This might not matter so much were it not for the eccentric economic policies of the Reagan administration and the huge budget deficits which have already accumulated. These create such a strain that the United States must think twice about adding to them. Moreover, the main losers in an export credit war could be neither the United

States nor the Community but the minor traditional exporters like Canada and Australia, which count among the closest associates of America (Anderson and Tyers, 1983, pp. 11–13). This leads to the third, political, strand in this complex equation. The United States' immense advantage not only in the division of the Community member states but in its leadership of the Atlantic Alliance makes most European governments very reluctant to let quarrels about agriculture spill over into broader relations. On the other hand, the United States too is tied. The politics of the introduction into Europe of Cruise and Pershing II missiles are turbulent enough without adding fuel to the anti-Americanism that is an important strain in the anti-nuclear movement, notably in Germany.

It is not surprising, then, that the sound and fury of 1982 has tended to abate in 1983. It is also significant that the Community has refrained from trying to expand its market share of world grain exports in 1983, it seems by agreement with Washington.[6] The United States, for its part, has kept very quiet in the second half of 1983. A delicate balance seems to prevail over trade in food. This implies an underlying search for accommodations. But the two may always fall foul of what are on both sides of the ocean major interests. Traditional postures also play a part. It is unlikely for example that the French would ever accept the American domestic grain price as any kind of yardstick for the Community.

Most Community products other than grains primarily affect either the Antipodes (dairy products, beef, and mutton), the Mediterranean (fruit, vegetables, and olive oil) or the tropical Third World (sugar). All of these lack the American bargaining power. Sugar is a classic case. In the late 1970s, the Community, not previously a net exporter, carved out for itself a share of a quarter of the world market largely at the other exporters' expense. The Community's subsidized exports of sugar not only deprived (mainly) poorer countries of markets, they drove prices down, and cut their competitors' earnings in the process. The Community refused to join the International Sugar Agreement (ISA) of 1977, and this has been one major factor behind the agreement's failure to stabilize the market. In the five years following the agreement, prices fluctuated between 5 U.S. cents a pound (c/lb) at the bottom of the cycle and over 40 c/lb at the top, the floor and the ceiling being each twice as extreme as those envisaged in the agreement. The ISA was due for renewal in 1984 and the Community offered to join a negotiation for the international management of stocks (Com-EC, 1983h; House of Lords, 1980a). One of the reasons is that even on sugar, now the Community has carved out a market share, there are limits to expansion. Potentially the most important of these involves the United States. Though an importer of sugar, the United States has been developing sugar substitutes for the food industry, by-products of maize, which could threaten present exporters much as the Community did in the 1970s.

The third case is dairy products, where the Community dominates world trade (Table 2.2), with the Netherlands in the lead, followed by France and Germany. A dominant supplier, who cannot well increase a preponderant market share is in some ways more constrained by the limitations of demand than a minor one who can. With New Zealand, the other major exporter, the Community managed to raise prices when the market was buoyant in 1980–81. But, with depression on the markets in 1983, sales have collapsed and dairy products have resumed their usual pride of place as the CAP's crisis sector par excellence. This tends to confirm the judgement of the "Europe" group for the French Ninth Plan that

> the outlets for the agricultural exports of the Community are uncertain [*fragiles*]. In 1973, only 43 percent of them went to Socialist states or the Third World. Today, 60 percent of them do, and some of the states in question face unprecedented balance of payments difficulties [Commissariat Général du Plan, 1983, p. 59].

In any case, no cartel is stable for long. Here the United States (again) enters the picture. Like the Community, a high-cost dairy producer, the United States has, since 1979, been accumulating surpluses though not, in 1983, on the Community's scale (Com-EC, 1983g). It has not yet dumped these on other markets, and to do so would be expensive, as American prices are every bit as high as European ones when the dollar is strong. But it could do so. An uneasy balance exists.

In short, the Community does not have a free hand on world markets whether or not it has become the dominant supplier of a particular item. The days of internally conditioned expansion onto world markets have become a lost paradise as a result of the very size of the Community's exports. It is also impossible to prevent the repercussions from invading the internal politics of the Community itself. Foreign goods can be kept out, but the financial costs of exporting cannot be insulated in this way. Given the role of subsidies in pushing sales of otherwise unwanted Community produce at home or abroad, or the still higher costs per unit of output of buying up surpluses for stock, the farm budget becomes virtually the thermometer of the market balance—or imbalance—of the CAP. This precipitates crises of financial shares between the member states still more telling than those of market shares with outsiders.

During the 1970s, world markets became notably more unstable than they had been. International prices, low in general before 1970, rose to the wild peak of 1974–75, down to a trough for most products in 1978–79, up again for some to 1981, and steeply down again in 1983. The exchange rate of the dollar also fluctuated wildly, which was important because it is the currency in which international contracts are drawn up. These vagaries were immediately reflected in Community finances through the changing costs of export subsidies, which have accounted at most times for over 40 percent of the Community farm budget. A weak dollar and world market push prices down and increase the subsidies the Community must pay to sell abroad (or even for some items at home, in competition with imports of oilseeds). A strong dollar and world market push prices up and cut funding on export subsidies.

These influences, important though they are, cannot always be neatly isolated, because of other factors. For instance, on the financial evidence, the CAP's managers seem, since 1978, to have become more adept in subsidizing exports to avoid having to pay the still higher costs of buying up stocks. But in 1983 dairy sales fell so badly on world markets that spending on stocks rose more than a third (in real terms) in a single year (Appendix Table 11). In effect, this helped to make the budget even higher than it would otherwise have been. Similarly, subsidies to production have tripled (at constant prices and therefore in real terms) between 1978 and 1983 after actually falling between 1975 and 1978. This development reflects the success of the Italians, and latterly the Greeks, in switching Community funding to the Mediterranean. It is also due to the new sheepmeat regime and the attempt to make the Community more self-sufficient in oilseeds. The combination of (1) rising help to southern products and oilseeds; (2) lower world prices resulting in higher sales subsidies; and (3) even then an inability to avoid higher stocks, which are particularly expensive, has meant that the Community farm budget increased almost a quarter (in real terms) in the single year from 1982 to 1983 (Appendix Table 11).[7]

The orders of magnitude of the variations in the Community budget can be seen in simplified form in Table 5.2, calculated in constant ECUs of 1975 and which excludes MCAs. This table, taking years which show the ups and downs of the budget at constant prices, brings out a number of important points. One is the fairly strong general growth of spending in the decade 1973–83 (equivalent to about 5.5 percent a year in volume). This is quite a high rate, although not as high as critics of the CAP like to make out; and it should be noted that the farm budget, in relation to GDP, has never, even in 1983, reached the levels attained by the Six as early as 1972 (see Appendix Table 11). It is clearly out of tune with the cost-cutting mood in the capitals, especially but not only Bonn and London, which has become evident since the second

Table 5.2   Variations in Size and Types of Expenditure of EC Farm Guarantee Fund, 1973–1983 (in percentages based on constant prices) (1975 = 100)

Year	EC Farm Guarantee Fund	Sales Subsidies	Stocks and Equivalent	Production Subsidies
1973	106	151	38	140
1974	91	80	64	104
1978	159	194	155	97
1980	160	234	121	174
1981	143	193	118	201
1983	180	216	172	262

Source: See Appendix Table 11. Table 11, however, covers the EAGGF (including the Guidance [Structural] Fund), MCAs, and Fish.

energy crisis. An obvious reason for the lack of consensus over the farm budget has been the incongruity between the efforts of deflationary-minded governments to curb public spending and the increase in the cost of a CAP more reminiscent of boom conditions. The table also demonstrates the sharp reduction in spending in 1974 and the milder one in 1981, as well as the steep rise from 1974–80 and again in 1983, generating crisis. The even steeper rise in sales subsidies from 1974–80 is also visible; as are the exceptional years of 1978 and 1983 for stocks; and the steady and rapid expansion of spending on production subsidies (largely aids to southern Europe) since 1978. All of these developments reflect political conditions or crises of some sort.

In 1974–75, the fall in the pressure on the CAP played a major role in the referendum of June 1975 in which the British public decided it was safer to stay in the European Community. In 1980, the Community budget crisis seemed imminent. Then changing conditions held it at bay till 1983. The fall in world markets in 1983 exhausted the funds provided by the agreement of 1970, which has underpinned the CAP at least as much as the original regulations setting it up.

Thus, both in the economics and diplomacy of world markets and in the financial politics of the Community, the limits on expansion seem to be fundamental and growing, not cyclical. The limits are elastic because of variations in the world market, and they do not altogether preclude growth, because world demand is bound in the longer term to expand. They are also elastic because political will can vary with developments and is to some extent unpredictable. But supply too is growing, with reserves of productivity that can be tapped by expansionary policies. The result is that the room for the Community to continue raising output on the scale which has become routine in the previous decades is becoming more and more thoroughly circum-scribed. This is a crucial change not only for the CAP and the Community, but also for Western Europe as an agricultural region.

SCOPE FOR NATIONAL EXPANSION

However, what is true for all agriculture and the whole region may not necessarily be the case for each commodity and for each individual member state. For instance, while there is virtually a Community consensus that milk and cereal output have to be controlled, expansion is being tried in a number of products where the Community is still in deficit: oilseeds are an outstanding example. More important politically, some member states might calculate they could afford to continue expanding, even if others could not. Such a conclusion could have far-reaching effects, for agriculture and the Commu-nity.

There are two archetypal—and opposite—cases where one might expect a country to envisage unilateral national expansion. The first is the strong world exporter, frustrated by collective CAP spending limits, who decides it might be better to accept the risks of operating alone. This most clearly points to France. The other archetypal case is where a net importing country feels it still has room for domestic expansion—and even a chance to occupy some international market niches—and that these possibilities will be foregone if Community restraints freeze the less favorable status quo. This could point to Britain, Germany, and Italy. It is far less likely to apply to the small Community member states, because they all specialize in intra-European trade and all depend more on this trade than do their larger neighbors (Appendix Table 9). Doubts, then, focus on the larger countries.

To take the case of the exporter first. France has for some time been pushing the Community to enter into long-term contracts, especially for cereals, with large buyers, mainly Egypt and the Maghreb countries. Public opinion polls in 1983 showed a surprising disaffection from, or indifference to, the CAP in France, of all countries.[8] French politicians are occasionally heard doubting the continuing value to their country of the CAP. France, with its large output of cereals and sugar is a force in its own right on the world market. Yet it is doubtful both for political and technical reasons that it could profitably exploit its food export potential alone.

The Community has somewhat different functions in its domestic and external faces. Domestically, the value of the CAP is as a preferential market for the farmers, traders, and processors of the member states. Externally, the value to the member states and lobbies is mainly as a source of funds and as a negotiating cooperative or export cartel. This is of particular importance to a new-found food exporter treading on the toes of the major established one, the United States. Unilateralism would throw away this protective cover. There are very few situations where a European exporting country would feel confident of its bargaining power alone against the United States. It is possible that France might be able to do so in cereals. It could, like Argentina, exploit its attractions to purchasers anxious not to become over dependent on the United States. It could, like the U.S. in grains or New Zealand in dairy products with the Soviet Union, enter into bilateral long-term contracts with importers. These are in effect preferential agreements and would give France priority against later entrants on the markets. But why these should offer a better prospect for the long-term expansion of outlets than would otherwise exist, or provide guarantees of better prices when world markets fall, is not clear. Contracts are invariably least committing on prices. In any case, it is not enough to be strong in a single commodity. France exports large quantities of dairy products and sugar as well as grains. On both, in isolation, it would be vulnerable to American spoiling tactics. Further, any country striking out alone would have to reckon on the potential rivalry on foreign markets of the very member states of the Community who hitherto increased their collective bargaining power in international negotiations by mutually backing each other up. Now these too might enter into trade competition based on export subsidies. An exporter would find itself in the same position as the U.S. today faced by the Community. Irrespective of its own comparative advantage, it would have to face subsidized competition it could not control. There is no profit to this. The risks seem incalculable and unattractive.

It would also be virtually impossible to insulate export policies from the operation of the internal CAP. At present, farmers or processors sell into intervention wherever the returns are best. The chosen intervention agency, often German because of the strength of the DM, then takes charge of the export sale. The Community is billed. However, the conditions in which the sale is made, and therefore in practice whether it can be made at all, are decided by the relevant Community commodity management committee in which the Commission, because of the procedural rules, plays a major role.[9] If export "restitutions" become even partly national, as they would have to under a national export policy, this system is likely to become unworkable. No country would buy up surpluses, and still less subsidize their export, on behalf of another with which it was in effect in open competition. Surpluses would become strictly national (and would have to be financed as such). Some countries would, of course, have more products available to sell than others. Some might also be more willing to subsidize sales (and stocks) than others. In any case, potentially low-cost exporters, by European standards, would be under pressure to lower their national prices to steal a march. This would reduce costs for the budget, make life harder for rivals, especially for European Community rivals exporting to the world market, and generally exploit the country's comparative advantages against higher-price sellers. By this time, common prices and common funding would both have clearly gone by the board. All that would remain would be the Community's mutual preference, and that too, with open national rivalry and prices, would be hard to sustain. Because the importing member states' self-sufficiency would be rising, maintaining even long-term contracts with Community partners might be beyond political reach. Yet it is precisely the exporters, the countries most under pressure to slip the leash on trade to the world, who also happen to be most dependent on maintaining their outlets within the Community itself. Cereals remain a major French export within the Community. Food trade with other member states still represents nearly two-thirds of total Community food exports and is not to be lightly jeopardized (Appendix Table 6). Contrary to popular mythology in Britain and Germany, it is the exporters, not the net importers, who most need to restrain the expansionist forces *within* the CAP. A choking up of the channels of food trade in the Community would be an admission of strategic defeat. After all, the exporters wanted the CAP in the 1950s precisely in order to open up these outlets.

The net importers could, arguably, take a different view. A net importer need, in theory, only limit contributions to the Community budget, maintain (or slightly reduce) real farm prices, and let nature take its course in the form of rising national self-sufficiency. Admittedly, the scope for expansion is not infinite and the limits will rapidly appear. But even on the most restrictive hypothesis, the net importer will be less under pressure to cut back output than the exporter and so will have a relatively larger market share in Europe, if not in the world, at the end of the process than now. So long as world markets are depressed, today's exporters are unlikely to lengthen their lead very much; and once world markets revive, erstwhile importers will at least have the option of expanding into a place in the sun, even if it is a modest one.

Whatever the theory might be, this is patently not an outlook that appeals to one of the net importers, Italy. Italy would gain advantages from a breakup of the CAP: cheaper food imports from outside the Community and room for more domestic agricultural expansion. But this would constitute a major political defeat for the ruling Christian Democrats, for whom European integration is one of the few ideological constants of a supremely pragmatic regime. It would also damage hopes that are common to all the countries that have traditionally been poor. All the poor countries of the Community, from Ireland to Greece—and Portugal in case of enlargement—look on it as a way of achieving higher standards of living in their poorest sectors, which are precisely in agriculture. All of them now obtain substantial funds for agriculture from the Community, and for all of them these sums represent not only invaluable capital and foreign exchange but sources of political patronage. Any damage to the CAP that affected these flows of funds and (for the Irish and Greeks especially) the hopes of expanding their most competitive products would constitute a grave national setback. For these reasons, all the poor countries are strong supporters of the Community and of the CAP in particular and oppose any kind of restraints on output. For the poor countries, this interest in taxing the rich, even in the limited and imperfect form of the CAP, overrides all other considerations, including whether or not they are exporters or importers. Any new arrangements aimed at resolving Community problems would have to maintain substantial transfers of funds.

The British also claim to be poor. If so, they are at most the new poor, or poor in declining industries, not in agriculture, where their farmers count among the largest and richest. Poverty seems in no way to cramp Britain's negotiating style. She seems in many ways the prototype for an "importer's policy." Being furthest of all the member states from self-sufficiency (Appendix Table 2), she could opt for unilateral food expansion more easily than any other. However, even for Britain, the operation would not be without costs. Like the Germans and Italians, the British have major sectors which already are, or soon will be, in surplus (Table 5.3). Calculations cannot be confined to Britain alone. On entry into the Community in 1973, she obtained a series of concessions for New Zealand in butter and lamb and for the Commonwealth sugar and to a lesser extent beef producers. These would fall back into her lap if the CAP were to subside. Because of expansion since 1973, supply balances in Britain are no longer what they were before Community membership. Taking into account traditional suppliers, including no doubt Ireland, whose goodwill is vital in Ulster, Britain is already in surplus, or on the edge of surplus, in cereals, in milk powder (that is, milk proteins), in lamb and even in butter (milk fats). The economic *Lebensraum* is not infinite.

Nor, though it is almost never mentioned, is the political. Britain, having failed to enter the Community when she could have done so on good terms, spent many years trying to retrieve her mistake. When she did so, the discomforts of operating in a system she had not herself shaped encouraged her to attitudes which are widely regarded by her partners as "anti-European." This means that if she carries through any self-assertive policy, she

Table 5.3   Self-Sufficiency of Supply in Germany and the United Kingdom for Selected Farm Commodities 1970 and 1981 (percentage of production to consumption)

Commodity	Germany 1970	Germany 1981	Weight in farm output 1981 Germany	Weight in farm output 1981 U.K.	United Kingdom 1970	United Kingdom 1981	United Kingdom 1981 including "traditional" imports
Wheat	78	107	4.7	9.0	45	88	
Other "home-grown" cereals[a]	78	95	4.1	7.8	92	123	
Sugar	87	123	4.0	2.0	32	45	96[c]
Beef and veal	89	108	17.2	16.3	67	83	
Mutton	100	60	0.3	4.1	42	67	107[d]
Dried skim milk	142	227			87	224	
Butter (product weight)	95	124	24.5[b]	22.5[b]	13	49	86[e] (105[f])

[a] Excludes maize, millet, sorghum.
[b] Milk (i.e., all dairy products).
[c] 1,225,000 tons imported from ACP (mostly ex-Commonwealth) sugar producers.
[d] 157,000 tons imported from New Zealand.
[e] 102,000 tons and 31,000 tons imported from New Zealand and Ireland respectively.
[f] Including additional 43,000 tons and 22,000 tons imported from Denmark and Netherlands.

Source: 1970—OECD, *Food Consumption Statistics 1964-1978,* Paris 1981; 1981—Com-EC, Eurostat, *1983 Yearbook of Agricultural Statistics,* 1978-81; Imports—Com-EC, Eurostat, *Analytical Tables of Foreign Trade, SITC Rev. 2,* 1981; Output Weightings —Com-EC, Eurostat, *ASC 1982,* pp. 194-195.

must have at least the complicity of Germany or France, and more probably of both. Otherwise, there is always the risk that the other two, who need each other more than either needs Britain, may bypass her once again. Their initiation—without Britain—of the European Monetary Scheme in 1978 was a clear sign of their potential readiness to do so. Britain's negotiating weaknesses were again demonstrated when her veto in the Community's annual farm price review was overridden in May 1982. This does not mean that Britain lacks all room for maneuver. Given German views of finance she has a good deal. France also has her hands tied, partly by gaullist tradition, in dealing with Germany. But Britain has to tread carefully in unilateralism. The implication, whether events bring this to the surface or not, is that Germany is the hinge of any reform of the CAP which touches the frontier between Community and national action.

Germany's position, despite some parallels with the U.K. on finance, is really rather different. True, if Germany maintained a rigid ceiling on her net budgetary contribution to the Community, she would dare France and other exporters to go down a unilateralist road. Objections to being the "paymaster" of the Community have become more and more of a political slogan in Germany. This reflects budgetary rigor at home and a reviving nationalism but beyond that, the similarities with Britain are small.

First, in the early 1980s, Germany has in effect ceased to be an importer at all (Table 5.3). Though overall she appeared a net importer still in 1981, this really depended entirely on fruit, vegetables, wine, and above all oilseeds for animal feed.[10] She was also a net importer in pork and poultry, but to disturb this arrangement would wreck the century-old links with Denmark and the Netherlands. In all the other major temperate foods, Germany is now an exporter. In dairy products, she is the biggest exporter in the Community. She cannot therefore play fast and loose with the trading channels built up under the CAP. This is a new economic factor, which has developed mainly in the last decade, but a crucial one.

Moreover, it is reinforced by nearly all the political factors in play, except the new radicalism with national overtones. An importer's policy is not only invalidated by Germany's emergence as a de facto exporter. It is also, implicitly, in contradiction, or potential contradiction, with at least two of the traditional goals of her policies: the enhancement of Europe's and her own influence in the Mediterranean and, more deeply still, the special relationship with France, which dates back not to de Gaulle but to the Schuman declaration of 1950.

The crucial factor is the relationship with France. For over thirty years, in the form of the European integration policy, this has come second only to the security relationship with the United States in German *Westpolitik*. The CAP cannot be divorced from it, for a host of reasons. For one thing, the French could abandon the CAP without this (at least in theory) sapping the relationship with Germany. But the Germans could not throw over, or be thought to be responsible for throwing over, the CAP without upsetting their relationship with the French. Much water has flowed under the bridge since the Treaty of Rome, and it could be argued that French needs and perspectives have changed. The fact remains that if the French themselves do not say they have lost interest in the CAP, the Germans would be taking a major political risk in saying it for them; and if any regime in Western Europe has "risk aversion," it is Bonn, especially under a Christian Democrat Chancellor who does not wish to be accused of betraying the inheritance of Adenauer. Germany has a huge surplus in her industrial trade with France, and this could be put in difficulties by a breakdown of the CAP. For Germany, any major reshaping of the CAP and Community must be part of an understanding with France. There is a reciprocal French need as well. France fears German neutralism. To play a lone hand on agriculture could weaken one of the few reins France perceives she holds on German policy: the European commitment.

Two presumptions emerge from this discussion. The first is that the world market, which now provides the main prospects for expanded farm sales, does not offer a free run. It differs basically in this from the preferential markets opened up by the CAP in Europe twenty years ago. The European producer now has far less control over prices and markets, especially when the Community dominates international trade. It ceases to be possible to treat output almost as a byproduct of farm income policies. In most years and for most commodities, the Europeans will have to gear the growth of their output to the vagaries of effective demand. The costs of failing to do so are likely to be political and cumulative as well as economic.

The second presumption is that the costs of unilateral expansion are likely to be such, even for an importing state such as Britain, that the option offers little room or time for expansion before the problems facing the CAP have to be confronted again nationally. A unilateral shift of member states to re-nationalization offers too many risks as against small returns. The main Community exporters might feel under greater pressure to take these risks. But they also happen to have invested most in building up outlets inside the Community and can least afford to jeopardize them. A member state alone would be far more vulnerable in international negotiations than is the Community as a whole.

Unilateral strategies of expansion might be more attractive if the CAP were the only constraint upon them. In fact, it is not. The CAP was itself set up in the 1960s to provide an escape route from constraints on national policies. For twenty years it has been very successful in providing just that. But now the road has led back, though at a higher level, to something very like the starting point. The constraints of external markets—world markets now, not as in the 1950s mainly European markets—are inexorably beginning to reappear. The limits are set by them, not by the Community, and will not be shed by dropping the Community. In these conditions, unilateral expansion may be a short-term temptation; it may be foisted on defensive governments by domestic uproar, which cannot be ignored in the equation; but it is not easy to see how it can be embraced as a settled strategy based on the cold calculation of national advantage.

Limits: Strategies

Once uncontrolled expansion is blocked, attention necessarily shifts to strategies of limitation. One might imagine that a wide range of them exists. In practical terms, they turn out to be surprisingly few: a mere three that matter.

The first, and nearest to the traditional CAP, is to maintain high price guarantees as in the past but, in contrast to the past, set limits to the amounts that qualify for support. Beyond the limits, various disincentives on production can be introduced. The limits are usually called "quotas" or, in the Commission's preferred term, "guarantee thresholds."

The second approach is to reduce guaranteed prices somewhat. In this case there are no quantitative limits. The reductions in guaranteed prices apply to all output of the item in question.

The third and most radical approach is to eliminate all guarantees and leave price levels to the operation of the open market.

All three strategies can be varied in different ways. The first and second can be mixed. Guaranteed prices for basic quantities can be lowered and "thresholds" applied in addition, beyond which further disincentives to production (price cuts) are introduced.

For present purposes, it is useful to discuss the strategies in inverse order, that is, from the polar opposite of the CAP—a free market policy—to the quantitative systems that most resemble it. The reason is that "free trade" provides some of the basic points of comparison by which the other two—politically more practical—contending strategies can be gauged.

OPEN MARKET POLICIES

An open market policy is so foreign to the ethos of the CAP and of nearly everything which has led up to it, in some countries for the better part of a century, that it could only emerge at the end of a long-drawn-out process with a host of changes not just in agriculture but in the rest of the economic and political context. Such a radical revision could hardly take place in the remaining decade and a half of the century. Yet this is no justification for passing on without comment. One reason is that the hypothesis of free, or at least freer, trade, casts a light on both the CAP and world markets and sets margins within which room for change can be assessed. A second reason is that in any case free trade in food cannot be understood in the same terms as for manufactures. It would imply a range of complementary actions, such as buffer stocks and guarantees against catastrophic short-term falls in prices, which are implicit in any reform of agriculture. A fortiori, they must be built in to other solutions. Third, however remote open market policies may be from the intent of any Community member state, the respective costs and gains they would entail for one nation would probably differ substantially from those for another; and these changed balances in Europe bring out some of the structural interests which exist.

There is nothing harder than to measure the economic effects of moving from one system to its polar opposite. The hypotheses on which any inquiry rests are bound to involve assumptions about elasticities of demand and supply with little basis in present evidence. Nevertheless, a number of econometric studies have been carried out since the late 1970s of the impact of free trade on Community agriculture. Two Australians in particular, Kym Anderson and Rodney Tyers, investigating grains and meat in 1983, have been more than usually comprehensive (Anderson and Tyers, 1983, pp. 11–13). Their conclusions (see Table 5.4), based on data for 1980, and assuming instant free trade that year, provide orders of magnitude both for the EC and for international trade. In effect, this research is an attempt to gauge the extent of protection under the CAP and the effects of its sudden withdrawal. The results would be quite different if the protection were to be phased out over a period. In that case, it would be necessary to take account of changes in productivity and costs during that period not only in the Community but in competing countries as well. Unfortunately, the research has excluded milk,

Table 5.4   Effects of Full EC Trade Liberalization for Grains and Meats, Hypothetical for 1980

Situation on Morrow of Full EC Trade Liberalization	Wheat	Coarse Grains	Beef/Veal and Mutton	Pork and Poultry
Weight of item in EC GAP 1980 (percent)	11.3	16.4	21.2	16.1
EC prices (percent)	−41	−39	−39	−25
EC net imports (million tons)	+14	+28	+3.3	
Percent EC Output item 1980[a]	26	40	44	
EC net exports (million tons)				+3.8
Percent EC Output item 1980[a]				29
World prices (percent)	+16	+16	+18	−3
World prices (percent)[b]	+23	+15	+25	−3
US exports (million tons)	+2.3	+22.5	+1.8	−2.8
Oceania-Canada exports (million tons)	+3.9	+1.0	+0.6	−0.4

[a] Derived from net imports.
[b] If all OECD liberalized.

Source: K. Anderson and R. Tyers, *European Community Grain and Meat Policies and US Retaliation: Effects on International Prices, Trade and Welfare.* Centre for Economic Policy, Australian National University (ANU). Discussion Paper 83 (revised) October 1983. Canberra.

which is related to the grain-meat complex and constitutes the biggest single problem in the CAP.

The results suggest that free trade would cut the returns of European grain and beef producers as much as 60 percent by reducing both prices and quantities produced. This alone explains why it is not likely to happen. On the other hand, while pork and poultry producers would not increase their gross returns, they would nevertheless raise both their output and exports very substantially. Moreover, though the research is not explicit on this point, their costs of production would be much reduced by lower grain prices, so that their net incomes would rise. The tendency for pork and poultry to gain at the cost of beef, already marked in the past decade, would be further accentuated.

As regards the relationships with the world market, the liberalization of EC grain and meat policies would mean that international prices would rise substantially but that EC prices and output would have to fall about twice as much to establish a market balance between the two. If North America and the rest of OECD (Oceania, the rest of Western Europe, and Japan) were also to liberalize, world market prices would rise further for wheat and beef, but with nothing like the same effect as an opening up of the EC. Similarly, the instability of world market prices from year to year would be reduced by about half for wheat and a third for coarse grains and beef, with wider OECD liberalization making little further difference. The conclusion follows that EC protection was in 1980 far and away the largest influence in depressing and destabilising world prices and markets for grains and meat.

Of course, the chief beneficiaries of liberalized EC grain and meat policies would be the traditional exporters, but the United States would gain much more than all the others put together. The (mainly Southeast Asian) exporters of cereal substitutes, whose sales of manioc have thrived on the Community's high-price cereals regime, would actually lose. So, on the whole, would importers, who are mostly the wealthier developing countries, though they would gain on pork and poultry; as matters are they gain from lower import prices. This takes no account of long-term export opportunities provided by more open European markets (for example, for sugar and beef); nor of the possible role depressed world prices may play in encouraging Third World governments to underpay their farmers. The fact remains that in immediate terms the Community's protectionism damages the other Western developed farm exporters rather than the rest of the world—sugar being the main exception.

The income losses in European agriculture from a general movement towards free trade in any relevant period—say of seven to ten years—would be so enormous and would be so far from everything European policies have striven for since the war, that the scenario is at first sight of purely academic and polemical interest. Yet it shows that some producers would gain on even the most extreme hypothesis: the pork and poultry farmers prominent especially in Benelux, Denmark, and Germany. This illustrates the wider principle, already put to forceful commercial use in the last century by Denmark and the Netherlands, that low prices of agricultural inputs—in this case grains—reduce costs for livestock producers; and lower livestock prices in turn encourage the development of competitive food industries. Much more value added is earned in the richer Community countries in livestock production than in crops; and more per worker is earned in the food industry than in agriculture (*ASC 1980*, p. 38; *ASC 1981*, p. 282).[11] Free trade, or some movement towards it, would be part of a strategy of increasing value added in food exports along the lines that have become intellectually fashionable in European industrial policies. The high price CAP is an obstacle to such strategies.

A similar policy, however, can be pursued more modestly by free trade not for agriculture in general but in grains as the basis of the livestock industry. This would amount to the adoption by the Community as a whole of the strategy successfully pioneered by the Danes and the Dutch a century ago. This might obtain many of the advantages of an open market policy without dealing such heavy blows to sectors with enormous social significance, such as milk. Home-grown grains fed to animals represent between a fifth and a quarter of the total value of output of dairy products, eggs, and meat in the Community.[12] This is a very high average proportion of the costs and all the higher for milk, pork, poultry, and eggs in that the impact on beef is much lower. Cuts in cereal prices by a third (to meet the world price levels implicit in a general OECD liberalization of trade) would cut the average costs of livestock production in the Community by 7 to 8 percent; and if beef is excluded, it would cut the costs of the rest of livestock production by 10 to 11 percent.

The President of the European Community's Court of Auditors, Pierre Lelong, writing in his private capacity, made an interesting suggestion along these lines in 1983. He proposed a cut of 40 percent in Community grain prices—that is, more or less to American levels. In French conditions, this would entail a fall of 20 percent in the production costs of pork and poultry and make it possible to cut CAP support prices for milk by 12 to 15 percent. (Beef prices would fall only 2 to 3 percent.) In all these cases, net returns to livestock would remain the same as before. Only grain incomes would fall. Because of lost import levies on maize, the main budget savings would take place not on grains themselves but on milk, where 1.2 billion ECUs of 1980 could be saved (or a quarter of spending on milk that year). The main beneficiaries on trade inside the Community would be the major importers of milk or meat—especially Italy but also Britain and Germany. The marginal grain producers most likely to be adversely affected would probably be in Germany. France herself would make the largest concessions in money terms both on the budget and on trade as the main producer and exporter of grains, but, proportionately, the only country that would lose substantial foreign exchange would be Ireland, to the tune of 1.7 percent of GDP. Because the absolute amounts in her case would not be very large, she could be compensated through greater development aid. For the rest, the problems of the CAP in the livestock sector would be substantially eased and so would the renegotiation of the Community budget. A basis would also be laid for a gentleman's agreement with the United States on the future conduct of world food trade in cereals (Lelong, 1983, pp. 552–58).

This suggestion raises all kinds of questions, apart from the details of the author's own figures or the evident opposition to be expected from the cereal growers. One problem, for instance, is that it is not possible to divorce cereal prices from those of livestock products, because there would be a trend for producers of crops to shift to milk and beef (already in surplus) if their profits from grains fell, as they clearly would. The repercussions would be complex. Nevertheless, the approach is much the most promising of all those made toward the reform of the CAP. It offers the basis for a long-term trade policy which links agriculture more effectively with industry. It makes substantial changes across the board in farming without upsetting all the sectors and regions. It affects a product where there are more substantial and economically robust producers than in others, and where prices could stimulate demand. It is generally agreed that cereal growers have made larger profits than other farmers. It would make trade diplomacy with other exporters, most of whom are close allies of the Community's member states, a great deal easier. All these factors help to explain why the Commission itself, in the most interesting and original of its proposals, has opted for a reduction, though certainly not of 40 percent, in the price of cereals. It is the main hint of a positive long-term strategy that has emerged from the confused and defensive debates on the future of the CAP.

LOWER PRICE SUPPORTS

The Commission has not put forward any precise figure for cuts in cereal prices. It has only referred to "narrowing the gap" between Community prices and "those applied by its main competitors in the world market," adding that in 1980 this gap was about 20 percent (Com-EC, 1981a, pp. 27–28, para. 59; 1983b, p. 14, para. 51). This is, in fact, an example of a milder form of the open market strategy, which would be to lower support prices without at least initially even contemplating free trade. Indeed, the aims would be quite different. They would be to hold the further growth of supplies to "self-sufficiency plus"—that is, plus an amount for the "normal" world market share of Community exports. The yardsticks of success would be the highly practical ones of keeping Community budgets within limits which the fragile consensus of the member states can bear; and perhaps of minimizing the wear and tear of "agro-diplomacy," above all with the United States. In effect, the criteria of performance would remain largely financial as in the past but, in contrast with that past, it would be recognized that budgetary problems are inseparable from prices and production. That involves a view of how fast demand grows, but perhaps the most difficult element is uncertainty about the effects of price changes on supply.

Farm prices can be as low as 10 to 30 percent of the price the shopper pays for food in the supermarket. Surprising as it may seem, the price of milk, for instance, seems to represent only 10 percent of the sales price of yogurt (at least in France) (Klatzmann, 1978, p. 85). Consumer responses to changes in food prices, across the range, tend to be sluggish. This would suggest that the effect of farm prices on domestic demand in the Community would be rather modest. On the other hand, this need not be the case for grains, which could regain some of their lost market for animal feed. And there are important foods—fresh fruit, vegetables, and meat—where farm prices represent a higher proportion of the sales price. This offers a little more scope for lower prices to influence demand.

The effects on supply of lower price supports are harder to gauge because of the uncertainty whether—and how much and for how long—they stimulate the more efficient farmers to launch into more output to make up for lower returns per unit produced. So long as the average return is higher than the farmer's average costs of production, lost earnings from lower prices can be recouped by producing more. Moreover, as general productivity on the farms rises over time, so average costs per unit of output tend to fall. Naturally, these vary from farm to farm and time to time. Across the board, supply will be held to the desired amount only when prices have been reduced to whatever level is appropriate for that purpose at the time.

Understandably, no one really knows what the appropriate price levels might be. Anderson and Tyers found, apparently to their own surprise, that a steady Community policy of cutting real prices 2 percent a year throughout the 1980s (by keeping annual price increases 2 percent below the rate of inflation) would make a significant cumulative impact (see Table 5.5). The main point of the Anderson-Tyers findings is that both output and consumption rise (except wheat consumption) whether real prices are stable or fall 2 percent a year; but that when they fall, consumption grows a little more and production a little less than when prices stay the same. These are not sensational results (though they are more marked for feedgrains and beef than for wheat and pork/poultry), but they are sufficient to be significant, in particular as regards trade (which is what Australia cares about). The Community remains an importer of feedgrains and beef and becomes a marginal one for white meat; while the tendency of wheat exports to grow is slowed down.

The moderation of the results is also politically important. If correct, the falling-price scenario argues that farmers might not lose as badly on incomes as they may fear. If one assumes that the rate of withdrawal of labor from the land will be about 2.5 percent per year, as in the recession years from 1975 to 1980 (*ASC 1982*, p. 285) and that costs of production of livestock, and especially of pork and poultry, will be reduced, losses should be small on average and white-meat farms should actually raise their net incomes. Even this leaves out the scope for farmers to use less expensive methods of

Table 5.5   EC Production, Consumption, and Trade Projections for Grains and Meats from 1978–80 to 1988–90, in Volume (assuming that Real Prices (i) do not change or (ii) fall annually 2 percent)

(in millions of tons)	Wheat	Coarse Grains	Beef and Mutton	Pork and Poultry
1978–80 (actual)				
Production	48.7	67.9	7.3	13.0
Consumption	44.5	74.7	7.4	12.8
Net exports (+)	+4.2			+0.2
Net imports (−)		−6.8	−0.1	
1988–90 (0 percent price change)				
Production	56.9	78.1	8.4	14.4
Consumption	44.6	80.9	8.0	14.5
Net exports (+)	+12.3		+0.4	
Net imports (−)		−2.8		−0.1
1988–90 (−2 percent price per annum)				
Production	53.9	72.3	8.2	14.9
Consumption	44.6	84.5	8.5	15.5
Net exports (+)	+9.3			
Net imports (−)		−12.2	−0.3	−0.6

Source: K. Anderson and R. Tyers, 1983, Table 5.

Table 5.6   **Cumulative Effects of an Annual Fall of 2 Percent in Real Prices of Grains and Meats on Prices, Output, and Gross Returns to EC Producers between 1978-80 and 1988-90**

	Prices	Output	Gross Returns
	(percentage 1978-80 to 1988-90)		
Wheat	−22	+11	−9
Coarse grains	−22	+6	−13
Beef and mutton	−22	+12	−8
Pork and poultry	−22	+15	−6

Source: Derived from Anderson and Tyers, 1983.

production. On balance, average incomes should not fall much, if at all, though there is little room for them to rise (except in pork and poultry) unless farmers are very successful in cutting costs. In short, this is, on the whole, a relatively reassuring scenario. It suggests that adjustment can be accomplished without too much upheaval. It does not, however, cover the crucial case of milk, where the Community's surpluses are higher than in grains and meat and the social pressures are much greater.

Perhaps the scenario is too reassuring. Comparisons between the Anderson-Tyers projections and the record from 1963–79 suggest it may be. Parallels can be drawn with two products, wheat (Table 1.5) and beef (Table 1.8). The resulting comparisons are shown in Table 5.7. Though for beef, Anderson and Tyers do indeed suggest an increased response of output to prices compared with the record, for wheat, where the average price reductions for the Nine are very similar, the 1980s projections assume a response which is only a third of the past.

It is very difficult, for lack of further information, to pronounce on this

Table 5.7   **Comparisons for Wheat and Beef of Anderson-Tyers Projections for EC for Ten Years from 1978-80 and Past EC Experience for Equivalent Periods (percentage changes)**

	Weighted Average for EC-Nine for 10 Years at 1963-79 Rates of Growth [a]		Anderson & Tyers Projections for 1978-80 to 1988-90	
	Prices	Output	Prices	Output
Wheat	−19	33	−22	11
Beef	+3	19	−22	12

[a]Weighted by proportion of EC-9 output in 1978-80.

striking difference. The major difficulty is that the effects in the past of national credits for farm investment and inputs are virtually unknown. In these circumstances, the contrast may well indicate the importance of national policies. Another imponderable is that perverse responses to price cuts in the past may well have been not economic at all but psychological—the well-founded belief that a sufficient pressure on policy-makers would sooner or later restore incomes. If a multiannual program could be established pointing to predictably lower real prices in ten years, this outlook might be modified. Much would depend on the political and technical credibility of the targets. This brings one back to assessments of the balance of power, and therefore of political will, in the member states and Community. When the margins between one outcome and another are fairly marginal, as compared to the total context, policy choices can be decisive. So is the determination with which they are pursued. A strategy with long-term targets is what Mansholt sought in the early days of the CAP. It is in fact the only way solid results can be achieved. But there was no support for it then among the member states, and he failed. The question now is not whether the Mansholt strategy is appropriate or not, but whether new circumstances have mobilized the political support in the national capitals to follow it.

As for trade, the implication of price cuts whose purpose is "self-sufficiency plus" is necessarily that conditions inside Community markets would not be much changed. The aim would be to slow down the rate of growth of national self-sufficiency and help preserve existing trade between member states. At the same time, Community exports should become more price competitive on international markets.

> If Community agriculture is to succeed—as it should—in expanding its exports and maintaining its share of world markets, it must increasingly accept the market disciplines to which other sectors of the Community's economy are subject. In this dynamic approach, which rejects any Malthusian limitation of agriculture's potential, the accent must be on production at a competitive price [Com-EC, 1983a, p. 7, para 18].

This no doubt enunciates an important principle: that competitive prices and expanding exports are bound up together. But what is a "competitive" price if it does not mean a world market price? And if prices have to fall to be competitive, how is that compatible with expanding exports?

In practice, in a "self-sufficiency plus" strategy, a "competitive" price is a diplomatic rather than a commercial concept. It means, presumably, one which the Community can defend in GATT when it is seeking to expand not only the amount of its exports but also its world market shares. It would be highly convenient to claim that European and American grain prices were not too far apart. The difficulties, however, are considerable. One is the combined effect of world market prices on American producer prices and of the dollar-European exchange rate. In practice, American support prices—the so-called "target prices"—are fairly close to world prices. World wheat prices, in current dollars, varied on average by 24 percent a year, up or down, between

1970 and 1981; and though the variation in ECUs was much the same, the swings from year to year were not the same. In these circumstances, it is not possible to aim at stable Community prices, say 20 percent below present ones for wheat, and assume an equally stable relationship with either American or world prices. This is not to say that reductions in price supports are useless. The mere fact of cuts would constitute a political argument. It could lay the basis for long-term understandings with the United States on grains and, because of the similarity of dairy prices, on other major sectors as well. But there could be no tidy view of just how effective, diplomatically, a cut in support prices that fell short of following world markets would prove to be at any given time. Markets and market-shares would probably count more than debating points about levels of prices.

There is an appearance of paradox in a price policy for exports whose main effects, if the econometricians are to be trusted, will be an increase in imports in key commodities. But this is only a short-term contradiction. It is clear that moderate price-cutting will not eliminate the growth of European output and that even if it raises demand, this will remain modest in the region. In the long term, this must mean that the expansion of Community exports will be resumed. The difference will be that while export subsidies are currently expensive and provocative, an export trade at lower prices will be more solidly based and sustainable.

Lower prices for northern products would also help to reduce the political pressures for higher prices for Mediterranean products in case of the enlargement of the Community to Portugal and Spain. This would discourage the emergence of new and unmanageable surpluses in the southern products where they threaten to pose new and potentially serious problems. It would in particular help in dealing with the difficulties Mediterranean exporters of fruit, vegetables, and olive oil who do not propose to join the Community, must face from the competition of Spain when she does join it. On the other hand, this is not really likely to ease the financial problems the Mediterranean poses for the Community. First, the Italian and French Mediterranean producers will feel the effects of Spanish competition anyway and will call for compensation. Second, since the ostensibly "northern" products are in fact important to all the actual and prospective Mediterranean members of the Community, lower prices for them would raise considerable problems for southern producers, and for smallholders and certain regions in trouble. One of the political questions involved in any steps to save money on Community budgets is whether the present flow of funds and patronage can be fed as fully through another system which is not only less automatic but also less responsive because of governments' general desire for retrenchment.

One important aspect of lower producer prices which is not immediately apparent is the potential scope they give for further policy changes. An instance is deficiency payments. In 1972, the United States, which previously ran a system of price supports for grains very similar to the CAP today and suffered from many of the same problems, switched to deficiency payments for producers. These had a number of advantages in the American setting.

They made it possible to keep export prices low without openly subsidizing them and also kept grain prices low for the livestock industries. Because they were associated with a whole pharmocopeia of further measures, they also saved money for the budget.

Potentially, deficiency payments might be attractive to the Community as a way of obtaining the advantages of really low cereal prices without incurring the insuperable opposition of the producers. This is impossible with prices as they are now. In 1981, EC sales subsidies for cereals came to about 60 ECUs a ton for about 20 million tons of exports: a cost of 1.2 billion ECUs in all. Given a total output of 120 million tons of grain, this is equivalent to a subsidy of only 10 ECUs per ton if spread across all grain production, as it would have to be with deficiency payments. To have paid out 60 ECUs per ton across the board in producer subsidies would have cost over 7 billion ECUs for cereals in a year when the total EC budget for price supports came to 11 billion ECUs, and would have been quite impossible. But if Community support prices for grains were cut by 25 percent, the cost of deficiency payments to all grain producers would fall to between 15 to 20 ECUs per ton across the board; and costs of storage would also be reduced because of increased demand. True, revenues would also fall, because levies on imported maize would be lower; but these losses could be more than recouped by the related savings in the dairy sector. It is still unlikely that the Community would move down this road, because 1981 assumed a strong market and strong dollar. A weak dollar in weak markets would change the whole basis of calculation. Since the Community puts a high premium on stable costs and prices, it would be unlikely to risk navigating on such an open sea. The fact remains that, with lower prices, options heave in sight that are unthinkable when prices are high.

There is no policy without costs, and those that lower prices involve make it no accident that there has been such marked reluctance to follow that particular route. The basic fact about price cuts is that all farmers would have to accept, at least initially, lower returns, and only the most efficient could hope to regain the lost ground. Substantial price reductions might be easier to contemplate if they could be confined to a few products, and farmers could be steered into new lines as they scale down or abandon old ones. But demand in the Community has been increasing markedly only for a few major products, such as cheese, pork, poultry, and quality wines, and production has more than kept up with these. Attempts to increase self-sufficiency through providing more protein-feed for animals, such as colza, peas, field-beans, and similar crops, offer some scope—at high cost—but not too much. The Dutch and Belgians, leading everyone else, stress higher value exports. There is certainly some leeway for luxury products. But the outlets are mainly luxury countries—a minority who tend to be protectionist. In processed foods, prospects are probably better for multinational corporations producing in many countries than for trade from region to region. There is, in short, only modest room for compensating in one sector for belt-tightening in another. In these circumstances, price cuts in one commodity simply drive farmers for relief into neighboring sectors and increase the pressures there. The process of decompression implicit in lower returns would have to be general and without escape to be effective. This makes the outlook socially more painful and politically more difficult.

Thus, compensation to farmers and regions, as well as the form it takes, is the fundamental problem of any strategy of lowering prices. This could even apply to the larger and more productive farmers who might on general grounds be thought well placed to adapt. They have been the main beneficiaries of the CAP. It might seem just that they should have to pay most of the costs of imposing limits. But politically they are the core of the farm lobbies. And some of them at least may face considerable difficulties. They have, naturally, expanded their productive base on the assumption that the good times would continue. Their capital wealth has greatly increased, reflecting the years of high prices. Land prices, for instance, have grown faster than general prices (Delorme and André, 1983, p. 331). Reduced prices could involve them in large capital losses. Some of these might only be accounting losses. But farmers would be hurt if they had to sell on the falling market. As their capital wealth shrank, many might find that their banks would begin to reduce their overdrafts or call in loans. Young farmers or ones who had recently expanded at costs geared to inflated expectations would be specially vulnerable to a narrowing of their credit base and the subsequent problems in funding their debt. This is not to suggest that most larger farmers could not weather the turn for the worse if given time to adapt and offered selective forms of compensation to take care of the hardship cases. This is another argument for long-term price targets involving moderate but cumulative price cuts that constitute a credible goal to which producers can adapt over time.

But larger farmers, who produce most of the goods, are in a relatively small minority. Welfare considerations are, obviously, still more important for smallholders who constitute the majority. To some of them, lower prices could spell catastrophe. Given the distribution of smallholders in the Community, this would mean a major concentration of loss around the Mediterranean, in Ireland, and in southern and western France and Germany. With enlargement to Spain and Portugal, the bill could become larger still. Independent commentators have generally tended to plump for the small producer's receiving income aids of various kinds, the main advantage of which is that they are divorced from, and in so far as possible do not influence, output. Yet in practice all such suggestions have met a barrage of objections from practitioners, nearly all of them ostensibly technical, many of them in fact indissociable from politics.

Who should be paid is no small problem in itself. Though half the Community's part-time farmers have no income off the farm, part-time farming in most of the northern countries tends to be a prosperous profession. The diversity of conditions between smallholdings and particularly part-time holdings, from the poorest to the richest end of the spectrum, around towns and in semi-deserts, makes it difficult to devise any generally accepted definitions. To build the bases of a system may call for cultural as well as administrative innovation. Farmers outside Britain, Denmark, and the Netherlands are generally taxed on the basis of unverified income reports and only a third of Community farmers keep accounts.[13] This means that the administrative base for income payments is largely lacking. It also opens a rich field for national prejudices to flower. Northerners are all too prone to assume that Latins cheat. The olive oil regime in Italy hardly discourages the stereotyped picture. If poor farmers benefited from the frauds, there might still be a case to press, but when traders or the Mafia do, persuasion fails. In any case, the administrative pitfalls would be severe:

> All the programmes have in common the fact that a register of interests would have to be established on day one of the scheme (a formidable administrative task) and all would suffer from the fact that a great deal of advance warning (in the form of lengthy Ministerial meetings) might encourage individuals to enter farming specifically to take advantage of the income supplements [Harris et al, 1983, pp. 337–38] .

If these administrative difficulties could be overcome, the problems of choice between categories would remain:

> how are the payments to be adjusted for inflation and is there to be a maximum annual payment per person (or family)? . . . Farm workers, landowners and farm machinery suppliers are likely to suffer some losses of income for instance; but it is unlikely that those groups will receive assistance. Some farmers will have been in business thirty years and will have no overdraft or mortgage payments outstanding. Others will have been in business for three months and will be heavily indebted [Harris et al., pp. 337–38].

Clearly, such problems are not merely administrative.

In fact, they do not seem to be insurmountable. In Germany, any farmer seeking credit has to provide detailed accounts. (CNASEA, p. 136). The Commission has found means to compensate a large number of small farmers in Italy and elsewhere because deliveries can be monitored through the dairies or sugarbeet factories. Production aids to hard wheat are based on acreage. Even olive trees have been registered by aerial photography! As long ago as 1970 a group of economists brought together by the Atlantic Institute produced proposals which could circumvent many of the problems:

> In essence, this would have made payments to farmers related to four elements: the average yield of the product in the Community, the amount each farm produced in the years preceding the decision to reduce prices, lifetime of the operator and the size of farms. Compensation paid in this way would create no incentive to increase output. Each farmer would have to make that decision in the light of expected costs and prices which would be lower than in the past. By giving compensation on the basis of average yields and making the proportion of production eligible for compensation less for large than small farms, the proposed scheme would tend to raise the incomes of some of the poorer of the Community's farmers. By continuing to pay compensation for price reductions, even if the farmer decided to produce some other commodity, the system ensured that production would be induced to respond to the new pattern of prices.[14]

While these problems are difficult, they are not insuperable.

They can also, of course, be costly. The second order of objection to income supports for smallholders in compensation for lower prices has concerned costs for the Community budget. However, the uncertainties about who would qualify for compensation govern to a great extent one's estimate of what the budgetary burden might be. If all price reductions were to be compensated and farmers paid for losses—in land values, for example—the costs would be impossibly high. On the other hand, if the smallest holders alone were to be compensated, the difference to the budget could be small. For instance, 52 percent of Community farmers occupy only 8 percent of the land sowed to cereals (Table 1.15). A rough calculation based on published figures suggests that in 1980–81 total Community spending on cereals and milk, with grain prices 25 percent lower and smallholders fully compensated for all losses on sales, might have balanced, even on conservative assumptions which make no allowance for lower costs of buying in surpluses.[15] More probable would be a graded system by which compensation would be geared in inverse proportion to the size of cereal harvest on each farm. The cost of income aids, unlike price supports, would fall over the years. This would require a register of the farms producing cereals in the base years. (Base years themselves are never neutral as between different claimants.) For milk and sugar, where the processing plants are reasonably few, this should not pose excessive difficulties. An embryonic system of income supports to smallholders producing milk has already been instituted. It is much harder for other products with less centralized sales patterns.

Administrative arguments, however, are often camouflage for political opposition. Income aids to small producers expose large ones to price cuts. Larger farmers have usually managed to associate the smallholders with themselves in a solid front against an alien urban world, so that whatever fissures there were between them did not come out in the open. This has changed since the French Socialists, once in power and with their clientele of smallholders began in 1981 to push for a difference of treatment in reform plans between large and small farmers. The British, Danes, and Dutch have adamantly opposed such schemes. Whatever the form discrimination between rich and poor farmers might take, they would have to pay for the Mediterranean and Ireland, and even for France and Germany, while getting little or nothing in return.

In any case, poor relief is not an adequate approach to the social problems of agriculture. The largest concentrations of smallholders tend to be in areas where other economic activities are also lacking or in trouble. As a result, the Commission has moved more and more towards "integrated development programs," involving policies for industry and services as well as farming. The first tentative batch was instituted in a small clutch of regions, north and south, in 1980. It was extended in the proposals of August 1983 for "integrated Mediterranean programs" amounting to some 7.5 billion ECUs in five years (Com-EC, 1983d and 1983e).

Here again, the problem is that however admirable the concentration of resources on the poorer regions may be, it has little appeal to those who pay. This is especially the case with Britain, which is too rich in agriculture to qualify for aid to smallholders but one of the poorer Community states. There has been a long tradition of seeking to meet this problem by extending the range of Community spending. The establishment of the Regional Fund was prominent in the negotiations for British entry into the Community before 1973. Edgard Pisani, one of the European Commissioners in 1983 and a former French minister of agriculture, adopted the same approach in a paper arguing for a systematic Community "integrated development policy" applying to all regions, those suffering from industrial senility at least as much as those lagging in rural backwardness and poverty. But this too encounters major obstacles. One is that Pisani favors an expansive route out of the Community's problems of financial balance at a time when governments are thinking in terms of cutting back the rate of growth of Community spending. Pisani meets this by arguing that the mass of general development spending in which the Community is already directly or indirectly involved is considerable, if one includes the operations of the European Investment Bank and other para-Community sources. The need is less for more money than to provide an overriding strategy for the commitments of the Community (Pisani, 1983 pp. 49–50). This raises a second major obstacle. It implies an extension of coordinated collective activity, and therefore of the role of the Community and Commission in particular. The nationalism so prevalent in the member states suggests that such an ambitious view of the problems is bound to encounter heavy opposition.

The long and short of the matter is that any attempt to lower the prices at which the Community provides support brings one up sharp against the social problems of the countryside and the division of interest between farmers and the rest of society, and between relatively prosperous rural regions and those that clearly pose a welfare problem. Moreover, the shift from price supports ultimately paid for the most part by consumers to development policies that appear more clearly in budgets, politicises finance even more than it is already. The countries where prosperous farming is preponderant, or where the problems do not arise in farming, are reluctant to foot the bill for the poorer farmers, areas, and countries. Moreover, serious approaches to regional problems demand a deeper level of coordination between national and Community development strategies (as well as between different directorates-general in the European Commission itself) than has existed hitherto. Precisely because lower prices pose the basic problems, they also confront basic difficulties.

QUOTA SYSTEMS

Given the resistance when price reductions are proposed, it is not surprising that policy discussion in the Community has veered toward quota systems that are, at least at first sight, less committing.

Systems which work by limiting price guarantees to specified quantities of output have a number of attractions. First, these are financial. Savings can be made. Budgets can at last be relieved of the automatic commitment to buy up whatever farmers find it expedient to produce at the public intervention price. At the theoretical extreme, payments beyond the historic guarantees could simply cease. Second, once automatic supports are withdrawn, possibilities open up of controlling output by varying the incentives both within the protected quota and the less protected sector outside it. It becomes possible to discriminate between different categories of output. Third, since historic guarantees are in practice maintained—that is the purpose of the device—the whole vexed question of compensation to farmers, which arises when prices are directly lowered, is finessed. Both in what they change and what they do not change, quotas have enormous practical advantages for hard-pressed policy-makers. Above all, such a reform is conservative. It minimizes the extent to which existing arrangements are upset. At the same time, it does introduce change at one vital point, by ending the automatic guarantees which turn farmers into pensioners who in effect fix the level of their own pensions simply by raising output. Risk at last enters the equation. This is a psychological factor which goes far beyond the mechanical calculation of costs. It makes it possible to envisage controls that were beyond the system before.

In practice, there are three techniques of handling such controls in connection with quantitative limits, or "thresholds."

The first is to reduce the support afforded to production beyond the threshold (that is, over the quota), or even withdraw it altogether. This can be done by offering different levels of price support for different quantities of deliveries, going from the basic price guarantee down to zero, as for sugar, where "producers pay the costs of disposal."

The second technique is to reduce prices across the board for all producers by a given percentage when output exceeds the threshold. Any percentage can, of course, be applied so that there need not be a one-to-one relation between excess output and cuts in price supports. This technique is like straight price cuts in that it has repercussions on the basic quota as well as on output beyond it. On the other hand, unlike price cuts, the reductions do not point to some predetermined level. Rather, they set out, step by step, from the status quo to apply a progressive price squeeze on output if it fails to stay within certain bounds. Indeed, this assumes that output will not stay within bounds; or, at least, it is designed to act as a deterrent against its doing so. It amounts to cautious price cutting. The only clear thing about it is that it is more closely related to controlling expenditure than production. It resembles the system of "standard quantities" in force in Britain for producer subsidies for grains and milk before that country entered the Community. The principle was to pledge a given total of money irrespective of the amount farmers produced. The subsidy per ton to each farmer therefore fell in exact proportion to the excess of total output from all farms above the target: the larger the total output from farms as a whole, the less the return per ton to each individual farmer. The difference between the British and Community proposed systems is that the British one applied to straight subsidies to farmers, while the Community point of reference is prices for given amounts of produce bought in by the intervention agencies. With that difference, the techniques are in close parallel. One may therefore speak, though with some impropriety, of "standard quantities."

The third technique, and a much more stringent one, is to impose penal taxes on producers for any output beyond the quota. If this were so high that it reduced farmers' returns below their profits on excess (marginal) output, it would amount to a veto on any production beyond the desired quantity. The "supplementary levy" imposed by the Community in 1984 on milk and the special levy on "factory" farms producing milk are examples of this approach (Com-EC, 1983b, p. 12, paras. 43–44; Council of the European Communities, 1984).

The choice of one or other of these approaches depends not only on the objective set but also on what might be called the technical and political authority of government as regards means. Technical authority corresponds to the ability to exercise effective control over the producers, wholesalers, and processors to see that the rules are observed. The Commission considers this possible for sugar, where quotas operate already, and for milk, because there are about 130 sugar factories in the Community and some 1,500 dairies, which is still reckoned to be manageable (Appendix Table 19). In other commodities, like cereals, the points of sale are deemed too numerous for effective supervision in current conditions.

Behind these administrative problems, and more important still, lie those of political authority. The Commission has a small corps of ten inspectors who do, with forewarning, visit the sugar factories. But where Community regulations do not specifically say so and supervision is delegated to the member states—which is the normal arrangement—the Commission has in effect no powers to check that what the governments say they are doing is in fact so. There have been occasions when nations administered Community regulations in ways suspected of contravening the rules and the Commission was refused all access to the wholesalers or agencies where the action was taking place. In the same way, the main obstacle to quotas applying directly at the farms, administratively monstrous as these might be, is the opposition of the national authorities, some of which themselves have this kind of access. From the national point of view, the risk is probably that such a register would allow the Commission to discriminate directly between different categories of farmers across the whole Community in ways the members states consider to be against their interests or in violation of their sovereignty. This would apply clearly to distinctions between small and large farms.

These obstacles determine the kinds of measures that can be proposed to deal with the surpluses. For instance, penal levies on overproduction imply either great power vested in the Community institutions, which is not the case, or a consensus of the member states on the need and measures to repress excessive output, which would probably be difficult to maintain indefinitely. The domestic protests within member states and differences of interest between them make it questionable whether such techniques can be applied over long periods. If so the Commission would have to fall back in many cases on the looser arrangements by which support beyond the "threshold" is reduced or withdrawn or, alternatively, the Community equivalent of "standard quantities" is applied.

In these conditions, it is highly relevant that the record of both the withdrawal of supports and of standard quantities in controlling output is very poor. As one witness before the House of Lords Select Committee on the European Communities put it: "all our experience of the standard quantity principle is that it is effective in cutting spending on farm support. But unless the cuts in producer prices are quite unacceptably severe, it is likely to have little effect on global output."[16] The key here is the refusal to countenance "severe" price cuts which might inhibit the more efficient farmers from recouping their losses per unit of output by higher production. The Commission's experience with milk in 1982 and 1983 was very similar. It operated the "threshold" system for milk and in 1982 reduced prices by 3 percent because the threshold was overshot by 3.5 percent. In 1983, output went up again by 3.5 percent so that "the threshold fixed for 1983 will be exceeded by at least 6 percent." But, like the House of Lords witness, the Commission was appalled at the formidable consequences of sufficient price cuts:

> The Commission estimates that, in order to offset fully the additional expenditure likely to arise from the guarantee threshold being exceeded in 1983, the milk price for 1984–85 would have to be abated by as much as 12%. A measure of this kind would evidently have grave and immediate effects on the revenues of producers, while there would be some delay before the full effect on production was achieved [Com-EC, 1983b, p. 12, paras. 43–44; see also Council of the European Communities, 1984].

In short, if standard quantities mean small price cuts to compensate for farmers overshooting the mark, they are likely to produce just the "perverse" producer reactions which aggravate the ill they purport to cure.

Similar difficulties arise from similar timidities when support is simply withdrawn for production beyond the basic high price "threshold." Graphic evidence of this comes from the Community's sugar regime, which is the only one that has for a long time relied on quotas. There is a basic A quota, corresponding to presumed domestic demand, support prices for which are high—consistently 10 to 20 percent higher than the *ceiling* set for world trade by the International Sugar Agreement. In fact, including the guarantees made to the sugar exporting islands of the Caribbean and the Indian and Pacific Oceans under the Lome Convention, output allowed under this quota exceeded a slowly declining Community demand in 1981–82 by 16 percent. There is a second, B quota, originally designed to cover exports, under which support prices may be, and have been, cut up to 39.5 percent. Output beyond these two quotas, sometimes called "C sugar," obtains no support at all: producers are left to earn what they can on the world market.

At first sight, this system might seem fairly liberal. In fact, developments in the late 1970s have shown just how profitable production in excess of the A quota is for a large part of the Community's sugar industry. Whereas between 1975–76 and 1981–82, the A quota increased moderately from 8.5 million tons to 9.1 million tons (though why, when demand was declining, is a fair question), output under the B and C sections in the same years nearly quintupled from 1.2 million tons to 5.6 million tons. By 1981–82, Community output, including the imports from the Lome partners who were treated, laudably enough, as Community producers, was 73 percent higher than domestic Community demand! Yet domestic Community prices were usually above two or even three times those on world markets. In 1982, 5.3 million tons of Community sugar were exported onto a world market experiencing (including that amount) an estimated 8 million ton surplus (Com-EC, 1982d, pp. 46–47). The Community was unquestionably a major cause of the difficulties of the established sugar exporters who, apart from Australia and South Africa, are all developing countries.[17] Their foreign exchange losses have been considerable (Curry, 1982, p. 32). Community sugar policy has been indefensible by any criteria of sensitive or even sensible dealings with the Third World.

The sugar regime does have built-in restraints. The main one is that exporters who find world prices too low to make it profitable to sell their C, or open market, sugar, can withhold it, but that if they do so for more than twelve months, it then counts against their allocation for A, that is, basic high-price sugar. This subtraction can go up to 20 percent of the A quota. In both 1980–81 and 1981–82, the producers held back about 1 million tons of sugar in this way in order not to sell at a loss. The result has been a 9.5 percent shrinkage in each of the following years in the area planted to sugarbeet, or 19 percent in all.[18] This is considerable. It is equivalent to a reduction in price supports and a sign that prices are beginning to be squeezed.

The trouble is that this happens only *in extremis*. The whole system operates on the basis of a large, secure home base no competitor can challenge and whose high prices fund producers' fixed costs so that it is easy for the more efficient ones to dump on foreign markets and still make a profit. This allows them to capture increasing market shares from rivals who may have lower basic costs but whose governments cannot afford to subsidize them to the same degree. The limits of this mechanism are only reached where a large market share has already been acquired and demand has fallen too low for dumping to provide a profit. In the Community's antitrust legislation, this would be arraigned as the abuse of monopoly power. In sugar, it is built in to the system. As a result, though, in constitutional terms, quotas may seem highly compatible with the international market-sharing agreements, their inner dynamics most certainly are not. Expansion stops only at the brick wall.

Moreover, when production is cut in a given factory and on the sugarbeet farms which supply it, this applies equally to all producers, irrespective of whether they were themselves responsible for extra output. As a result, smallholders who did not increase production, or increased it less than the average, are penalized proportionately as much as major growers who did. Their prices are in effect cut with the rest and they obtain no compensation. In this way, it is not only developing country exporters in the Third World but also smallholders in the Community who have to pay part of the bill for the expansion of the larger-scale European beet-growers. This is no basis on which to conduct social policies at home any more than foreign policies abroad.

Thus, while quota systems are useful in achieving financial targets and limiting costs fairly quickly, their long-term effects are much less satisfactory and uncertain. Quota systems which stop short of penal taxes are unlikely to restrain the more efficient producers from expanding their output. The constraints only appear either through trade conflicts or the failure of demand once the exporters are already overextended. At that late point producers will at long last be under overwhelming pressure from shrinking markets and falling prices to cut back output. But before that point is reached, other weaker exporters, most obviously but not only in the Third World, will have been ruthlessly pushed aside, which is not compatible with Community claims to worldwide views or sympathy with the poor; and after it is reached, smallholders in the Community are likely to have to foot part of the bill without any provisions for compensation. If, on the other hand, and as for milk in 1984, penal taxes are applied, they demand great political authority not only to introduce but even more to maintain. They do not reduce the political pressures for higher output as lower prices cumulatively would. They build them into the system by institutionalizing the status quo. The grievances farmers nurture against governments for reining them in are not moderated by an adjustment of the productive structure towards more competitive output. The dangers of an explosion against the system remain hardly diminished. In fact, they are potentially increased by the head of steam that builds up with time. Further, all quota systems, penal or permissive, encourage producers to find alternative outlets. One of the fears for milk quotas imposed in 1984, for instance, is that clandestine deliveries to consumers direct from the farms will increase at the cost of the deliveries to the dairies which are now under control.

For all these reasons, quotas are technically, socially, commercially, and politically inferior to progressive price reductions. They put a lid on the previous evolution, but they offer minimal incentives to the long-term adjustments which alone can resolve the underlying tensions. It should not be assumed, simply because penal taxes on output have been imposed in 1984, that it will be politically possible to maintain them indefinitely. Price reductions offer better prospects of long-term adjustment, and they seem also to have a wider potential range of application. If the arguments adduced against quotas where processing is too decentralized are to be taken seriously, it follows that quotas can apply only to a limited range of commodities, excluding some of the most important, such as cereals.

Having said that, some problems are likely to be common in one guise or other whether a price or quota approach is chosen. This is obvious in some of the political aspects of the change of direction, such as the fall in the growth of incomes. It also applies to the structural responses of the system to policy. For instance, inadequate price reductions, like insufficiently stringent quotas, will encourage lower-cost farmers to produce more than is required, in hopes of making up by higher volume for losses on each individual ton produced. Again, both quotas and prices, by reducing incentives to operate within the lines of farming subject to control, stimulate farmers to seek compensation in other lines. One of the drawbacks of the Community waking up so late to the need to restrain output in the CAP is that there are now very few lines (and virtually no major ones) in which farmers can expand without generating surpluses. Controls are likely, therefore, to spread from one line to other adjacent ones in a potentially endless chain.

Of course, it is also possible to combine different approaches so long as these have roughly equivalent effects—price strategies in one commodity with quota systems in another. The Community's decisions for the 1984–85 farming year implicitly do this by applying tight quotas on milk where the budget situation has become most desperate; and reducing real prices (by failing to compensate for inflation) for most of the other commodities, including cereals, olive oil, wine, and some fruit and vegetables (Council EC, 1984). In all these cases, the acid test will be the length of time for which the Community and the member states can mobilize the political determination to maintain the course which, in 1984–85, they have apparently chosen.

Limits: Political Themes

It is difficult to overstate the extent to which limits transform the environment for agriculture and the CAP.

For a generation, production was treated almost as a byproduct of income policies for farmers. Now the balance is reversed and farmers, many of whom are in effect small businessmen, are beginning to find they have to adjust to demand and markets like other entrepreneurs.

On top of this, limits on budgets have shifted the initiative in the Community from the food exporters to the main bankers, Britain and Germany. The expanding Community budget was anomalous in a context of national retrenchment. The politics of constraint are now beginning to affect it too, and the consequences could be far-reaching.

Together, limits on markets and budgets mean that the growth of the incomes of farmers, rural regions, and the poorer countries is put in doubt and so poses major problems for the balance of development within and between member states.

Finally, limits are likely to influence the division of powers between the member states and the institutions of the Community because they have now to face political and social problems expansion was designed to conceal.

Changes on this scale clearly open a new phase in the history both of European agriculture and of the CAP.

FINANCE

Budget limits reverse the old balance of power in the Community. When the CAP was established, France, at the head of the food exporting nations, was able to persuade Germany to act as virtual banker to the farm regime. Germany accepted this as the price of her industrial advantages in the common market and of a necessary politico-economic balance with France. This understanding was sealed by the Luxembourg agreement of 1970, which secured ample funds for the Community in anticipation of the entry of Britain, who was known to be no enthusiast for the CAP. But by the time these funds ran out in 1983, the situation had profoundly changed. Since the second energy crisis in particular, Germany had lost some of her old economic self-confidence and belief in capacity to pay. The other major net contributor, Britain, far from needing to pay a price for the industrial common market, registered that year her first deficit on trade in manufactures since the industrial revolution. Both countries, pursuing deflationary policies, were determined to limit public spending at home and in the Community, and most governments of the member states, including the French, were following suit.

If Germany and Britain, as the main net contributors, insist on applying narrow limits to future Community spending, the balance of bargaining power is bound to shift to them. It was evident from the negotiations in 1983 that they were not aiming at completely rigid ceilings on Community spending. There was talk of raising the ceiling of the tax base of the Community from 1 percent of VAT receipts to 1.4 percent. But this seemed designed to provide only a few years' grace, especially if one takes account of the enlargement of the Community to Portugal and Spain, before concessions would have to be paid for again. What it points to is a determination to make the bankers' will felt at frequent intervals, especially as the tax base could only be widened after parlimentary ratification. Financial power had taken a long time to surface in the Community, but by 1983–84 it seemed to have done so.

A great deal therefore depends on what Germany and Britain want. This is, of course, a matter of speculation. Nevertheless, in Britain's case it would not be surprising if it included a desire to limit commitments to welfare spending on foreign smallholders and more generally the southern states whose claims will rise with the entry of Portugal and Spain; and a lack of enthusiasm for subsidizing the world exports of France, the Netherlands, and Germany, who are the three main beneficiaries of Community export aids. There might even be a preference for "re-nationalizing" agriculture, but that would not be so necessary if the other aims were satisfied. It is not, however, at all sure that Germany is in a position to embrace these goals with the same wholehearted-ness. She has lately become a substantial exporter of most commodities. Though she is no doubt far from overjoyed to assume more financial commit-ments in the poorer countries, the Mediterranean has a far greater importance in her security policies than in those of Britain. It seems likely, therefore, that the British and German motives are what they seem to be, primarily financial, and do not conceal elaborate ulterior motives. That does not make them any less significant for the future of the Community.

The first issue that arises is the difference between restoring control over agriculture policies which are out of hand and budget restrictions for their own sake. There are advantages in moving to committing funds as the result of deliberate decisions on priorities and away from a mechanism in which spending grew almost despite budgetary considerations. A budget without a consensus behind it cannot remain politically legitimate for long. Reducing the automatic growth of one item—agriculture—is also the precondition of more funding for others. But if money-saving becomes an end in itself, the result can be simply to cut down real benefits without redirecting effort to better purposes. A budget strategy has to be defined.

There have been hints of this in recent years. More has been spent on regional policies and the Social Fund, not least in the Mediterranean.[19] There is a new emphasis on industrial research and development, much pressed by France. There are obvious arguments in favor of shifting effort to high technology at one end of the range and depressed industrial areas at the other. Such a broadening of functions can also alleviate some of the problems of the British deficit. Strategic lines, it seems, are being laid down. But the efforts are still very modest. In the present climate, they could remain so.

The second issue is what happens to those parts of the agricultural policy which provided funds to the poorer countries, in ways both largely autonomous and automatic. The Irish benefited enormously from the common market organizations for milk and beef; the Mediterranean areas have received far more funds since 1978. The poorer countries have an interest in high Community budgets because they are politically fairly well placed to be net beneficiaries from them. The same will apply to Portugal and Spain. A shift in priorities away from agriculture could damage the prospects of the poorer regions and countries for whom agriculture is much more important than for the richer ones.

The third issue also arises out of the loss of agricultural benefits but is more general. The beneficiaries of the old CAP have been mainly the more productive farmers in the richer regions at the cost of the urban consumers of food. These richer farmers still have considerable electoral and political influence in several Community countries. If the Community pays out less to them, one must, from past experience, expect the pressures for higher national payments to be intensified.

In short, the shift in financial power to the bankers raises questions about the basic budget strategies of the Community, and for agriculture not only about farmers' incomes but also about the potential de facto transfer of funding to the national budgets.

INCOMES

In the last resort, sustaining farm and rural incomes was what the 30 years of expansion were all about. High prices were supposed to close the gap between farm and other average incomes that existed in most countries. They did not in fact do this; and when saturated markets and constrained budgets make it plain the whole approach has reached the end of the road, there is not only a sense of defeat. There is the more concrete fear of falling incomes in future. The old apparently easy way to raise returns has been eliminated. The most obvious alternative is to reduce production costs of all kinds. There seems to be plenty of room for this in West European agriculture as a whole. Farms are often heavily overcapitalized in relation to their size.[20] It has been shown that less intensive methods of farming can give earnings that are in some cases comparable with the high-input, high-output techniques (Milk Marketing Board, 1978, 1979a, 1979b). But new methods require investment and a learning period. They also lack the potential of the old. Whatever the initial margins for restoring net returns by cutting costs, they certainly are not, like high growth, openended. They are not even appropriate in all cases.

There is no need to jump to apocalyptic conclusions from these disappointments. The Anderson-Tyers scenario for a reduction in real Community prices of 2 percent a year for a decade is relatively encouraging in this respect. It shows that it may be possible, if an appropriate and steady policy is pursued, to achieve significant results with fairly modest sacrifices of incomes if not expectations. It is, in fact, almost an econometric orchestration of the Mansholt theme, already quoted at the outset of this chapter, of long-term price restraint. But, of course, the results may be based on misleading assumptions and do not chime in with past results on grains. And even if they could be proved correct, some will gain in the process while many others will lose. Restriction is never easy. At best, it cannot avoid taking place in a climate of anxiety and invidious comparisons.

In practical politics, relative incomes matter just as much as absolute ones, and in many situations more. People look less at what they are earning than at where they stand compared with neighbors, for this also affects the esteem in which they are held, and to some extent in which they hold themselves. If there is expansion in the economy but limits in agriculture, incomes outside agriculture will rise faster than the stagnant or falling ones inside. During the 1970s, average incomes per head in farming fell behind those in other sectors. (On the other hand, farming does not have open unemployment.) Between 1973–75 and 1983, real incomes per active worker in the general economy rose 16 percent; in farming, they fell 4 percent (Com-EC, 1984d, Graph 1). This is discouraging enough in itself, especially given the growth in output, and is a sign of the misdirected efforts of the old CAP. It is the more so when one recalls that average incomes per head in Community agriculture in 1973–75 were themselves about half those of the employed in general. Too much weight should not be given to such comparisons, because it is difficult to compare the farmer, who is self-employed, with wage-earners in other professions. The patterns of capital and income are quite different. Nevertheless, it is plain that a period of restriction, coming on top of a situation where, for all but the highly productive farms, income comparisons are not too favorable, will be experienced as depression.

In principle, the producers who lose most from the foreclosing of the prospects of openended expansion are the larger ones who benefited most from the old regime. In principle, also, quotas protect the smallholder's income because he will be paid fully for the same output as before. But the previous discussion of the likely operation of quotas shows that there is no guarantee, nor even probability, that this will be permanent. In such circumstances, average figures, such as those that the Anderson-Tyers scenarios necessarily deal in, are not representative. There will continue to be an implied competition for market shares between large and small farmers (as well as producers in different lines more or less restrained) in which the small are at a huge disadvantage. In the period of expansion, this was not too noticeable because the smallholder himself may have been modestly increasing his output and returns. The fact that the large farmer was doing so much more was not of immediate relevance to him. But when the total returns to agriculture are rationed, the effects become apparent at once. Overproduction by some leads to the threat of reduced prices per ton for all; and those who have increased output less than the average perceive a direct and unrelieved loss.

Such a situation may bring out the implied competition between large and small farmers which was muffled by general expansion. It will certainly draw attention to the regional problems of the Community. This is not only the matter of rich–poor contrasts and related ones between north and south. It concerns the emphasis several of the member states have placed upon having a diffused population of farmers spread as widely as possible across the landscape. The emphasis that should be placed on this is not universally agreed even in countries like France where the policy prevails (Klatzmann, 1978, pp. 120–23; Bergmann, 1979, pp. 19–20). Nevertheless if incomes decline in farming, they will be felt to threaten the healthy social structures of the countryside as well. It is a normal enough concern anywhere; it will be stronger in some countries than others because it will work against longstanding priorities. If the Community provides substantial compensation, it may be regarded as an important prop. If not, the political opposition will channel demands towards national governments.

On the practical side, this will obviously by expressed as calls for funds. But the underlying political message could well be a much wider one. To farmers who have known high levels of support and guarantees for three decades, the reduction of their levels of secure income is an assault on established rights; and the less mercantile the national farming tradition, the more outrageous the assault appears. Governments are not, of course, the source of the farmers' troubles. But having administered food markets in one way or another for generations, it is natural they should be regarded as failures, or worse, when expectations are disappointed. Declining incomes may well be interpreted as the failure or refusal of the Community or governments to carry out their traditional and therefore bounden duties.

Poujadism is never far below the surface of producer-oriented systems which encourage the beneficiaries, real or supposed, to believe they have inalienable rights which are being snatched away. It is easy to envisage domestic turmoil hitting governments at vulnerable points and depriving them of room for maneuver. There could be turbulence, even violence. There is, of course, a histrionic element in such rituals, because that is how political will is mobilized in modern bargaining via the media and public opinion. There are also restraints. Both the base and the apex of corporatist decision-making systems are adept at the gentle art of knowing just how far to go too far. At some point in generating surpluses at the cost of the rest of society, farmers could lose the crucial sympathy of the public. Nevertheless, when basic changes are in the air, in however limited a way, they arouse fears of larger ones to come and give politics an undertone of ferocity. In many countries, the farm sector is still identified with Mother Earth as well as with the national interest. Such sentiments, given the appropriate conditions, can rapidly turn to xenophobia. Governments could lose control of the political process. That knowledge could even become an element in negotiation, a dangerous one that encourages escalation.

NATIONS AND COMMUNITY

In short, the fear of loss of incomes and of depression in the countryside raises the issue which has lain just below the surface ever since the CAP has been visibly off balance: whether it is possible to reconcile national and collective policies in agriculture once the uncontrolled expansion of output and openended price guarantees come to an end. As soon as one raises such a question, another follows: whether there may be forms of agricultural policy in Western Europe which redistribute powers between the member states and the common institutions, and for what purposes.

There is, for instance, a fairly widespread view in Britain that the diversity of the Community is too great for a truly common agricultural policy. It is also argued that the only way to force governments to restrain blind expansionist policies is to make them pay the costs their farmers generate. Since much of the force behind such arguments comes from the desire to limit payments into the Community budget, the practical form they take is to suggest that some types of farm spending, such as income aids, should become national responsibilities.

There are at least four ways in which countries can maintain traditional levels of support to farmers by supplementing what the Community pays:

1. Farm prices can be fixed by the Community, as in the past, but the Community itself may pay only part of the costs for buying up stocks or subsidizing sales at home or abroad, the rest being borne by the member states.

2. A relatively low "trading price" can be set for intra-EC trade, as suggested by John Marsh some years ago, while national prices will be set by the member states, who will bear any of the extra costs that result (Marsh, 1978).

3. Quotas for volumes attracting Community price supports can be agreed, dictated by the limits of the common budget, but subsidies to producers (deficiency payments) can be added nationally to bring their returns up to whatever levels the domestic politics of each country demand.

4. Community price limits can be strictly observed, but any shortfalls in the returns to farmers each country desires to maintain can be made up by income supports from national budgets.

In practice, all of these, as has been said of the income aids which governments have already accorded, "can be viewed as an alternative to

(Community) price supports. Indeed, their growth in recent years is probably the consequence of the tighter price policy adopted by the Commission." (House of Lords, 1982, p. vii, para. 11). Part at least of any extra funds placed in the hands of farmers is likely to be invested in the business and will usually add to production capacity. Extra output will only be inhibited if the penalties on unwanted production are stringent and applied. If not, supports will amount in effect to the prolongation of policies of national expansion. They would only differ from the past in that Community financial responsibility would be diminished, and from unilateral policies in that there would be a kind of collective hunting license to pursue such policies. For the rest, the success of such approaches depends either on the bet that the costs would prove prohibitive for national governments, or on the establishment of effective and collective (in practice Community) controls to limit the quantitative and qualitative distortions to which they might lead.

It is not clear why the bet on national self-restraint should come off. Governments will be under a diversity of different pressures once they have a license to apply their own measures in free variation on those of the Community. In some countries, farmers will be able to apply much more pressure than in others. The lure of larger market-shares will be stronger and a more practical proposition for some than for others. Rich countries will be better able to compensate this or that category of farmers for losses in earnings than the poorer ones which are least able to pay but are in greatest need. In general, such policies (some of them suggested when circumstances were not what they have become today) would be at least as likely to debouch on unilateral national expansion as on restriction imposed by cost. Insofar as costs had an effect, it would be likely to fall first on the poorer countries. Moreover, it is obvious, from the political energy the French have been investing in trying to persuade the Germans to abrogate MCAs, and the pressure the French farmers have been bringing on their government, that national supplements also increase mutual jealousies based on the belief that conditions are skewed in favor of neighbouring countries. Such systems would, therefore, stimulate rivalry and suspicion between member states and usually favor the strong against the weak. Far from causing restraint, national supplements could rapidly cause disruption.

National supplements might, however, be viable so long as they were free variations on Community policies but reflected collectively agreed and defined arrangements under equally collective supervision. Such criteria would have to be collectively set and apply to all (however ingeniously they were tailored to meet special needs). Ad hoc measures are not possible on a permanent basis because they institutionalize discrimination, which sooner or later is seen, and resented, as privilege. Thus, it is perfectly possible to imagine national income aids which conform to Community criteria. But payments would have to be selective, not general—say to smallholders with no earnings off the farm, or young farmers in danger of bankruptcy because of debts inherited from a recent expansionary past. Rich countries would have to contribute, on known and agreed lines, through the Community budget to the national costs in poorer ones of subsidizing smallholders. Such a collective discipline would not be so much a new division of responsibilities as a decentralization of Community regulations. If such codes worked (reluctance to enter into them might reflect fear that in practice they might not), they would reinforce and even extend common policies, not weaken them.

The balance to be struck between common and national priorities is particularly delicate in the case of quotas. Quotas are basically the frozen version (and the equivalent in a world of limits) of the market-shares which have always been a prominent aspect of expansive national ambitions in the CAP. It is hard to conceive of any member state willingly losing its market-share in any plan of quotas. Thus, even if they are administered at the farm or processing plant, quotas are bound in some sense to be national. It is only a short step from this to national governments seeking to administer quotas themselves. There are national agencies in plenty to do this. Can they be prevented from monopolizing control? The question is how closely the Commission is allowed to regulate what goes on. The main problems are triggered when there are signs of overproduction. Will national governments alone judge what restraints (or lack of restraints) are necessary, and whether to keep their country in line with common targets? There were clearly suggestions of this kind in the negotiations leading to the decisions of 1984. Commission spokesmen strongly repudiated schemes to let governments police quotas and pay whatever extra amounts would be necessary for the Community to dispose of, or store, the excess national output.[21] At the opposite extreme, one could have a system of quotas based on individual farms, where the Commission would discriminate between farmers and products according to social priorities or the technical requirements of the sector, irrespective of the implications for national market-shares and financial balances between member states in Community budgets. In existing conditions, such federalism would clearly not recommend itself to the governments. In practice, then, something between federalism and nationalism has to be devised. National balances must perforce be respected; but the Commission must be able to supervise whatever minimum collective disciplines are required to keep the system going.

Once again, sugar offers a precedent. It is significant that the most constraining rule in the sugar regulations concerns what happens when sugar exports can no longer earn a profit even for farmers with sufficiently low marginal costs to dump abroad. The question that then arises is what to do with the unsellable sugar. Keeping it is no solution, unless markets revive. In fact, its very existence (if the quantities are large enough) makes it harder for the markets to improve. Excess supplies hang over them and keep prices low. Unwanted surpluses are also very expensive to hold in store. The excess can be destroyed, of course, as some commodities were in the 1930s. If conditions are bad enough this can make considerable commercial sense. But politically it is too appalling a confession of failure to be tried. The only remaining solution is to absorb the excess on domestic markets. This is the policy which has been adopted for sugar.

In the Community's sugar system, excess supplies which cannot be exported within a year count against the quota of domestic high price, A sugar for the following harvest of each factory holding unsold stocks. In this way, excess output (or some of it) is absorbed; prices, in effect, are cut (because there is that much less support for new high price sugar delivered to the factory); and threats to the balance of national market shares are held in check. A minimum collective discipline is maintained even though the system amounts to a cartel of national quotas. Without such minimum rules at the Community level, one would soon be back, once again, to the national, subsidized expansion that threatens both the CAP and relations in agriculture between the member states.

The upshot of all this is that limits radicalize the basic options of policy-makers. On the one hand, they encourage a drift back to national solutions, or at least the temptation to resort to them. On the other hand, if relations between the member states in agriculture are not to break down altogether, the policing of arrangements requires that the role of the common institutions—and of the initiatory and supervisory body, the Commission, in particular—should in some important respects be reinforced. This is not so much a matter of political conflicts of jurisdiction between member governments and the Commission. It is more that if the member states are to regulate their relations effectively with each other, they will have to tighten up their mutual commitments inside their collective. The powers of the Community's institutions are not the cause but the consequence of the need of the member states to act together. This has in fact been the case at every stage in the chequered history of European integration, not excluding the establishment of the CAP itself. There would have been no need of elaborate management committees run by the Commission for a few long-term German contracts for cereals with France and for dairy products from the Netherlands.

The need for tighter mutual commitments goes further than the administration of quotas. It also applies to the investment policies the member states have traditionally all but monopolized. Relatively little is at stake when expansion is general. When every hope and every ton of a commodity can find a market niche, violations of, and exceptions to, the general rule do not make much difference. No one suffers an immediate loss and the precedent can often be filed away for one's own use at a suitable later time. When limits appear, this tolerance fades. Countries or interest groups which have to observe restraints themselves do not take kindly to anything that smacks of sharp practice among their partners. Concupiscence gives way to potentially embattled paranoia. Far from becoming looser, a CAP under pressure and proposing to survive has to become stricter and visibly equitable. This means, in one way or another, more restraints over each member state's actions by the collective as a whole.

This is no small innovation and it goes beyond relatively obvious issues such as national income aids. Since the CAP is in effect a dual policy—a Community policy for prices and a conglomeration of largely separate national policies for investment—it is impossible to make any limitative strategy stick unless there is a more or less concordant approach on the ubiquitous national aids and structural policies. As Chapter 3 makes evident, these too are far from covering the whole picture, because many of the developments most relevant to agriculture are dealt with under quite different headings, such as regional or manpower or environmental policies. So far, this flaw in the system has simply been ignored in the general dash for growth. Once growth is reined in, there can be no common policy without national activities—either by spontaneous and angelic self-discipline or by collective vigilence—being effectively folded into the whole.

This is the most difficult and profound question posed by any effort to control Community farm production. It is essentially political. The traditional CAP was enough of an obligation on national policies for it to require years of struggle to set up. But the collective discipline was only fragmentary and in practice proved more theoretical than real. Any discipline in time of slowing up would pose the problem of relations between the national and Community policies with a searching intrusiveness that has previously, and not by accident, been missing. It is not only a question of deliberate national policies to flout common purposes. It concerns the sheer difficulty, political and administrative, of bringing vast and obscure structures of power and patronage, with deep roots in national history and ways of doing business, under minimum control.

Any approach to the problem will certainly have to be minimalist and evolutionary. The criterion is not primarily who does what. The core of the matter is that what is done nationally should not negate collective purposes. A supposedly central system undermined by national activities will collapse. A decentralized system in which countries cooperate to common ends might be much less tidy, but it would further integration in a deeper sense.

The problem is how to do this. The Commission has been given the constitutional powers in Article 92, paragraph 1, of the Rome Treaty, which states

> save as otherwise provided in the Treaty, any aid granted by a Member State or through State resources whatsoever which distorts or threatens to distort competition by favouring certain goods shall, in so far as it affects trade between Member States, be incompatible with the common market.

This is the kind of provision which has served federal government so well over a couple of centuries against states' rights in the USA. The Commission has duly staked a claim in its 1983 proposals for a revised policy on agricultural structures:

> under the new basic regulation (to be presented to the Council), it is proposed to ban all investment aids at both Community and national level if they increase the output of products with market difficulties, particularly milk, subject only to certain very limited exceptions in some less favoured areas [Com-EC, 1983c].

The fact remains, not altogether surprisingly, that the Commission has so far gained extraordinarily little hold over the national structural and investment systems. One witness before the British House of Lords Select Committee on the European Communities in 1981 referred to a responsible Eurocrat who reckoned that less than half of national aids were registered with the Commission (House of Lords, 1982, p. 65., para. 185). The Commission's confidential register, shown to the Committee, nevertheless ran to nine volumes. It has been much criticized for its gaps, outdated facts, inadequate definitions, and confusing presentation. But whereas the House of Lords Committee accepted that this was better than nothing and called for improvements, the member states have taken the opposite tack. Criticism by them has led not to more transparency but to withdrawal from public, or semipublic, scrutiny of those figures that have been published (Appendix Table 10). The Commission's own actions have related for the most part to structural programs in which Community funds were involved. Though significant, these are far from covering the field.

So long as expansion has been the order of the day, no government has been willing to grant the Commission the means to carry out its job. The Council has even withheld the funds that would be necessary for the Commission to set up an effective monitoring service. To give the Commission any practical extension of power in this area would imply a change, however quietly effected, of major significance. It would already be something to give the Commission some of the basic means, including personnel, to monitor national investment and structural policies. It is likely that this will only develop if the Council enacts stricter regulations, along the lines the Commission has proposed, and national governments begin to show more interest in what their partners are doing. A broader definition of what is relevant to agricultural investment is also necessary. The case of the Breton plant set up in 1980 with a capacity to supply the whole British market with turkeys and which was established with 75 percent of subsidies, all of which were legal under national and Community rules, has demonstrated how different policies overlap (House of Lords, 1982; Riley, 1982, pp. 61–62, paras. 159–68). The more the Community itself contributes to regional and development policies along the lines suggested by Pisani, the more it will enter this difficult field. The Commission must have earlier information on regional plans across the member states. As for sanctions, the Commission is already empowered to withhold payments from countries which provide forbidden subsidies sub rosa. This power has been little used because of the obvious risks of retaliation, but in a situation where evasion is less happily tolerated, the political support for rigor could be greater than it has been in the past (Com-EC, 1983a, p. 20, para. 83).

CARDINAL POINTS AND CRISIS MANAGEMENT

Limits on expansion, then, set up a circuit of political choices around the circumference of which there seem to be at least four cardinal points.

One of them is the continuation of national policies of growth even when these have to be renounced in the Community as a whole, because social pressures or ambitions in a given country are not to be denied. If that option is chosen, by a strong enough state or states, and for a long enough time, there will be nothing but a husk of a CAP. It will also be hard to avoid trouble in relations between the member states and in international agro-diplomacy.

Because of these risks, governments will probably prefer to move to some system of restraints based on quotas. This marks a quarter shift around the circle to a position in which an attempt is made to freeze market shares, at least between the members of the Community. This implies a cartel of national policies under the auspices of the Community for whatever commodity receives the treatment. The most obvious sectors are milk and sugar, but once the precedent is set the pressures may well mount for other economically connected sectors, such as beef, to follow suit.

It is unlikely that systems of national restraint can work without common controls to see that they do in fact conform to collective norms of perceived equity between the member states. This pushes policy into the next quarter of the compass where, in some important respects, the rules and supervision of the system under the common institutions are tightened up. If limits are to work at all, the collective aspects of the Community will almost certainly have to be reinforced.

Even so, the pressures for excess production can be lastingly deflated only by reducing prices. This pushes policy into the last quarter of the circle. At this point, two choices are possible. Either price policies are adopted which are sufficiently lasting and cumulative, in which case there is escape from the circuit towards what the OECD calls "positive adjustment": if so, Community policies will have to be reinforced to handle the social and regional problems in farming. Or the compressions of income, and even more the fears of further compression, will lead to revolt in the countryside. In this case national policy-makers are likely to take matters back into their own hands, even against their better judgment, and so move into the first quarter of the circle and return to the original point of the compass.

The mere enunciation of such alternatives shows that the issues posed by the advent of limits in European agriculture are not going to be settled by a single package deal, however momentous and decisive it may seem at the time. The decisions reached in the crisis of 1983–84 are only the beginning of the end of a long phase and the hint of the opening of a new process, not a once-for-all shift from imbalance to equilibrium in agriculture, nor even from one kind of CAP to a new CAP or set of national policies adapted to new conditions.

The behavior of governments left to themselves will probably be fairly predictable because of the difficulties of moving rapidly in a Community of Ten or Twelve states, because of the interlocking interests in the Community in agriculture and beyond, and because, whatever happens, the member states will have to live on in close association. These factors all, on the whole, favor accommodation and, insofar as accommodation requires effective action, and effective action implies a minimum of common disciplines, the slow and untidy reinforcement of the Community system. On the other hand, the reactions of the farmers themselves in the face of constricted and, for many falling, incomes are much more unpredictable and may well produce recurrent upheavals which put all calculations into the melting-pot.

In such an unstable environment, the key factor may well be the spirit and quality of crisis management by the governments and the Community institutions. It may seem easier at any given moment for a country to deal with its farm problems in isolation. In the long run, the costs are likely to be prohibitive, because the limits are set by a total environment and not by the CAP. Contracts of cooperation are usually the result of decision-makers flinching from conflicts with incalculable risks and realizing they have to go beyond their problems and beyond responding to angry constituents. But leadership, which is at best surrounded by difficulties, is sometimes weak, particularly in diffuse confederal systems where the general interest is not consistently perceived as overriding. Governments may at times simply lose control of their domestic pressure-cooker and step back for fear of an explosion. The future of agriculture in the Community is likely to be decided by considerations such as these. While governments will try to make sense in terms of the sector, their choices will to a great extent be decided by general political perceptions and priorities: the evolution of public opinion in the member states, itself linked to changing social structures; the security of Western Europe; the special Franco-German relationship; and the hopes vested in, and fears exorcised by, European integration.

Conclusions

A number of simple but not always familiar themes have emerged in the course of this inquiry, most of them virtually of their own accord.

One such theme is that the CAP is itself the symptom rather than the cause of the problems which assail it. National governments first introduced price support policies as the easiest way of raising farmers' low average incomes to levels nearer those of the rest of society. They initiated these policies, which now unbalance the Community, well before the Treaty of Rome was devised, let alone the CAP was elaborated and established. By this time, it had begun to dawn on policy-makers that the industrialization of agriculture, revolutionizing supply at a time when demand in the Community was increasingly turning to satisfactions other than food, was basically driving prices and farm incomes down. Encouraging production by artificially high prices was, paradoxically, aggravating the problem of oversupply at the root of falling prices and incomes. The problems of a declining industry and countryside were thus soon added to those of welfare for farmers.

For two decades, governments managed to mask these dilemmas. The moment of truth was postponed by the CAP, which provided exporting countries with new markets in Germany, Italy, and Britain, the main importing areas of Western Europe; and then by subsidized exports to world markets in the 1970s. But once these sources of relief began to run out, the underlying problems of oversupply, falling prices and declining relative incomes could not help but reappear. The problems of the 1980s are in essence the same as those first faced by the exporting European countries thirty years ago, well before the Common Market and CAP were mooted.

Moreover, under the umbrella of the CAP, national policies have continued to flourish to a surprising degree and well away from the Community's effective control. Despite public differences which might suggest that national policies have diverged, in fact they displayed remarkable similarities. All the member states of the Community have pursued the national expansion of farm production to sustain farm incomes, to increase food exports or for other reasons. Parallel policies do not, of course, mean compatible ones. When everyone stokes up the pressure in the boiler, sooner or later it bursts. In the early 1980s, crisis has duly erupted. The fact remains that its origins are older than the CAP and that its evolution shows the policy to have been much less of a common one than is usually supposed. National purposes have lain at the base of the CAP without their potential incompatibilities being subordinated to collective goals.

A second theme is the force with which the Community has emerged on world markets in the most recent decade. This has been another expression of the pressures for growth within the member states. Becoming a major world exporter, in its turn, profoundly changes the environment for policy-making in the Community and its member states. This is partly a diplomatic issue with competing exporters, the United States at their head, with whom the basic level of confrontation on food trade has slowly but surely been rising. More important, however, as soon as the Community has acquired major world market shares it comes up hard against the realities of world demand, which it can only manipulate within narrow limits. When manipulation fails, as it did from 1982–84, farmers, national governments and Community alike face limits on prices and growth they can no longer ignore.

All the other themes of this inquiry derive from the basic changes in the environment for the farms which limits imply—even where these are elastic and variable in accordance with the swings of the international market. Expansion itself, when neither continuous nor as steep as in the past, breaks with the old guaranteed conditions. It demands flexibility and powers of adjustment that were ignored. The old modes of policy and expansion, though they seemed dynamic, were in reality largely defensive. They were designed to push back and postpone the problems of agriculture as a "declining" industry. Once limits appear, these can no longer be evaded. Accordingly, limits mark a fundamental turning-point.

Limits are bound to be experienced in the countryside as depression. Some studies suggest this may not be as painful as farmers, in natural alarm, will no doubt assume. Moderate but steady long-term price reductions might not cut net incomes much and even, when farmers are successful in cutting costs, leave room for some improvement. But the projections may be too optimistic in the light of past experiences with prices and output. There will in any case, at least for a period, be little prospect of average incomes rising much. If the general economy revives and earnings in nonfarm jobs move forward when those on the land do not, relative returns from the land will continue to fall, as they have done since the later 1970s. And the collapse of former expectations, however artificial these may have been, tends of itself to engender a psychology of depression. Life in the profession will be harder than it has been for a generation.

Reduced growth will slow down the trend towards the concentration of output on a small minority of highly productive farms which high price supports encouraged. It will favor lower-cost and less intensive farming. The drift from the land will nonetheless continue, if only for demographic reasons. Though more gradually, the transformation of the old peasant society into an industry in many ways like any other will go on. Yet Community farming in 2000 will still be largely in the hands of medium-sized family farms, on average much smaller than British holdings in 1975. There is still, for all the changes since the war, a large remnant of the old peasant agriculture. It is much more than a remnant in the Mediterranean, in Ireland, and even in southern and western France and Germany. Its relative weight will be further increased by the accession of Portugal and Spain. The reduced prospects for agriculture will accentuate the problems of farmers, regions, and countries who rely more than the rest of society on agricultural incomes.

Limits make plain what has in fact always been true of the CAP: low incomes in poor regions cannot be improved primarily by channeling funds to agriculture through price supports. A declining industry cannot be the standard-bearer of the future in less productive areas. There has already been a shift in the thinking of the European Commission towards "integrated" development in "less favored" regions, including industry, services and infrastructures as well as farming. But this is still not reflected to any extent in financial flows through Community budgets. A serious commitment to "integrated" development will imply a relative reduction of the excessive emphasis on agriculture in Community funding. It will not imply a reduction in general Community spending, rather the reverse. The political conflicts surrounding the budget will not disappear with limits on agriculture. They may well increase with enlargement.

The political effects of limits will not be confined to budgets. Until farmers are convinced that limits are inevitable, the stability of farm policy will always be in doubt. It is always possible in a crisis year to impose "prudent pricing." This has been quite traditional, even a recurrent pattern, in the old CAP. The test of restraint is not behavior over one to two years, but the ability to maintain control for five to ten years. That is a political feat of a different order. Left to themselves, governments will probably prefer accommodation within the CAP to the dubious prospects for member states of striking out alone. But limits will exacerbate differences of interests not only between farmers and society but between farmers themselves, at different levels of income, in different countries, and in different lines of production. Political resistance and even violence may at times force governments into channels they would, of their own free will, much prefer to avoid.

Ultimately, however, the political issues generated by limits in the Community go even deeper than the obvious difficulties of maintaining control over the constituency. Limits on expansion bring out into the open the dilemma in policy-making as between national preferences and Community disciplines. So far, the CAP has been much less common than its title suggests. It has been a dual system, mainly *communautaire* for prices, mainly national for investments. There has been little collective regulation of the latter. This has not mattered much in an expansionary climate. Each country, preoccupied by its own growth, paid little attention to that of others. The accent was not on disciplines at all. This changes with limits. Countries or interest groups forced to observe restraints themselves will not take kindly to actions by others which smack of sharp practice. Behavior will have to be tightened up. The dual policy, in one way or another, will have to become more coherent and unified. Channels of action may well remain national—bank credits can hardly be anything else. The guidelines, however, will have to be genuinely as well as formally common. There can be no general restraint without national investment priorities being, de facto, folded into the common one.

Whatever form it takes, the control of investment policies implies an enormous practical extension of the writ of the collective. Since the lack of such controls in the past has been anything but accidental, their affirmation means a pooling of sovereignty far beyond that in the traditional CAP. However obscurely this is faced, or not faced, in the interstices of a complex, opaque, and multinational administration, the political issue is a decisive one. Accordingly, there is a clear potential for a reversion, initially covert and then increasingly open, to national agricultural policies. But if the risks of these are felt to be too great (for a range of economic and political reasons), the reciprocal prospect is of an equally significant increase in the practical primacy of collective government. The crisis is a source of potential integration in strict proportion to the risk it bears of the reverse. Paradoxically, this could be the indispensible condition of the CAP becoming effectively and not just formally common. It holds out the possibility for the first time of national authorities having to accept priorities compatible with operation as a collective, that is, of a genuinely common agricultural policy. Limits are a major political issue for the Community as much as an economic and social one for the sector.

It can be argued that a tighter CAP is incompatible with a Community which has become looser over the years. The opposite and reciprocal proposition, that the CAP made economic unity inevitable, was certainly an article of faith in Community circles in the 1960s. Bitter experience, however, has tempered such mechanical expectations. The CAP did not prevent the economic chaos and divergences between member states of the inflationary 1970s, but surprisingly it also weathered them and survived. Today, with the tacit but apparently increasing European acceptance of German leadership in macroeconomic policies, monetary relations between member states seem to be converging again. Economic policies are more compatible than they were. A stronger collective approach to agriculture, though difficult to apply over the years in its own terms and unlikely, even if successful, to transform the Community, nevertheless seems quite possible. The issue as between national and European policies will remain open perhaps for years to come.

The final theme thrown up by limits is that the Community can no longer escape a new relationship with the rest of the world consequent on becoming one of the world's dominant farm exporters. The horizons of the CAP have in the past been essentially confined to the Community's own region. With massive exports, the Community has to acquire some sense of the world politics of food. This would be true even if the Community were a low-price, obviously competitive exporter. It becomes doubly so when Europe exports on a diet of subsidies which are provocative to rivals and play a significant role in depressing world markets.

This is more than a balance of terror with the United States inducing stalemate. Once the Community depends on world markets, it becomes involved in how effectively they work. Given the difference between Community interests and those of other countries, such a situation does not point clearly to a single set of priorities. These will depend on how narrowly the Community defines its farm interests and how far it tries to integrate them with broader policies, not least toward the developing countries. Even on farm issues, strictly defined, there can be differences between minimal approaches—say, caution in expanding market-shares in one commodity for fear of competitors retaliating in another—and maximal ones, such as attempts to set up international buffer stocks to iron out damaging swings of prices from year to year. What choices will be made is a matter for speculation. What is not speculative is the fact that henceforth the Community cannot avoid giving thought to the international dimensions of its farm policies. This is already evident in the crisis of 1983–84.

Thus, a complex of agricultural policy problems which gradually matured towards crisis in the 1970s under the heading of surpluses, begins to appear, once the various strands knot together in the 1980s, as something much broader and deeper. Domestically, it means recognizing that agriculture cannot expand as it has done for a generation, and that, for the poorer regions, this demands a bigger commitment to broad development policies than in the past. Externally, it implies limits and a greater concern for world food markets and the effects of policy, especially on developing countries. For European integration, it raises the stakes either to a greater cohesion of policy in the Community or a disguised dislocation. All of this plainly goes well beyond agriculture in the strict sense. It is also bound to test the political resources of the Community and its member states for years to come. It is not the end of a crisis so much as the beginning of a new and widely ramified process, full of continuing strains and uncertainty. One of the prizes at the end of the process could well be, with apparently paradoxical logic, a more strongly and deeper-rooted European Community. In this sense, what is needed now is a common agricultural policy. It has never truly existed in the past.

Notes

1. Table 5.A shows the trade in fuels (SITC 3) in billion ECUs in 1980.

Table 5.A.

	Imports	Exports
France	25.8	3.3
Germany	30.2	5.2
Italy	20.0	3.2
Netherlands	13.3	11.8
United Kingdom	11.3	10.7
Rest of EC-10	16.0	4.9

Source: Basic Statistics of the Community 1981.

2. Koester, 1982, using results of Manfred Köhne, *Getreidepreis, Einkommens—oder Kostenfaktor für die Landwirtschaft?*, MFI Schriftenreihe, Bonn 1978, concludes that 0.18 tons of soya substitute for 1 ton of maize, p. 35. USDA sources have estimated that in 1981, at world prices, the EC might have imported 7.5 million tons more grains and 1.5 million tons less soyabeans.

3. EC-10 output of cereals rose from 95 million tons in 1970 to 124 million tons in 1980. See *ASC*s.

4. An important factor was the high level of taxes imposed by European governments on petroleum products. The result was that even large changes in crude prices had a much reduced effect on consumer prices.

5. Com-EC, 1983b, p. 6, para. 14. "There is a constant improvement of crops and breeds of animals, machinery and techniques which mean that the factors of production can be combined more and more efficiently and at lower real cost. These trends will continue and even accelerate in the coming years."

6. Scotto, 1983, and note 7, Ch. 2 supra.

7. See note 3, Ch. 4 supra.

8. "Image de l'Agriculture dans le Grand Public," *France Agricole*, 1983, a poll based on interviews carried out from June 20 to July 10, 1983, found that only 6 percent of non-farming Frenchmen and 8 percent of French farmers thought their country's agriculture "benefitted substantially" from the CAP, while 40 and 59 percent respectively thought it suffered from the CAP.

9. In the agricultural management committees, the Commission has the decisive voice unless there is a qualified majority of the representatives from the member states against the decision proposed.

10. On the basis of grain equivalents, German self-sufficiency in the main categories of food production in 1981 is shown in Table 5.B.

Table 5.B

Commodity Group	Final Production × 100 / Domestic Demand for Food and Industry	Percent Value of German Farm Output, 1981
Crops		
Grains	107	9.1
Sugar	120	4.0
Other	30	12.6
Livestock		
Milk and beef	112	41.7
Other meat and eggs	81	26.4

Source: Com-EC, *Crop Production 1-1983*, pp. 139 and 143; *ASC 1982*, pp. 194–95.

11. In 1978, value added per employee in agriculture in six EC countries for which data are available (the big four, Belgium and the Netherlands) was 7.5 thousand ECUs, and in the food industry it was 22.4 thousand ECUs (*ASC 1980*, p. 38).

12. Given output of 118 million tons of cereal and prices 5 percent above the intervention price (i.e. 160 ECUs per ton), the value of EC-10 grain output in 1980 was about 18.9 billion ECUs. About 73 million tons were used for animal feed, worth approximately 11.7 billion ECUs. The value of livestock production that year, excluding beef and mutton, was 45 billion ECUs and including beef, 64 billion ECUs. This gives a lower proportion for grains of 18 percent and a higher proportion of 26 percent. *ASC 1981* figures for 1979–80.

13. House of Lords, State Aids, 1982, pp. 100–103, and 130–31. Ian Reid, Director of the Centre for European Agricultural Studies at Wye College, London University, presented a memorandum which put the percentage of farms taxed on notional income at 75 percent in Germany, 95–98 percent in France and all farms in Belgium-Luxembourg and Italy.

14. Marsh, 1975, pp. 9–10, summarizing the results of Uri and Bergmann, 1970.

15. In 1980–81, EC exported 21 million tons of grain for which export refunds cost 1.2 billion ECUs. The intervention price was 156 ECUs per ton. A quarter cut in this would reduce export refunds to 17 ECUs per ton. This would save over 800 million ECUs. In addition a 25 percent cut in intervention spending would shave 100 million ECUs off the stocks account. A related cut of 12 percent might reduce the cost of refunds for milk, skimmed milk, etc. by 500 million ECUs. The total saving would be a little short of 1.5 billion ECUs. Against this, income aids to smallholders would cost less than 400 million ECUs (25 percent of the intervention price of 156 ECUs per ton for 8 percent of output of 120 million tons). This would leave rather more than 1 billion ECUs to meet the reduction in the import levies of cereals, worth 1.1 billion ECUs in 1980, resulting from a 25 percent cut in prices (the data do not allow one to break the figure down further). At the least there would be no budget loss, and there would probably be a gain.

16. House of Lords, 1981, D. S. Johnston, Director and General Secretary of the National Farmers Union of Scotland, "Reflections on the CAP," 28 January 1981, pp. 63–65.

17. House of Lords, 1980a, p. 69: the main sugar exporters are Cuba, Australia, Brazil, the Philippines, Thailand, South Africa, and the Dominican Republic. In relation to size, the producers most dependent on exports seem to be the Lome Convention countries and the Dominican Republic.

The difficulties of the world sugar exporters are somewhat reduced because both EC and the USA offer access at their domestic prices to favored suppliers within quotas. In the case of the EC, this applies to the sugar island states which have signed the Lome Agreement. In the case of the USA, quotas are extended to a number of suppliers including Australia. (*Financial Times 1984c*).

18. Sugarbeet plantings in the Community (in thousands of hectares) have been as follows of recent years: 1978–79—1796; 1979–80—1800; 1980–81—1805; 1981–82—2026; 1982–83—1839; and 1983–84—1667. Only the fall from 1982–83 to 1983–84 brings a change. The previous year merely compensated for the leap the one before.

19. Annual Reports of Court of Auditors in *Official Journal* of EC, Vol. 22, C326, p. 230 of 31 December 1979; and Vol. 27, C348, p. 18 of 31 December 1984.

Table 5.C

	Agriculture	Regional Social Industry	Other	Total
1978	9124	1334	1804	12262
1983	16431	5182	3195	24808
1983 ÷ 1978	1.80	3.88	1.77	2.02

20. Hectares cultivated per tractor tell an interesting tale: USA—43; UK—16; France—12; and Germany—5. (FAO, *Production Yearbook 1980*.)

21. Claude Villain, Com-EC, 1984c, p. 9: "the Commission *cannot* accept a system in which each country does what it likes within a national quota, and gives the Community a financial contribution for excess production. That is a recipe for ten different systems, all conflicting. It is a recipe for overproduction. It is not a common market."

Glossary

Terms

Agrarbericht (German). Annual report on agriculture which the German Federal Government is bound by law to present to the Federal Parliament (*Bundestag*).

Benelux. Customs union of Belgium, Luxembourg and the Netherlands, predating EC and used to designate them as a group.

European Currency Unit. The unit of account used by EC, a weighted average of the currencies of the states in the European Monetary System (infra).

European Monetary System. Set up in 1979 to maintain stable exchange rates between member countries. All EC states except Greece and UK belong.

Eurostat. Statistical Office of the Commission of the European Community.

Green rates. Special exchange rates for food trade between EC states after 1969 (see Chapter 4).

Hectare. Basic measure of land area in the metric system, equal to 2.47 acres.

Indicative planning. A form of government economic planning in which targets are not mandatory but designed to give a frame of reference to economic actors. Closely associated with France.

Land (German). A (regional) state, one of the 11 into which the German Federal Republic is divided.

Lome Agreement(s). Renewable 5-year preferential and otherwise special economic arrangements between EC and African, Caribbean and Pacific (ACP) states, numbering 64 in September 1984.

Monetary Compensatory Amounts. When "positive" are subsidies, and when "negative" are taxes, on cross-border food trade in the EC since 1969 (see Green rates supra and Chapter 4).

Nimexe. One of the two widely used international codes for the breakdown of trade statistics (see note 19, Chapter 1).

Real prices. Sometimes called "constant,"—prices corrected for inflation in comparisons between different years.

Treaty of Rome. Signed in 1957, established the European Economic Community and Euratom, now fused, with European Coal and Steel Community of 1952, in the European Community.

Value added.   Value added to resources in manufacture by working them up into more finished goods; i.e., differences in value between outputs of production and inputs into it.

Valued added tax.   Tax imposed on value added (supra), now general in the European Community states.

Abbreviations

ALU	Annual Labor Unit, a measure of work based on standard annual hours of labor. It is designed to take account of differences between full-timers and part-timers in statistics of the labor force.
ASC	Annual reports on the agricultural situation in the Community issued by Com-EC (infra).
CMA	Germany's central marketing organization for farm and food products.
Com-EC	The Commission of the European Community.
DM	Deutschmark, the German currency.
EAGGF	European Agricultural Guarantee and Guidance Fund; i.e., the Community's farm fund.
EC	European Community. Technically, the European Communities, the fusion of the European Coal and Steel Community (set up 1952) and the European Economic Community and Euratom (set up 1958). The fusion took place in 1967.
ECU	European Currency Unit (supra).
EEC	European Economic Community till 1967, now fused in EC.
EMS	European Monetary System (supra).
EUA	European Unit of Account, used by EC for statistics until superseded by ECU in 1979.
FAO	Food and Agriculture Organization of the United Nations
FAP	Final Agricultural Production, results from deducting from gross agricultural production (infra) that part of it (e.g., cereals and oilseeds) which is used as inputs in agriculture itself (e.g., in feeding livestock).
GAP	Gross Agricultural Production, total output as distinct from FAP (supra).
GATT	General Agreement on Tariffs and Trade, which regulates international commerce; also the organization that implements the agreement.
GDP	Gross Domestic Product.
ISA	International Sugar Agreement.
MCA	Monetary Compensatory Amounts (supra).
MEP	Member of the European Parliament (of the EC).

OECD	Organization for Economic Cooperation and Development, established 1962, of which industrial societies (Australasia, Japan, North America and Western Europe) are members.
OEEC	Organization for European Economic Cooperation, Western European predecessor of OECD (supra) set up in 1947, initially to share out Marshall Aid funds between West European recipient states.
SITC	Standard International Trade Classification of the United Nations, one of two widely used international codes for the breakdown of trade statistics (see note 19, Chapter 1, and Nimexe, supra).
UAA	Utilized Agricultural Area, used by EC, covers arable land, permanent cropland and permanent pastures, as distinct from cultivated area which excludes pastures.
UN-ECE/FAO	Joint office in Geneva of two United Nations bodies, the Economic Commission for Europe and the Food and Agriculture Organization.
USDA	United States Department of Agriculture
USDA-ERS	Economic Research Service of USDA (supra).
VAT	Value Added Tax (supra).

References

Agence Europe. Daily News bulletins. Brussels.

Agra-Europe. 1978. *Special Report No. 2: Political Change in the European Community: Implications for the Common Agricultural Policy*. Agra-Europe. November. London. Mimeographed.

Agrarbericht. 1980–1984 (yearly Agricultural Report). Bundesministerium für Ernährung, Landwirtschaft und Forsten. Bonn.

———. 1980, 8/3635–36, January.

———. 1981, 9/140–41, January.

———. 1982, 9/1340–41, January.

———. 1983, 9/2402–3, January.

———. 1984, January.

Agricoltura. 1977. No. 59. December.

Allen, G. R. 1981. *The Food Sector in an International Context*. Allen Associates and Reading University. Mimeographed.

Allen, Rosemarie, 1982, "The Common Fisheries Policy." Ph.D. dissertation, Oxford University. Mimeographed.

Anderson, Kym, and Tyers, Rodney. 1983. *European Community Grain and Meat Policies and US Retaliation: Effects on International Prices, Trade and Welfare*. Centre for Economic Policy, Australian National University (ANU). Discussion Paper No 83 (revised). October. Canberra.

Anuario de Estadistica Agraria. 1980. Ministerio de Agricultura, Pesca y Alimentación. Madrid.

ASC (Agricultural Situation in the Community) 1972. Com-EC. (yearly reports). Luxembourg.

ASC 1978. Com-EC.

ASC 1979. Com-EC.

ASC 1980. Com-EC.

ASC 1981. Com-EC.

ASC 1982. Com-EC.

ASC 1983. Com-EC.

Attwood, E. A. 1979. "The Consequences of Participation in the Common Agricultural Policy to the Irish Economy." *The Net Cost and Benefit of EEC Membership*. Centre for European Studies, Wye College, London University. Mimeographed.

Auberger, B. 1980. "Quelle politique agricole commune pour demain?—un point de vue français." *Revue du Marché Commun* 41. November.

Barna, Tibor. 1980. *Agriculture Towards the year 2000: Production and Trade in High Income Countries*. Sussex European Paper 6. Brighton: SERC, Sussex University.

Bergmann, Denis. 1979. *L'Agriculture Française: Perspectives, Stratégies et Politiques à Long Terme*. Institut National de la Recherche Agronomique. August–December. Paris.

———.1983a. "French Agriculture—Trends, Outlook, and Policies." *Food Policy*. November.

———. 1983b. "Pour une politique agricole 'productiviste'." *Le Monde*. 18 January. Paris.

Best, Geoffrey. 1971. *Mid-Victorian Britain 1851–75*. London: Weidenfeld and Nicolson (also Panther 1973).

Bideleux, Robert. 1979. *Tsarist/Soviet Food and Fibres Production*. University of Southampton. Mimeographed.

Bourrinet, Jacques, and Stioui, Raoul. 1982a. *L'adhésion de la Grèce, de l'Espagne et du Portugal aux Communautés Européennes: Contraintes et possibilités nouvelles vis-à-vis du bassin mediterranéen.* CERIC, Université d'Aix–Marseille III.

————. 1982b. *Problèmes Agricoles d'une Communauté Européenne à Douze.* CERIC., Université d'Aix–Marseille III.

Brown, Lester R. 1982. *U.S. and Soviet Agriculture: The Shifting Balance of Power.* Worldwatch Paper 51. Washington, D.C.: Worldwatch Institute.

Butler, David, and Kavanagh, Dennis. 1975. *British General Election of October 1974.* London: Macmillan.

Cipolla, Carlo M., ed. 1976. *Fontana Economic History of Europe,* 6 volumes. London: Collins/Fontana.

CNASEA (Centre National pour l'Aménagement des Structures des Exploitations Agricoles). 1980. *Contribution à une nouvelle politique de l'exploitation agricole.* Ministère de l'Agriculture. Paris.

Commissariat Général du Plan. 1983. *Quelle Stratégie Européenne pour la France dans les Années 1980?* April. Paris.

Commission of the European Communities (hereafter Com-EC). *Agricultural Situation in the Community* (yearly report). *See* ASC.

Com-EC. European Statistical Office. *See* Eurostat. (Luxembourg).

Com-EC. *Official Journal of the European Communities.* Various volumes from 1977 to 1983. Official Publications Office of the European Communities. Luxembourg.

Com-EC. *Price proposals* (annual). *Commission proposals on the fixing of prices for certain agricultural products and on certain related measures:*

————. 1977, for 1977/78. COM(77) 525. 8 December. Brussels.

————. 1979, for 1979/80. COM(79) 10. 31 January. Brussels.

————. 1980, for 1980/81. COM(80) 10. Vol I 7 February, Vol II 15 February. Brussels.

————. 1981, for 1981/82. COM(81) 50. Vol I 20 February, Vol II 3 March. Brussels.

————. 1982, for 1982/83. COM(82) 10. Vol I 27 January, Vol II 5 February. Brussels.

————. 1982, for 1983/84. COM(82) 650. Vol I 21 December, Vol II 23 December. Brussels.

————. 1983, for 1983/84. COM(83) 500. July. Brussels.

————. 1984, for 1984/85. COM(84) 20. 17 January. Summarized in Com-EC 1984. *Green Europe Newsletter* 24. Brussels.

Com-EC. 1958a. *First General Report on the Activities of the Community* (yearly reports). September. Brussels.

————. 1958b. *Report on the Economic Situation in the Countries of the Community.* Brussels.

————. 1968. *Mémorandum sur la Réforme de l'agriculture dans la Communauté Economique Européenne: Agriculture 1980.* COM(68) 1000. 21 December. Brussels. (= Com-EC. 1969. q.v.)

————. 1969. *Plan Mansholt.* Brussels. (= Com-EC 1968.)

————. 1971. *Yearbook of National Accounts 1960–1970.* Luxembourg.

————. 1975. *Stocktaking of the Common Agricultural Policy.* X/167/75-E. Brussels.

————. 1977. *Pizzutti Report.* SEC(76) 4450, 7 January. Brussels.

————. 1978a. *Economic Effects of the Agri-Monetary System,* COM(78) 20. 10 February. Brussels.

————. 1978b. *Survey on the Structure of Agricultural Holdings,* Vol II. 1975. Luxembourg.

————. 1978c. *Economic and Sectoral Aspects of Commission Analyses supplementing its Views on Enlargement* (so-called "Fresco") COM(78) 200. 27 April. Brussels.

————. 1978d. *Future Development of the Common Agricultural Policy. Communication of the Commission to the European Council.* COM(78) 700. 29 November. Brussels.

————. 1979a. Finn O. Gundelach, European Commissioner for Agriculture. "The common agricultural policy and the community budget." Extracts from a speech before the Agricultural Committee of the European Parliament, 2 October 1979. *Green Europe Newsletter* 5. November. Brussels.

————. 1979b. *Reference Paper on Budgetary Matters.* COM(79) 462. 12 September. Brussels.

———. 1979c. *Economic Effects of the Agri-Monetary System.* COM(79) 11. 14 March. Brussels.

———. 1980a. *Australia and the Community.* Background Report ISEC/B35/80. 10 July. London.

———. 1980b. *Agricultural Markets: Special Number—Prices received by farmers.* (1959/60–1978/79). June. Brussels.

———. 1980c. *Reflections on the Common Agricultural Policy. Communication from Commission to the Council.* COM(80) 800. 5 December. Brussels.

———. 1981a. *Guidelines for European Agriculture. Memorandum to Complement the Commission's Report on the Mandate of 30 May 1980.* COM(81) 608. 23 October. Brussels.

———. 1981b. *Olive Oil.* COM(81) 610. 15 October. Brussels.

———. 1981c. *Répercussions de l'Elargissement de la CEE sur les Régions Italiennes.* Documentation Interne de la Politique Régionale de la Communauté, No. 13, XVI/244/81. October. Brussels.

———. 1981d. *Report on the Mandate of 30 May 1980.* COM(81) 300. 24 June. Brussels.

———. 1981e. *L'industrie Alimentaire dans la Communauté Economique Européenne,* III/100/81 February. Bruxelles.

———. 1982a. *Differential Rates of Inflation and the Common Agricultural Policy.* COM(82) 98. 11 March. Brussels.

———. 1982b. IBI. *Relations with the United States.* 1 October. Brussels.

———. 1982c. *Problems of Enlargement: Taking Stock and Proposals. Bulletin of the European Communities.* Supplement 8/82. December. Luxembourg.

———. 1982d. *The Situation of the Agricultural Markets, Report 1982.* COM(82) 794. 8 December. Brussels.

———. 1983a. "Adjustment of the Community Agricultural Policy". *Bulletin of the European Communities,* Supplement 4/83. July. Luxembourg.

———. 1983b. "Adjustment of the Community Agricultural Policy," "Annex III, Milk." *Bulletin of the European Communities,* Supplement 4/83. 29 July. Luxembourg.

———. 1983c. "Commission Proposals for a Revised Policy on Agricultural Structures." Spokesman's Group. P-89. September. Brussels.

———. 1983d. *The Commissions Proposals for the Integrated Mediterranean Programmes, Parts I and II.* COM(83) 24. 23 March. Brussels.

———. 1983e. *Proposals for a Council Regulation Instituting Integrated Mediterranean Programmes.* COM(83) 495. 16 August. Brussels.

———. 1983f. "Sale of Products." Spokesman's Group. IP(83) 271. 29 July. Brussels.

———. 1983g. Spokesman's Group Sources. November. Brussels.

———. 1983h. *Vers un Nouvel Accord International sur le Sucre.* Spokesman's Group, Information Memo P-8. January. Brussels.

———. 1983i. *European Economy* (Quarterly.) November 1983. Luxembourg.

———. 1983j. *Twelfth Financial Report on the European Agricultural Guidance and Guarantee Fund (1982).* COM(83) 531.15 September. Brussels.

———. 1984a. The Farm Accountancy Data Network: *Farm Accounts Results 1978/79–1981/82.* Luxembourg.

———. 1984b. *Agricultural prices 1984/85 and rationalisation of the CAP—Council Decisions* (of 31 March 1984). Newsflash, *Green Europe Newsletter* 27. April. Brussels.

———. 1984c. "The Outlook for Europe's Agriculture." Claude Villain. *Green Europe Newsletter.* 25 February. Brussels.

———. 1984d. *European Community Commission proposes agricultural prices for 1984/85. Green Europe Newsletter 24.*

Council of the European Communities. General Secretariat. 1984. *921st Meeting of the Council: Agriculture.* Press Release 6131/84. 30–31 March. Brussels.

Curry, David. 1982a. *The Food War.* European Democratic Group of European Parliament (UK Conservatives). London.

———. 1982b. *State Aids to Agriculture.* House of Lords Select Committee on the European Communities. 7th Report of the 1981–82 Session. 23 February 1982 (cover misdated 1981). London.

Debatisse, Michel. 1981. *EEC. Organisation of the Cereals Markets: Principles and Consequences.* Occasional Paper 10. Wye College, London University.

de Bruin, Robert. 1978. "Les Pays Bas et l'Integration Européenne 1957–1967." Ph.D. dissertation. Institut d'Etudes Politiques de Paris.

Delorme, Robert, and André, Christine. 1983. *L'Etat et l'Economie.* Paris: Seuil.

Dvoskin, Dan, and Heady, Earl O. 1976. *U.S. Agricultural Production under limited Energy Supplies, High Energy Prices and Expanding Agricultural Exports.* CARD Report 69. Ames: Iowa State University Center for Agricultural and Rural Development. November.

European Parliament. 1982. *Report on the Proposals from the Commission of the European Communities to the Council (Doc 1-1033/81) on the fixing of prices for certain agricultural products and on certain related measures (1982–1983), Part A, Explanatory Statement.* Rep. David Curry. Document 1-30/82/B. 19 March. Luxembourg.

Eurostat (Statistical Office of the European Communities) (a). *Analytical Tables of Foreign Trade.* SITC Rev. 2. annual, 1960 onwards. Nimexe, annual 1973 onwards. Luxembourg. (For SITC and Nimexe see note 19, Ch. 1)

————. b. *Basic Statistics of the Community.* (normally yearly). Luxembourg.

————. c. Cronos. Data base (time series) of foreign trade and agricultural production statistics. Luxembourg.

————. d. 1958 onwards. *Monthly External Trade Bulletins.* Luxembourg.

————. e. *Yearbooks of Agricultural Statistics* (annual). Luxembourg.

————. 1976. *National Accounts 1960–1975.* Luxembourg.

————. 1977. *Population and Employment 1950–1976.* Luxembourg.

————. 1978. *Regional Accounts 1973.* Luxembourg.

————. 1980. *Review 1970–1979.* Luxembourg.

————. 1982a. *External Trade Statistics, User's Guide 1982.* Luxembourg.

————. 1982b. *Monthly External Trade Bulletin: Special Number 1958–1981.* Luxembourg.

————. 1982c. *Sectoral Income Index 1981.* Doct. D/SX/53.26 January. Luxembourg.

————. 1982d. *National Accounts ESA* (European System of Integrated Economic Accounts) *1960–1980.* Luxembourg.

————. 1983a. *National Accounts ESA, Detailed Tables by Branch, 1970–1981.* Luxembourg.

————. 1983b. *Crop Production, 1–1983.* Luxembourg.

————. 1984a. *Review 1973–1982.* Luxembourg.

————. 1984b. *Regional Statistics.* Luxembourg.

————. 1984c. *Crop Production 3—1984.* Luxembourg.

————. 1984d. *Animal Production 2—1984.* Luxembourg.

FAO (UN Food and Agriculture Organisation). 1950–1982. *Production Yearbooks* (annual). Rome.

————. 1950–1982. *Trade Yearbooks* (annual). Rome.

————. (FAO I and II). 1979 and 1981. *Agriculture: Towards 2000.* C79/24. July 1979. Mimeographed. Revised 1981. Rome.

————. 1980a. "The Commodity Trade Implications of EEC Enlargement." *Commodity Review and Outlook 1979–80.* Rome.

————. 1980b. *Production Yearbook 1980.*

————. 1980c. *Trade Yearbook 1980.*

Financial Times. 1981. "National Aid Undermines Common Farm Policy." 15 May. London.

————. 1982a. "Brezhnev points hopefully towards greener pastures." 27 May. London.

————. 1982b. "Cresson stands firm." 6 July. London.

————. 1982c. "New New Zealand Butter Row Looms." 6 July. London.

————. 1982d. "World's Sugar Market: Why Europe's Rivals Are Sour." 17 August. London.

————. 1982e. "Compromise Statement from GATT Attacked for 'Papering Over' Issues." 30 November. London.

————. 1982f. "Olive Oil 'Fraud' in Italy May Cost EEC $230m a Year." 20 December. London.

————. 1983a. "Flour Sale to Egypt Adds Force to Farm War Threats to EEC." 9 January. London.

———. 1983b. "Wheat Flour Sale to Egypt Threatens EEC–US Ceasefire." 20 January. London.

———. 1983c. "France Offers a Chance to the Young Farmer." 21 January. London.

———. 1983d. "Brussels Sues Paris Over Farm Decision." 23 January. London.

———. 1983e. "Thatcher urges higher food exports." 17 February. London.

———. 1983f. "European Community Spending: France Seeks Tighter Control." 29 November. London.

———. 1984a. "Milk scheme delays aggravate discontent." 18 July. London

———. 1984b. Colina McDougall. "Bumper Harvests boost Exports." China Report, p. xi. 29 October. London.

———. 1984c. "Why the sweet talking had to stop." 24 July. London.

Finansierengsproblemer i Landbruget: fra Udvalget vedroerende Landbrugets Finansierengs/og/ Skaggeforhold. 1981. Committee on financing and taxation of agriculture. Report 941. Danish Ministry of Agriculture. November. Copenhagen.

Fontaine, André. 1982. *Un seul lit pour deux rêves: Histoire de la "détente," 1962–1981.* Paris: Fayard.

France Agricole. 1983. "Image de l'Agriculture dans'le Grand Public." October. Paris.

Gardner, Bruce. 1982. "The Economics of U.S. Agricultural Policy." *U.S.–Japanese Agricultural Trade Relations,* ed. E. N. Castle and K. Hemmi with S. A. Skillings. Washington D.C. & Tokyo: Resources for the Future.

Gonod, P. 1969. "Evolution de la Productivité de l'Agriculture dans la CEE" (1951–1964). Com-EC. *Informations Internes sur l'Agriculture No. 44.* Brussels.

Guardian. 1983a. "A Hot Time Ahead for Planet Earth." 19 October. London.

———. 1983b. "EEC Ministers Again Fail to Agree on Herring Quotas." 27 July. London.

Gutachten zur Einkommensbesteuerung in der Landwirtschaft. 1978. Schriftenreihe des Bundesministeriums der Finanzen, No. 24. Bonn.

Harris, Simon; Swinbank, Alan; and Wilkinson, Guy. 1983. *The Food and Farm Policies of the European Community.* Chichester (Sussex) & New York: John Wiley & Sons.

Heidhues, T.; Josling, T.; Ritson, C.; and Tangermann, S. 1978. *Common Prices and Europe's Farm Policy.* London: Trade Policy Research Centre.

Henry, P., and RICAP group, eds. 1981. *Study of the Regional Impact of the Common Agricultural Policy.* Regional Policy Series 21. Com-EC. Luxembourg.

Hicks, N. 1977. "Ireland: Commitment to the EEC." *Span* 20 (3), pp. 108–10.

———. 1978. "Agriculture in the EEC. 2 France." *Span* 21 (1), pp. 9–11.

Hill, Berkeley. 1983. "Farm Incomes: Myths and Perspectives." *Lloyds Bank Review.* No. 149, pp. 35–48. July. London.

Holmes, Peter, and Duchêne, François. 1981. *Spanish Agriculture and the Common Agricultural Policy.* Brighton: SERC, Sussex University, Mimeographed.

Hopkins, B. P. 1979. *A Comparison of Dairy Farming in Brittany and England & Wales.* Milk Marketing Board, LCP Information Unit. Report 21. November.

House of Lords, Select Committee on the European Communities. 1978. *Enlargement of the Community.* 17th Report of 1977–78. Vol. II, Minutes of Evidence. London.

———. 1979; 1980a. *EEC Sugar Policy.* Session 1979–80. Minutes of Evidence, 27 June 1979; and 44th Report with Minutes of Evidence, 19 March 1980. London.

———. 1980b. *The Common Agricultural Policy.* Session 1979–80. Report 32. November. London.

———. 1981. *The Common Agricultural Policy—Directions of Future Development and Proposals for Prices and Related Measures.* Session 1980–81. 19th Report. Vol. II, Minutes of Evidence. 26 March. London.

———. 1982. *State Aids to Agriculture.* 7th Report of the 1981–82 Session. 23 February (cover misdated 1981). London.

Hu, Yao-Su. 1979. "German Agricultural Power: The Impact on France and Britain." *World Today.* November.

Hughes, H. C. 1978. *A Comparison of the Economics of Milk Production in Eire and Great Britain.* Milk Marketing Board, LCP information Unit. Report 17. November. Reading.

IAMM (Institut Agronomique Méditerranéen de Montpellier). 1980. Allaya, Mahmoud, and Vassilis Bontosoglou. *Tunisie: le secteur agricole et ses perspectives à l'horizon 1990.* September. Montpellier. (also Com-EC. same date. VIII/1/1119/80-Fr. Brussels).

Institut d'Economie Régionale du Sud-Ouest, France. 1979. *L'Elargissment de la Communauté Européenne: L'Impact de l'adhésion de l'Espagne sur certaines régions françaises, notamment ses régions frontières continentales: Approche sectorielle.* Pessac (Gironde).

Inter-Departmental Committee on Land Structure Reform. 1978. *Final Report.* Government Stationery Office. May. Dublin.

International Dairy Arrangement (GATT). 1982. *The World Market for Dairy Products, at 30 September 1982.* Geneva.

IEA (International Energy Agency). 1982. *World Energy Outlook.* Paris: OECD.

Johnson, D. Gale. 1973. *World Agriculture in Disarray.* London: Fontana/Collins.

Johnston, D. S. 1981. "Reflections on the CAP." House of Lords Select Committee on the European Communities. *The Common Agricultural Policy—Directions of Future Development and Proposals for Prices and Related Measures.* Session 1980–81. 19th Report. Vol II, Minutes of Evidence. Evidence of 29 January 1981, pp. 63–68. March. London.

Jørgensen, Erik Juul. 1978. "Alternatives for Danish Agriculture." *Food Policy.* November.

Josling, Timothy E., and Pearson, R. Scott. 1982. *Developments in the Common Agricultural Policy of the European Community.* USDA, ERS. Foreign Agricultural Economic Report 172. June 1982. Washington, D.C.

Kelly, T.J. 1979. *Trends in Dutch and British Dairying 1975–1978.* Milk Marketing Board, LCP information Unit. Report 18. February. Reading.

Klatzmann, Joseph. 1978. *L'Agriculture Française.* 2nd edition. Paris: Seuil.

Koester, Ulrich. 1982. *Policy Options for the Grain Economy of the European Community—Implications for the Developing Countries.* Int'l Food Policy Research Inst. (IFPRI). Research Report 35. November. Washington, D.C.

Koester, U., and Tangermann S. 1977. "Supplementing Farm Price Policy by Direct Income Payments: Cost-Benefit Analysis of Alternative Farm Policies with a Social Application to German Agriculture." *European Review of Agricultural Economics* 4.

Köhne, Manfred. 1978. *Getreidepreis, Einkommens—oder Kostenfaktor für die Landwirtschaft?* Bonn: MFI Schriftenreihe.

Lancelot, Alain. 1975. "Opinion Polls and the Presidential Elections, May 1974." *France at the Polls: The Presidential Election of 1974,* ed. Howard R. Penniman. Washington, D.C.: American Enterprise Institute.

Lelong, Pierre. 1983. "Politique Agricole Commune et Structure des Prix." *Commentaire.* Autumn–Winter. Paris.

Lindberg, Leon N. 1963. *The Political Dynamics of European Economic Integration.* New York: Stanford and Oxford University Presses.

McCrone, Gavin. 1962. *The Economics of Subsidising Agriculture: A study of British Policy.* London: Allen & Unwin.

McDougall, Colina. 1984. "Bumper harvests boost exports." *Financial Times.* China report, p. xi. 29 October. London.

McDougall, Sir Ian, et al. 1977. *Report of the Study Group on the Role of Public Finance in European Integration.* Com-EC. Studies in Economy and Finance. Luxembourg.

Marsh, J. S. (rapporteur). 1975. *European Agriculture in an Uncertain World.* Paris: Atlantic Institute for International Affairs.

————. 1978. "European Agricultural Policy: A Federalist Solution." *Federal Solutions to European Issues,* ed. Burrows, Denton, and Edwards. London: Macmillan.

Marsh, J., and Ritson, C. 1971. *Agricultural Policy and Common Market.* London: Chatham House–PEP.

Milk Marketing Board (U.K.). 1978, see Hughes; 1979a, see Kelly; 1979b, see Kelly.

Ministère de l'Agriculture. 1982. *L'Aide au revenu agricole assise sur le chiffre d'affaires de 1980.* Service Central des Enquêtes et Etudes Statistiques. Collections de Statistique Agricole, Etude 208. November. Paris.

Ministry of Agriculture (Denmark). 1978. *Note on the Agricultural Sector of Denmark.* Copenhagen. Mimeographed.

Mitchell, B. R. 1976. "Statistical Appendix 1920–1970." *Fontana Economic History of Europe*, ed. Carlo M. Cipolla. Vol. 6 (2). London: Collins/Fontana.

Murphy, J., O'Connell, J. and Sheehy, S. J. 1979. *Alternative Growth Rates in the Irish Food Industry to 1990*. Dublin: The Economic and Social Research Institute.

Neville-Rolfe, Edmund. 1984. *The Politics of Agriculture in the European Community*. London: European Centre for Policy Studies, P.S.I. May.

O'Brien, Patrick M. 1981. "Global Prospects for Agriculture." *Agricultural Food Policy Review: Perspectives for the 1980s*. USDA. April. Washington, D.C.

OECD (Organisation for European Cooperation and Development) (a). *Main Economic Indicators*. (monthly). Paris.

———(b). *Statistics of Foreign Trade, Series C, Trade by Commodities* (yearly). 1962 onwards. Paris.

———. 1973. *Agricultural Policy in the Netherlands*. Paris.

———. 1974. *Agricultural Policy in Denmark*. Paris.

———. 1975. *OECD Food Consumption Statistics 1955–73*. Paris.

———. 1976. *Study of Trends in World Supply and Demand of Major Agricultural Commodities*. Paris.

———. 1977. *Agricultural Policy in Denmark*. Paris.

———. 1978. *Meat Balances in OECD Member Countries 1963–76*. Paris.

———. 1980a. *Review of Agricultural Policies in OECD Member Countries 1979*. Paris.

———. 1980b. *The Instability of Agricultural Commodity Markets*. Paris.

———. 1981a. *Food Consumption Statistics 1964–78*. Paris.

———. 1981d. *Food Policy*. Report by OECD Working Party on Agricultural Policies and by the Committee on Agriculture. April. Paris.

———. 1983a. *Issues and Challenges for OECD Agriculture in the 1980s*. April. Paris.

———. 1983b. *Review of Agricultural Policies in the OECD Member Countries 1980–82*. May. Paris.

OECD, Interfutures. 1979. *Facing the Future*. Paris.

OEEC (Organisation for European Economic Cooperation). 1959. *Agricultural and Food Statistics*. Paris.

———. 1961. *Statistical Bulletins of Foreign Trade, Series C, Trade by Commodities 1960*. Paris.

Owen, David. 1978. "The Enlargement of the Community". *New Europe*. Summer.

Paarlberg, Don. 1980. *Farm and Food Policy: Issues of the 1980s*. Lincoln and London: Nebraska Univ. Press.

Pepelasis, A. 1980. "Greek Agriculture in the EEC." *The Tenth Member—Economic Aspects*, Pepelasis et al. Sussex European Paper 7. Brighton: SERC, Sussex University.

Pisani, Edgard. 1983. *Réflexions sur une politique agricole et alimentaire commune et ses liens avec une politique structurelle de développement régional*. Com-EC. April. Brussels. Mimeographed.

Plan Vedel. 1969. Ministère de l'Agriculture. Paris.

Priebe, Hermann. 1976. "The Changing Role of Agriculture." *Fontana Economic History of Europe*, ed. Carlo M. Cipolla. Vol. 5 (2). London: Collins/Fontana.

Read, Magdalena. 1979. *The Impact of the Age Distribution on the Future Supply of Agricultural Labour in the Community*. Brighton: SERC, Sussex University. Mimeographed.

Rehrl, J. 1979. "Prognose der kuenftigen Agrarstrukturentwicklung. Ergebnisse und Erfahrungen: einer Delphi-Umfrage." *Agrarwirtschaft 28*.

Ries, Adrien. 1978. *L'ABC du Marché Commun Agricole*. Paris and Brussels: Fernand Nathan, Editions Labor, Collection "Europe."

Riley, K. P. 1982. House of Lords, Select Committee on the European Communities. State Aids to Agriculture (q.v.) 7th Report of the 1981–82 Session. 23 February (cover misdated 1981), pp. 45–69. London.

Rollo, J., and Warwick K. 1979. *The CAP and Resource Flows among Member States*. UK Government Economic Service Working Paper No. 27. November. London.

Ryan, Pierce, 1983. "Impact of the CAP in the Irish Economy." *Revue d'Intégration Européenne*. Montreal.

Sanderson, Fred H. 1982. "Managing our Interdependence." *U.S.–Japanese Agricultural Trade Relations*, ed. E. N. Castle and K. Hemmi with S. A. Skillings. Washington and Toyko: Resources for the Future.

Scotto, Marcel. 1983. "Politique Agricole Commune: Il ne s'agit pas seulement de maîtriser les dépenses." *Le Monde*. 2 August. Paris.

Sharpe, Wayne W. 1982. "The Role of Agriculture in Transatlantic Relations." Speech to Int'l Federation of Margarine Assn's. 8 June. U.S. Mission to EC. Brussels.

Sheehy, S. J. 1980. "The Impact of EEC Membership on Irish Agriculture." *Journal of Agricultural Economics* 31 (3).

Sociaal-Economische Raad. 1966. *Statutory Organisation of Industry in the Netherlands*. The Hague.

———. 1976. *Industrial Organisation under Public Law in the Netherlands*. The Hague.

Strasser, Daniel. 1975. *The Finances of Europe*. Praeger. New York & London. (Revised edition, Com-EC. 1981. Luxembourg.)

Strauss, Robert. 1983. "Economic Effects of Monetary Compensatory Amounts." *Journal of Common Market Studies*. July.

Szczepanik, E. F. 1976. *Agricultural Policies at Different Levels of Development*. Rome: FAO.

The Times. 1982. "Brezhnev's radical farm Cure." 25 May. London.

Thiede, Günther. 1970. "Die Versorgungslage der EWG mit landwirtschaftlichen Erzeugnissen." *Berichte über Landwirtschaft* 48 (2). Bonn.

———. 1972. "La Révolution technique agricole devant la CEE et ses conséquences." *Economie Rurale* 91. January–March.

———. 1975. *Europas Grüne Zukunft*. Econ-Verlag. Duesseldorf and Vienna.

———. 1980. *Overall Accounts on the Community Supply Situation, based on grain equivalents*. Com-EC, Eurostat. Agricultural Studies No. 22. Luxembourg.

———. 1981. "Mengenmaessige Gesamtrechnungen zur EG-Versorgungslage 1979." *Agrarwirtschaft*. Bonn.

Tovias, Alfred. 1979. *EEC Enlargement—The Southern Neighbours*. Sussex European Paper 5. Brighton: SERC, Sussex University.

Tracy, Michael. 1964. *Agriculture in Western Europe: Crisis and Adaptation since 1880*. Cape. London. (Revised 1982. *Agriculture in Western Europe: Challenge and Response 1880–1980*.) London: Granada.

U.K. HMSO. 1975. *Food From Our Own Resources*. Command 6020. London.

———. 1979. *Farming and the Nation*. Command 7458. London.

U.N. *Yearbooks of National Accounts Statistics* (annual). New York: UN.

UNCTAD. 1981. *Trade and Development Report. 1981*. New York: UN.

UN ECE (Economic Commission for Europe). 1968. *Review of the Agricultural Situation in Europe at the end of 1967. Vol II. Dairy Products and Eggs*. ST/ECE/AGRI/29/Vol II. New York.

UN ECE–FAO. 1954. *European Agriculture: A Statement of Problems*. Geneva.

———. 1967. *Prices of Agricultural Products and Fertilisers in Europe 1965/66*. ST/ECE/AGRI/21. Geneva.

Uri, Pierre, and Bergmann, Denis. 1970. *A Future for European Agriculture*. Paris: The Atlantic Institute for International Affairs.

U.S. Congress, Joint Economic Committee. 1981. *Consumption in the USSR: An International Comparison*. Washington, D.C.: USGPO.

USDA. (U.S. Department of Agriculture), ERS (Economic Research Service). 1981a. *Agricultural Situation: USSR*. Supplement 1 to WAS-24. April. Washington, D.C.

———. 1981b. *Fall 1981 Baseline Projections*. Washington, D.C. Mimeographed.

———. 1981c. *Problems and Prospects for U.S. Agriculture in the 1980s*. November. Washington, D.C. Mimeographed.

———. USDA I. 1981. O'Brien, Patrick M. "Global Prospects for Agriculture." *Agricultural Food Policy Review: Perspectives for the 1980s*. April. Washington, D.C.

———. USDA II. 1981. *Problems and Prospects for U.S. Agriculture in the 1980s*. November. Washington, D.C. Mimeographed.

———. 1982a. *Agricultural Outlook*. November. Washington, D.C.

———. 1982b. *Outlook and Situation: Fats and Oils*. FOS-309. October. Washington, D.C.

———. 1982c. *Review of Agriculture in 1982: Western Hemisphere*. Supplement 5 to WAS-27. Washington, D.C.

———. 1982d. *USSR: Review of Agriculture in 1981 and Outlook for 1982*. Supplement to WAS-27. May. Washington, D.C.

U.S. Department of Commerce, Bureau of the Census. 1982. *Statistical Abstract of the United States 1981*. Washington, D.C.

U.S. Mission to the European Communities. 1981. *US–EC Agriculture in Brief*. Brussels.

Vanous, Jan. 1982. "Why Russia would rather not feed itself." Letter to *The New York Times*. 19 November. New York.

Wade, Robert. 1982. *Regional Policy in a Difficult International Environment: The Italian Case*. Brighton: Institute of Development Studies, Mimeographed.

Webb, Alan J. 1981. *World Trade in Major U.S. Crops—A Market Share Analysis*. USDA, ERS. ESS-7. April. Washington, D.C.

Weinschenk, G. 1979. "Zur problematik der Fortsetzung gegenwärtiger Entwicklungstendenzen im Agrarbereich." *Agrarwirtschaft* 28.

Willer, H., and Haase, F. 1978. *Der Landwirtschaftliche Anpassungsprozess unter veränderten Rahmenbedingungen*. Bonn: Arbeitsgruppe des Bundesministeriums für Ernährung, Landwirtschaft und Forsten.

World Bank. 1981. *World Development Report 1980*. Washington, D.C.

Zeller, Adrien, with Giraudy, Jean-Louis. 1970. *L'Imbroglio Agricole du Marché Commun*. Paris: Calmann-Levy.

STATISTICAL
APPENDIX

Appendix Table A   Dollar-ECU Exchange Rates, 1962-1983

The US dollar value of the ECU (European Currency Unit) has varied greatly from year to year. Tables in values must be read with this in mind. The average variations from year to year have been as follows since 1962:

Year	Value of ECU in US dollars
1962–66 inclusive	1.06981
1967	1.06482
1968	1.02889
1969	1.02219
1970	1.02223
1971	1.04776
1972	1.12178
1973	1.23173
1974	1.19270
1975	1.24077
1976	1.11805
1977	1.14112
1978	1.27410
1979	1.37065
1980	1.39233
1981	1.11645
1982	0.98208
(1983) estimate	0.88979

Source: Com-EC, *European Economy*, November 1983, Table 41.

Appendix Table 1 Average Annual Rates of Growth of Agricultural Output and Consumption in EC-9, 1953–55 to 1981 (percent)

	Output (final production)			Consumption (food and industrial uses)		
	1953–55 to 1959–61 (a) (national accounts)	1957–61 to 1969 (b) (grain equivalents)	1973 to 1981 (c) (grain equivalents)	1953–55 to 1959–61 (a) (national accounts)	1957–61 to 1969 (b) (grain equivalents)	1973 to 1981 (c) (grain equivalents)
Belgium–Luxembourg	2.8	2.4	1.1	2.7	1.3	1.5
France	1.9	3.5	2.6	2.6	2.5	1.7
Germany	2.9	2.9	2.1	6.7	2.1	0.9
Italy	3.4	2.7	2.6	3.7	3.8	1.6
Netherlands	4.5	3.2	4.6	2.7	1.7	3.0
EC-6	(2.8)	3.1	2.6	(4.1)	2.6	1.5
Denmark			3.1			2.6
Ireland			3.5			2.1
UK			2.5			-0.3
EC-3			2.7			0.03
EC-9			2.6			1.2

Note: 1973–81 columns exclude rice, sugar, fruit and vegetable oils, for which the EC basis of calculation changed in 1980. The remaining items accounted for 91 percent of all EC-10 agricultural output in 1981 and the excluded items for 7 percent.

Sources:

(a) For output: Pierre Gonod "Evolution de la Productivité de l'Agriculture dans la CEE," Com-EC, Informations Internes sur l'Agriculture No. 44–1969, pp. 309–13; For consumption: UN, National Accounts (in constant national currencies. Since "real" food prices fell in the 1950s, figures in value, such as the national accounts provide, understate the growth of the physical volume of output. Series by value (national accounts) cannot be compared with series by volume (grain equivalents). See note 5, Ch. 1, supra.

(b) Günther Thiede, "Die Versorgungslage der EWG mit landwirtschaftlichen Erzeugnissen," Ministry of Agriculture, Bonn, *Berichte über Landwirtschaft*, XLVIii, 1970, 2, pp. 228–75 in grain equivalents. These are figures, by definition, in physical volumes.

(c) Günther Thiede, "Overall accounts on the Community supply situation based on grain equivalents," Com-EC, Agricultural Statistical Studies No. 22, 1980, with supplementary figures for 1979–80 (1980) and 1980–81 (1981) in Com-EC, Eurostat, *Crop Production 1 1983* (March 1983), pp. 129–153.

Appendix Table 2 **Aggregate Self-Sufficiency Ratios in Agriculture in Member States of EC-10 1959–1981 (calculated in grain equivalents)**

	1959	1969	1973	1980	1981
Belgium–Luxembourg	87	89	96	101	94
France	98	114	124	127	135
Germany	79	84	82	91	91
Italy	91	85	78	89	91
Netherlands	114	115[a]	147	155	161
Denmark	–	–	242	251	246
Ireland	–	–	184	231	202
UK	–	–	61	73	77
EC-6	91	96[b]	99	107	110
Denmark, Ireland, U.K.	–	–	80	98	99
EC-9	–	–	94	105	107
Greece	–	–	–	117	126

[a] 1968: 122. For the Netherlands, 1969 was a year of exceptionally low production.
[b] 1968–69.

Note: These figures do not take account of imported feed for livestock. If this is included the EC-9's self-sufficiency ratios for 1973 was 83 percent and 96 percent for the EC-10 in 1981 (Greece making only a minor difference).

Source: See Appendix Table 1, sources (a) and (b).

Appendix Table 3 Production of Major Commodities in the EC-10 and in Member States, 1960, 1980, and 1982 or 1983

Commodity/Year (million tons)		EC	Belgium	Denmark	France	Germany	Greece	Ireland	Italy	Netherlands	UK	Weight in EC-10 FAP, Percent
Cereals	1960[a]	67.9	1.9	4.5	20.4	14.0	2.3	1.3	13.0	1.7	8.8	12.6
	1980	124.3	2.0	7.1	47.9	23.1	5.1	1.6	17.0	1.3	19.2	
	1983	122.9	1.9	6.4	45.9	23.0	4.3	1.9	16.8	1.3	21.3	
Sugar	1960[a]	5.9	0.3	0.3	1.5	1.5	negl.	0.1	1.0	0.5	0.7	2.7
	1980	12.3	0.8	0.4	4.2	2.7	0.2	0.1	1.8	0.9	1.1	
	1983	14.0	1.1	0.5	4.8	3.3	0.3	0.2	1.2	1.1	1.4	
Milk	1960[a]	79.1	3.9	5.2	19.1	20.8	0.4	3.1	8.3	7.0	11.6	19.2
	1980	104.5	4.0	5.1	26.9	24.8	0.7	4.9	10.4	11.8	15.9	
	1982	108.1	4.1	5.2	27.9	25.5	0.7	0.5	10.5	12.7	16.7	
Beef	1960[a]	4.3	0.2	0.2	1.3	0.9	negl.	0.2	0.5	0.2	0.8	15.8
	1980	7.2	0.4	0.2	1.8	1.6	0.1	0.4	1.1	0.4	1.1	
	1983	6.9	0.3	0.2	1.9	1.5	0.1	0.5	0.9	0.5	1.0	
Pork	1960[a]	5.3	0.3	0.5	1.1	1.8	negl.	0.1	0.4	0.4	0.7	11.5
	1980	10.1	0.7	1.0	1.9	3.2	0.1	0.2	1.1	1.1	0.9	
	1983	10.5	0.7	1.1	1.7	3.2	0.2	0.1	1.1	1.5	1.0	
Poultry	1960[a]	1.0	0.1	negl.	0.4	0.1	negl.	negl.	0.1	0.1	0.2	4.2
	1980	4.0	0.1	0.1	1.1	0.4	0.1	0.1	1.0	0.4	0.7	
	1982	4.4	0.1	0.1	1.3	0.4	0.2	negl.	1.0	0.4	0.8	

a = Average 1956-60.

negl. = negligible (i.e., more than 0 and less than 50,000 tons).

Source: For milk, for all countries: Eurostat, *Cronos* series.
For EC-6, all other products: Eurostat, *Yearbook of Agricultural Statistics 1973* and *ASC 1981.*
For 1960 Denmark, Greece, Ireland, U.K., all other products: *OECD Food Consumption Statistics 1955-1973.*
For 1980 and 1982-83: *ASC 1983*; Eurostat, *Crop Production* 3, 1984, and *Animal Production* 2, 1984.

Appendix Table 4 World Trade in Agricultural Products (1982 billions of U.S. dollars) (excluding intra-European Community trade)

IMPORTS

Country or Group	$ billions
European Community	44.4
USSR	19.4
USA	16.9
Japan	16.2
PR China	7.4
Including in European Community:	
Germany	11.3
United Kingdom	9.4
France	7.6
Italy	7.4

EXPORTS

USA	38.2
European Community	24.5
Australia	8.7
Brazil	8.0
Canada	8.0
Argentina	5.0
Including in European Community	
France	6.4

Note: FAO definitions: SITC categories 0 (food including 03 fish), 1 (beverages), 21 (hides and skins), 22 (oilseeds), 26 (natural fibers and excluding 266, 267, and 269), 29 (miscellaneous agricultural raw materials as well as plants and flowers), 4 (fats and oils).

Source: FAO, *Trade Yearbook 1982*, Rome; Com-EC *Eurostat, Analytic Tables of Foreign Trade, SITC Rev. 2, 1982* (denominated in ECUs; the average ECU: $ exchange rate in 1982 was 1 ECU = $.98208).

Appendix Table 5 Commodity Breakdown of EC-10 Food Trade with the Rest of the World, 1981 (by value-current ECUs)

SITC Category	Commodity	Imports	Exports	Exports as Percent of Imports
00	Live animals	481	504	1.05
01	Meat	2204	2107	0.96
02	Dairy products	614	3802	6.19
03	Fish	2211	642	0.29
04	Cereals	2980	4736	1.59
05	Fruit and vegetables	7083	1604	0.23
06	Sugar	1015	2648	2.61
07	Tropical beverages and spices	5389	875	0.16
08	Feedstuffs	4232	1137	0.27
09	Patent foods	190	882	4.64
11	Drinks	760	3589	4.72
12	Tobacco	1129	625	0.55
22	Oilseeds	3728	43	0.01
29	Agricultural materials, including plants and flowers	1123	820	0.73
4	Fats and oils	1631	816	0.50
Total		34770	24830	0.71

Note: The average US $ value of the ECU in 1981 was 1 ECU = $1.1645.

Source: Com-EC, Eurostat, *Analytical Tables of Foreign Trade, SITC, Rev. 2,* 1981.

Appendix Table 6 The Agricultural Trade of the EC-9 in 1960, 1970 and 1980 (SITC Categories 0 + 1 + 22 + 29 + 4)

	1960	1970	1980	1970	1980	1980
	(billions of ECUs of 1980)c			(1960 = 1)	(1970 = 1)	(1960 = 1)
Trade Between Member States[a]	10.5	20.4	34.3	1.94	1.68	3.2
Trade with the rest of the world						
Imports[b]	33.5	32.3	31.7	0.96	0.98	0.95
from Developed Areas		15.0	14.5		0.97	
from Developing Areas		14.7	15.4		1.05	
from Centrally Planned Economies		2.5	1.8		0.72	
Exports	7.9	10.8	18.5	1.37	1.71	2.34
to Developed Areas		6.2	7.2		1.16	
to Developing Areas		3.8	9.1		2.39	
to Centrally Planned Economies		0.8	2.2		2.75	

[a] Average of results by exports and imports.
[b] Corresponds to Classes 1, 2 and 3 of EEC Country code.
[c] One ECU of 1980 was worth, on average that year, US $1.39. In 1960 and 1970 the ECU, or European Unit of Account (EUA) at that time, was worth $1.00.

Note: SITC Categories as follows: 0 = food; 1 = beverages and tobacco; 22 = oilseeds; 29 = agricultural materials, including plants and flowers; 4 = vegetables, oils and fats.

Source: OEEC/OECD (Paris) *Statistical Bulletins of Foreign Trade, Series C, Trade by Commodities 1960, 1970, and 1980.*

Appendix Table 7 The Coverage of Food Imports by Exports between EC Member States and with the Rest of the World, 1960, 1970, 1980, and 1983, (percent—SITC 0 + 1 + 4 + 22 + 29)

	B/L	F	G	I	N	6	3	D	U	E	9	H	10
1. Intra-Community Trade													
1960	66	182	13	160	892	104	89	1213	11	611	100		
1970	98	180	29	63	328	101	86	663	23	408	100	259	
1980	86	143	52	46	233	98	107	380	54	215	100	144	
1983	101	141	57	43	241	101	95	354	48	162	100	90	100
2. Community Trade with Outside World													
1960	13	41	8	34	57	29	17	79	12	40	24		
1970	23	53	14	27	57	33	35	130	24	71	33	77	
1980	53	107	33	39	61	58	61	118	43	265	58	100	
1983	40	106	35	46	70	60	75	159	51	356	63	185	65
3. Total Community Trade													
1960	33	60	10	63	151	48	33	262	12	214	41		
1970	67	98	21	41	152	62	49	244	24	219	59	125	
1980	76	125	43	43	138	79	82	212	48	226	80	142	
1983	80	125	47	44	151	83	85	246	49	200	83	115	84

B/L = Belgium-Luxembourg, D = Denmark, E = Ireland, F = France, G = Germany, H = Greece, I = Italy, N = Netherlands, U = United Kingdom, 6 = Six founder states of EC, 3 = Three members of first enlargement, 1973, 10 = Ten EC states after entry of Greece, 1981.

Source: 1960: OEEC, Statistical Bulletin of Foreign Trade, Series C, Trade by Commodities, 1960; 1970: OECD, same title, 1970; 1980: COM-EC, Eurostat, Analytical Tables of Foreign Trade, SITC, Rev. 2, 1983; Eurostat, Monthly Bulletin of External Trade, 1984. Greece 1970, and 1980: OECD, Statistics of Foreign Trade, Series C, 1970 and 1980.

Appendix Table 8   Evolution of Farm Trade between EC-9 Member States and with the Rest of the World 1960-1970 and 1970-1980, with Shares in EC-9 Total in 1960 and 1980 (based on constant ECUs at 1960 prices; SITC 0 + 1 + 22 + 29 + 4)

	Imports				Exports			
	$\dfrac{1970^a}{1960} = 1$	$\dfrac{1980^a}{1970} = 1$	Share in EC-9 Total Percentage		$\dfrac{1970^a}{1960} = 1$	$\dfrac{1980^a}{1970} = 1$	Share in EC-9 Total Percentage	
			1960	1980			1960	1980
1. Intra-Community Trade								
Belgium–Luxembourg	2.7	1.8	8	12	4.0	1.6	5	10
Denmark	1.4	2.5	2	2	0.8	1.4	23	8
France	3.2	2.1	7	15	3.2	1.6	14	22
Germany	1.8	1.3	36	27	4.2	2.4	5	14
Ireland	1.9	3.1	1	2	1.3	1.7	8	5
Italy	3.5	2.0	8	16	1.4	1.4	12	7
Netherlands	5.3	2.1	3	11	1.9	1.5	29	26
United Kingdom	1.0	1.4	35	15	2.1	3.2	4	8
2. Community Trade with Outside World								
Belgium–Luxembourg	1.1	1.2	4	6	1.9	2.8	2	5
Denmark	1.0	1.2	3	4	1.7	1.1	10	8
France	0.9	1.1	15	16	1.2	2.2	26	30
Germany	1.2	1.1	20	26	2.0	2.6	7	15
Ireland	1.1	0.7	1	1	1.9	2.7	2	3
Italy	1.6	0.9	8	13	1.2	1.4	12	9
Netherlands	1.2	1.4	8	15	1.2	1.5	19	16
United Kingdom	0.7	0.7	41	20	1.4	1.2	21	15

[a] $\dfrac{1970}{1960}$ = values in 1970 divided by values in 1960 (both at constant prices of 1960); etc.

Source: See Appendix Table 7.

Appendix Table 9   Food Exports and Gross Value Added in Agriculture and the Food Industry in the Member States of the EC-10 in 1980 (percentage of Gross Domestic Product)

	Food Exports 1980		Gross Value Added in Agriculture and Food Industry
	Intra EC	To Rest of World	
Belgium–Luxembourg	4.0	1.1	5.5
Denmark	5.5	3.0	7.1
France	1.6	1.2	7.3
Germany	0.8	0.5	4.6
Greece	1.4	2.0	16.9
Ireland	12.9	4.6	14.7
Italy	0.9	0.6	9.8
Netherlands	7.3	2.4	6.3
United Kingdom	0.7	0.7	4.7

Source: Com-EC, Eurostat, *ASC 1981*, p. 178–79 and 281; *National Accounts ESA, Detailed Tables by Branch, 1970–1981* (1983).

Appendix Table 10   National and EC Expenditure on Agricultural Policies in the EC-9, 1978

Authority Type of Expenditure	(millions of EUAs)	Share in Value of Final Agricultural Production of EC-9 (percent)
National		
General measures, production processing and marketing	4,275.1	4.44
Food consumption	394.7	0.41
Tax relief	1,757.9	1.82
Social security	6,279.3	6.52
Other	908.3	0.94
	13,615.3	14.13
Community		
Guarantee and guidance funds	6,959.1	7.22
Total	20,574.4	21.35

Note: 1978 was the last year for which detailed national breakdowns were published by the European Commission.

Source: Com-EC, *ASC 1980*, pp. 186, 234, 243.

Appendix Table 11   Annual Expenditures of the European Agricultural Guarantee and Guidance Fund (EAGGF) (millions of constant ECUs; 1975 = 100)

European Community of	Year	EAGGF millions ECUs of 1975	Expenditure Percent GDP	Subsidies to Sales [a]	Subsidies to Output/Income [a] (millions of constant ECUs)	Buying-in of Stocks [a]	Percent of VAT in EC receipts [b]
Six	1967	595	0.10				
	1968	1514	0.23				
	1969	3206	0.45				
	1970	3745	0.50				
	1971	1959	0.25				
	1972	5611	0.68				
Nine	1973	4869	0.38	2877	1150	377	
	1974	4192	0.34	1515	848	642	
	1975	4587	0.45	1904	819	1004	
	1976	5445	0.44	2171	934	1170	
	1977	5474	0.46	2842	773	1028	
	1978	7314	0.61	3701	796	1557	
	1979	7570	0.61	4446	1205	1248	0.79
	1980	7335	0.60	4460	1424	1211	0.73
Ten	1981	6573	0.53	3684	1649	1188	0.79
	1982	6761	0.54	(3585)	(1793)	1280	0.92
	1983	8260	(0.65)	4122	2144	1726	0.99

a = Excludes MCAs.
b = From 1979 only.

Source: Com-EC, *European Economy*, November 1983, Tables 17 and 48; European Community *Official Journal*, C313, Vol. 21, pp. 162-163, 30 December 1978 and C357, Vol. 26, p. 178, 31 December 1983, Reports of the Court of Auditors; *ASC 1983*, p. 155; *ASC 1982*, p. 159.

Appendix Table 12 EC Budget Support to Final Agricultural Production (FAP) in 1982 (payments from Guarantee Section of European Agricultural Guidance and Guarantee Fund—EAGGF)

Product(s)	Product Share in FAP (percent)	Product Share in EC Guarantee Expenditure (percent)	Ratio of Guarantee Expenditure to FAP (percent)	Main Beneficiaries of EC Farm Guarantee Expenditure (percent)[e]			
Tobacco	0.7	5.0	61	I 46	H 33	F 14	
Oilseeds	1.0	6.5	55	G 37	F 27	U 15	N 10
Seeds, hops and textile fibers	0.3	1.2	37	H 59	F 13		
Sugarbeet	2.4	10.0	36	F 41	G 19	B 15	
Olive oil	1.2	4.0	28	I 84	H 15		
Table wines[a]	2.4[a]	4.6	16	I 68	F 28		
Dairy products	19.2	26.9	12	G 24	N 23	F 21	D 9
Rice	0.3	0.4	11	I 97			
Cereals (excl. rice)	12.9	14.8	10	F 37	G 16	U 13	
Mutton (and goatmeat)	1.8	2.0	10	U 91			
Fruit and vegetables[b]	10.6	7.4	6	F 69	H 15	F 12	
Beef and Veal	14.6	9.4	5	F 24	E 23	I 21	G 15
Pigs, poultry and eggs	19.3	1.7	<1	D 30	F 29	N 20	G 11
Non-supported items[c]	13.3	–	–				
Total	100.0	93.9[d]	9[d]	F 24[d]	I 21[d]	G 16[d]	U 11[d]
Country's share of EC FAP (percent)	–	–	–	F 26	I 20	G 18	U 13

[a] Table wines and quality wines are only partially distinguished in *ASC 1983*. The proportions for 1979 *(ASC 1980)* have been used. Quality wines are not supported.

[b] Some fruit and vegetables are not supported and appear under "Non-supported Items."

[c] "Other" fruit and vegetables; potatoes; flowers; quality wines; and miscellaneous.

[d] Except (i) monetary compensatory amounts (ii) subsidies to inputs of food manufacturers to compensate for high CAP prices.

[e] B = Belgium, D = Denmark, E = Ireland, F = France, G = Germany, H = Greece, I = Italy, N = Netherlands, U = UK.

Source: *ASC 1983*; Com-EC, *Twelfth Financial Report on the European Agricultural Guidance and Guarantee Fund (1982)*, COM (83) 531 final, 15 September 1983. Brussels.

Appendix Table 13   Expenditures by EAGGF in Each of the Member States of the EC-9, 1980

| | | ECUs per | | | As Percent of | |
	(millions of ECUs)	Agricultural Holding	Hectare of UAA[b]	Annual Labor Unit	Gross Value Added[a]	Final Agricultural Production (FAP)
Belgium	571	6275	395	5827	34.9	14.5
France	2830	2493	89	1749	16.5	9.0
Germany	2453	3078	200	3058	24.6	11.0
Italy	1841	840	103	977	10.6	7.5
Luxembourg	11.6	2417	89	1275	16.1	9.8
Netherlands	1543	11961	761	6247	37.7	16.6
Denmark	616	5133	212	4190	32.3	14.0
Ireland	565	2511	99	1883	42.5	22.8
United Kingdom	885	3404	48	1595	13.7	6.1
EC-9	11315	2284	122	1999	18.9	10.0

[a] Gross value added at market prices.
[b] UAA: Utilized Agricultural Area.

Note: Most expenditures (e.g., export subsidies, storage costs, etc.) do not go directly to farmers, though they have the effect of indirectly sustaining internal producer prices from which farmers benefit.

Source: Com-EC, Eurostat.

Appendix Table 14   Estimated Net Cash Flows between EC Member States, 1979 (millions of ECUs)

	Net Budget Receipts	Net Trade Receipts	Total Net Cash Receipts
Belgium/Luxembourg	76	−464	−388
Denmark	520	580	1100
France	394	928	1312
Germany	−719	−193	−912
Ireland	524	425	949
Italy	6	−1083	−1077
Netherlands	509	503	1012
UK	−1364	−348	−1712

Source: J. Rollo and K. Warwick, *The CAP and Resource Flows among Member States*, U.K. Government Economic Service Working Paper No. 27, November 1979; and House of Lords Select Committee on the European Communities, 1980–81 Report 19, *The Common Agricultural Policy – Directions of Future Development and Proposals for Prices and Related Measures*, Vol. II Minutes of Evidence, 26 March 1981, pp. 191–94 (including method).

Many other calculations have been made: Wynne Godley, "The System of Financial Transfers in the EEC," paper for Wye College Workshop Report on *The Net Loss and Benefit of EEC Membership* (Martin Whitby, ed.), 1979. Data derived from Ch. 2 of the Cambridge *Economic Policy Review*, 1978, No. 5; Paolo Blancus, "The Common Agricultural Policy and the Balance of Payments of the EEC Member Countries," Banca Nazionale del Lavoro, *Quarterly Review*, December 1978; U. Koester, "Effects of the Common Agricultural Financial System," *European Review of Agricultural Economics*, Vol. 4, No. 4, p. 327; C. N. Morris, "The Common Agricultural Policy," *Fiscal Studies* Vol. 1, No. 2, Institute of Fiscal Studies, London, March 1980.

Appendix Table 15   The 1950s and 1960s: Annual Average Growth of Agricultural and National Product (income) per Head in EC-6 in Constant Prices (percent)

	Per Capita Gross Value Added in Agriculture at Factor Cost			GDP per inhabitant	GDP per active worker
	1951–59 (1)	1959–64 (2)	1965–69 (3)	1953–58 (4)	1958–68 (5)
Belgium	6.8	5.4	8.5	2.0	3.9
France	4.8	5.7	6.3	3.7	5.0
Germany	5.0	5.1	8.8	5.7	4.8
Italy	4.8	5.2	7.7	4.6	6.3
Netherlands	4.0	2.8	7.8	2.8	4.2
EC-6	—	—	7.5	4.4	5.2

Source: Cols. 1 and 2: Com-EC, Pierre Gonod "Evolution de la Productivité de l'Agriculture dans la CEE" *Informations Internes sur l'Agriculture*, 309-13. National prices at average 1952-4 rates.
Col. 3: Com-EC, *The Agricultural Situation in the Community: 1972 Report (ASC72)* Vol. II, 25.
Cols. 4 and 5: Com-EC, *Basic Statistics of the Community*; 1965, 35; 1968-69.

Appendix Table 16   The 1970s: Annual Average Growth of Real Agricultural and National Product per Head in EC-9 in Constant Prices (percent)

	Before energy crises 1968–73		First energy crisis 1973–76		Between energy crises 1976–79	
	(1)	(2)	(1)	(2)	(1)	(2)
Belgium	9.4	5.0	−1.4	2.8	−4.0	1.6
France	11.7	5.0	−6.0	2.6	3.1	2.8
Germany	4.9	4.4	−0.6	3.5	−5.7	3.0
Italy	4.6	4.4	0.9	1.2	4.0	2.6
Netherlands	2.9	5.0	−0.1	2.8	−2.3	1.8
Denmark	2.8	3.7	−6.5	1.5	−0.1	1.8
Ireland	9.3	—	2.2	3.3	2.1	3.7
UK	5.5	2.9	−2.8	1.0	−5.9	1.5

Source: Col. 1: "Average annual increase in 'real income' per agricultural worker" (date of price and exchange rates not specified in source), Com-EC, *ASC 1980*.
Col. 2: GDP per head of occupied population for 1968-76, Com-EC, Eurostat, *National Accounts* 1960-75 (1976) at price and exchange rates of 1970; and 1976-79 at prices and exchange rates of 1975 (1980), Com-EC, Eurostat, *Review 1970-1980*.

Appendix Table 17   **Average Net Value Added on EC Farms per Annual Labor Unit (ALU), 1981–82, According to Area of Farm**

	Net Value Added (thousands of ECUs) per ALU[a] per Farm Size (hectares)		GDP per head All Employed (thousands of ECUs) 1981
	2 – < 10 ha.	> 50 ha.	
Belgium	11.2	26.3	20.2[e]
Denmark	10.7	24.7	18.6
France	10.3	13.7	21.8
Germany	8.1	12.3	22.1[e]
Greece	3.2	(13.2)[d]	8.9
Ireland	3.1[c]	10.2	12.0
Italy	3.6	12.9	14.6
Luxembourg	6.0[b]	10.3	20.1
Netherlands	15.9	36.1	23.2[e]
United Kingdom	8.7	15.3	14.1[e]

[a] Agricultural work done in the year by one full-time worker (at least 280 days or 2380 hours per annum) and seasonal work are attributed fractions of an AWU.
[b] Farms of 2 to < 5 ha. only.
[c] Farms of 5 to < 10 ha. only.
[d] Farms of 30 to < 40 ha.
[e] 1980

Source: Com-EC, FADN (Farm Accountancy Data Network), *Farm Accounts Results 1978/79–1981/82*, Luxembourg, 1984; Eurostat, *Regional Statistics*, Luxembourg, 1984, pp. 104–6.

Note on Structure:
Size of Categories of Farms Chosen in Their Country and the EC

	Farms of 2 – < 10 hectares		Farms of > 50 hectares	
	% Farms in Country	% Category in EC	% Farms in Country	% Category in EC
Belgium	21.4	1.3	5.9	1.4
Denmark	8.4	0.7	11.4	3.4
France	7.1	4.2	17.4	38.6
Germany	4.7	1.7	6.3	8.5
Greece	81.7	24.2	—	—
Ireland	11.8[c]	1.8[c]	16.8	9.7
Italy	63.0	64.0	2.3	8.7
Luxembourg	2.7[b]	0.01[b]	23.9	0.2
Netherlands	6.8	1.7	3.1	1.2
United Kingdom	2.7	0.4	52.1	28.2
EC-10	35.8	100.0	9.5	99.9

Source: FADN, as above.

Appendix Table 18 Ratio of Gross Value Added per Person Employed in Agriculture to That in Non-Agriculture in Member States of the EC-12 1960, 1970 and 1980 (percent of national average)

	1960	1970	1980
Belgium	75	71	67
Denmark	90[a]	51	68
France	42	49	47
Germany	41	39	41[c]
Greece		46	61
Ireland	69	64	91[b]
Italy	41	44	48
Luxembourg	46	41	35
Netherlands	77	83	61
Portugal			
Spain		43	37
UK	88	71	100

[a] Total occupied population of 1966.
[b] 1978.
[c] 1979.

Note: Because of the substantial non-farm earning of many farm families, this gives little indication of households' average total revenues.

Source: Com-EC, Eurostat, *National Accounts ESA, Detailed Tables by Branches 1970-1981* (1983); *Comptes Nationaux 1960-1970* (1971); *Population and Employment 1950-1976* (1977); *ASC 1981,* p. 282 and *ASC 1982,* p. 285. OECD, Committee for Agriculture, *Issues and Challenge for OECD Agriculture in the 1980s* (1983), Table 3, p. 150. UN *National Accounts Statistics.*

Appendix Table 19   EC-9 Food Industries, by Sector, 1976 (firms of more than 20 employees)

Sector	Gross Value Added (billions of ECUs)	Number of Enterprises	Employment (thousands)	Average Gross Value Added per employee (thousands of ECUs)
Processing	11,9	—	924	12,8
Dairy	3,4	1,568	259	13,0
Meat	3,2	2,369	303	10,4
Fruit and vegetables	1,6	865	153	10,6
Sugar	1,6	136	71	22,3
Manufacturing	14,8	—	1,074	13,7
Brewing	4,3	927	209	20,6
Beverages (not wine)	2,7	1,145	147	18,1
Bakeries	2,5	1,751	331	7,5
Confectionery	2,5	722	205	11,9
Specialty foods	2,1	667	133	15,5
Others	4,0	—	234	17,1
Tobacco	2,0	172	118	16,6
Animal foodstuffs	1,6	990	90	17,8
Total	30,7	12,951	2,232	13,7

Source: Com-EC, DG III, *L'Industrie Alimentaire dans la CEE*, 1981.

Appendix Table 20   EC-9 Food Industries, by Member States, 1976 (firms of more than 20 employees)

	Employment (thousands)	Gross Value Added per Employee (thousands of ECUs)	Gross Rates of Change, 1972-76 (percent)		
			Gross Value Added (Constant ECUs)	Employment	Number of Firms
Belgium	85	15.3	28	−11	−36
Denmark	64	15.7	15	−9	−32
France	400	14.8	16	−7	−38
Germany	479	16.7	−22	−11	−10
Ireland	55	12.7	3	3	−20
Italy	253	11.1	3	−1	−2
Netherlands	153	17.7	35	−2	−6
UK	741	10.9	−1	−5	−24
EC-9	2,232	13.8	−1	−6	−22

Source: Com-EC, DG III, *L'Industrie Alimentaire dans la CEE*, 1981.

Index

The Authors

François Duchêne, an Anglo-Swiss born in London in 1927, has worked as a Paris correspondent and editorial writer for both the *Manchester Guardian* (as it then was) and *The Economist* (London). He joined the precursor of the EEC, the European Coal and Steel Community, at the outset in 1952 and later became *chef de cabinet,* or principal personal assistant, to the founder of the European Communities, Jean Monnet, from 1958–63 at the Action Committee for the United States of Europe. He directed the International Institute for Strategic Studies in London (1969–74) and the European Research Centre at Sussex University, SERC (1974–82). He has published widely on international economic and security issues in such journals as *Foreign Affairs, Foreign Policy,* and *The World Today.* He is the editor of *The Endless Crisis* (1970), on America and Vietnam, and the author of a study of W. H. Auden, *The Case of the Helmeted Airman* (1972). He is a Governor of the Atlantic Institute.

Edward Szczepanik, who fought in the Polish army at Monte Cassino in World War II, is Professor of Economics at the Polish University in London. From 1963 to 1977 he was Senior Economist at FAO in Rome and previous to that Harvard University adviser to the Planning Commission in Pakistan. He has been a consultant to the International Coffee Organisation and several UN agencies. He was a Senior Research Fellow at SERC from 1977 to 1981 and has taught economics in the universities of Warsaw, London, Hong Kong and Rome. He is Chairman of the Polish Society of Arts and Sciences Abroad.

Wilfrid Legg is a Principal Administrator in the Agricultural Policies Division of the OECD (Paris) working primarily on European agriculture, on food policy and on Issues and Challenges for OECD Agriculture in the 1980s. He was previously Research Fellow in agriculture at SERC and Economics Lecturer at Lanchester Polytechnic, Coventry (UK).

The views expressed in this book are those of the authors and do not necessarily reflect those of the OECD or of its member governments.